BIG RED DYNASTY

THE CHAMPIONSHIPS, TRADITION AND DOMINANCE OF WEBB CITY FOOTBALL

BIG RED DYNASTY

THE CHAMPIONSHIPS, TRADITION AND DOMINANCE OF WEBB CITY FOOTBALL

BRENNAN STEBBINS

Copyright © 2015 by Brennan Stebbins

All rights reserved. This book or any portion thereof may not be reproduced or used in any manner whatsoever without the express written permission of the publisher except for the use of brief quotations in a book review or scholarly journal.

First Printing: 2015

ISBN 978-1-329-00102-2

Edited by Chad Stebbins
Photographs by Bob Foos
Cover photo by Bob Foos
Back cover photo by King Jack

Contents

Introduction	7
Chapter 1 - A Party on Main Street	10
Chapter 2 - The First Football in Webb City	14
Chapter 3 - The Early Years	18
Chapter 4 - The First Great Team	25
Chapter 5 - The Roaring Twenties	29
Chapter 6 - Webb City's Best Team Ever?	40
Chapter 7 - Pearl Green and a Lot of Luck	45
Chapter 8 - Bill Jackson and the Lights at Hatten Field	47
Chapter 9 - The Forties	51
Chapter 10 - The Blue Top Cafe	55
Chapter 11 - Henry May Goes Out On Top	61
Chapter 12 - The Merlyn Elder Years	68
Chapter 13 - The Tom Gosch Era Begins	76
Chapter 14 - The Seventies	83
Chapter 15 - Into the Eighties	93
Chapter 16 - The Post-Gosch Era	99
Chapter 17 - Begin the Drive in '85	105
Chapter 18 - The Jerry Kill Years	114
Chapter 19 - Jerry Kill For President	120
Chapter 20 - The First State Championship	127
Chapter 21 - A Surprise Hire?	138
Chapter 22 - The Mud Bowl	145
Chapter 23 - The 'Outlaw Class'	152
Chapter 24 - Defending Their Title	162
Chapter 25 - Grant Wistrom	171
Chapter 26 - The Mid Nineties	179
Chapter 27 - John Roderique's First Championship	194
Chapter 28 - The New Millennium	206
Chapter 29 - A Title Drought	226
Chapter 30 - Cardinal Stadium is Rebuilt	235
Chapter 31 - Back to the Title Game	249
Chapter 32 - An Old Nemesis	261
Chapter 33 - The Streak Begins	264
Chapter 34 - The Tenth Title	277
Chapter 35 - Richard Correll	283
Chapter 36 - Undefeated Again	287
Chapter 37 - The 'Quad Squad'	292
Chapter 38 - Five in a Row	344
Afterword	365

INTRODUCTION

Since 1985, Webb City High School has been the greatest football team in the state of Missouri. In the last 30 years, no team has won more championships or as many games. No school has been as dominant for such an extended period of time.

The Cardinals went to the playoffs for the first time in 1985. They've been to the postseason a total of 24 times. They won their first state championship in 1989. They've won a dozen more.

Webb City's graduates have gone on to star in college. They've been All-Americans, they've won national championships, and they've played in the Super Bowl. Its coaches have coached at major universities. Webb City football has made a reputation for itself across the state and even at a national level.

What might be forgotten is how the Cardinals came to be this good. There was a time when a state championship or a trip to the playoffs felt like a once-in-a-lifetime event. There were losing seasons and bad teams. There were losses to Carthage. A bulldog was once the team's mascot.

Of course, even before 1985, there were plenty of good years, standout athletes and legendary coaches. Football has been played in Webb City for more than 115 years. Fans used to take the electric trolley or a train to away games.

The fact is, while no school has been as good on the gridiron as Webb City has in the last 30 years, neither can very many point to a history and tradition as rich as Webb City's over the last century and beyond.

It will surprise some to learn I played high school football a few miles to the west, at Carl Junction High School, where I graduated in 2006. Carl Junction is one of Webb City's two biggest rivals, and from the time I moved there before junior high until I finished high school and left for college, I despised Webb City football. The Cardinals were just too good, they won too many games. And they didn't even play for a state championship while I was in high school.

We only played Webb City in the preseason jamborees, as the schools were in the midst of a decade-long period where they didn't play even once. When I was a sophomore, in 2003, the jamboree was at the old Cardinal Stadium, and Carl Junction had a pretty loaded team that season. Each team ran 12 offensive plays against the other's defense, starting at about the 40-yard line. No official score was kept.

But on the Carl Junction sideline, I guarantee you everyone was keeping score when we scrimmaged Webb City. When we scored a touchdown, you'd have thought we'd just taken a lead in the fourth quarter of a playoff game. We were probably more enthusiastic for that scrimmage than we were for most of our regular season games. In the end, we scored one or two more touchdowns than Webb City did. It was one of the season's big highlights.

The next season, I was playing in the varsity jamboree, at defensive end. I recall being blown away – literally and figuratively – by the speed with which Webb City's offensive linemen got off the ball. They were the quickest linemen I'd ever played against and I was pretty helpless against them. I did manage to make an open field tackle on quarterback Brayden Drake, as he rolled out to his right and scrambled. I was about 10 yards down the line of scrimmage and came face to face with him. I knew he'd try to juke and I was conscious of not jumping in the wrong direction. In the end, I think he just bulldozed right through me, but I was enough of an obstacle to bring him down. It was a proud moment.

In those years I disliked Webb City football, but I was also in awe of it.

I moved back to the area a couple of years after high school and enrolled at Missouri Southern State University. I had been working for some local newspapers since I was 14 – first for the *Jasper County Citizen*, and then I was something of a stringer for the *Webb City Sentinel*. Editor Bob Foos was a great mentor for an aspiring young journalist. In 2008 I started writing for the *Sentinel* again, this time covering Webb City football. The Cardinals went 15-0 and beat Jefferson City Helias for the state title. A year later, the Cardinals went 13-1 and lost in the state semifinals. In 2010, they were undefeated state champs, again.

I covered the team for three seasons. In high school I didn't like Webb City football. In the years after, I was indifferent. But when I started covering the Cardinals every Friday night, I grew to respect it immensely.

I realized Webb City has been the greatest team in the state since 1985, for 30 years, not because of something nefarious or unfair, but because the Cardinals do things the right way. Their execution is nearly flawless. Players maximize their abilities. Physically, they are often the smaller team, but they are always the more physical team. While the Cardinals do often have some spectacular athletes with a natural gift, the bulk of their teams are comprised of players who won't ever set foot on a college football field. Often they get to start for only one season, but they make the absolute most of their chance to shine. They are motivated by living up to the lofty standards set in the program's past, by their older brothers, dads and uncles.

Another significant reason Webb City has been so good is that it has the best coaching staff in the state of Missouri. I wholeheartedly believe this. I have never seen a Cardinals team out-coached in a game. The coaches, as they have for 30 years, will heap credit on their players, but just as the coaches need players to play, the players need coaches to coach.

Watching Webb City football really is a beautiful thing.

It has been a very enjoyable experience researching and writing this book, from sorting through old yearbooks and newspaper archives to interviewing some of the people responsible for making Webb City football what it is today.

I'd like to thank the coaches: Merlyn Elder, Tom Gosch, Jerry Kill, Kurt Thompson, John Roderique, Mike Smith, Richard Correll, Rich Adkins and others. I'd also like to thank Bill Jackson, Grant Wistrom and everyone else who took time to talk about their playing days. Special thanks go to the Webb City Library, especially to the volunteers in the genealogy room upstairs, and to Bob Foos and the *Webb City Sentinel*. To everyone else who assisted with or supported this project in any way, I haven't forgotten; thanks.

My biggest regret with this project is that I wasn't able to talk to more people or include everybody's name. There simply wasn't enough space or time in the day to get to everyone who's contributed to what Webb City football is today. So, to everyone who's ever played, coached, managed, taught, cheered and watched, I'd also like to thank you.

1. A PARTY ON MAIN STREET

It's almost lunchtime on a Monday at Webb City High School, and a P.E. class is running sprints on the wood floor in the gymnasium.

Through a door on the east end of the gym is the weight room, and in the weight room is an office, where John Roderique sits at a desk with his back to the door, his keys hanging from the lock on the outside.

"Turn them to the left to unlock it," he says.

Barely three weeks ago, on the Saturday after Thanksgiving, the Webb City football team took the field at the Edward Jones Dome in St. Louis, the players wearing their white jerseys with red lettering and Columbia blue pants.

When the players walked off the field a few hours later, they had just put an exclamation point on a perfect season with a 49-14 victory against Jefferson City Helias in the 2012 Missouri Class 4 State Championship game.

It's now December 2012 and the Cardinals have won 45 games in a row and three state championships since their last defeat. They haven't lost a regular-season game since 2003, a streak of 90 games. They have 11 state titles in the trophy cases at the high school, tying them with a small Catholic school on the other side of the state for the most in Missouri history. Roderique, in 16 seasons, has won eight of them.

Now, after three weeks of interviews and catching up on his duties as athletics director, Roderique is finally able to reminisce.

"As a football coach, I don't know how many classes have ever graduated here that didn't win a state championship," he says. "I remember thinking about that some time ago. 'This group here hasn't had a chance to win one yet and we want to give them an opportunity to play for one.' It's one of those things that's not necessarily a burden, but it's pressure you put on yourself."

And it's true that not many classes have graduated from Webb City without a championship ring, at least in the 23 years since Webb City football became synonymous with winning.

There was a five-year span without a title early in the new millennium. Since that point, the Cardinals have brought home five of the last seven championships, and the senior class that just won No. 11 will graduate with three rings and one loss in four years.

And each time, the buses turn onto Main Street and the town celebrates.

Roderique has driven home from St. Louis on his own the last two seasons, but he remembers a time, maybe the first state title he won, or the second or third, when the team was due back in Webb City well after midnight.

"I remember one kid in particular," he says. "He jumped up and saw we were heading in on 171 over the bridge east of town. I remember him getting up and I said, 'Are you a little bit excited about this?' He said, 'Coach, I've been dreaming about this. I've been dreaming about driving down Main Street forever. I've been dreaming about this day. Not just the game, but being on the bus that drives downtown.'"

Roderique gets goose bumps just thinking about it.

"It's one of those once-in-a-lifetime things," he says.

Well, at least it used to seem that way. Winning a state championship is a once-in-a-lifetime opportunity for almost every high school football player, coach and team in the state. It used to be viewed that way in Webb City. But now, that moment when the buses stop on Main Street isn't a rare occurrence. It's a rite of passage.

John Roderique's first season as head coach at Webb City was 1997. The Cardinals went 14-0 and won a state championship. In 16 seasons, he has never coached a team with a losing record. His second year on the job was his worst season, when Webb City went 5-5. The team went 8-2 in his third year, but missed the playoffs again. The Cardinals haven't missed the playoffs since.

In those 16 years since Roderique took over, Webb City has 14 playoff appearances, eight state titles, eight undefeated seasons and a record of 193-18. Roderique's winning percentage is 91.4, the highest in state history by a comfortable margin. The legendary Pete Adkins, who spent most of his career at Jefferson City, won 405 games with a winning percentage of 86.8.

Of the eight seasons when the Cardinals haven't won a title under Roderique and his coaching staff, Webb City has finished as a state runner-up once, a state semifinalist three times, and the Cardinals have also ended seasons in the sectional and quarterfinal rounds.

"You see the things in the programs, but I really don't know what to say about it," Roderique says. "It's very humbling to be considered one of the better programs in the state, I guess. Each and every year is different. That's the unique thing about it. That's what drives you as a coach, and that's what makes it exciting."

Right now it's December, and the holiday break is right around the corner. In January, the coaches will be talking to the junior class about next season. They'll spend winter, spring and summer working with next year's senior class, a group hoping to leave high school with a state title for every year they were there.

It's that offseason process that might be the highlight of coaching for Roderique. If it only comes down to winning, the wins become empty, he says.

"We've been very blessed and very fortunate to have good players, good coaches, good administration in our school, good support with our school community as well as our town, but it's more about the kids and trying to prepare them and, like my son for example, letting the kids realize how much they can really do. So many of our kids come in as freshmen and sophomores and we're kind of scratching our heads, wondering if they'll ever be good enough to play. Then, by the time they're a senior, they're an example like my son John. Heck, he turns into a pretty darn good player. It's just that process of developing those kids and seeing their maturity. That's probably what means more to me."

But it's also hard to ignore the wins, and most people know full well the kind of numbers Webb City has been racking up. The Cardinals have posted winning streaks of 24 and 28 games before. They won 30 straight from 1999 to 2002. Right now, they haven't lost since 2009, and playing the full 15-game schedule it takes most years to win a championship, the Cardinals have won 45 in a row. That's the longest streak of Roderique's tenure. That last defeat came at home, too, and in the state semifinals. Visiting Kearney took it to Webb City, winning 38-13, and then capturing a championship a week later. The Cardinals finished the year 13-1.

When most people talk about Webb City football and "the streak," though, they talk about regular season games. Roderique is asked about it every year. Since losing 30-3 to Columbia Hickman High School in week seven of the 2003 season, the Cardinals haven't lost before the playoffs.

Tied for the most titles in state history, with the longest winning streaks of Roderique's career; with all the percentages and statistics and the machine that Webb City football is today, this would seem as good a point as any to declare this as the peak of the sport in this town.

That's not saying the Cardinals won't continue to rack up wins and titles, even at their current pace. There's no telling what the future holds, and no reason to believe they won't be dominant for years more to come.

But if this right now isn't the highest point in the proud history of football in Webb City, then what is?

"Gosh, it'd be hard to say it's not," Roderique says. "People ask a lot of times, 'What's the best team?' And that's not even fair, I think, to rank teams like that, but our football team this year was probably about as dominant as we've ever had since I've been here."

And you can't just compare seasons by statistics, either. In 2012, the team's starters played all four quarters in maybe two games, Roderique guesses. A lot of times they only played a half.

"It was a very dominant team and it had good, talented kids," he says. "It had really smart kids. We've got a smart group of seniors, a really athletic group of seniors. And good people, good families, good parents so we didn't have a lot of issues off the field or within the team. It's hard to think it could get much better, honestly. But again, if it was just about the winning…" He pauses. "But that's kind of setting yourself up for failure and disappointment because it can't always be about that."

Webb City has had teams with less talent, and they've still won. They've won with teams that didn't have the star players or the college talent, and those years are especially rewarding for the coaches.

There have also been plenty of seasons like this one, where the Cardinals were ranked No. 1 in the state all year, and everybody expected it.

"You can look at it from a lot of different ways, but it would be hard to say that things can get much better," he says. "How much better can it be?"

The only thing left for the Cardinals to do is maintain the success. They've already climbed the mountain.

"The numbers are so staggering," Roderique says. "Ninety consecutive regular season wins. To me, all the pressure's off. That's how I look at that. We've far exceeded what any of us even dreamed would be possible. Five out of the last seven state championships. Those things are far more than what we ever expected. But there's always pressure outside from what people expect every year. We really enjoy the process. Enjoy the preparation and getting kids ready, just seeing the development of the kids and seeing them grow and mature over each and every step of the way."

Roderique, with a smile, has one last thing to say. To be honest, he says, he's ready for the streak to be over. Not that he wants to lose. His team will face some tougher competition next year, and some teams laden with seniors. In 2013, the Cardinals will travel to Springdale, Arkansas for a rematch with Har-Ber after beating them at home last year, and the Wildcats will be out for revenge.

2. THE FIRST FOOTBALL IN WEBB CITY

Elijah Webb moved in 1856 from his home in Tennessee to an area just south of the clear, pure running waters of Center Creek. A year later, his son, John C. Webb, claimed 200 acres of the area that is now Webb City, paying just a few hundred dollars for the land. He became one of Jasper County's most substantial farmers.

The Webb family was one of four prominent pioneer families who would go on to play major roles in the formation of the city, along with the families of William Armstrong Daugherty, Charles Jabez Tall Foster Hatcher and Dr. David M. Whitworth, who was the area's only doctor.

Webb City owes its existence not to the fertile soil on the ground, but to the rich mineral wealth below it. As the story goes, or at least one of the stories, J.C. Webb was plowing a field near Ben's Branch and turned up a chunk of lead. The story is feasible; much of the mineral content of the Webb City area was just beneath the surface.

Another account, still involving Webb, says he told his grandson he was once visiting with a man who was crossing his land in a wagon. As the pair visited, several chunks of lead fell out of the wagon, which gave Webb the idea to look for ore on his land.

Webb dabbled in mining, along with his neighbor, Daugherty, but didn't make any money. Instead, his fortunate came in real estate when he laid out the town of Webb City, which was chartered in 1876.

A year later, *The New Century*, one of Webb City's earliest newspapers, detailed the history of the young town. One of the "finest school houses in southwest Missouri" was nearly completed and a smelter was running full blast as local mines produced $70,000 worth of mineral ore each week.

"Situated upon a beautiful high and rolling prairie, about two miles and a half south of the Missouri and Western Rail Road, it presents a commanding view from all parts of the compass," the newspaper wrote in describing the town. "Where a year ago was nothing but fields and crops, where now is seen a city of over eleven hundred inhabitants, well built and beautifully laid off."

That school house was considered one of the city's chief ornaments and also its most useful building, and was expected to accommodate between 400 and 500 students when it was completed.

The Missouri Pacific Railroad came to town in 1881, and it was in a field where the railroad station was later built that E.T. Webb, son of John, said his father had discovered lead.

By 1893 Webb City had electric trolley service. Alfred H. Rogers owned a mule-drawn streetcar line between Webb City and Carterville, and after adding electricity to the mix, he formed the Southwest Missouri Electric Railway.

As mining operations in and around Webb City grew, so too did the population of the town. It had 9,201 residents in the 1905 census, and that population grew to nearly 12,000 in just five years.

Written accounts of the early years of the sport of football in Webb City are sparse. It certainly started before the turn of the 20th century. When Walter Harry Tholborn, a lifelong Webb City resident and civic leader, died at his home on South Madison Street in 1946 at the age of 63, his obituary stated he had been a stellar athlete on the undefeated team of Webb City High in 1899. Tholborn, who went by Harry, was born in 1883 to some of the original Webb City pioneers. He became a prominent member of the local Republican Party, served two years as town mayor and eight years on the local school board, including a stint as board president.

At least as early as 1904 football was being covered by the town's newspapers. *The Daily Sentinel* announced, on Oct. 5, 1904, a "picked" team would play the first game of the season against Webb City College and the "picked" team was expected to win. Two days later the paper reported the college had lost 5-0 at Joplin, but still had plenty of time to rack up some wins. The *Webb City Daily Register*, another of the city's early newspapers, wrote at least two stories in the fall of 1905 about the high school football team. Webb City lost a game 5-0 against Joplin on the evening of Oct. 20 at the league ballpark. As often seemed to be the case, the team was "greatly outclassed in weight." Webb City traveled to Carthage in early November 1905 for the second game of the year between the two teams, but the contest was called off when Webb City discovered an experienced team awaiting it, not an amateur squad like itself. The Webb City boys simply refused to play.

Around this time, in the few years after the turn of the century, Webb City High School students published something like a monthly school newspaper, called *The Review*. An issue published in October 1905 speaks briefly about the football season, noting a number of the "more husky fellows" were preparing for action. Webb City had played two games already, the first on Oct. 6 against the Webb City Normals at League Park. The high school team, although outweighed, managed to "push a man over the goal" in the second half of the game and won 5-0. A week later Webb City played on the road in the first game against Carthage and won 10-0.

"They intend to play the season to a finish and are looking for a supper after their fourth or fifth victory," *The Review* wrote.

In November 1905 *The Review* published its Thanksgiving edition. The high school had lost two football games, 5-0 against Joplin, and 48-0 against Columbus. Games consisted of two 20-minute halves.

"You could see the stern visages harden as the ball was placed in position for the kick off," *The Review* wrote of the triumph against Columbus. "Every back bent in unison as the umpire called 'Ready Columbus,' and the deep tuned answer 'Yes' came rolling back across the intervening space. Every eye shot a baleful gleam: every hand clinched tighter as the umpire called 'Ready Webb City,' and like an answering echo rolled back the word 'No.' The ball had rolled out of position."

Around this time there was a building boom in Webb City, and Walter Stemmons, a Carthage resident, wrote an extended piece for the *Joplin Daily American* in September 1906 outlining all of the improvements to the town. The *Daily Register* referred to Stemmons as one of the "brightest young newspaper men in the county." According to him, by the end of the year 1906 more than $1 million would have been spent on improvements within the city alone, and at least 300 residential properties had been constructed that year at an average cost of $1,500.

He cited the new Webb City Northern Electric Railway line as one instance of the town's prosperity; the line connected with Alba, Neck City and Purcell. The Missouri-Kansas-Texas Railroad was also expected to extend its lines through the city. Stemmons guessed that, among every town in the country the size of Webb City, none had experienced as much building. It wouldn't be long, he wrote, before the city limits of Joplin and Webb City would meet.

Later that month, Webb City High School won its first football game of the season at Galena, beating the Kansas champions 10-0. Webb City had practiced only three times before the game, the *Register* reported, while Galena had practiced for three weeks. Of interest: the game was played by 1905 rules, as neither team was yet familiar with the revised rules of 1906, which were "supposed to prove advantageous to teams whose players are nimble on their feet rather than to avoirdupois."

The year 1905 had been a particularly deadly one in the sport of football, with more than a dozen players dying, and president Teddy Roosevelt called to reform the sport after his own son was injured. The American Intercollegiate Football Rules Committee was formed, adopting new rules in the spring of 1906 meant to "open" the game where possible and eliminate unnecessary rough play.

One of the biggest changes under the new rules was the requirement to gain at least 10 yards in three downs, as opposed to five yards as the game was previously played. The rules also allowed forward passes. Rules also reformed methods of tackling and created harsher penalties, and limited the number of players situated on the line of scrimmage to six.

According to *The Review*, Webb City scored both of its touchdowns in the Galena game in the first half. After that, Galena substituted three "town boys" for three of its high school players, which enabled the team to play better.

Webb City had arrangements to play every Friday afternoon until Thanksgiving that year against teams like Joplin, Neosho, Carthage, Lamar, Columbus and Seneca, which Webb City would play at home on Thanksgiving Day. When the team played Joplin a week after the Galena game, the *Daily Register*, in previewing the game, wrote that the team would play its first game under the "new and debrutalized rules." That contest was scheduled for 3:30 p.m. at Joplin's Barbee Park, which featured a race track and grandstand. Roughly 50 young spectators from Webb City accompanied the team to Joplin for the game, which was played on a muddy field in the rain. Joplin won 2-0.

Webb City's first home game was set for Oct. 19 against Galena, which was expected to be much stronger than the first meeting, *The Review* wrote.

"It is rumored that she will bring the town team which made such a record in 1904. This is expected by Webb City, who has gotten together such a 'bunch' of players as will enable them to give Galena 'a good run for their money.'"

By the first week of November, however, the enthusiasm surrounding the football team was dealt a "crushing blow" when the school board decided that no student could play football unless he had at least an 80 percent in three subjects. The rule was apparently harsh enough that *The Review* reported it would likely lead to the disbandment of the team, although several of the players were still going to play in the Thanksgiving game against Seneca.

Members of the 1909 Webb City High School football team, as pictured in the high school yearbook, King Jack.

3. THE EARLY YEARS

By Saturday, Sept. 14, 1907, the Webb City football team was officially ready to commence winning games from opposing teams. Such was declared in a headline on the bottom of the front page of the *Daily Register*.

The news brief, likely submitted by the team, sounded a cautious, though confident tone. The team was ready to meet any and all "strictly high school" football teams of the area on the gridiron. According to the article, "the question now is, Who will it be?"

While several dates had been planned, no games had yet been finalized, and the article boasted that the team had been greatly strengthened under the guidance of head coach Chas Holloway and would "undoubtedly give all the teams a good chase for their money."

The following Friday, the paper announced on the front page that the second high school football team had been organized and would challenge any team with a lineup not averaging more than 110 pounds. Those wishing to play the team could write to Lawrence Dick, who was the team's left end.

The 1907 season finally got under way in early October when Webb City hosted Carthage on the afternoon of Friday the 11th. The newspaper announced the game more than a week in advance, writing that Webb City was believed to have a fast team but was lacking in weight, as was Carthage. Players from Carthage High School had been hampered in their practice routine when they were banned from using the Grammar school play ground to scrimmage on, and were left with virtually nowhere to host a game without venturing to the remote corners of Carthage.

More than 250 spectators attended the game, but with Webb City handicapped by the absence of three regular players, Carthage left town with a 5-0 victory. Webb City came close to tying the score, moving within 20 yards of the goal line following a 30-yard run, but time expired.

The day before Thanksgiving the *Daily Register* announced there would be a Thanksgiving Day football game between the Webb City High School first team and the local Y.M.C.A. at the local ball park. The Y.M.C.A. team was composed of grown men who had played football for several seasons, and though the high school squad was younger in both years and practice, "the High School lads are not daunted by any such an array of players and expect to win the laurels of victory on the field tomorrow afternoon."

Friends of the teams had tried to secure a game between both squads in Webb City, though they apparently had offers to play in other towns like Monett and Galena. Roy Purkhiser, the high school team captain, declared the game must be played in Webb City and refused the other offers.

Seven hundred fans gathered at the ballpark for the Thanksgiving Day game against the Oronogo Giants, who won the toss and defended the east goal. Webb City received the ball to start, with a player named Teel receiving the opening kick. When he was tackled, he passed the ball to Mallory, who ran another 20 yards. Ten-yard gains by Carnes and Teel started the drive, and Purkhiser ran to both sides and up the middle for good gains before Oronogo got the ball on a fumble. After the teams exchanged possession a number of times, Carnes finally ran around Oronogo's left end and scored, with Mallory making the extra point. In the end, Webb City won the game 18-6. The next morning, the team left on an early train from Joplin on their way to Neosho to play in a game Friday afternoon. "The boys expected to hand them a package done up, which spells defeat, but they were confident they would have to work hard. After the game, a reception will be given the Webb City boys," a newspaper reported.

The game was played in a "sea of mud," and Neosho gave the visitors their most difficult game all season as Webb City lost 2-0. But even in defeat, it wasn't all bad for the players. The Neosho girls gave the Webb City boys a reception "which they enjoyed very much." The team returned to Webb City on the 3:45 a.m. train Saturday morning.

The account of the season differed slightly in the first issue of *King Jack*,

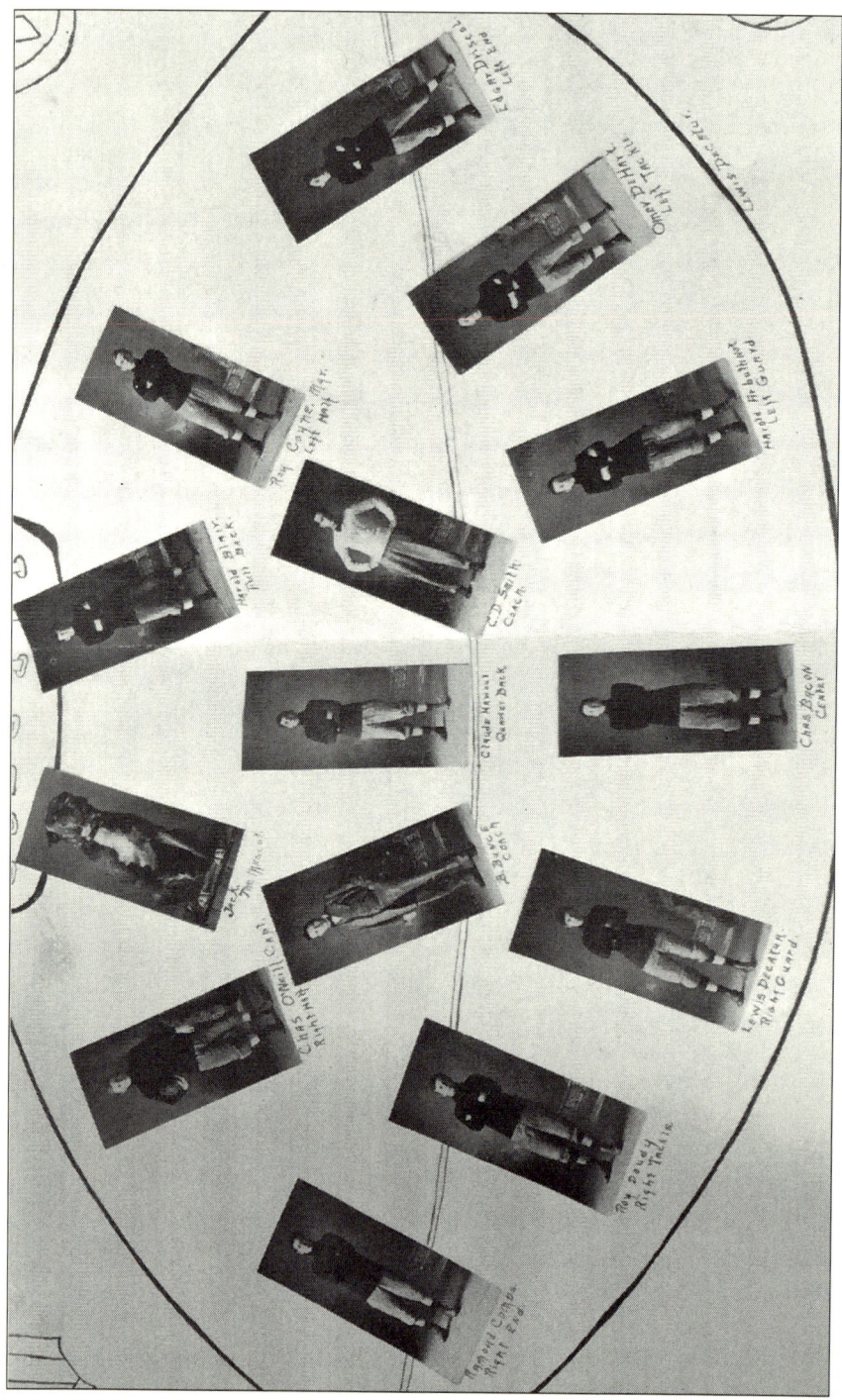

The 1909 Webb City football team, along with 'Jack,' the team's canine mascot.

the high school yearbook, which was published in 1908. According to the yearbook, the team had elected Elmer Stevison as captain and Albert Chenoweth as manager, and it had been a very successful year for the "Foot Ball" team. The yearbook mentions games not written about in the newspaper, such as a 5-0 victory against Carterville the week before the Carthage game. The team played Carterville again in its third game, this time winning 27-0, then beat the Joplin Seventh Street Grays 12-11 in a game that featured "many brilliant plays." In a second game against Carthage, Webb City avenged its first loss with a 28-0 thumping of the rivals. The best game of the year, however, was a contest against Joplin High School. Webb City successfully used many trick plays, as well as "masterly head work and hard playing" in beating Joplin 7-5.

Those early years of Webb City football featured numerous head coaches, which were at first elected by the players. Holloway didn't coach again after the 1907 season; he was replaced by Dr. M.S. Slaughter, who would spend many years with the program. Even he took years off, though.

The 1908 team was organized on Sept. 28 and elected W.L. Miller as the faculty manager, Vance Thralls as the student manager and LeRoy Mountjoy as team captain. It took just two weeks of constant practice to select what was considered a very strong team. Perhaps the team was too strong, though, as the yearbook reported that other high schools had formed an agreement not to play Webb City. The team was forced to play schools from further away, which happened to be better than any of the local teams. Even some of those teams turned down Webb City, saying the team was too strong for them, but teams from Springfield, Baxter Springs, Neosho and the Carthage town team accepted challenges.

The season opened with a 1-0 win against Carterville at the Tri-city park; Webb City won on a technicality. Behind star plays from Purkhiser and Mountjoy, Webb City defeated Springfield 11-0 on Oct. 10. Springfield won the return game on Oct. 24, 10-6. The team also worked to arrange games against Monett, Lamar, Aurora and Pittsburg, with the Pittsburg game slated for Thanksgiving Day. No word on if any of those teams accepted the challenge.

Maybe it was something in the water, or there just wasn't enough food to go around, but Webb City's lack of weight was again an issue in 1909, though what the team lacked in weight, it reportedly made up for in speed. They weren't quite fast enough, apparently. The team lost 10-5 to Galena in its first game of the year, due to "tough luck," then faced Columbus in game two. Webb City attempted an onside kick, but fumbled the ball and Columbus scored a touchdown to win 6-5.

The team's biggest rival in those days, and for many years, was not Carthage but Joplin. And Webb City lost that game, too, in 1909, falling 12-0 after two hours and 50 minutes of "swimming and fighting." The team then journeyed to Columbus and "played in another lake," losing that one 17-0. A player named Brown was playing well that game, but was ejected for "rapping" a Columbus

Doc Slaughter and his winless 1915 football squad.

player named Tub Jones too hard.

Even though they weren't huge rivals yet, the team delighted in winning 11-5 at Carthage for its first victory of the season. It was also apparently the best game of the year; it even featured forward passes. Webb City finished that season with a 4-4 record, though the Carthage game was really the only win in head-to-head competition. Joplin, Galena and Carthage each forfeited later games.

By the spring of 1910 the big news was Webb City's admittance into the Inter-High League after a year's absence. The team had been kicked out of the league on charges of playing dirty ball, but since being reinstated, *King Jack* said the players had been "the nicest little fellows."

"True, we did have a little trouble, but in both instances the trouble was on foreign grounds, the first at Joplin and the second at Carthage. The league is more of a success this year than ever before."

The league was composed of schools from Columbus, Carthage, Galena, Webb City, Carterville and Joplin. Webb City High School also formed an athletic association to encourage more students to attend the games, and that, too, was a successful effort. Clarence Lively served as head of the association, and Roy Coyne was secretary and treasurer.

Chas. Smith and Beverly Bunce coached a winless team in the fall of 1910, though the coaches believed they would "carry away everything in sight" the next season, as the yearbook wrote.

Chas. Smith, Slaughter and Beverly Bunce were the coaches in 1912, when the team went 3-3-1. Slaughter alone was listed as the coach a year later, and despite a bad year on the field, the yearbook found no fault with his coaching, instead citing bad luck. Slaughter was said to be faithful and loyal to the team. The team was winless in 1915, but again, it wasn't Slaughter's fault. He reportedly had such odds against him that he couldn't make the team a winner.

The greatest game that year was against Joplin, "our old enemy," which sported an undefeated squad when it came to play winless Webb City at Lakeside Park. Joplin had planned to "white-wash" Webb City, and 500 spectators rode trolleys to the park and watched the game, which was scoreless after a half of play. Injuries to Webb City's linemen finally mounted in the second half, and Joplin escaped with a 27-0 win. Nearly all of the players were due to return in the fall of 1916, though, and "Doc" was planning for a championship team. *King Jack* offered some helpful advice: "Don't disappoint him, boys. Get into the game and make Webb City loom up so big that Joplin can't hold a candle by the side of us."

Doc Slaughter in the 1917 issue of King Jack, left, and in the 1920 issue of the yearbook, at right.

4. THE FIRST GREAT TEAM

After Webb City failed to win a single game in 1915, Doc Slaughter set the bar high for the following season. The team returned almost everyone, and Slaughter had used the word "championship" to describe his expectations. Slaughter knew what he was talking about.

The team of 1916 was the first greatest team in school history. Enough players turned out to field two teams, and the captain and manager convinced local merchants to donate enough money to buy 20 jerseys, which were worn proudly by both teams each time they played. It was also reported in 1910 that merchants had generously paid for the team's uniforms.

The uniform was a red, long-sleeved shirt with two white stripes across the chest and on each arm. Players also wore baggy pants that came down just below the knee, starting halfway up the torso, and striped socks. They were a big deal; the yearbook printed photos of the players proudly wearing them.

Chalmers Smith was the team's quarterback and team captain. A senior, he weighed 168 pounds, and was nicknamed "Buzz." The left halfback was junior Forest Smith, who weighed 165 pounds and was nicknamed "Slim." At left tackle was post-graduate Harlie Smith, who also weighed 168 pounds. He just went by "Harlie." Senior Wesley Claypool played the other tackle position and he weighed just 155 pounds. Nicknamed "Whistle," he "didn't tell them what he'd do but went ahead and did it and everybody knew about it."

The two ends were senior Raymond Schoenherr and junior Claud Daniels. Schoenherr, nicknamed "Shinney," weighed 148 pounds and was known as a flying tackler. Daniels weighed 140 pounds and just went by Daniels. He played good ball. A third end was senior Dewey Imes, who went by Dewey and weighed 130 pounds. He had a big performance in the Joplin game. Shirley Myers, the hero of the Joplin game, was the senior right halfback and weighed 138 pounds. He was known for his "educated toe," which won the game.

Paul "Doc" Rose played right guard at 160 pounds. A junior, he was also a self-made prize fighter. Sophomore Don "Pedro" Rafferty played left guard at 155 pounds. He was best known for being red-headed, and also played good ball.

Junior Dale McCoy was the heaviest player on the team at 185 pounds, earning him the nickname "fat." He played center and "always managed his opponent." Senior Charles "Chick" Keys weighed 154 pounds and was a "steady man" at fullback.

There was plenty of excitement around the program that fall, and the slogan of the season was simply "Beat Joplin." The teams would meet at Joplin on Thanksgiving Day, the last game of the season. Webb City won six of its first eight contests leading up to the Joplin game, the only losses coming against Carthage, who won 18-7 in Webb City and 7-0 in Carthage. Home wins came against Neosho, Aurora and Pittsburg, and the team won road games at Galena, Neosho and Aurora. The win against Pittsburg came the week before the big game, and was held at Lakeside Park. Slaughter played several second-team players in the 14-7 win to rest his regulars for Joplin.

Despite the two losses, Webb City was a confident team when Thanksgiving rolled around, and fully planned to go to Joplin and win. A week in advance, the *Daily Register* printed a story, citing accounts from a Joplin newspaper, that Joplin's coach Marr expected the clash to be Joplin's hardest game of the season, and Joplin officials expected a record crowd. Marr was also greatly interested in the outcome of the Thanksgiving Day game between Carthage and Springfield.

"If Springfield wins, he maintains that the county seat athletes will be automatically eliminated from the championship struggle, basing his assertion on the fact that Joplin defeated Springfield," the article stated. "If Carthage wins, Marr will demand another game with them to be refereed by four neutral officials."

At least 1,500 people turned out for the game at Joplin, and both Marr and his Joplin squad were supposedly visibly nervous before kickoff. Slaughter and the Webb City boys were "easy and confident."

Two long forward passes for Joplin put the ball at the Webb City 3-yard line early on, but the Webb City defense stopped them on four straight plays. It was the closest Joplin would come to scoring all day. After this, the crowd saw some of the best high school football ever seen in Joplin, the *Daily Register* wrote. In the fourth quarter, Webb City had the ball near the Joplin end zone, but a 20-yard penalty pushed the ball back to the 25. Facing into the wind, Shirley Myers dropped back to the 30 and kicked one of the "prettiest thirty yard kicks ever seen at a high school game." That was the difference, and Webb City ended the season with a 3-0 win at Joplin.

"The main feature of the game was Imes fast work at end; Rose at center James at quarter and Myers kicking," the newspaper wrote. "Altho the team work of every man was perfect and C. Smith out kicked Johnson of Joplin by about ten yards on each punt, Johnson the supposedly fast quarter back for Joplin failed to show Webb City anything and the first Webb City gains were made thru Dorman, the *News Herald* all star tackle, showing that in picking the All Star team, that Webb City had not been considered."

With the win at Joplin, and Springfield's defeat of Carthage, Webb City also won that season's championship. The newspaper explained the math:

"This leaves Webb City with seven games won and two lost, Carthage with six won, one lost and two tied Webb City winning over both teams that Carthage tied, while Joplin win five and lost two and tied two, so altho Webb City lost two games to Carthage, taking the entire season, and the fact that Joplin beat Springfield, 14 to 0, while Springfield beat Carthage 13 to 0 and Webb City beat Joplin 3 to 0, giving Webb City an advantage over Carthage for the championship."

FOREST SMITH
Junior
Wt. 165—Left Half Back
"Slim," the third member of the tribe, who was known the district over for his remarkable scoring ability.

CHALMERS SMITH
Senior
Weight 168—Quarterback (Capt)
"Buzz," another member of the tribe, who came into public notice and won his spurs at Joplin.

HARLIE SMITH
Post Graduate
Wt. 168—Left Tackle (Mgr)
"Harlie," left tackle, who could always be depended upon to get his man and some one else's. He is the first member of the tribe.

(Top) Chalmers Smith, Forest Smith and Harlie Smith show off the team's new uniforms in 1916, which were donated by local merchants. (Bottom) Members of the 1918 team, from left: Sam "Shinny" Shaner, Harry "Jonesy" Jones, George "Wildcat" Rutledge, Floyd "Fat" Freeman, Jack "Flop" Flournoy, Orin Reece, Cecil "Zeke" Herrod, Ray "Sody" Stewart and Herbert "Eagle Beak" Kerr. Reece, according to King Jack, was "too steady for a nickname."

Three seniors from the 1919 football team. At left is captain Herbert Kerr, who played fullback; quarterback Pat Boyer is in the middle, and manager Sam Hoffman is at right.

5. THE ROARING TWENTIES

Webb City "repeated the annual defeating of Carthage" in 1919, according to the yearbook, though the team lost its claim on the Southwest championship that season by losing to Joplin by an "overwhelming" score. Doc Slaughter was back as head coach, still reportedly "very" efficient and faithful.

Thirty-five players turned out for the first day of practice in 1920, and Slaughter had whipped the team into shape when the first game was called against Galena. Webb City would win 19-0. In week two the team traveled to Neosho and *King Jack* wrote that Webb City showed the "pumpkin-growers" something about football in a 6-0 win that included Frank Freeman's initiation into football – he received a bloody nose.

The team outscored its opponents 156-79 that season, posting another big win against Galena, 51-7, and a 53-6 win against Baxter Springs. The team was shut out in two games against Carthage – 6-0 and 12-0 – and finished the year with a record of 4-4-1. The first loss to Carthage was blamed on clay and mud on the field, while the second was the annual Thanksgiving Day game that featured the largest crowd all season. Weight was still an issue; the heaviest player on the team was tackle Warren "Pap" Hill, who was 5-foot-11 and 170 pounds.

The 1920 season would be Slaughter's last as head coach, and the program saw a bit of a coaching carousel for the rest of the Twenties. There was a man named Henry Grigsby, a science instructor, in 1921, though he coached for just one year, a poor one on the field. Doc Slaughter was back in the picture a year later, though as an actual doctor, serving as the team physician with Gene Reel the team's head coach. Forty players answered Reel's call to report to practice, and after three weeks a team was chosen. According to *The Joplin Globe*, superintendent J.A. Hale authorized all grade students to be released early in time for them to reach the field that season; in previous years they needed parental permission if they wanted to leave early enough to see the beginning of the games. Long overhead passes were adopted as an offensive tactic, and Webb City won three of its first four games that season and tied against a heavier Pittsburg team. In the team's first three games, not a single touchdown was scored by opponents, and by the time Reel's players took on Baxter Springs in the season's fourth game, both players and coach alike were confident of a win. The solid start to the year set up a big match-up with Carthage. The team's 16-0 loss was blamed on hot weather and a dusty field. Webb City also played Sarcoxie in 1922, winning 53-6, but lost the very next week at Monett on Armistice Day, Saturday, November 11. Field conditions were once again to blame; the playing surface was described as "rough." Webb City won two more games, against Aurora and at Seneca, before the big Thanksgiving Day game, a rematch with Carthage. Webb City was hurt by the loss of its quarterback, Bailey Harrison, who was injured, and though the team lost 16-6, Webb City was one of just two teams to score on Carthage all season. A cooked goose banquet was held for the team in the dining hall of the First Methodist Episcopal Church after the 6-3-1 season and was attended by 19 of the team's 22 players and 16 guests. Reel was praised for putting together a strong team, and everyone said goodbye to the six graduating seniors: J.T. Herrod, the left halfback; Max Miller, the center; Frank Barlow, the right guard; Wright, at left tackle; Mummey, at left tackle; and B. Jones, another right guard.

Reel coached again in 1923, and Slaughter again looked after the team's physical condition as the size of the program grew steadily over previous years, with 50 players reporting for the first day of practice. Harrison was back at quarterback, and along with Marcus Harrison, Kenneth Gregory, Virgil Sherman, Paul MacFarlane, Horace Cruse, Robert James and Albert Cobb, the strongest team in the history of Webb City High School was built, at least according to the yearbook. Things started off strongly: Webb City hosted neighboring Carterville, "a snappy little team," and won 35-0 to open the season, then picked up wins against Galena, at Baxter Springs, and against Nevada and its "one-ton team."

Barely two decades since the high school began playing football – when it was considered more of a club than anything, with faculty and student managers – the sport was growing quickly in popularity. *The Daily Sentinel*, the day before the week four game with Nevada, reported that Webb City businesses would close at will the following afternoon for the football game. At a meeting the day before, business owners were urged to let their salespeople leave work early. Adding more hype to the game than Webb City's undefeated record alone, Nevada reported that when its team trotted onto the field the next day, it would be an unusually large team in terms of weight; its line averaged 170 pounds, and its backfield 165 pounds. Nevada, also unbeaten, had outscored opponents 113 to 7 in its first two games. Reel, replying to Nevada's claims in the same story, declared that Webb City would meet the "one-ton team" with speed and high-tempered steel, though Webb City averaged just 145 pounds on the line. Businesses even offered prizes to the team if it could defeat Nevada. One owner offered to give the team a dinner the next week, and Jimmy Malloss, of the Minerva Candy store, offered each player a pound box of candy. The high school teachers were excited, too. The faculty agreed to award a gold pencil to one player. It went to Paul MacFarlane, who would score the first touchdown of the game. When game day finally arrived, the stores closed at 2:30 that afternoon, and the massive crowd was delighted to watch a 25-12 Webb City victory.

"It came as a surprise even to Webb City folk who looked over the local's adversary before the game," the *Sentinel* wrote. "Nevada seemed to have the power but were unable to make it function. And the one-ton team as has been nick-named, went down to defeated before a much swifter and headier bunch of Webb City boys."

That night the team celebrated with a bonfire at the corner of Main and Daugherty streets, followed by a shirt-tail parade through the downtown area.

Things went downhill from there, though. Webb City lost 9-6 at Aurora, and it was reported the "Houn' Dawgs" used rough tactics and outsiders in the game. Webb City was also debating whether Aurora even belonged in the league, and the loss would count against the team in the league standings. In late October, the team from Carthage ventured to Webb City and tried everything it could think of but was unable to cross the Webb City goal line. Webb City couldn't score, either. The game ended in a scoreless tie, disappointing those Carthage fans who had ridden a special electric trolley chartered by the high school for the team and its supporters for the trip. Webb City expected to send 1,000 fans to the Thanksgiving game at Carthage weeks later. Webb City was also lobbying to have Aurora disbarred from the league as the team was still bitter about the loss a week earlier. the *Sentinel* reported that even if Aurora was declared a member of the league, Webb City would protest the game on the grounds that Aurora used ineligible players.

For the seventh game of the season the team hosted Neosho, but Webb City's players weren't in very good "trim" and the contest ended in another scoreless tie. After that game, the Board of Education fired Reel as coach, and it was becoming evident how big of a sport football had become. The board met in a special meeting the Monday after the game, and, yielding to pressure from the players, made the move to relieve Reel of his coaching duties. At the same time the board elected Otto Wilkerson to serve as "city school physical director in order that he may officially and legally assume, immediately, the duties of coach to the football team," the *Sentinel* wrote. "Football has become that important."

The timing of Reel's firing was odd. The team was 4-1-2 but had played in two straight scoreless ties. Only three games were remaining. But, according to the paper, the game against Neosho had developed a great amount of dissatisfaction and disaffection among players, who accused Reel of failing to coach and develop any new plays. His dismissal may have had more to do with politics. School board politics reportedly inspired the players' opposition to their coach.

Doc Slaughter was fervently opposed to the coaching change. He declared in the meeting that "football in Webb City is now at an end after this season." He walked out in the middle of the meeting, refusing to vote to hire Wilkerson. Wilkerson was an insurance salesman in Webb City, but also a former college athlete and he had coached the previous season at Fort Smith, Arkansas. The football team was to hold a ratification meeting that same afternoon to express its "hearty" approval of his hiring.

Wilkerson's first game at the helm was the team's third-straight tie, but this time the team managed to score 13 points against Monett in the Armistice Day game. Two weeks later, Webb City was blanked 30-0 at Joplin with four starters sitting out due to injuries. And Bailey Harrison was hurt again, this time suffering a broken rib. The Thanksgiving Day game at Carthage was postponed due to a deep snow, and when Webb City took part of the regular team there a week later, it lost 30-0.

Several months after the 1923 season had ended, Reel announced he would not return to the high school faculty, and would instead go to Washington, D.C. at the end of the school year to take his final examination to enter the United States diplomatic service. He had been preparing for the career move for three years, and hoped to obtain an overseas assignment; in the summer of 1924 he was appointed as U.S. consul in Cologne, Germany.

Otto Wilkerson's stint as head coach was a short one, lasting just three games. By 1924, Tom H. Grant had taken over as head coach, and Webb City lost its first game of the year against Carterville at Lakeside Park, on September 26. The team played Pittsburg, Neosho, Joplin, Miami, Monett, Nevada and Seneca, as well as two games against Carthage that season, but won just one game, a 9-0 defeat of Seneca.

By now the forward pass was becoming slightly more common, and a long forward pass was the difference in a 6-0 loss to Joplin at the Ball and Gunning Field on north Madison Street. The game between the "white-heat rivals" was played as a part of the harvest show celebration.

"There is some tradition of several years' standing for the Red and Green to uphold and for the Red and White to smash," *The Globe* wrote before the game. "Webb City has not won a game from Joplin since 1916 when they took in a 3 to 0 victory. Not since that day have they scored a point against a Red and Green eleven. This makes an ideal setting as the locals will endeavor to keep the slate clean and their opponents will be battling for all they are worth to crack through such a jinx."

A large crowd witnessed a 21-6 loss to "The County Seaters" in October, and two more forward passes were again the difference in a 13-6 loss to Miami; one was intercepted. By the time Webb City took on Carthage again, on Nov. 27, several players were sick and the team's morale was shot. The result was a 70-0 Carthage trouncing.

There was also controversy on the team that season. According to an account in *The Globe*, Grant was forced to "reorganize" the team three times that season, and election of a team captain was deferred until late October, when tackle Albert Cobb received two-thirds of the team vote. Francis Jones, another tackle, ran in opposition. Many of the team's most dependable players missed key games due to either insubordination or ineligibility, and two days before the Carthage game two backfield players and a lineman were kicked off the team.

A more detailed roster included in the yearbook sheds an interesting light on the sheer difference in size between players back then and those playing now. In 1924 the team's tallest player was Benard Clayton, who stood 6-foot-2 and played guard. Only three others were 6-feet. The biggest difference, though, is in weight. Freshman Lawrence McMechan, the team's other guard, tipped the scales at 175 pounds. Senior Walter "Woggie" Leib, another guard, weighed 177 pounds. They were the two heaviest players on the roster. The average weight of the whole team was just 153 pounds.

The team's mascot was a dog that looked to have some bulldog in it. It was pictured wearing its own sweater in the yearbook.

There was yet another head coach in 1925 when the school hired Max L. Cherry, of Mount Vernon. His team once again played Carterville, Joplin, and Nevada and had two games against Carthage, and also played Baxter Springs, Aurora, Lamar, Neosho, and even a road game at Quapaw, which the team lost 19-0. In the Quapaw game, Cherry coached for the first time against his old friend, John Phillipe. The two had played together at Mount Vernon and at Springfield teachers college.

In 1926, for the first time in Webb City High School history, a student Athletic Association was organized to promote interest in athletic events among students who weren't participating. Tom Lowe was elected president of the association, and Elda Bigley served as secretary. Cherry and Mr. Grigsby were the organization's sponsors. The group drew up a constitution that barred any officer from holding office if he or she was a member of an athletic squad, and in order to be a member of the organization, one must be a season ticket holder.

The association also handled all of the athletic funds, and presented receipts and expenditures for the 1926 football season. The association began the year with $326.69 on hand, and added $945 in cash gate receipts and $160 from other athletic associations. Officials were paid a total of $168 for the year, and Webb City paid visiting schools $315. The association paid $321 for supplies, $50 to rent the football field, and $48 to repair the team's shoes.

The association reported its financial situation was better than ever by the spring of 1927, with more than $300 on hand and rent on the new field already paid. The association also purchased new equipment for the basketball teams, and new jerseys for the football team.

Things were good for the athletic association, but not for the football team, which didn't win a game in 1926. It was especially disappointing because the team had expected to finish with a winning record and returned several key players, like Everett Bishop at halfback; Clayton, the captain, at center; Willis Lawson, another backfield player; as well as Turnor and Archie Ellsorth. On the line the team returned McCullough, Veatch and Davis, and a guard from Oronogo High School, Neff, had transferred in. On the bright side, the team scored points against Joplin for the first time in a decade, and Max Cherry was elected as president of the Southwest Missouri Inter-High School Athletics Association, which also voted to align itself with the Missouri State High School Athletics Association.

The team's backfield was on the lighter side, averaging 140 pounds, but the line was "unusually" heavy, averaging 165 pounds.

On the baseball diamond in 1926, the St. Louis Cardinals won their first National League pennant and went on to beat the New York Yankees in seven games to win the World Series. The Redbirds won eight straight games in the month of August and finished the season with a record of 89-65.

In response, Webb City chose a new mascot: the Cardinals.

James Gardner served one year as head coach in 1927, which was the best year of Webb City football in more than a decade. Captain Willis Lawson was back at fullback for the fourth season, and other returning lettermen were Gene Crocker at tackle, Roy Stark at end and halfback and Everett Bishop at halfback. Other players had seen playing time in 1926, like Archie Ellsworth, Philip Hardy, Thelbert Cagle, Lee Daugherty, Jr., Clifford Geer, David Buxton, Roy Johnson, Henry Damron and Bob Sellinger. The team won seven of nine games, with a loss and a tie. Webb City also finished second in the Southwest Missouri Class A Conference, something that hadn't been done since 1916. Lyle Turner and Henry Damron made the All-Southwest Team, and Willis Lawson, Everett

Bishop and Roy Stark received honorable mention.

"He knew football, he knew boys, and he knew how to make football players out of green boys," the yearbook wrote of Gardner.

As usual, Webb City played Carterville to open the season, blowing out the rivals 37-7. In a first-person account of the season in the yearbook, one of the players wrote that the team had been put through a "very hard practice" for a month leading up to the game, and the players were in great shape.

The team had grown overconfident when it hosted Neosho in week two, and it nearly cost Webb City the game, which ended in a 6-6 tie. The player wrote that the team lacked its "old fighting spirit," which it regained in time to host Nevada for its third game, an 18-6 victory.

"Our fourth game was our first one away from home; this time we went to Aurora, the town which last year beat us 20-0. The people as a whole were afraid that we could not play as well away from home as we did at home, but in this game we showed them that it did not make any difference whether we were at home or at Aurora. Aurora scored first, but just then we heard our yells from both sidelines and, looking around, we saw all of Webb City there. From then on they could not hold us back, and when the final whistle sounded we had swamped them."

A one-point win against Mount Vernon, a "real fighting bunch of fellows," and a blowout against Carl Junction in which Webb City played all of its bench, including freshmen, set the stage for a big homecoming game against Monett, played on Armistice Day. The players considered it the biggest game of the year. Despite outplaying the visitors, a fumble picked up by a Monett player, who fell over the goal line, was the difference, and Webb City lost 6-0.

"The following Monday we made up our minds we would win the two games left, one of which was with Carthage," the player wrote. "We practiced like we never practiced before, and that Friday we took the bus for Lamar. When we got there we had to wait almost an hour for the officials, but finally the only one we had came. We went out to warm up and, to our surprise, it was snowing. We were very slow to start, and Lamar scored on us and held us for downs the first and second quarters, but the second quarter our center got through and blocked a fumble, which resulted in a touchdown. We played until dark and had to cut off ten minutes, but we won, 20 to 6.

"Our last game, and the biggest game of the season, was on Turkey Day, when we went to Carthage, with no other thought than bringing home the bacon. However, we had not won from Carthage in nine years. Like all our other games, Carthage scored first, and we were still trailing 6 to 0 at the end of the first half. At the middle of the third quarter a pass from Lyle to Daugherty, right end, made a gain of fifty yards, and with four more downs, resulted in our first touchdown, making the score 6 to 6. We then picked up and fought for the deciding score. Lyle passed to Red in the final quarter, which made the score 12 to 6 in our favor. When the final whistle blew at the end of the game we were within just a few inches of their goal line, but we did not need the extra touchdown."

J.T. Herrod, a Webb City graduate, took over as head coach in 1928 after coaching at Carterville. His first team featured Lee "Junior" Daugherty at fullback, who, when in "fighting trim" tipped the scales at 187 pounds. Unfortunately for Daugherty and for the team, he broke a bone in his foot early on and was limited by the injury the rest of the year. The rest of the backfield was full of speed, with Lyle Turner at halfback – one of the district's "foremost broken field runners" – and others like Goff, an "eleven-second man" and Huckaby, a freshman who promised to equal Turner in speed. Bishdorff was at fullback and Miller at end. Linemen were Denron, an all-southwest guard; Johnson at center; Bettis and Maness at ends; and Gallagher at tackle.

Webb City opened that year with an exhibition game against the alumni, winning 6-0. The team didn't allow a point until week four of the regular season, and scored at least 44 in its first three games against Galena, Carl Junction and Carterville. Carterville, considered another traditional rival, proved no match for the Webb City backfield as the Cardinals won 52-0. Carterville had 23 passing attempts and only completed two; Webb City registered 20 first downs and gained 352 yards of offense while holding Carterville to one first down and 32 yards.

"In past years the blue and white had been able to hold Webb City to a comparatively low score, but the powerful Card aggregation was just too much for the lighter and less experienced team," the yearbook wrote.

As the season went on, though, the losses mounted – to Lamar, Mount Vernon, Monett, Joplin and Aurora. The yearbook wrote that Webb City's "impregnable defense, the smashing offense, and superb broken field running that had been formerly present in the Webb City machine was missing," in the 25-0 home loss to Mount Vernon.

Games weren't always played on regular weekly intervals as they are today. The team lost to Monett on a Friday, then took on the "Red and Green" at Joplin the following Monday, a game in which the Cardinals lost due to an "absence of punch." Still, the semi-annual defeating of Carthage was again repeated, 6-0 on Nov. 29.

"This game was played before the usual large Turkey Day crowd in a sea of mud," the yearbook wrote. "Neither team was able to show any powerful attack of any kind, but Webb held the upper hand throughout."

As the Twenties came to a close, the Cardinals had yet another new face at the helm, with Lloyd O. Samuels assuming the coaching duties for the 1929 season. But by early September, Samuels declared a "lack of football material" and spent the first two weeks of practice doing nothing but punting, passing and working on other technicalities. Senior Bob Sellinger appeared a favorite to start at center, as long as he could develop more aggressiveness and more accuracy in passing the ball. At guards Samuels had Mammen, Lewellyn and Bischdorff to choose from, and tackle was well taken care of by Gallagher, Byler and Thomas. Damron, the all-southwest guard for two years, didn't look well in practice early in the season. The ends were Bettis, the team captain, and Wright, with Lofton and Bruce showing promise; Kirby wasn't quite living up to expectations at quarterback, but other backs were showing promise like Silvara, Shouse, Terry, Huckaby, Harding, Smith, Davis and Kneeland. On the line, prospects were Hughes, Freeman, Sellinger, Mammen, Robinson, Lewellyn, Bischdorff, Sweetland, Gallagher, Byler, Thomas, Damron, Bettis, J. Wright, Lofton, Bruce and Hendry.

Despite the "lack of football material," Webb City was considered a dark horse to win the conference.

The Red and White played Joplin that year, which was coached by James Gardner, Webb City's former head coach. Like so many of his predecessors from the decade, he coached just one year. Webb City won only three games all season, during which the stock market crashed in late October and the Great Depression began.

From the top: The 1923 football team and the 1924 football team (King Jack). An overflow crowd at a Webb City game in the twenties, and a season ticket from 1922 (Webb City Area Genealogical Society).

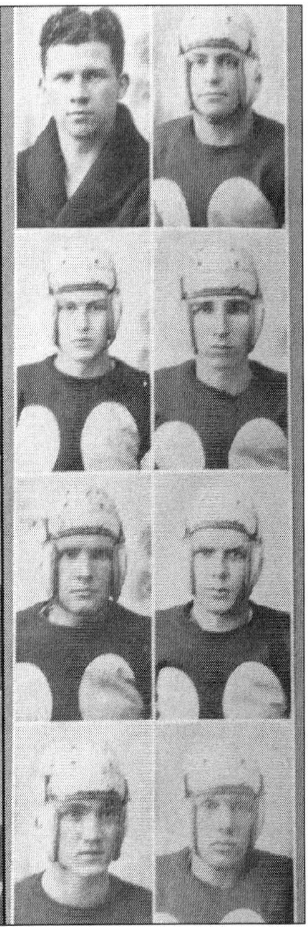

(Top left) The 1923 team, coached by Otto Wilkerson, who is pictured next to quarterback and captain Joe Ragland. *(Top middle)* Members of the 1926 team. *(Top right)* The 1928 team, pictured with head coach J.T. Herrod. *(Right)* The team's mascot in 1924.

Charles Cummings as a Webb City player in 1924, and as the program's head coach in 1932.

6. WEBB CITY'S BEST TEAM EVER?

Finally, with the arrival of 1930, came a sense of stability for Webb City's football program, as the school hired Carterville coach Charles Cummings to lead the team; he had graduated from Webb City in 1925. He would guide the Cardinals for the next six seasons and coach some of the school's best-ever teams. And his legend only grew after he left Webb City.

Webb City won five games his first season and ended the year on a high note with a 12-6 defeat of Carthage. A young man with dark hair and big ears, Cummings posed for his yearbook photo in a white shirt and dress pants, holding a football at his side. By now the team's jerseys incorporated a large 'W' into the design.

Cummings' 1930 team featured players such as Emmett "Mutt" Hughes, who was one of the best centers in the league and who also blocked nine punts that season, two of which led to Webb City touchdowns. Offensively, the Cardinals were led by Louis "Louie" Kirby at quarterback, who was also a sure tackler on defense with a knack for breaking up passes, and also the team captain. He was "a friend of every man on the team," *King Jack* said.

After defeating Lamar 7-0 in the team's third game of the season, football players celebrated with their first bonfire in "many moons" in downtown Webb

City, soaking wood with gasoline in an old barrel in the alley just north of the *Sentinel* building. Firemen arrived and put out the blaze, and the players were forced single-file into a theater to continue the festivities. The bonfire caused enough of a ruckus that the *Sentinel* noticed, and the celebration made the front page of the paper the next day.

In Cummings' second year, the fall of 1931, the Cardinals were even better, winning eight of nine games and tying one. The yearbook wrote that it would probably be considered the greatest football season in school history, past, present and future.

"With the coaching of Mr. Cummings, the perfect teamwork and spirit of the team, it is not surprising," *King Jack* wrote. "They accomplished three things principally: broke the Joplin and Monett jinxes and won the first conference championship. Joplin had been the reason why coaches turn grey, ever since the historic game of 1916, when the valiant Webb City gridironers defeated them, 3-0; W.C.H.S. had one of her best teams that year."

An enthusiastic writer in *King Jack* proclaimed the season as the "greatest in the history of Webb City's gridiron sport."

Little could the yearbook editors have imagined how successful Webb City football would become more than half a century later.

That championship season of 1931 began on a clear, bright and warm day in late September with a thrilling game against rival Joplin, who broke a scoreless tie with a safety in the third quarter. In the final eight minutes of the game, the Cardinals began a long drive toward the Joplin end zone. Frank Hanna, previously a star player at Carterville and one of the hardest-hitting backs in the conference, carried the ball four straight times, plunging over the goal line on fourth down to give the Cardinals the 6-2 victory.

As an example of the intensity of the Webb City/Joplin rivalry, the win was considered the highlight of the season, even ahead of winning the conference championship for the first time. Webb City's 1919 squad had come within a game of the conference title when the team still played in the Big Ten Conference of Southwest Missouri, but a loss to Joplin prevented it. That conference, in 1928, became the Big Eight, omitting Joplin and Springfield.

Lamar challenged the Cardinals for the Big Eight title, playing Webb City to a 7-7 tie midway through the season, but the Tigers lost to Nevada in the final game of the year, giving the Cardinals the outright bragging honors.

"However, the general opinion, in Webb City anyway, is that the game rightfully belonged to us," the yearbook wrote of the tie. "Several scoring chances were missed by fumbles, and we made more yardage and first downs than Lamar did."

As far as breaking the Monett jinx, Webb City's 38-6 trouncing was the first time the Cardinals had won that match-up in at least a decade, coming only as close as a 13-13 tie in 1923. The losing streak ended on Monett's "slanting" field.

"It was a cloudy day, especially for Monett," the yearbook wrote. "Finding straight football was not getting them anywhere, and trick plays as ineffectual, Monett attempted a wild passing game, sending about half the team down the field on every play. The referee could not be convinced that this was not in accordance with the rule book, so the only thing to do was to win the game anyway, which is now a matter of history."

Just three times did the Cardinals score in single digits all year. Otherwise, they posted at least 34 points in four games, and even scored 48 against Mount Vernon. When the season was done, Webb City had outscored its opponents 223-30, the highest scoring total in team history. Again, the yearbook provided some context.

"The highest total score any previous team had managed was 212 in 1922, but they also allowed 87 points to be rolled up against them, and got an average of only about two and one-half as much. The team of 1928 also obtained an average of two and one-half. With these statistics it is possible to get a better idea of where this year's team stands. The first team to beat Joplin since 1916, the first championship team, and the only team so far to beat Monett, made an average of eight times the opposing score, collected the greatest aggregate score of any W.C.H.S. team, held four teams to no score, and had no greater a score than 8 points made against them. Besides which the margin between the total scores of Webb City and the opponents was 193 points, the team was unbeaten, with but one tie, and they surpassed all previous teams."

Cummings gave the team a turkey banquet and invited several citizens to attend the event, where the team's lettermen were announced and Kenneth Kneeland was elected as an honorary captain. Some 150 people attended another large banquet for the team, this one sponsored by the Webb City Chamber of Commerce, and turkey was again the pièce de résistance. Past graduates of the high school told stories of the "greatest team in the history of Webb City" that they had played on, though there was no topping the squad of 1931.

"Perhaps in the future, members of this year's squad will explain to their children or grandchildren how they made the winning touchdown in the most important game of the most successful team ever to bring home the bacon to W.C.H.S.," *King Jack* concluded.

(Top) Webb City in 1934. (Bottom) The 1935 Cardinals.

(Top) Webb City in 1936. (Bottom) The 1937 Webb City team. Head coach Wilburn Morris is on the top row, third from the left. Bill Jackson is wearing No. 76 in the middle row, and his younger brother, Eugene Jackson, is sitting on the ground with a football. Next to him is the team mascot "King."

7. PEARL GREEN AND A LOT OF LUCK

Obviously, the assertion that no team in Webb City history ever would be as good as the 1931 unit turned out to be incorrect. And it only took one year to prove it, as the Cardinals were even better than before in Cummings' third season at the helm. Granted, that 1932 team didn't post the gaudy statistics and didn't win by big margins, but the Cardinals went undefeated again, this time with no ties, and won another Big Eight conference title. Even more importantly, Webb City beat Joplin for the second year in a row, 6-0. And that old tradition, the annual defeating of Carthage, was repeated to close out the season, 19-0.

The largest margin of victory was just three touchdowns, and the team eked out wins against schools like Aurora, Lamar, Monett and Nevada. Webb City was said to be blessed with "Pearl Green and a lot of luck," but *King Jack* considered a more accurate description to be "eleven football players and a never-say-die spirit."

That spirit was on full display in a 13-7 win against Aurora. After leading early, the Cardinals found themselves locked in a 7-7 game against a team with all the momentum and a referee who was "generous" with his penalties. With the ball on the 50-yard line at the end of the game, quarterback Pearl Green fired off a long pass to Bill Byers, who caught it as the final gun sounded and Webb City emerged victorious. Two more close games, a 7-6 win against Lamar and a 13-12 victory against Monett, ended in similar thrilling fashion.

"These three games were examples of the strong determination to win, which was the greatest virtue of this year's team," the yearbook wrote.

A boost in attendance that season was due in part to the Queen of Football contest sponsored by the student council. Three candidates, Sylvia Bouser, Maxine Giles and Helen Peek, were in the running, and votes were obtained by the sale of football tickets. Bouser was crowned queen at the football field before the Thanksgiving Day game with Carthage.

The winning streaks ended in 1933 when the Cardinals lost to Carthage and didn't even play Joplin. Three losses in the middle of the season took them out of the conference race. The schedule was different, too, even beyond the absence of Joplin with games against Galena and Jasper. They played Jasper again a year later, but it was just one of three wins for the team in 1934. Cummings turned the team around by 1935, though, and the Cardinals earned second place in the

Big Eight with a record of 7-1-1, tying in week two with Pittsburg and losing a 7-6 heartbreaker against Nevada in November. The 1935 squad had an especially stout defense, allowing just 23 points in nine games and posting five shutouts, including a 20-0 defeat of Carthage on Thanksgiving.

For the first time in at least a couple decades, the Cardinals had an official assistant coach in 1936, Cummings' last season with the program, when he hired Wilburn Morris, a newcomer to the school faculty. Unfortunately for Cummings, his tenure ended with a lackluster year; the Cardinals won three games, lost four, and tied twice. The only positive was yet another win against Carthage in his final game as coach. After that, he left for Indiana.

Cummings also coached basketball, and his 1946 Anderson High School team won the Indiana state championship by defeating Fort Wayne 67-53. His father, John Cummings, 61, who had worked for the *Joplin Globe* and *News Herald* for 23 years, listened to the title game on the radio in Webb City; when it was over he went back to his home at 120 North Jefferson Street and died later that night of an apparent heart attack.

Charles Cummings, who had moved to Crawfordsville, Indiana in 1937 after leaving Webb City, coached basketball there for four years, his teams advancing to the semistate twice and the final four once. After Crawfordsville, he took the job at Anderson and coached another four years. There he made the state finals in 1944 and won the state championship in 1946. The best player on that team was the legendary "Jumping" Johnny Wilson, the only player on the team who was able to dunk. In the state title game, he scored 30 of the team's 67 points. After graduating that spring, he hoped to play basketball at Indiana University but wasn't recruited; the Big Ten conference had an unspoken policy not to recruit African-American basketball players. He instead attended Anderson College, where he was a two-time All-American. He played for the Harlem Globetrotters from 1949 to 1954.

With a coveted Indiana state championship under his belt, Cummings was in demand as a head coach, and he accepted the head coaching job at Boston College before the 1948 season began.

He returned to Anderson in 1960 where he served as athletics director until he retired in 1974. He was inducted into the Indiana Basketball Hall of Fame in 1971, and he was inducted into the Webb City High School Hall of Fame in 2000. He died in 2003 at the age of 94, and is buried in Mount Hope Cemetery in Webb City.

Wilburn Morris was the team's head coach in 1937, and he, too had an assistant in Lonnie Adams, but Webb City finished with a losing record for the second straight season with only four regular players back from the year before. Still, the Cardinals beat Carthage, and at least 13 lettermen were expected to return in 1938; hopes were high once again.

At left, Bill Jackson during his playing days for Webb City in the 1930's (Webb City Area Genealogical Society). On the right, Bill Jackson gives a thumbs up to the crowd while John Roderique speaks during a 2008 pep rally at the high school. (Photo by Bob Foos.)

8. BILL JACKSON AND THE LIGHTS AT HATTEN FIELD

For many, many years Bill Jackson has been a familiar face on the sidelines at Webb City football games. Always decked out in Cardinals attire, including a Webb City ball cap, Jackson can likely count with a hand or two the number of football games he's missed since 1978. That's the year he moved back to Webb City after he retired from the Beech Aircraft Company in Wichita, where he worked 26 years. In that time, Jackson has seen coaches come and go; he's watched players go on to play professional football; he's seen an old stadium torn down and a new one built in its place; he's witnessed hundreds of Webb City wins, dozens of conference and district titles and more state championships than he can count on two hands.

Jackson's connection with Webb City football goes back much further than 1978, however, and he's done much more than stand on the sidelines in his Cardinals gear. He was born in 1921 in a house that still stands on Second Street, and 15 years later he made the football team. Jackson played for the Cardinals in 1936, '37 and '38; he was on the first team ever to play under the lights at

Hatten Field, and he played in the first Webb City game broadcast on the radio.

He lived longest in a house at 11th and Jefferson Street, and still remembers riding the streetcars through town – up and down Daugherty Street, to Carthage and back, out to Lakeside Park. His father played baseball at Lakeside, and when the streetcars quit running, Jackson rode the buses back and forth.

"Them old streetcars was quite an experience," he says now.

As Jackson grew up, Webb City's mining industry was coming to an end, and he remembers running around in the tailing piles in the Sucker Flat area with his friends and brothers. A neighbor boy nicknamed "Poss" was usually in on the shenanigans.

"Where we lived on 11th Street was right next to a filling station and they had little one-room cabins they rented out at night," Jackson recalls. "In this yard there was a tree with an iron pipe across it and he'd get up there and hang by his legs and one of the neighbors come down and said, 'That's just the way a possum is.' That's where he got his name and he still goes by it."

Jackson is the oldest of his three brothers, Eugene, Bob and Roy, and he also has a sister. Each of the brothers played football for Webb City, and Eugene is even listed as the team mascot in team photos from 1936 and 1937, along with a dog named King. The 1936 season was Jackson's sophomore year of high school, and he played for Charles Cummings, who was in his last year at the head of the program before leaving to coach in Indiana. Jackson recalls Cummings as a sharp dresser who wore a jacket and tie to the games. He was nice, but firm.

"I mean he never hit you, he never kicked you, but when he told you something you knew he meant what he said," Jackson says.

The team wore dark maroon jerseys, and in practice the players wore old khaki-colored pants. The uniforms were "fair," Jackson says, but nothing like what the team wears today.

"We had a good time playing ball just as much as they do today," he says. "We didn't have the equipment. We had helmets, but they didn't have much padding in them. They were about like a motorcycle helmet. You didn't have much protection, no face guards or masks or anything. Our center got his nose broken and they put a nose protection on his helmet, but he was the only one who ever had one that I know of. We didn't have shoulder pads like they have today. We had thigh pads and hip pads and there wasn't much shoulder padding. We had pretty good equipment."

After Cummings left, Jackson played his last two seasons under the direction of Wilburn Morris and Lonnie Adams, both of whom, like Cummings, were firm coaches, though Jackson says he never heard either cuss anybody. Adams could kick a football a mile, according to Jackson.

"They were firm when they talked to you," Jackson says. "That's the way John Roderique is today. I've never seen him ever come up and hit you on the back. He gets in your face and says, 'You did this wrong.' That's the way you learn. You learn from your mistakes. The coach today we've got I would put him right along with my first coach. I had a lot of good coaches."

Jackson still remembers Webb City's plays, too. The offense usually operated in a single-wing formation, and "No. 1" was a run right through center and "No. 6" was a run off tackle. The team had only a few plays. Odd-numbered plays went to the left, and even numbers were plays to the right.

"We had a guy who played running back name of Ray Hill," Jackson says. "Jay Fussell was quarterback. He wasn't much bigger than I am but he was a good passer. Bill Waring – his dad was a miner from Oronogo; he ran the Oronogo Circle Mine at one time – he played guard. Verlie Abrams played tackle right next to me. Claude Burke was our center and he's about the only one that I've seen after I got home from the service. Mickey Smart was the other guard. Both of us pulled out and led interference or protected the passer. Only time we ever carried the ball was when we played Aurora one time. Our two guards pulled out to go down to cover the ball receiver when we punted; when we got down there, why, this kid who was gonna catch the punt, it just went right down through his arms and bounced up in my arms. I took off on the run toward the goal line and a guy hit me from the back and let the air out of me. The only time I ever had to come off the field for getting hurt."

Abrams, like Jackson, started playing in 1936, though as a freshman. He lettered each of his first two seasons, and had the reputation of being the toughest guy on the team as a sophomore. Waring lettered as a freshman in '37, reportedly showing up plenty of upperclassmen in the process.

Hatten Field wasn't much, Jackson says. Just "that old rock wall" around it. Some of the kids who didn't have any money were allowed to crawl over the wall to get inside. By 1938, with night games becoming popular, Webb City erected light poles at the stadium.

"When they started putting the light poles up we were practicing out on the field and we had to watch for the holes they were digging," Jackson says. "We thought it was great to have lights to play football. We didn't have school buses. If we had a car we loaded up our car and took the guys to play football."

But even with an illuminated playing surface and Joplin WMBH broadcasting games, Webb City didn't have locker rooms at the stadium. Instead, players dressed at the old high school on Broadway and walked to Hatten Field. Teams just stayed on the field at halftime.

That 1938 season, Jackson's last, started off with a bang. There was plenty of hype with all of the returning varsity players from the prior season, and in the first game the Cardinals beat Baxter Springs 13-7. The week two game against Joplin is the game that stands out the most to Jackson. It was the first time Webb City had played Joplin in a handful of years, and though the teams tied 6-6 in a "thriller," according to the yearbook, it was considered a moral victory for Webb

City. Of course, the Cardinals had one of the lightest teams in the conference and district, *King Jack* wrote, but made up for it in "hard, aggressive offense and a strong, determined defense."

"They had a pretty good passer," Jackson says. "I remember knocking down a pass or two that could have been a touchdown pass to win the game. That was probably my outstanding game. We played offense and defense both back then; we didn't have enough for both teams. I played left half back on defense. When they go around the right end, that's when they was coming at me. Man, we had a lot of fun."

Fussell and Burke were elected co-captains that season, and Abrams was considered the "roughest" player on the team. As for Jackson, *King Jack* wrote: "Although light in weight he played an excellent, hard game at guard position. He lettered two years for the Cardinals."

Webb City finished with a 6-2-1 record in Jackson's senior year and took second place in the Big Eight, with seven of 15 lettermen set to graduate the following spring. Jackson was supposed to be one of them, but instead he graduated a year later.

"I played too much football and didn't get my grades," he says. "I wouldn't give a book report and my English teacher flunked me. She said, 'Why don't you learn your lessons?' I said because I was learning my football plays. She just wouldn't pass me."

Jackson joined the military in 1942, the same year he married his wife, Freeda, who was from Granby. They had two sons, one of whom now sells football lighting equipment, among other things.

So, what makes Webb City football so good?

"The coaching and all the staff," Jackson says. "The whole school. The superintendent. The coaches, they just treat me like I'm one of the team. I guess it's because I played ball for Webb City. It gets into your skin, I guess."

In 1939, with Jackson gone – from the football team at least – the Cardinals won four games, losing three and tying three others. Wilburn Morris was still the head coach, and like so many times in the previous years, the Cardinals closed out the decade with a 13-0 shutout win against Carthage.

Jim Wynne scores a touchdown during Webb City's 28-7 victory over Carthage in the last game of the 1946 season. The Cardinals finished 5-4.

9. THE FORTIES

The 1940s marked a downturn for Webb City football. In the yearbooks, more thought was given to the annual Football Queen coronation than what happened on the field. The program went through a handful of coaches during the decade, and though the Cardinals finished with winning records in five seasons, they were winless in two more. Even worse, after dominating rival Carthage a decade earlier, the Tigers returned the favor in the 40s, winning eight of the 10 games between the teams. Webb City's rivalry with Joplin was coming to a close, as well. The teams only played in 1940, a game Webb City won 6-0. That was also Wilburn Morris' last season as the team's head coach. He was replaced by his assistant, Lonnie Adams, who coached for three seasons.

Adams' first year coaching couldn't have gone worse. The Cardinals lost all nine games they played, were shut out three times and never scored more than one touchdown in a game. But Adams' second season, in 1942, was probably

Webb City's best year of the decade. Despite having just 35 players on the team, the Cardinals posted a 6-2 record, beating the likes of Sarcoxie, Lamar, Aurora, Mount Vernon, Nevada, and – finally – Carthage, 18-6. It was good enough for third place in the Big Eight.

The Cardinals were in the thick of the conference race in 1943, but an 18-10 loss to Carthage in the final game of the season ended Webb City's hopes of a title. The highlight of the seasons, Adams' last, was a 20-14 victory over Monett in the sixth game of the year, ending Monett's undefeated season. Adams would finish with a career record of 11-14, though he was 11-5 in his last two years.

In came William Pierce in 1944, and like his predecessor, the Cardinals were winless in his first season. The program got back above .500 for the next three years, but never by much. Webb City was 4-3-1 in 1945, 5-4 in 1946 and 5-4 in 1947. The 1946 team finished third in the conference, and drilled Carthage 28-7 for the second, and final, win against the Tigers that decade.

Tom Dunphy coached the team in 1947, when the Cardinals won their first three games but finished 5-4, and Palma Hunter finished out the decade as head coach, but Webb City won just two games in 1948 and three games a year later when Jack Mayfield was named to the Big Eight All-Star Team. By now Webb City had enough players out to field a 'B' team every year, and it played four games in 1949, including three against other schools' 'A' teams. Webb City's B's tied with the Jasper A team and lost a second matchup. It also lost to Alba's A team, but beat Alba's B team by 10 points.

The coronation of the Football Queen at the Thanksgiving Day game between Webb City and Carthage in 1944. Pictured, from left, are Webb City captain Jim Hicks, Maxine Hancock, Janice Lamb, student body president Bob Woodard, Janie Duncan, Curtis Childress, Carthage captain Kennie Johnson and Shirley Palmer.

(Top) Webb City's 1945 football team. (Middle) The 1947 team pauses for refreshments. (Bottom) Action shots from the 1948 season. On the left, Jack Day goes around the end in the Mt. Vernon game. On the right, Bennie Leonard runs "Play No. 44."

The 1947 Cardinals in action.

10. THE BLUE TOP CAFE

Every time Webb City traveled north to play at Nevada or Lamar, the team bus would stop on the way back at the Blue Top Cafe off Highway 71 in Lamar. The place had great big rolls, and the school would pay the three dollars or so to feed each player there. Meals were served family style, and the coaches usually ordered chicken for everyone. Merlyn Elder remembers one night there in particular.

"They put the green beans and potatoes and gravy and chicken on the tables," he says. "Then they'd pass out these great big rolls and they'd give you butter and honey. They just ate lots of rolls and butter and by that time everybody was full and they didn't eat much chicken."

After having their fill the players boarded the team bus in the parking lot and started the drive south, back to Webb City. They had just beaten Lamar 19-13 in the final game of the 1961 season, Webb City's best year in well more than a decade, and the win capped an 8-1 year and solidified the team as Big 9 Conference champions. Elder doesn't know who suggested it, but as the team bus approached Carthage, someone suggested they take a spin around the square.

"We were two blocks from the square so we just drove up and around it," Elder says. "We went around the square and it was after midnight and there wasn't anyone down there, no cars, nothing down there but we just drove around the square honking the horn and making lots of noise and we came home and that was it."

Carthage had beaten the Cardinals 7-0 in the third game of the year, Webb City's only loss, but when the season was over it was Webb City who was crowned conference champion and the players were eager to rub it in a little bit with their neighbors to the east. After all, they hadn't won a conference title since 1932.

In 1961 Elder was still an assistant coach and Henry May was the team's head coach. May had taken over in the 50s and played a big role in reversing the program's decline throughout the 1940s. Palma Hunter, who took over in 1948, would become one of the longest-tenured coaches in school history to that point, leading the program for seven years. He was not, necessarily, one of the most successful. His first two teams combined to win just five games, but as a new decade arrived, the Cardinals were at least average on the field.

Hunter guided Webb City to a 4-5 record in 1950 and a fifth-place finish in

Jim Hunter in 1952. Hunter is one of the greatest athletes in Webb City history. He was an all-state football player, earned 12 letters and was one of four players in Missouri to have his number "retired" by legendary University of Missouri head coach Don Faurot.

the Big 8. Monett, usually a strong team, won the conference, while Mount Vernon, Nevada and Lamar rounded out the top four, and Carthage (6th), Neosho (7th) and Aurora (8th) finished at the bottom. That team only returned one veteran lineman, Floyd Shirk, but by Thanksgiving had greatly improved – enough to end the year on a high note with a 6-0 whitewashing of Carthage in the 54th game played between the two rivals. One of the best players on the team was Jack Mayfield, a "backfielder" who was named the "outstanding backfield-man of the year" by Webb City's Athletic Association. The association also provided a banquet the following January at the First Presbyterian Church annex to honor the players. John C. Simmons, the freshman football coach at the University of Missouri, served as guest speaker.

The 1951 gridders won just three of eight games, but were supposedly feared by every opponent and even claimed a few upsets, particularly a 6-0 win against a powerful Nevada squad. In addition to the usual conference opponents, Webb City played Rogers for the first time that season. Hunter's best season was in 1952, and it was also his only winning season when Webb City went 5-3 and outscored its opponents 214-122.

"Although there were some drawbacks especially in having a light and somewhat inexperienced team, the spirit and determination of the boys carried them to high scores in most of their games," *King Jack* wrote.

Yes, the Cardinals still didn't weigh much.

The team was led by Jim Hunter, Bob Burris, Bill Terry and Garry Huffman, and beat Carthage 27-12 on Thanksgiving Day, though it would be just the second and last win against the Tigers in the 1950s. Jim Hunter, who played fullback despite posing for a yearbook photo in a quarterback's pose, was elected team captain and was also the son of head coach Palma Hunter. He was one of the greatest athletes to pass through the halls at Webb City High School, earning first-team all-state honors in both football and basketball. He was also a leading scorer on the track team in '52 and '53, played baseball and golf and earned 12 letters during his athletics career – three in football, three in basketball, three in track, two in baseball and one in golf. Hunter was also a member of the All-American Football Squad of the Wigwam Wisemen of America, and was even distinguished by having his football number, 48, "retired" by Missouri's legendary head coach Don Faurot at a Lions Club banquet honoring Webb City athletes. Only four players in the state earned that honor. Hunter also became the latest Webb City player to play football at Missouri, joining others such as Lloyd Buehner, Verlie Abrams and Bob Teel. It is no surprise he was named Webb City's Outstanding Athlete in the spring of 1953. Teel, a 1941 graduate of Webb City, eventually served as Missouri's head track coach for 17 seasons. He coached 42 All-Americans, was selected once as the National Track Coach of the Year, and is in the University of Missouri Sports Hall of Fame.

After the success of the 1952 campaign, the school's first winning season in so many years, the fall of 1953 couldn't have been a bigger letdown for football fans in Webb City. Plagued by injuries all year long, the Cardinals didn't win a game, though they earned the reputation as one of the conference's hardest-fighting teams behind the leadership of Jerry Rusk, the team's captain, and Wesley King, Jerry Burk, Bob Peek, Bob Restivo, Gary Baker, Danny Kulp and Howard Phillips. The team also played Altamont for the second time ever. Hunter's last season at the helm, 1954, was only slightly better; the Cardinals went 2-6 with Lloyd King as captain, Dee Conner as co-captain and Don Scott as student manager.

With 1955, in came Henry May as head coach at Webb City. May was originally from Monett and was a big guy, 6-foot-4 or taller, and had played football at the college in Springfield, now Missouri State University, and even played a year of professional football in Chicago before suffering an injury, a pinched nerve in his neck. During his high school career at Monett, May played for coach Kenley Richardson during the 1945-46 season. Ironically, Richardson and his Monett team would be May's first opponent at Webb City, and May's team won, 22-0, beating Monett for the first time since 1942.

"We are proud of you Coach May; did you remember all of Mr. Richardson's good plays?" *King Jack* asked.

As a freshman at Springfield, May lettered for the Bruins, who were 7-2-1 overall. He then played at Monett Junior College for a year and returned to Springfield in 1949. His best season was his senior year, 1950, when he was a team co-captain. He was named to the MIAA all-conference first team, was an Associated Press all-conference selection and was named the conference's outstanding lineman. In 1951, May was a 17th-round selection in the pro football draft, taken by the Chicago Cardinals as a center.

At Webb City May coached football, basketball and track, and though his first football team won just two games, the Cardinals' win total improved for four years straight after he took over. With a record of 3-5-2 in 1956, Webb City earned sixth in what was now the Big Nine conference, consisting of Lamar, Monett, Cassville, Aurora, Mount Vernon, Carthage, Nevada and Neosho. Their record could have been even better; they outscored their opponents by 35 points and even held Carthage to a scoreless tie. Things were looking bright, especially considering the success of the "little Redbirds," the B team that won four of five games with assistant coach Merlyn Elder and Mervin Hight at the helm.

May's team won four games in 1957, beating Bolivar for the first time, and still maintained sixth place in the Big 9, which was won by Aurora despite having an identical 7-0-1 record with Neosho. Webb City was 5-5 a season later and especially talented on offense; the Cardinals scored 62 points against Carl Junction, 38 against Cassville, 39 against Mount Vernon, 40 against Pierce City and 39 against Nevada. They still finished sixth in the conference. More help was on the way. The Cardinals' freshman team went 4-1 that year and scored 62 points in two straight games against Carl Junction and Lamar. Other than losing 20-14 to Joplin, they scored at least 34 points in two more wins against Neosho and Carthage.

Finally, in 1959, the Cardinals got back above the hump, winning six games, losing three and tying Aurora. The Cardinals won their first four games, allowing a combined 12 points, and were 5-0-1 before tripping up against Carthage. They blasted Pierce City 54-0 but ended the season with losses to Nevada and Neosho. Bruce Waggoner and Phil Armstrong were co-captains that year, and the Cardinals had momentum as yet another decade of Webb City football came to a close. And May's best season was still ahead.

(Top) Howard Phillips carries the ball around the left end while Bob Burris looks for someone to block during the Thanksgiving Day game against Carthage in 1952. (Middle) The Thanksgiving Day game at Carthage in 1953. (Bottom) Head coach Palma Hunter walks the sideline in 1954.

(Top) The 1954 game against Nevada. (Middle left) Quarterback Bob James, center Phil Armstrong, guard John Rawson and back John Powell in 1957. (Middle right) Gary Goswick carries the ball in the 1955 game against Mount Vernon. (Bottom left) Henry May and Monett coach Kenley Richardson pause for a photo in 1955. May played for Richardson in high school. (Bottom right) The coaching staff of Henry May, Merlyn Elder and Mervin Hight in 1957.

11. HENRY MAY GOES OUT ON TOP

The nine-game schedule for Webb City's 1961 season was released in mid August that summer, and 70 players had reported for the first practice a week earlier. Gear was distributed and coach Henry May announced a week of two-a-day practices. Hopes were high for the Cardinals; they returned nine lettermen from the 4-4 squad of 1960: quarterback Harold Benford; halfbacks Ralph Frizzell, Jerry Damer and Claude Divine; end Ronnie Crutcher; tackles John Vest and John Goodman; and Jim Laster, a guard. Three-fourths of the backfield from 1960 was back, including fullback Wayne Hodges. A month after the first practice, Webb City traveled west to Carl Junction for its first game of the year, a nonconference game set for 7:30 p.m. on Friday, Sept. 8.

It was another light team for the Cardinals. Goodman weighed 180 pounds at left tackle and was the team's heaviest lineman. In the backfield, Hodges and Damer were the biggest players at 160 pounds. Benford was just 150 pounds at quarterback, and Frizzell only five pounds heavier. Carl Junction, meanwhile, had two lineman topping 210 pounds, but the Bulldogs returned just three starters from the prior year and their inexperience showed early in the game. Early on, Damer returned a punt 45 yards for a touchdown, then Frizzell romped 55 yards for a score and Benford kicked both extra points. Hodges made it a 20-0 game in the second quarter with a 37-yard score, then Divine rushed 42 yards for a touchdown as the romp continued. Damer added a 35-yard interception return for a score, and another 15-yard touchdown run, and the Cardinals led 41-0 by halftime. Backup quarterback Wayne Williams threw a 45-yard touchdown to Divine in the third quarter, then Alex Spencer scored on a 26-yard scamper. For good measure, Damer dropped Carl Junction's quarterback for a safety and Benford scored on a 16-yard run. When it was all over, the Cardinals headed home with a 64-6 victory.

A week later Webb City opened the conference season, and its home slate, with an 8 p.m. contest against Neosho at Hatten Field. The Wildcats were considered the preseason favorite to win the conference crown, even after losing to Springfield Central by 10 points in a nonconference game. The praise for Neosho didn't mean much to the Cardinals, though. They built a 13-0 halftime lead behind a Benford-to-Jack Divine touchdown pass for 28 yards and a Ralph Frizzell run, and the Webb City defense, led by Hodges, kept the Wildcats in check throughout. The Cardinals quickly racked up five first downs to open the second half with Damer and Hodges handling most of the workload, and Damer scored on an 18-yard run after Neosho had cut the score to seven to give Webb City a 19-6 win.

In week three, Webb City traveled to Cassville for a game with another bunch of Wildcats. The Cardinals were without left end Jack Divine, who suffered a hip injury in practice, but other than that were in good shape for their second conference game.

"According to the coach the Cards had a good week of practice and seem to display good spirit," the *Sentinel* reported that Friday. "May thinks they are ready to go tonight."

They played Cassville tough, but suffered their first loss of the year when the Wildcats scored on a touchdown by fullback Bobby Reams in the fourth quarter and won 7-0.

With the arrival of week four of the season came another greatly-anticipated event: the annual rivalry game with Carthage, one of the oldest grudge matches in the area. The game was no longer played on Thanksgiving Day as had long been tradition, but the 1961 game would be the 66th time the foes had met. Webb City went into the game with Frizzell a question mark; he had pulled a leg muscle that week, and Carthage knew it would be missing its starting left end to a knee injury. The Tigers started the season 1-1-1, losing to Joplin by 11, tying Mount Vernon and beating Lamar. The game lived up to the hype.

After a closely-contested first half, Webb City managed to take a 7-0 lead after the first two quarters, scoring when Damer rushed 60 yards for a touchdown. Harold Benson added the conversion. In the third quarter a high snap sailed over Benson's head with the Cardinals lined up to punt, resulting in a safety that pulled the Tigers to within 7-2. Carthage's Stan Davis returned the free kick back 17 yards to the Webb City 25-yard line, and after four plays Carthage went ahead 9-7 on Davis' 1-yard run. The Cardinals got the ball back and worked it to their own 35 on several running plays. May called for a handoff to Hodges, who took the ball and was hit twice at the line of scrimmage by Carthage linemen. He shook the tackles off and his teammates provided key blocks downfield, and his 65-yard touchdown run proved to be the difference in a 13-9 Webb City win at Hatten Field.

In early October Webb City traveled to Nevada and spoiled the Tigers' homecoming with three touchdowns in the air and two on the ground in a 33-6 win. Benford's first-quarter touchdown to Frizzell, and Benford's extra point made it 7-0 after a quarter of play, and Frizzell hauled in a 25-yard scoring pass from backup Wayne Williams in the second quarter as the Cardinals built a 14-0 lead after two quarters. A touchdown from Hodges made it 20-0, and Williams threw another touchdown pass, this time to Claude Divine later in the game.

After five weeks of the regular season and four weeks of conference play, the competitive Big 9 had a logjam at the top. Monett, now the favorite to win it all, was 3-0 with a tie. Aurora, too, was 3-0-1, while Webb City and Neosho were each 3-1. Cassville was 2-1, Mount Vernon was 2-1-1 and Carthage, Nevada and Lamar each had losing records. The conference race would gain some clarity in week six, though, with Monett visiting Hatten Field and the Cardinals hoping their team speed would help offset the disparity in size with the Cubs. Monett, a defensive-minded team, held an 11-pound advantage per player, on average. Aurora was the only team who had scored on Monett all season, and it managed only six points. Webb City was averaging 25 points per game through five weeks, and its defense was pretty good, too, allowing just four.

"The Cubs though have not been faced with the quickness of the Webb City line or the speed of the Cardinal backs. The Cards halfbacks, Jerry Damer and Ralph Frizzell, have the speed and ability to score from anywhere on the field and their 160 pound fullback, Wayne Hodges, runs with the authority of a 190 pounder. Quarterbacks Harold Benford and Wayne Williams can both throw for the distance," the newspaper reported.

The following Monday, the *Sentinel* ran a bold two-deck headline on the front page: "Cards & Neosho Tied For Big-Nine Lead." Indeed, the conference race had begun to sort itself out. Neosho, tied with Webb City for second place, had defeated Nevada 24-13. Aurora, who had been tied for the conference lead, lost to winless Lamar 26-13. And Webb City rose to the occasion, using its quickness to overcome Monett's size, and the Cardinals beat the Cubs 20-13. Webb City's running game was especially effective; the Cardinals outgained Monett 256-96 on the ground. As the newspaper pointed out, the game wasn't even as close as the final score indicated.

Webb City drove to the Monett 1-yard line in the first quarter but fumbled the ball. In the second quarter, the Cardinals returned a punt to the Cubs' 41, and nine plays later scored on a 1-yard run by Frizzell for a 7-0 lead. Monett drove to near midfield on its subsequent possession, but Damer intercepted a pass and returned it to near the 50-yard line. With less than a minute to play, it appeared Webb City would settle for a touchdown lead at halftime, but Benford tried to catch the Cubs off guard and threw a pass. The play backfired when Monett intercepted his throw. With 25 seconds left in the second quarter, Monett quarterback Mike Wilks ran to the left and threw across the field to his halfback who raced to the end zone untouched. The half ended in a 7-7 tie.

The game remained close through the first half of the third quarter. After a Monett punt, Webb City took over at its 20-yard line and needed eight plays to cross midfield to the Monett 47. Benford faked handoffs to Hodges and Frizzell, then gave the ball to Damer who ran the distance for a touchdown. Monett answered with a 90-yard scoring drive but missed the extra point and trailed 14-13 with just one quarter remaining. It remained a one-point game until Webb City's final drive of the game, which covered 66 yards. With the ball on the 5, Hodges ran around the right end and scored, but Benford's kick was blocked, allowing

Monett a chance down by just 7. The Cubs threatened to tie it up, too. They got near Webb City territory before Damer picked off a pass at the Webb City 40, and the Cardinals ran for two first downs before running out the clock.

With Webb City tied for the conference lead and just three games remaining, the buzz surrounding the Cardinals only grew. They were ranked seventh in the state, and the coverage of the team now dominated the front page of the *Sentinel*. As they had done two weeks earlier at Nevada, the Cardinals were again attempting to play spoiler when they traveled to Aurora to face the 'Houn Dawgs on their homecoming night, Oct. 20. Aurora was tied with Monett for third in the conference with a 3-1-1 record.

"Coach Henry May said his boys are up both mentally and physically for what he termed the peak game of the season for his club," the paper wrote the day of the Aurora game. "May said 'if we can win tonight the schedule is with us to go all the way.'"

Only games against Mount Vernon and Lamar remained. But playing at Aurora on homecoming night would be a test. Aurora was the defending conference champion, after all. And when the first half ended that Friday night in October, the Redbirds found themselves down by a touchdown after being shut out for the first two quarters. Webb City, though, regained its championship look when the third quarter started, scoring on its first two possessions; the first a 10-yard touchdown pass from Harold Benford to Ralph Frizzell, and the second a 50-plus yard Benford-to-Frizzell connection. It remained a one-touchdown game into the fourth quarter. Webb City drove to the Aurora 1-yard line before being held on downs, but the Cardinals lengthened their lead when the 'Houn Dawgs punted and Jerry Damer returned the kick 70 yards for a score. Late in the game, Benford came up with an interception and added a 10-yard scoring run to cap the 27-7 victory. The win was Webb City's sixth overall and fifth in the Big 9, and Monett had assumed sole possession of second place in the conference after beating Neosho by 15 points. The Cardinals would return home for Homecoming against Mount Vernon, who had just lost 28-0 to Lamar.

A week later John Goodman, Wayne Hodges and Jerry Damer, the team's three captains, served as escorts for the homecoming royalty in a ceremony at Hatten Field, and Gretchen Told, a senior, was crowned queen. Damer scored the first touchdown of the game, and a bad snap into the Mountaineers' end zone quickly gave the Cardinals a 9-0 lead. Webb City held Mount Vernon scoreless until the third quarter. With the game all but decided, May played his reserves for most of the final quarter, and backup quarterback Wayne Williams led a drive deep into Mountaineer territory with less than two minutes left in the game, but the Cardinals were already leading big. Final score: Webb City 29, Mount Vernon 7.

The conference race was all but decided, too. Webb City stood at 6-1 in the Big 9, while second-place Monett was 4-1-1 and third-place Neosho was 4-2.

Lamar, the Cards' final opponent, had won just two conference games. But to make things official, the Cardinals still needed to beat the Tigers to clinch their first conference title in 29 years. Lamar, 3-4 overall, still could have posed a challenge after picking up each of its wins in the previous three games. Lamar's single-wing offense couldn't get rolling early in the season, the paper reported, but was in fine shape by week nine. May thought the weather might play a big part in the outcome of the game. If the field was in good shape, he believed his fleet backfield would do enough offensively to win, but it had rained for two days before the game and if the field was soft the Cardinals might be in trouble; they hadn't played on a muddy field all season.

Jerry Damer turned out to be the hero of the game. He scored three times – every Webb City touchdown – to help the Cardinals to a 19-13 win. Harold Benford threw a 40-yard pass to Damer for the Cardinals' first score, and Damer ran 19 yards around the left end for the team's second touchdown, which came in the second quarter. Webb City had missed its first two extra points, though, and when Lamar intercepted a pass deep in Cardinal territory in the third and scored, the Tigers trailed by only five points, 12-7. That put fear into the Webb City fans in attendance. Damer, though, quickly calmed everyone's nerves by returning the ensuing kickoff 80 yards for his third touchdown. After his first two extra points were blocked, Benford finally made the third and the Cardinals led 19-7. Webb City's defensive line stuffed Lamar on its next possession and the Cardinals got the ball back with barely seven minutes left in their season. But a fumble gave the ball back to Lamar and the Tigers scored quickly to make things interesting, though Webb City then ran out the clock.

When it was over, the team filled up on those great big rolls at the Blue Top Cafe off Highway 71, then went for the infamous stroll around the Carthage square in celebration.

A few weeks later, 200 people turned out for a banquet honoring Webb City's Big 9 conference championship at the Lion's clubhouse that was sponsored by the coaches' wives and players' mothers with fried chicken, potato salad, baked beans, garlic bread and relishes, cake and hot chocolate for dinner. After the dinner, master of ceremonies Lawrence Miner, the school district superintendent, introduced the evening's dignitaries, ending with Henry May. The coach introduced his coaching staff and members of the team, and then high school principal Fred Daugherty introduced guest speaker Carney Smith, the legendary Pittsburg State football coach whose Kansas State College of Pittsburg team had earned a No. 1 ranking that season and won the national championship. He spoke on "what a coach looks for in a college athlete," and stressed three things: a good student, good habits and attitudes, and the courage to play and to stick it out. One member of Smith's 1961 national title team was Tom Gosch, who would become a familiar name in Webb City just a few years later.

At least eight different Cardinals earned all-conference honors in the Big

9 in 1961, and fittingly so after Webb City had just completed its best season in almost 30 years. Earning an all-conference nod were players like Wayne Hodges, who played fullback and was the team's second-leading rusher; tackle John Goodman; quarterback Harold Benford; center Jim Bradfield; halfback Ralph Frizzell; guard and linebacker Jim Lassiter and halfback Jerry Damer, who led the team in both tackles and yards gained.

Henry May had returned Webb City football to prominence during his seven-year career as head coach. He finished with a winning record of 36 wins, 31 losses and three ties and in 1961 he accomplished what no Cardinals coach had done for nearly three decades. He would end on a high note; the conference championship team was the last he coached at Webb City.

In March 1962, a 32-year-old Henry May beat out more than 40 applicants for the head coaching position at Ottawa High School in Kansas. He told Ottawa officials he'd bring his T-offense, and that same spring would earn his master's degree in education from Pittsburg State. Only a few days later, though, May told Ottawa officials he couldn't sign the contract. The local superintendent told the *Ottawa Republic* May had requested a higher salary than the school board thought was proper.

Instead, May ended up at Millikin University in Decatur, Illinois for a year, coaching and teaching physical education. At some point he reportedly took a job selling textbooks. In 1979 he was inducted into the Southwest Missouri State University athletics hall of fame.

The 1961 Big Nine champions. Front row, left to right: J. Damer, R. Crutcher, J. Vest, J. Laster, J. Bradfield, B. Baker, J. Goodman, M. Fisher, R. Frizzell. Second row: J. Steel, R. Nichols, D. Simpson, L. Lundien, H. Benford, W. Hodges, D. Waggoner, J. Black, D. Bond, Coach Elder. Third row: Coach May, R. Stanford, P. Green, E. Long, K. BeVier, D. Lofton, M. Grissom, J. Newman, J. Sanders, G. Boyd, A. Spencer, W. Williams.

(Left) Quarterback Harold Benford, who earned second team All-Conference honors. (Right) Ends Ron Crutcher and Marion Fisher, and All-Conference tackle John Goodman and All-Conference fullback Wayne Hodges.

(Left) Henry May in 1956. (Right) Henry May and Merlyn Elder in 1960.

12. THE MERLYN ELDER YEARS

Merlyn Elder went to work in 1956 for Webb City High School, teaching math and physical education. During football season he coached Webb City's linemen, while Henry May and his other assistant, Merv Height, worked with the ends and backfield. In the winter May coached the basketball team and both Elder and Height assisted him, and in the spring everybody had their own sport to coach. Elder coached golf one or two years, he coached tennis once and he also coached baseball. The pay wasn't great; assistant coaches were paid $200 for the whole year.

"My first contract was $3,600 for the year, including the extra $200," Elder says. "They divided that up into 12 equal payments and that's what you got each month."

Elder, who spent four years as an assistant to May, was the logical choice to become Webb City's next head coach when May left following the 1961 conference championship season. Elder had played more basketball than football when he was in school and was interested in taking over the basketball program, but Webb City hired someone else instead.

"It kind of hacked me off," he says. "I said, 'How come I didn't get the job?' I guess it just wasn't meant to be. I got the football job, so I guess that's the way it was meant to be."

Not that Elder wasn't excited to coach football. He had played for the legendary K.E. "Doc" Baker in Carthage, the man the Tigers eventually named their stadium for. Baker, in turn, had been an assistant coach for Joplin's legendary Russ Kaminsky, whom the Eagles would eventually name their basketball gymnasium for. Elder was originally from Lamar, but moved to Carthage as a child and attended Mark Twain Elementary. He entered Carthage High School in the fall of 1946 and played basketball, but his mother wouldn't let him go out for the football team until he was a senior. It was then, while playing for Baker, that Elder got his first football education.

Baker's father was a doctor with an office on the second story of a business on the Carthage square, and he would send his players there for physicals. They would climb the stairs to the top and the doctor would say, "Did you make it up those stairs? Yep, well you're in good shape. OK."

"None of us ever died on the field but he worked us hard, boy," Elder recalls. "Sometimes you kind of wished you had died because he'd just almost run you to death."

Baker was also a strict disciplinarian. He allowed his players to go on one date during football practice, but girls were mostly off limits. He told his players not to drink soda pop and if they wanted something carbonated they could have a limeade with plain water. He instituted a curfew the night before games, and the players quickly found out the repercussions if they were caught out on the town. Baker would go into the movie theater at night to look for any of his players. One night he caught one of his basketball players there on a date and the next day asked the player if he'd seen him in the movies with a girl the night before. The player said he'd been there, and Baker told him to turn his gear in.

"It made a believer out of the rest of us," Elder says. "I did the same thing when I was coaching in Webb City. An assistant coach found a guy in a bowling alley and the next night we had a ballgame. I told him, 'Turn in your gear, you're not playing for us anymore.' He did and we went to the ballgame and got beat because we didn't have a starting center. That's the way it used to be in the old days."

Baker did have a soft side, too. In basketball he told his players every year if they could beat Joplin or Springfield or win the conference he'd take the entire team to Kansas City to watch the NIT basketball tournament. Carthage never beat Joplin or Springfield, and never won the conference, but Baker took the team up to the NIT every year.

Carthage went 4-4 with two ties in 1949, Elder's senior year. He played linebacker on defense and tackle on offense, and also a little bit of end and halfback. He helped the Tigers beat Webb City 40-6 that season, and when he graduated the following spring he enrolled at Joplin Junior College to continue his football and basketball careers. He stayed there for a year and a half, then left school and worked until he got married.

"When I was in high school we were rivals with Webb City then and it just grew on us," Elder says. "Webb City, we had to beat them. So what'd I do? I went over and married a Webb City girl. A Webb City cheerleader at that."

One of Elder's good friends married a Cardinals cheerleader, and when Merlyn went with him to visit he caught sight of a girl named Patricia who went by Patsy. "She had big blue eyes and I guess that was it," he says now. She graduated two years after Elder, and they started dating while he was still a student at Joplin Junior College. Her parents would bring her to watch Elder play. He was 19 when they married and she turned 18 the very next day. They've been married more than 60 years. A few years later Elder decided to return to school and enrolled at Kansas State College in Pittsburg as a physical education major and a math minor. Though he wasn't playing football, he was still learning more and more about the sport from another reputable source: Carney Smith, the legendary coach at Pittsburg, who taught a football class at the college. In 1956 he graduated and was soon hired to teach at Webb City High School, beginning his stint as an assistant coach to Henry May.

When May left to sell textbooks after the 1961 season, his other assistant, Merv Height, left too, for a coaching job at Baxter Springs. The coaching staff took on a completely new look in 1962: Elder as the head coach and Tom Gosch and Charlie Land as his two assistants. Gosch had graduated from Pittsburg earlier that year, and both he and Land were hired in May to teach at the high school. Gosch had played football for Carney Smith and won a national championship, while Land had coached at both Carterville and Jasper high schools. They each were hired to teach industrial arts and physical education.

By the end of August the new-look coaching staff was ready to show the team to the public. Elder scheduled a scrimmage game under the lights with the price of admission a bar of "sweet-smelling" soap. The school also released the schedule for 1962 that week, which would feature nine games and open with the season's only nonconference game, at home in early September against Carl Junction.

The Cardinals lost all four starting backs and three starting linemen from the 1961 championship team, though nine returning lettermen and five provisional lettermen had participated in early drills that summer. Dwight Simpson, a senior guard, dislocated his shoulder and was expected out for six to eight weeks. Bob Fisher and Dick Bond both were looking good at quarterback, Elder told the newspaper, and two of the team's four halfbacks – Marion Fisher, Claude Divine, Joe Hensley and Ronnie Linder – were destined for starting roles. Fisher had played end in 1961 but looked good at left half in practice. Darrell House had the fullback slot nailed down. Three players were battling for the starting end positions: Ron Crutcher, Jack Divine and Gary Hertwick; and Bill Baker, Ricky Adkins, David Waggoner and Jim Sanders were competing for the starting guard positions. Mike Grissom and James Bradfield appeared to have the starting tackle positions, while Larry Lundien was expected to start at center.

"We didn't have too many coming back but we had a few players who were juniors when they won the conference," Elder recalls. "We tried to keep everything our kids knew – the plays – most of them. We just continued running the same thing, we didn't change it a lot. That's what most of the kids had grown up with. They had been running it in their sophomore and junior years. We changed up some things. Once in a while we made some new plays ourselves when we ran into a seven-man front on defense."

The single-wing offense Elder had played in for Doc Baker at Carthage was going by the wayside, and teams were running the "T" offense, splitting out the ends and putting flankers way out in the backfield.

The Cardinals tied Carl Junction 7-7 in Elder's first game as head coach, but with the relative inexperience of the team, it was a long season. Webb City won two games but lost six others, including 21-12 to Carthage.

About 40 players showed up for the first day of practice in Elder's second season, and a total of 65 – including nine seniors – were expected to be on the team after physicals were completed. Elder announced that a season ticket plan was being worked out. They would eventually go on sale for $4. He also announced his coaching staff: Ed Nealy would supervise the 8th grade football program, Charlie Land would coach the 'B' team, Tom Gosch would work on the varsity team as well as the 'B' team and Ken Gentry would head the 9th grade squad.

Nealy, a 1953 Webb City graduate, was also the Cardinals' head basketball coach for five seasons before leaving for Bonner Springs (Kan.) High School in 1968. He's the father of Ed Nealy, a 6-foot-7 power forward from Kansas State University who went on to play 10 seasons in the NBA. The 6-foot-3-½ Nealy Sr. was a basketball standout himself, starring at Joplin Junior College under coach Buddy Ball and then earning Central Intercollegiate Conference first-team honors at Pittsburg State University in 1956 and 1957.

By the time two-a-day practices began in late August 1963, there were 64 players on the team but just two seniors who had earned letters – Pat Green and Mike Grissom. Green had turned heads in his time at quarterback a year before. The Cardinals also returned junior lettermen Joe Hensley, Darrell House, Bob Goddard, Ricky Adkins and Carl Moback. Provisional lettermen returning included senior Gary Hertwick and juniors Bobby Fisher, Gary Brake, Gale Newby, John Cochran, Mike Reeder, Odus Ross and Glen Barlow. Other returnees included John Damer, Terry Keeton, O.J. Moss and Ron Goodman.

When the Cardinals opened the season against Carl Junction at Hatten Field, Elder's starting lineup included both Ray Stults and Pat Green alternating at quarterback; Joe Hensley at right half; Glen Barlow and Doug Corner at fullbacks; Gale Newby and Bob Dean at left halfbacks; Bob Goddard at center;

and Rickey Adkins, John Damer, Darrell House, Gary Hertwick and Odus Ross rounding out the offensive line. Rusty Stanford, Gary Brake and Carl Moback would see action on the defensive squad. Webb City's line averaged roughly 175 pounds.

The Cardinals led 7-0 until the very end against the Bulldogs, who picked off a pass and returned it for a touchdown with just 1:42 remaining in the game to force a 7-7 tie. After losing 26-0 to in week two, Elder exclaimed that the team needed "a lot of work." While Neosho gloated that it would win the conference, now the Big 10, the Cardinals were optimistic they would be the closest contender for the conference crown.

"We had a nice sell-out," Elder said after the home game against Neosho. "Ticket sales totaled near $1,196, which is more than twice last year's total of $594."

Several players had sold more than $50 worth of tickets, and the team planned to take a Saturday off later in the year to go see an Arkansas football game.

The rest of the 1963 season didn't go very well, either. Webb City lost every conference game it played, and by the time the final game against Carl Junction arrived, the Cardinals' roster was down to just 28 players due to injuries and other reasons. Webb City had run into trouble scoring points all season, managing a high of just 18, but 12 points were enough to end the season with a win against Carl Junction, 12-7.

Things were looking up in 1964, especially after the annual soap scrimmage on the first Friday of September, which was covered by the *Sentinel*.

"In taking a good look at this year's line-up, this writer sees why coach Elder has such optimism in stating that our men have a very promising season ahead. Fourteen lettermen are returning to make our a team to be reckoned with in the Big Ten Conference," a reporter wrote.

Returning lettermen included quarterbacks Ray Stults and Bob Fisher, fullbacks Darrell House and Doug Corner, halfbacks Jerry Walker and Ricky Adkins, centers Ron Goodman and Bob Goddard, halfback Gale Newby, guard John Damer, tackles Lynn Swoveland, John Cochran and Mike Faulkner, and end Odus Ross.

Webb City clobbered Carl Junction 25-0 to open the '64 season, but lost 43-18 to Neosho in week two. After beating Cassville 13-0 in week three, hopes were once again high with Carthage on the slate for week four; that game turned into a disappointment, a 7-6 loss. Still, a win against Nevada at Hatten Field would get the Cardinals back above .500.

"Tonight's match on the gridiron will certainly be a very exciting one," the newspaper wrote. "When asked about the game with Nevada, Coach Elder said that the Card's chances were 'GOOD!'"

Elder was right; the Cardinals won 27-13. And after a 14-13 win at Monett, Webb City was 4-2 with momentum on its side with a home game against Aurora up next. The 'Houn Dawgs would win by 20 points, and a loss to Mount Vernon evened the Cardinals' season mark at 4-4.

Webb City rebounded to beat Carl Junction again in its last game of the year, giving Elder his first winning season.

A year later the Cardinals played at Raytown for the first time anybody could remember, and the players spent the night there with members of the opposing team after they played on Saturday night. Webb City lost the game 34-0.

The 1965 Cardinals returned seven lettermen from Elder's winning season. Among them: senior quarterback Ray Stults, junior halfback Scott Fetters, senior halfbacks Jerry Walker and Gary Summers, and linemen like Stan Walker and Mike Faulkner. Faulkner, at 223 pounds, was the biggest player on the team and he played tackle. Webb City by now had also introduced Columbia blue to its color palette.

The Cardinals returned home to host Neosho in the team's first conference game of the season and bounced back from the loss at Raytown with a strong defensive effort. Lynn Swoveland made 10 tackles and Fred Davis finished with eight; the Cardinals limited the Wildcats to just 61 rushing yards and won 6-0.

After losing to Cassville by a point, 7-6, in week three of the season, Swoveland was big again in a game against Carthage. Originally a tackle, Elder had moved him to end and he hauled in a 20-yard touchdown pass from Stults that was the difference in a 6-0 Webb City win. As Elder recalls, the score came on the last play of the game.

"Every year at the ballgames I had a bunch of friends over in Carthage I played ball with and they'd come over and say, 'Merlyn you had a good game,' but the year we beat them nobody showed up to come over and tell me anything. Even the coach was mad because it was 0-0 and we had run out of timeouts; they had the ball and the guy fumbled it and he called timeout only it was our ball and so we got the extra play there so that's how we beat them. Their coaches walked off the field. Never even came over or anything. It was different."

Elder remembers a game at Carthage when he was still Henry May's assistant. He wanted to beat the Tigers more than any other team and shut up his old friends who liked to give him a hard time, and this one year it looked like the Cardinals might pull it off. They had the ball on the 1-yard line and needed a touchdown to win, but the lights at the stadium went out and the game ended.

"Merlyn, you almost beat us, you played a good game," he heard afterwards.

After finally beating the rivals on the last-minute play in 1965, Webb City headed to Nevada and the Cardinals took a commanding 19-6 lead behind a 1-yard run by Stults, a five-yard pass from Stultz to Swoveland and a three-yard run by Doug Corner. Nevada scored twice in the second half to win 20-19.

Corner scored twice and Joe Sanders, Stults and Scott Fetters each added touchdowns in Webb City's 34-27 win against a big Monett team, and the Cardinals sat at 3-3 more than midway through the year. But the up-and-down season continued against Aurora, which won 45-12, and the Cardinals lost to Mount Vernon to drop to 3-5 overall. A third-straight loss, to Lamar, had served to drain what momentum the team had left, but the Cardinals rallied to cap the season with a 20-0 win against Carl Junction.

Elder's Cardinals would finish the year 4-6 overall. After the last game of the year the team traveled to Fayetteville to watch the second-ranked University of Arkansas football team play ninth-ranked Texas Tech in the school's 44th homecoming. The Hogs won 42-24.

One day after the 1965 season Elder was with his wife at her parent's house in Webb City and the district superintendent and high school principal drove by and stopped in the middle of the road. They called him over to the car and told Elder there would be a position coming open for assistant principal and asked him if he'd take the job.

"This wasn't going to be a great big raise, but it was going to be more than I was making as a coach," Elder said. "I said, 'You bet.'"

Thus came an end to Elder's tenure as head coach. Tom Gosch, who Elder describes as a "sharp guy," was the obvious choice to replace him, and he would begin a decade-plus run leading the Cardinals starting in 1966. Elder says he didn't really miss coaching when he was done.

"I had never been real successful," he says. "Back in those days we'd lose a lot of kids who would be working and get a car and then they wouldn't show up for football. That didn't really bother me."

At a school board meeting in August 1966, Elder was officially made assistant principal of the junior and senior high school complex. He later spent more than 20 years as a principal in Wellington, Kansas.

As he looks back on his career, both as a player and a coach, Elder knows he's learned from some of the biggest names in coaching in southwest Missouri and southeast Kansas. "I had a lot of good coaches I played for," he says. "I had some good coaches that gave me lots of good pointers. I worked with some good people. That's just kind of been the story of my life."

The coaching staff in 1965. From left: Tom Gosch, Ed Nealy, Charles Land, Merlyn Elder, Larry Swindle, Carl Coleman.

The crowd at Hatten Field in 1963.

Tom Gosch gives a sideline pep talk in 1968.

13. THE TOM GOSCH ERA BEGINS

Tom Gosch played six-man football in high school at Norwich, Kansas, a small town 35 miles southwest of Wichita, and he'll tell you there's a big difference between playing six-man football and the standard 11-on-11 most are familiar with.

"Nothing really transfers other than blocking and tackling," he says. "It was quite a change."

And it was quite a change when he found himself a freshman football player for Pittsburg State University in 1957, back when the school was still called Kansas State Teachers College of Pittsburg. The Gorillas won their first-ever national championship in football that fall, beating Hillsdale 27-26 in the NAIA title game, known then as the Holiday Bowl.

Gosch's uncle had attended the college, and his older brother had transferred there from a junior college.

"He liked it so I thought since he was going there then I'd go there, too," he says. "We only had one car and if I wanted a ride to school I thought I better get in with him."

Like Merlyn Elder before him, Gosch took the football theory class taught by legendary Pittsburg State coach Carnie Smith, and it was here he learned about the game. On the field Gosch played tight end for the Gorillas, during a time when almost everyone ran the power ground game with both tight ends in on the line. Throwing was a rarity; Pittsburg passed maybe nine or 10 times a game, and on occasion Smith would split a tight end out to spread out the defense.

"Nothing very fancy," Gosch says. "Tight ends were glorified tackles."

Gosch's senior season at Pittsburg, the fall of 1961, proved to be one of the greatest campaigns in school history. A 12-7 victory against Linfield College of Oregon in the Camellia Bowl at Sacramento, California, on Dec. 9 completed a perfect 11-0 season and gave Smith and his Kansas State College team their second NAIA national championship in five years. The Gorillas scored on their first offensive play that game and led 12-0 early in the fourth quarter. That team would later be inducted into the university's athletics hall of fame in the inaugural class of 1988. Smith himself was inducted into the NAIA Hall of Fame in 1963 and the Kansas Sports Hall of Fame in 2002. He ended his 17-year coaching record with 116 wins, 52 losses and two ties. He died in 1979, four days shy of his 68th birthday. After the 1961 season, he spoke at Webb City's football awards banquet in honor of the Cardinals' conference championship

"I've got all kinds of memories," Gosch says of the national title. "I think probably the greatest thing is the friendships that developed from that time frame. We still get together and play golf, a bunch of us, but the tightness, the close relationship of that team was quite evident and on good teams I think that's a quality that's pretty common. Closeness. The camaraderie we developed."

After lettering in football for three years in Pittsburg, Gosch graduated with his bachelor's degree at midterm that year, in January 1962, and started graduate school in the spring. By the following fall, he was serving as an assistant coach on Merlyn Elder's staff at Webb City. He served as an assistant for three years, but by the spring of 1965 Gosch felt he was ready for a head coaching job. He found one at Thornton High School in Denver, Colorado.

"I wouldn't have left Webb, but I thought Merlyn was going to keep on coaching and I felt like I wanted a head coaching job," he says. "My wife had an uncle in Colorado and he made me aware of an opening out there. I applied and got the job so we moved out there."

Gosch coached in Denver for one season, but after Elder stepped down from coaching after the 1965 season, Webb City officials contacted Gosch and asked if he'd be interested in coming back. It was an easy decision, and he moved back in the summer of 1966.

"Winning was really not that common," he recalls. "They had won a championship in the fall of '61 in the old Big 10, but in any case Webb really didn't have that much of a winning tradition. When I came there the kids were hungry. They wanted success, and Merlyn had done a pretty good job in regard to motivation, but they really didn't have anything they could lock onto in terms of continuity in their offense or continuity in their defense. We locked in and the kids bought in to it."

Gosch transferred Carnie Smith's offensive and defensive philosophies into his own and installed the power T offense and the 5-2 defense. The results were seen immediately: Webb City went 6-4 that first season, and it seemed as if another conference title were within reach.

Gosch won his first conference game against Cassville in week three of the 1966 season, 39-6. It evened Webb City's record at 1-1 in conference play after losing 20-0 to Neosho a week earlier in a game in which the *Sentinel* said the team "deserved more credit than they received. Yes, their play was marred by fumbles and penalties, but that could be blamed on over anxiety and the excitement of the game ... Along with the hometown crowd and what they've learned in their first two games, the Cards should be 'Up' and ready to win. Let's all go out and cheer them to victory tonight at 8:00 at Hatten Field."

And ready to win they were. Gale Mahurin, the team's hard-running fullback, "charged" his way to "Cardinal paydirt" for four touchdowns against Cassville, and Bill DeMoss scored another touchdown in the third quarter before Steve Lightle recovered a fumble and returned it 70 yards for Webb City's final score. They only led 13-6 at halftime but scored 20 unanswered points in the third quarter.

Webb City then lost two straight to Carthage and Nevada, but spoiled Monett's homecoming and evened its record at 3-3 by winning 27-14 on a Saturday afternoon in October. After beating Aurora 13-6 behind strong running from senior halfback Scott Fetters and Mahurin, the junior fullback, the Cardinals were finally above .500. They won two of their final three games to seal the winning year.

The offensive philosophy Gosch had learned from Carnie Smith was simple: continuity. It's what Smith always preached in his football theory class. Three backs in the backfield. You start out with a dive play. Off the dive play, you fake the dive and give to the fullback, who runs off tackle. From that you fake the dive, fake to the fullback and run the option with the quarterback and a third running back. Then you run trap plays.

"Everything starts out the same but it can change," Gosch says. "The continuity thing is what he really preached on. Make them think you're doing one thing but you can do something else off of it based on what they do. That's basically it."

To defend against the other power running games his Cardinals faced, Gosch used Smith's 5-2 defense, with five down linemen. It was a read defense; that is, the players reacted to what their offensive opponents did when the ball was snapped.

"You could stunt out of it; you could play straight if you could whip them playing straight," Gosch says. "I always felt there was something you could do out of that defensive set to compensate for what the offense is doing. It was really pretty simple to teach, and I always felt like if the kids didn't understand what they were doing they were going to make a lot of mistakes so we made sure it was simple."

Gosch's second team was even better than the first. In 1967 Webb City won eight games and tied for the conference championship. The offense consisted of Robert Allen, Gale Mahurin, Don Collins, Bill DeMoss, Bob Wynne, Ken Clement, John Nickelson, Less Sapp, Larry Fetters, Steve Fullmer and Don Poor. Defensively the Cardinals had Jim Morris, Gary Brown, Fetters, Mahurin, Allen, DeMoss, Poor, Fullmer, Arnold Baker and Clement. They tied Carthage and Nevada in back-to-back weeks, the only games they didn't win, but won their final five games of the season and allowed a total of 26 points in the final four games combined, while scoring a total of 227 points on the season. It got everybody excited again about Webb City football.

Shortly after the conclusion of the 1967 football season the school district began discussing plans to replace Hatten Field with a new stadium. The school board held a special meeting in December and discussed the stadium project as the first step in construction of a new high school. Members distributed copies of a master plan for the high school, along with floor plans, and the board had recently purchased the 52.70-acre tract where Hatten Field was located as a site for the proposed new high school. The board estimated the new stadium would seat approximately 3,000 fans and would also include a track, dressing rooms and coaches' offices. In January the board approved a plan to seek bids for a locker room project and to begin work on the stadium. The locker room would be a boys' dressing room and would be attached to a future high school. It would be located at the northeast corner of Hatten Field. A parking lot would serve both the new stadium and high school. The project came with a price tag of $85,000, but superintendent Lawrence Miner emphasized that it would not require a bond election or tax increase. It would be paid for from the school's building fund. The project was estimated to be completed by the start of the 1968 season.

When asked what Hatten Field was like, Tom Gosch laughs and says one word: dark.

"It had that old rock wall, and the field was low and flat and held water, and there was poor lighting," he says. "The seating was just on concrete."

When the new stadium was built just north of Hatten Field the field was leveled with a bunch of "junk" dirt, according to Gosch. It wouldn't even grow dandelions, he says, and despite attempts to seed it, the grass never would take. Eventually the school scraped away the dirt and put better soil down, but again the grass wouldn't grow very well and there were dead spots. Gosch would take his son, Bret, in an old panel truck that belonged to the school district and they'd drive to a sod farm in Bolivar. The truck wouldn't go more than 55 miles an hour. The two would haul back a truckload of sod – the trip would take all day – and the next day father and son would roll in new sod in the dead spots.

By April 1968 the board was ready to propose a bond issue and it voted unanimously to pursue an $800,000 bond issue for construction of the new high school.

"Overcrowded conditions of the present high school and rising construction costs and school reorganization were given as the reasons for calling the election at this time," the newspaper reported.

If approved, the high school would be completed around January 1970. A few weeks later, the city overwhelmingly approved the bond issue, 774-121. Voters in Alba approved 54-23, and in Oronogo the vote was 41-4. Meanwhile, in May construction was slated to begin on the locker room facility for a cost of $84,149. That August the school board approved preliminary plans for the high school and the cost had risen to $976,602. That figure included construction of a building for the gymnasium, auditorium, cafeteria, shop, music and ROTC rooms and construction of bleachers for the new football stadium. A third phase in the high school development would include construction of an academic wing with classrooms and offices and would cost between $600,000 and $800,000.

In 1968 Carterville High School merged with Webb City High, giving the Cardinals a total of 13 returning lettermen – seven from Gosch's conference championship squad, and six from Carterville. The biggest returners were end Bob Wynne and guard Larry Fetters. Each had earned all-conference, all-district and honorable mention all-state honors the year before. Bob Allen, Don Poor, Les Sapp, Larry Snider, Bob Morris, John Vandergrift, Steve Richardson, Bob Dikens, David McCloud and Steve Gannaway were among those returning.

Gannaway had started at quarterback for Carterville in 1967 and played quarterback for the Cardinals in 1968. Behind him were Alan Spencer and Bob Allen, along with David McCloud at fullback. Spencer had a breakout game in the season-opening win at McDonald County – the first at the new Mustang Stadium – scoring two touchdowns in the second quarter of the 34-12 win. He had a rushing touchdown and a receiving touchdown in week two, a 28-20 loss.

He was key in getting the team back above .500, scoring a 71-yard touchdown and finishing with two touchdowns and 140 yards on five carries in a 33-7 win against Cassville. He also returned a punt for a touchdown. Bob Allen, now playing quarterback, scored twice.

Allen and Spencer provided most of the offense the rest of the season. The Cardinals lost big to Carthage, but won four of their final five games in finishing 6-4. Spencer scored a touchdown in an 18-6 homecoming win against Nevada, and he returned an interception for the team's only score in a 31-7 loss at Monett. In a 14-7 win against Aurora, Spencer scored a 60-yard touchdown in the first quarter and later returned a punt 60 yards to the 1, setting up another score. In a 20-7 win against Lamar, Allen scored two touchdowns on the ground and threw a 47-yard touchdown pass to Spencer. Allen added two more touchdowns in the 27-0 win against Carl Junction to close out the year.

(Top) Bill DeMoss rushes the ball in a 1967 football game. (Right) 'B' team and backfield coach Charles Land, and head coach Tom Gosch, in 1968.

Webb City's top offensive performers in 1968: Bob Allen, above, and Alan Spencer, below. Both started in the backfield, with Allen eventually moving to quarterback.

14. THE SEVENTIES

Tom Gosch was a disciplinarian as a head coach, and his practices were organized and structured. He typed up a practice schedule every day divided into different segments, a far cry from earlier years when coaches would meet at a restaurant and write out a practice schedule on a napkin. Structure was important, and discipline was very important. Gosch always believed if his players weren't paying attention they weren't going to learn.

"We liked to have a good time but not at the expense of the practice schedule. We had certain things we wanted to cover and we'd make sure we covered them," he says.

Those practices were even cited in the 1970 edition of *King Jack*, and though the Cardinals had a few down years after winning the conference championship in 1967, the work was laying the groundwork for more success in the 1970s. They managed to win just one game two years after winning the conference championship in 1967, but tied three others. A 50-point loss to Carthage was hard to swallow, and *King Jack* described the 1969 season as "disheartening."

"For many players this was their first year of real action. Many on the team were plagued with injuries throughout the season which proved hard on morale. The Cardinals lacked experience but this year gave them the experience needed for a winning team in the future. The coaching staff has produced winning seasons in the past and they soon will have the experience and material needed for another season at the top. However being at the top is never as important as what the individual learns by playing."

Gosch was determined to make the team better. On a "hot" August day in 1970 at 7 a.m. he began summer practice by making the team run a mile in seven minutes. Those who didn't make it had to do extra sprints for a week.

"Coaches Gosch and Collins spent countless hours preparing their men both physically and mentally for the games," *King Jack* wrote of the 1970 season. "Closely related to the performance of the Cardinals were the three captains – Jackie Allen, Bob Brown, and Eric Cunningham. Some times were rough, like those hot summer practices, but victory was sweet. Sweat, grime, pushing to the last ounce of strength – all were part of the 1970 gridiron season, now only a memory."

The Big 10 Conference voted to increase admission prices for its football games that fall to $1.50, though most conference schools were set to provide season tickets for a reduced rate. Only Carl Junction had decided not to boost the regular ticket price.

"Our board voted prior to the conference meeting last December not to raise the admission price and we're sticking by our guns," Carl Junction Superintendent Jack McCracken told the *Sentinel*. "We lost money every year on athletics. I don't believe raising the admission price is going to put us in the black. I think the increase will hurt the attendance of our fans when Carl Junction teams play away from home."

Carl Junction was sticking with its old rate of $1 a ticket. Student admission conference-wide remained at 50 cents.

The Cardinals went 3-7 that year, a small improvement, and reinforcements were on the way; Webb City's 'B' team went undefeated in five games, tying Carthage once, and only allowed more than eight points one time.

Webb City opened the 1971 season against McDonald County at home. With 1:20 left in the fourth quarter the Mustangs held a 16-14 advantage and had the football, but five seconds later the Cardinals recovered a fumble, and a minute after that won the game when quarterback Bob McAfee threw a 22-yard touchdown pass to split end Bill Isenberger as time expired. McAfee ran for one touchdown and threw for two more, and also converted a pair of two-point conversions in Webb City's 36-0 throttling of Lamar in week two. Two of his touchdown passes were long bombs to Isenberger, a favorite target. Feeling good after the 2-0 start, the Cardinals played at Carl Junction in week three in what turned into a defensive struggle. The Bulldogs struck for the game's only touchdown in the fourth quarter when quarterback Mike Larson, who would go on to a career as athletics director at Carl Junction, threw a 70-yard pass to Ron Kegerries. It was Carl Junction's first win against the Cardinals in 14 years, the Bulldogs having won 25-13 in 1957.

"We played a good defense, with exceptions of course," Gosch told the newspaper.

His Cardinals improved to 3-1 with an 11-point win against Neosho, and he said he would be very pleased to spoil Cassville's homecoming the following week. Webb City ended up losing 13-8 on a touchdown with 50 seconds left in the game.

In week six the Cardinals hosted Carthage and sought their first homecoming win in two years. Alan Spencer, the former Webb City standout who was then playing for Kansas State College, told the newspaper he was confident of a Webb City win.

"I know they have real good stuff," he said. "Back in 1969, we were the underdogs against Nevada, but we still won. Last year our college team won our homecoming even though we were the underdogs. So even if the Cards are rated the underdogs, there is still a good chance we will win. I'm looking forward to a real good game."

Spencer had caught a touchdown pass in Kansas State College's 21-7 win against Missouri Southern College a week earlier.

Webb City's homecoming was spoiled by its rivals, 20-7, but the Cardinals improved to 4-3 overall with a two-point win at Nevada. But the schedule was getting tougher; Webb City next faced a Monett squad that Gosch said was the best he had ever seen in the conference. They lost the game, and two more, finishing with a 4-6 record and in fifth place in the conference. They were expected to finish about the same a season later. With a lack of depth, he opted for a platoon system in 1972 at several positions. The team returned McAfee at quarterback and eight seniors on the offensive unit, but were forced to rely on sophomores on the defensive side.

"We have some pretty scrappy sophomores on defense and they are pretty darn good," he told the paper. "The only problem is they lack experience on offense if they have to go both ways."

By the time the season was finished, many of the team's players had compiled impressive years. Matt Spencer, a senior defensive back, earned all-conference honors for the second year, and McAfee, also a senior, set school records for completions and passing yardage. Junior split end Danny Campbell established a school record in pass receptions and also led the conference in catches.

Gosch's rebuilding effort gained steam in 1973. His team finished the season 5-5, including blowout wins against Lamar (48-6), Carl Junction (35-0) and Monett (40-7). The team outscored its opponents by 46 points. Linebacker John Hoffman, split end Danny "Bo" Campbell, offensive guard Harvey Hough and defensive back Tom Campbell each received all-conference and all-district honors, and Jim Roth, Wade Stefka and Eddie Hafner earned all-conference selections and punter John Wynne was an all-district player.

Bo Campbell, 40 years later, is a familiar face at sporting events in southwest Missouri. As a popular umpire and referee at the high school level, Campbell can often be seen at area softball, baseball and basketball games. He still thinks fondly of Tom Gosch.

"I don't think a high school coach understands, but it's been 40 years since I played at Webb City and there's probably not a week that goes by where I don't think of something he said or a lesson that is crystal clear today that he tried to teach," Campbell says. "His footprints were all over the Webb City athletic program long after he was gone. For those of us who played in the '70s, we thought Tom Gosch walked on water.

"I came from a broken home," Campbell says. "My stepdad stepped in and did all anybody could do, but as far as a male influence that I admired in my teen years, it was Tom Gosch. I'm approaching 60 years old, I graduated with the class of 1974, and we all speak to what a profound influence he had on us, even today."

On the field, Campbell thinks his senior class helped bridge the gap between a few years of losing and the success that would follow later on in the decade. A year after his senior season, the Cardinals were back in the win column.

"The Big Red succeeded in re-establishing football as a major school sport and are ready to prove themselves in the '74 campaign," the yearbook wrote. "With the fine crop of sophomore linemen and junior backfield returning from last year's squad the Big Ten had better beware in 74-75."

The yearbook was right; 1974 would prove a banner year for Webb City football, and three games would be key. The first came at Neosho. Webb City opened the season with four straight wins, and coming off a 40-point win against Carl Junction took on the Wildcats in a defensive struggle. The game ended in a 14-14 tie. After beating Cassville and shutting out Carthage, the Cardinals were 6-0-1 and set to do battle with Nevada in the conference's biggest game of the year. Nevada had a 20-game winning streak on the line, as well as the conference championship and a state playoff berth. The Cardinals had the Big 10 title and a playoff berth on their minds, as well, and their execution proved better than the Tigers as Webb City won 13-9. At that point it appeared the Cardinals were headed for an undefeated season and conference title of their own, but a week later Monett dispatched Webb City 28-0. The Cardinals then scored 62 points against Aurora in the final game of the season and finished with an 8-1-1 record.

Having returned to the program's winning ways, the middle '70s saw Webb City sport some solid, though not necessarily spectacular, teams. The Cardinals went 6-2 in '75, 5-3-2 in '76, and 5-5 in '77.

In 1975 they finished second in the Big 10 Conference and were led by four all-conference players, each named to the first team: Ed Hafner, Wes Waggoner, Lloyd Walker and John Wynne. Wynne also earned first-team all-state honors. Hafner played offensive guard, Walker was an offensive tackle, Waggoner was a tight end and Wynne was the team's halfback. Wynne was also a standout in the defensive backfield, while Waggoner played linebacker.

And the Cardinals beat Carthage by a point, 22-21. They also beat Carthage in 1977, 24-19. That year's team was led by inexperienced juniors, but won three of its final games.

"With experience being gained this year, Coaches Mark McDonald, Tom Gosch, and Jerry Archer have the base to form an even great team in the future," *King Jack* wrote.

The offensive unit averaged almost 20 points a game, but the top-ranked defense gave up fewer than 15 points. And the freshmen team of 1977 went 5-1 and was the best freshmen team coach Charles Meadows had ever led. Their play would spell future success for Webb City's varsity team.

That big junior class, and the talented freshmen of 1977, made a splash a season later. Fourteen of the 22 starters were seniors in 1978, and the team set six offensive and defensive records ranging from team marks to individual records. It was a very close-knit team. The Cardinals won against East Newton to open the season, but suffered a week two loss to eventual state champion Mount Vernon. After that the team won six straight games and was 7-1 before the streak was snapped by fourth-ranked Carthage. Webb City ended the year with a 28-3 win against rival Carl Junction and finished 8-2 and in second place in the Big 13 west division. Despite the winning record, the Cardinals still were plagued by that age-old problem: a lack of size.

"This year was by far one of my smallest teams ever," Tom Gosch was quoted as saying in *King Jack*. "But they made up for this lack of size by displaying more heart and will to win than any team I have ever coached. This football team was also one of the most dedicated in the off season."

It was a fitting end to Webb City's time in a conference that for so many years was the Big 8, and then the Big 10, and by the late 1970s the Big 13. The Cardinals were leaving for what they hoped would be greener pastures in the Ozark Conference, which included teams from Joplin and Springfield.

"So this year was goodbye to our neighborly rivalries that have become rather intense over the years," the yearbook wrote.

The following winter the school district began planning for an expansion of Cardinal Stadium. In February the Board of Education approved a motion to apply for funding to increase the seating capacity by 1,200 by installing a section of aluminum bleachers 132 feet long and 34 feet high along the stadium's east side.

The 1967 season was a highlight of Gosch's coaching career, but he believes he got better as a coach as he spent more years leading the program.

"When I finished up I think I was a lot better coach than when I started out and in '67," he says.

He adapted his coaching philosophies as times changed and the game of football evolved. On New Year's Day in 1979 Gosch was at home watching the Cotton Bowl, which pitted Houston against Notre Dame, and he watched as Houston and head coach Bill Yeoman rolled to a 34-12 lead behind Yeoman's split-back veer offense. Yeoman had invented the offense in the 60s and it had revolutionized the offensive game. Against Notre Dame, it was working like a charm.

"He was ripping them with it. Ripping them," Gosch recalls.

Notre Dame had scored the first 12 points of the game, but Houston scored a touchdown off a turnover and by the second quarter had taken a 20-12 lead. The game was played a day after one of the worst ice storms Dallas had ever seen, and Notre Dame quarterback Joe Montana was battling the flu. At one point during the game he became so cold he was forced to the locker room where medical staff fed him chicken bouillon to warm his body temperature.

Montana returned to the game with 7:37 left in the fourth quarter and led Notre Dame to a dramatic comeback. With six seconds left Montana threw an incompletion out of bounds to stop the clock with two ticks remaining, and he found receiver Kris Haines for a touchdown as time expired to tie the game at 34. Joe Unis had to kick the extra point twice because of a penalty, but his kick was good and Notre Dame won 35-34 in what is now referred to as the "Chicken Soup Game" and an instant classic.

Even though Yeoman's Cougars had lost, Gosch liked the veer offense he'd seen. He contacted Yeoman, who in turn sent Gosch a book he'd published in 1975: *University of Houston Football: Veer-T Offense*. It was a guide to the offense which Yeoman's Houston team had used to average 271 rushing yards per game, an average of five yards per carry.

"I've still got the darn thing somewhere," Gosch says. "It's very, very simple in regard to implementing it. It was a read offense. You read the defense and it's very similar to what John does now, but he's tweaked it a little bit more than we did. We were a true split back team, and as I progressed we put in a power sweep off of it. It really made exciting football at Webb City. We were the first in the area to run it."

Monett had installed a wishbone offense in the '70s, inspired by the wishbone offense developed by head coach Darrell Royal at the University of Texas in 1968. The wishbone debuted, ironically, in a game against Houston, which Texas tied, and after the Longhorns lost their second game utilizing the new offense they rattled off 30 wins in a row and two national championships. Much of the wishbone philosophy is built into the split-back veer offense, but when Gosch's Cardinals adopted the veer they were the first and only team in southwest Missouri using it.

"It wasn't that much different than the wishbone," Gosch says. "It was a read and they had played against Monett, but they read it out of a wishbone. Other teams just weren't willing to go to it because it's completely different than the old power T or the power I, things they were doing at that time. They were reluctant to go to it and they had a lot of trouble defensing it, especially the outside veer. The outside veer was a money maker. It took them a while to adjust and adapt their defenses to slow it down. I don't think you can stop the veer. There's always something you can do to offset what they're trying to do defensively. John does a good job with it. He throws more out of it than what I ever did; I still had that Carnie Smith philosophy of running the ball and if you throw it three things can happen and two of them are bad."

The new-look offense debuted against Carthage in the 1979 season opener. The teams had finished at the top of the Big 13 Eastern Division in 1978, with Carthage finishing 5-0 in conference play and Webb City 4-1 with identical 8-2 overall records. A year later, though, both teams were inexperienced.

Carthage had a new head coach in Ray Harding, while Gosch had added Richard Correll to his staff, which included Mark McDonald coaching receivers and defensive backs and Jerry Archer as defensive coordinator. And Webb City was no longer in the Big 13 after leaving for the bigger Ozark Conference, which included teams in Joplin and Springfield and also Lebanon and Sedalia. Webb City was one of the smallest schools in the conference.

"Sure we're going to see teams with good athletes," Gosch told the *Sentinel*. "And more athletes than we have."

But he thought his team's intensity and desire to win would help even things out.

The 1979 squad was captained by Greg Philpot, Curt Divine and Gale Perry. Philpot was slated to start at linebacker and tight end, but after undergoing surgery to repair torn knee ligaments suffered in the second week of practice, he was expected to miss most of the regular season. On offense, Jeff Archer was slated to start at center, Randy Rhines and Divine at guards, Steve Brown and Perry at tackles, Kelly McDowell at split end, Danny Carter at tight end, Doug Humphrey at quarterback, Rick Mobley and Ronnie Campbell at running backs, and Robbie Clute at flanker. On defense the Cardinals went with Archer at nose guard, Curt and Phil Divine at linebackers, Rhines and Perry at tackles, Craig Giliam at end, Gary Berliew and Humphrey at cornerbacks, Randy Jones at weak safety and Hirsch at strong safety.

Webb City lost that first game 20-2 and went on to complete a 3-7 season in the final campaign of the 1970s. One highlight was the Sept. 14 game against Joplin Parkwood – Webb City's first Ozark Conference opponent – in week two of the season. Not only was it a big deal because of the proximity to Parkwood and that school's legendary run of success that decade, but it was also a reunion for Webb City's teams of 1931 and 1932. The team went undefeated in 19 straight games over the two seasons, tying one game in '31. The 1932 team was the last undefeated and untied team in Webb City history. Head coach Charles Cummings was expected to attend the reunion, which consisted of a dinner at 6 p.m. and then the Parkwood game at 7:30 p.m., and so were several players, including J.E. Wommack, Elmo Webb, Pat Tarrant, Bud Rountree, Frank Martin, Woody Mahurin, Ray Mahurin, John Lofton, Bob Kungle, Ken Kneeland, Jene Julian, Mutt Hughes, Dink Huckaby, Bud Huckaby, Carrol Gregory, Pearl Green, Roland Davis, Colby Bradshaw and Harry Bishop.

"Mutt" Hughes, whose first name was actually Emmett, was considered one of the best centers in the league in his time, and blocked nine punts in the 1930 season. And remember Pearl Green, the quarterback of that legendary 1932 team. *King Jack* wrote that Webb City was said to be blessed with "Pearl Green and a lot of luck," though it wrote that a more accurate description would be "eleven football players and a never-say-die spirit."

"The 1931-32 group is sure to be hoping for an upset to match their 6-2 and

6-0 wins respectively over Joplin High School," the paper wrote.

But Parkwood had been selected as the top team in southwest Missouri by local sportswriters, and the Cardinals lost big. Webb City did get its first Ozark Conference win later that month, a six-point home win against Springfield Central. The Cardinals, thanks to the veer offense, racked up 316 rushing yards. The running attack was led by Randy Jones, who ran for 133 yards on 16 carries.

"We've worked hard and good things are finally happening," Gosch told a *Sentinel* reporter, in the "calamity" of the locker room. The team had just finished its best week of practice all season.

Webb City rushed for 327 yards the next week in a 37-31 loss to Springfield Hillcrest. Both Jones and Keith Hirsch totaled 137 yards. A week later, when the Cardinals blasted Lebanon 27-6, the team's "surging offense" was the lead story after accumulating 338 yards. Hirsch went for 116 yards and Jones had 102. The offense had averaged 28 points per game in the team's last three outings. The running game also enabled the team to end the losing season on a high note, a 19-0 win against Joplin Memorial at Cardinal Stadium. Jones rushed for 135 yards and Hirsch tallied 133 yards.

According to the newspaper: "This marks the high point of our season of frustration, beamed the Cardinal Coach Gosch in an ecstatic Redbird locker room after the contest. Gosch's crew racked up a booming 23 first downs for a season high compared to only 9 in the contest for the Eagles. Those first downs were the most ever racked up against a Memorial team. Emotion dominated the game as the Cardinals outdistanced one of the few rivals they have faced this year as newcomers to the Ozark Conference."

Hirsch finished the season with 50 points scored and 766 rushing yards on 152 carries, and he was just a junior. Jones, the 165-pound senior back, rushed for 651 yards on 118 carries. Junior quarterback Doug Humphrey passed for 524 yards and four touchdowns. His primary target was senior Kelly McDowell, who hauled in 20 passes for 246 yards and two touchdowns. Junior Danny Carter finished with 166 receiving yards.

Another interesting item in the *Sentinel* that fall was about football, but not about Webb City High School. Twelve-year-old John Roderique had taken first place in his age division in the Punt, Pass and Kick zone playoffs at Joplin's Junge Stadium, allowing him to advance to the district playoffs at Arrowhead Stadium in Kansas City to compete against other zone finalists from Kansas City, Missouri and Arkansas. The son of Mrs. Jenell Roderique, John won the event with a 44-foot punt, a 71-foot pass and a 69-foot kick. He had to win the area playoff a week earlier to compete at the zone level.

(Top) The exterior of Cardinal Stadium as it appeared in 1970-71, complete with the Cardinal sign out front (at right). (Left) Danny "Bo" Campbell with the ball in 1972. (Bottom left) Head coach Tom Gosch and line coach Jerry Archer in 1971. (Bottom right) The coaching duo in 1972.

Matt Spencer leads the team onto the field in 1972.

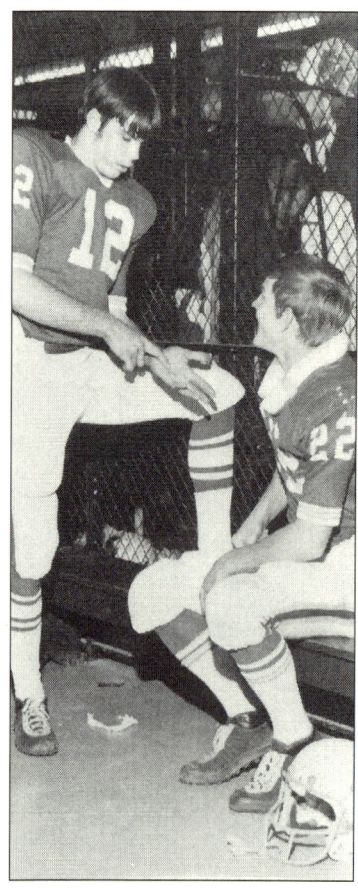

(Left) Co-captains Bob McAfee and Matt Spencer in 1972. (Above) Kent Williams bursts onto the field in 1974.

15. INTO THE EIGHTIES

By February 1980, after completing only one season in the Ozark Conference, Webb City was already considering a return to what was now the Big 12, and high school principal Ron Lankford was expected to appear before members of the conference that month to discuss possible re-entry within two years.

Webb City officials cited the distance between teams and travel expenses suffered that year as reasons for the possible move. In January 1978, when the school board decided to leave for the Ozark, gas prices averaged 46.9 cents per gallon, but by February 1980 had risen to 109.9 cents per gallon. The entrance of Sedalia into the conference, and that lengthy road trip, was another major point of concern, the paper reported.

Overall finances of the athletics department had suffered because of the move, according to Gosch, who also served as athletics director.

"It's not going to get any cheaper...just more expensive," he said in the paper. He also believed competition in the Big 12 and Ozark conferences was very comparable and clarified in the newspaper that Webb City was not being "scared out of the Ozark Conference."

"We were hoping to find a more difficult level of competition," Lankford said, "but it hasn't necessarily been that way."

A month later the school board unanimously approved a resolution to rejoin the Big 12 and begin competing against those schools in the fall of 1981. In August 1980, as the Cardinals prepared for the second and final slate of Ozark Conference competition, Gosch told the newspaper that summer two-a-day practices were going really well.

"Apparently the teammates absorbed too much shade during their vacations but worked their way back into shape quickly," he said.

In year two of the Ozark Conference, and of Gosch's new experiment with the split-back veer offense, the results were much better. The Cardinals blanked Carthage 6-0 in week one with Keith Hirsch, the senior running back, scoring the only touchdown. That 1980 team had several vacancies on the line after six linemen had graduated, but also some returning lettermen in guards Phil Divine, Craig Gilliam and Garry Harris, all seniors, and junior Derek Johnson. Tom Chaney was back as center, and Tony Williams, Gary Veach and David Wood were back at tackles. There were others considered good prospects on the line, like seniors Mark Elliston and Paul Moser, juniors Matt Baldwin and Tim Chaney and sophomore Aaron Spencer.

The Cardinals were in great shape at the skill positions. Hirsch was back in the backfield, and he had been an all-conference and all-district strong safety, as well. Doug Humphrey was back at quarterback, and the team also had backs Rick Mobley, Gary Berliew, Ronnie Campbell and Brian Benford.

By the time the week one game against Carthage rolled around, the lineup was set and the Cardinals had six players going both ways: Bret Gosch, Tom's son, at offensive and defensive end; Danny Carter at tight end and linebacker; Phil Divine at linebacker and offensive guard; Humphrey at quarterback and cornerback; Gary Berliew at running back and corner; and Keith Hirsch at running back and strong safety.

In their second game against Joplin Parkwood the Cardinals were blown out 53-0. Alan Cockrell, Parkwood's incredible quarterback, ran for three touchdowns, passed for two and booted five extra points. The loss put steam under the players' collars, Gosch said, and his team planned to release that steam against Glendale. They won that game 14-3. The Cardinals upped their overall record to 3-1 and their conference mark to 2-1 after edging Springfield Central 16-14. After a homecoming win against Hillcrest, 14-7, an overtime loss to Lebanon, a one-point defeat to Kickapoo and a 21-7 win at Sedalia, Webb City was 5-3 overall. They beat Parkview by five points to earn a tie for third place in the conference.

The Cardinals ended the season with a game at Junge Stadium against Memorial High School, and Webb City's defense was huge in the team's 14-13 victory. Webb City trailed 13-7 at the half, the only score coming on a three-yard run in the second quarter by Rick Mobley, but Tony Williams put the team ahead in the third with a fumble recovery in the end zone and David Wood's extra points were the difference. The win allowed the Cardinals a tie for third place in the conference with Parkview, and they finished the year 7-3 overall and 6-3 in the Ozark.

By March 1981, Gosch decided to call it quits after 15 years as head coach and three more as an assistant, but he maintained his role as athletics director.

"There were a lot of years that we won eight and seven games, but we never won the conference championship again," he was quoted as saying in the *Sentinel*.

"After you put your heart into something for 19 years it's hard to step out," he said. "But it won't be like I'm totally stepping back from it because I'll still be able to contribute to the athletic program as athletic director."

In his final season at the helm, Gosch shared district coach of the year honors with Parkwood coach Dewey Combs, who won the 4A state championship that season.

When Gosch first came to Webb City in the early 1960s he made $4,700 a year to teach and serve as an assistant coach in three sports. His coaching stipend was a measly $500 per year, but by the time he stepped away from coaching his assistants received a stipend more than 10 times that amount. In the early days you only worked with each sport during the season; offseason weight lifting and conditioning were unheard of. The football team gathered each August a few weeks before the start of the season and got into shape. But if you want to get better you've got to do more, and by the time his coaching career came to an end he was spending 11 months out of the year focused on football. He had also developed a weight room and a lifting program at Webb City that started with one weight machine in a janitor's room.

"We were working hard," he says. "We were working hard. I felt like maybe I needed to do something else. I was getting a little bit – not burned out, but just repetitious – and the high school principal at the time was Ron Lankford. In the spring he asked me if I'd be his assistant principal and I said, 'No, I don't think so. I'm tired right now but I think I'll continue coaching.' He said, 'Well, you want to do this all your life?' I said, 'No, not really but I'm not sure this is the time.' As it turned out I changed my mind and decided to retain the athletic directorship and be assistant principal. It turned out to be a good decision."

Gosch's son, Bret, had also finished his high school career in 1980. Playing on both sides of the ball he had earned second team all-conference honors as defensive end.

"He was a pretty good football player," Tom says. "He was a good high school player, especially on defense. He played both ways but, he was a tough nut on defense."

Bret went on to play football for Pittsburg State, just like his father. In 1982 he and Randy Jones, the former Webb City standout, were on a Gorillas' team ranked second nationally in the preseason NAIA Division 1 poll.

A few months after he announced he was quitting coaching, his conference champion football team of 1967 "brought tears of joy" to Gosch for a second time when they presented him with a shotgun in appreciation of his decade-plus of coaching. They made the presentation during a banquet honoring Gosch, and he entertained the crowd with bits of game footage he had spliced together with segments of footage from every team dating back to the late 60s. He also received a painting of Cardinal Stadium by John Fitzgibbon, which still hangs on a wall in his home.

"You never know how good a person a player is until 10 years after school," Gosch said at the banquet. "And I've had some good ones."

He's still got the shotgun, too.

As Tom Gosch reminisces about his 15-year run with the Cardinals, he still remembers the specifics of many games. He recalls one contest against Carthage sometime in the 1970s, played in Webb City, and he remembers Carthage had some "big ol' kids," it was raining and nobody had scored in the first half.

"We got in the second half and it was just miserable conditions," he says. "We ran an option play and my fullback slipped and he and the quarterback just ran into each other. The fullback knocked him through the center-guard gap and he went straight upfield about 60 yards for a touchdown and that was the only damn score that was made and it was a fluke and we beat them 6-0. We had some real close, competitive games. When I first came to Webb, Carthage was tougher than nails. They beat us my first year and we tied them the second year. Then I think they beat us two or three in a row and then we got the four or five in a row.

"There's a lot of Webb City guys working with Carthage guys at Hercules and Atlas and those places around," he continues. "I think there's some pretty good bets going on every year on those games based on conversations I've had."

He remembers all the great players he coached, too many in number to name them all, but he recalls Gale Mahurin was a tough fullback and linebacker. He remembers a good athlete in Alan Spencer, who played at Pittsburg State and had tryouts with professional football teams; he later coached Monett. There was John Wynne, who played at Tulsa and later at Missouri Southern. There was John Hoffman, who played at Drake and beat Colorado; he was a good, tough player.

"A lot of them didn't go to college," Gosch says. "There's a lot of them who weren't outstanding athletes but they were just tough. Just hard-nosed, blue collar-type kids who just liked to play and so many of them you look back on and I think football made a difference in a lot of their work habits. Their success, I think, was based on discipline and doing the right things. We had a lot of good kids come through, but not a lot of them were outstanding athletes."

This is another trademark of Webb City football. The Cardinals have had players with incredible talent, for sure; players who went on to start and star for big-time Division I colleges and even in the National Football League. But the vast majority aren't superior athletes. They're talented, yes, but they also play with maximum effort, utilizing 100 percent of their talent. That's how a program marked by so many undersized players going all the way back to the earliest days of football manages to beat so many teams with superior size and athletic ability and win more state championships than anyone else in the state. That hard-nosed, blue collar-type attitude described by Gosch can be traced all the way back to the days when Webb City was a mining town and miners swung pick axes and loaded bucket after bucket of crushed rock all day.

"I think that has a lot to do with it," Gosch says. "A lot of these kids have never had a lot of things given to them. They've had to work their butts off for everything they've gotten. Some communities [that are] a little more wealthy, the kids have been given maybe a little more. In Webb City, the only way you get more is you earn it. That's how you win championships. You earn them. They're not going to be given to you. I do think the blue-collar atmosphere the community has developed is a big part of it. Look at a place like Seneca. They have some tough old kids, but they don't have any wealth down there. Those kids just work their butts off. That's something they take pride in and that's something these kids take pride in."

There are other reasons for Webb City's success, of course. Reasons that go beyond just the talent and effort on the field. Gosch believes another key has been support of the administration. When he started coaching, the administration wanted to win but didn't want to go to the lengths needed to really develop a program. Over time that has changed.

"The superintendent's office has been very, very supportive in trying to make Webb City successful in all activities," he says. "It starts at the top but then you've got to look at teaching and coaching. They have excellent coaches, well-schooled, and they teach football. They teach football and the offseason programs have gotten so intense and thorough.

"John [Rodrique] doesn't leave a stone unturned. He's a teacher, but he's also hired good people. The peewee program is made up of a lot of his former players and coaches, and they teach Webb City football through the youth programs right on up through junior high and into high school. It's a selling job. The kids, they just want to be Cardinals when they're in second grade. He just does a great job selling it."

Seniors from the 1980 football team present Tom Gosch with a plaque for their appreciation. Gosch was named Co-District Coach of the Year along with Parkwood's Dewey Combs.

Tom Gosch, left, speaks with Webb City High School principal James Paullus. Photo by Bob Foos.

16. THE POST-GOSCH ERA

Through the program's first 80 or so years, Tom Gosch was by far the longest-tenured football coach Webb City ever had. With his decision to step away from coaching and into full-time administrative duties, there was now a void at the top of Cardinals football. There was a huge amount of interest in the job; the school received 31 applications for the position in the winter and spring of 1981. But in the end Webb City would find Gosch's successor only a few miles away. Enter Mike Hutchison, a 34-year-old assistant coach on Dewey Combs' staff at Joplin Parkwood. He had spent the previous five years at Parkwood, where he also coached golf. In 13 seasons of coaching football to that point, he had spent the previous decade as an offensive line coach. A native of El Paso, Texas, he had also played at Joplin Junior College and then Pittsburg State before starting his coaching career at East Junior High in Joplin. Hutchison spent time on Charlie Cooper's staff at Joplin Memorial, and he had followed Cooper to Coffeyville Junior College before deciding college coaching wasn't for him. He then coached a year at Jay, Oklahoma before unexpectedly coming to Parkwood when Combs called him two weeks before two-a-days and asked him to join his staff.

"I hope I'll be as successful as Tom Gosch has been," he told the *Sentinel*. He hesitated to guess a win-loss record for his first team, but did promise the Cardinals would be competitive. He inherited a relatively inexperienced squad; Gosch's 7-3 team a year before had 15 seniors filling most of the starting positions, including tri-captains Keith Hirsch, Danny Carter and Phil Divine. Bret Gosch, Divine and Hirsch had earned all-conference honors and Hirsch and Divine were named to the all-district team. Divine, a linebacker; Gosch, a defensive end; and strong safety Hirsch had led a strong Webb City defense that allowed just 13.2 points per game in 1980, registered one shutout and held opponents below their scoring averages in 70 percent of their games. While the defense was clearly the team's strength, the offense was pretty good, too. Hirsch, a running back, averaged 5.6 yards per carry and finished just 17 yards short of 1,000 for the year.

So it was a rebuilding year of sorts for Hutchison and the Cardinals, though he did have four experienced seniors on the team.

"It could be worse, but not much," he said in the newspaper.

Brian Benford was moving from center to fullback, and Bruce Humphrey was set to start at quarterback with junior Dean Edwards as the backup. Defensive tackles Derrick Betebenner and David Wood were also returning. Benford and Humphrey would play both ways. Forty-four players went through two-a-day practices that August.

Hutchison did have an experienced coaching staff behind him. Richard Correll was back to coach the offensive line, and Mark McDonald was still on staff coaching the defensive line and serving as defensive coordinator. Jerry Archer had left, though; he was replaced by Chris Christman, who coached the defensive secondary.

Hutchison's coaching philosophy was simple: "All I expect out of them is to be competitive, which means putting out a little more than their last effort," he told the *Sentinel*. "And if they're competitive, success will usually follow. We're just trying to be successful."

He was noted for his quiet manner on the sidelines. He believed a coach should act restrained as a reflection of mediocre play, saving outward expressions of emotion for notably good or bad play. He installed the wing T offense, sometimes with a flanker set.

The 1981 season would mark Webb City's return to the Big 13 conference after a two-year stint in the Ozark Conference, and the Cardinals' first test would be a road game at East Newton. The Patriots reportedly sent scouts to Webb City's soap scrimmage in late August, and Hutchison said he'd seen "100 percent" improvement over a scrimmage a week earlier.

"There were a lot fewer mistakes and the excitement was up," he said. "They're rising to the task. We've had spirited workouts this week and we'll reach a peak by game time, hopefully.

"We realize we don't have much weight, so we'll have to make up for it with enthusiasm."

Starters set for that first game were Bruce Humphrey at quarterback, Randy Carney at wingback, Ron Wallace at running back, Brian Benford at fullback, Tom Chaney at right guard, Derek Johnson at center, Terry Corbaley at left guard, Phil Roderique and David Wood at offensive tackles and Troy Dilworth at tight end.

On defense the Cardinals went with Tim Chaney, Stuart Hughes, Doug Heiniger and Benford at linebackers, Derrick Betebenner and Wood at tackles, Andy Thompson and Chris Gilliam at cornerbacks, Bruce Parks and Larry McReynolds at ends and Humphrey at defensive back.

Chaney, Benford, Wood and Humphrey were selected as captains.

"Like I told my players, it's nice to be able to make as many mistakes as we did and still win." Those were Hutchison's words after he opened his coaching career at Webb City with a 7-0 win at East Newton. Andy Thompson's 15-yard touchdown catch from Bruce Humphrey was the game winner, coming with about seven minutes left in a defensive struggle of a game. Defensive end Larry

McReynolds ended the Patriots' final charge with a fumble recovery at the Webb City 30.

The Cardinals then blew out Monett in their first home game of the year, coming from behind to tie the game 7-7 at halftime and then scoring three times in the third quarter – each time after a Monett turnover – to win 33-7. Sophomore Bruce Parks' fumble recovery set up a 42-yard scoring run by Humphrey. Three minutes later, Andy Thompson intercepted his second pass of the night and ran 55 yards for a touchdown. His first pickoff had ended a scoring threat. Later in the third quarter sophomore Stuart Hughes recovered a blocked punt and ran 65 yards for a touchdown, and sophomore Teddy Harre added a 45-yard scoring run in the fourth quarter. Humphrey's 22-yard pass to Greg Tarrant in the second quarter had tied the game at 7.

In week three against McDonald County, the Cardinals gained steam as their offensive players became more comfortable with the new wing T offense. They beat the Mustangs 22-6.

Webb City edged Carthage 15-9 to improve to 4-0, and took its winning streak on the road to face the Pittsburg (Kansas) Purple Dragons a week later in what would be one of the season's most exciting games. Pittsburg was the toughest team the Cardinals had faced to that point, and Webb City trailed 14-7 late in the fourth quarter. Bruce Humphrey's 60-yard pass to Greg Tarrant set up a six-yard touchdown run by Ron Wallace that brought the Cardinals to within a point with less than three minutes left in the game. Hutchison opted to go for the two-point conversion and the win, but the ball was fumbled and Pittsburg escaped with a 14-13 win.

That was the first of three straight losses, but Wallace, the junior tailback, got the team back in the win column with a herculean homecoming effort against Mount Vernon, rushing for 177 yards and three touchdowns in the 29-6 win. That made Webb City's record 5-3 as they prepared to play rival Carl Junction for the first time since leaving the conference two years earlier. It would also be their final game of the year.

"No matter what their record, they always play their best game against Webb City," Hutchison said.

And the rivalry had moved beyond the football field. A week earlier, prior to Webb City's homecoming game with Mount Vernon, several Carl Junction girls were sent to Cardinal Stadium on a bus to paint over graffiti they had painted on the ticket booth.

The Cardinals shut out the Bulldogs 20-0 to end the season with a 6-3 record. They had won 16 of their previous 20 meetings with Carl Junction, and tied twice. But the future of the rivalry was now in jeopardy, as was the future of the Big 13 Conference.

The *Sentinel* reported in November 1981 that the conference could die at the end of the year due to a split between small and large schools. The conference was divided into two divisions, Eastern and Western, with small schools in the Eastern and larger schools, including Webb City and Carl Junction, playing in the Western Division. The eight members of the Eastern Division called for a meeting that month in Carthage and requested to secede and form their own conference. During an informal meeting a few days before the meeting in Carthage, Eastern Division schools had met in Monett and decided to break away.

Webb City at that time had the fifth-highest enrollment in the conference with 749 students. The other Western Division members and their enrollments at the time: Neosho (1,104), Carthage (950), Nevada (755) and McDonald County (735). Joplin Memorial, with an enrollment of 1,034, was set to join the Western Division of the conference in 1982.

At a conference meeting in September, Carl Junction's request to jump from the Western to Eastern Division was approved by conference members. The Bulldogs would join Aurora, Seneca, East Newton, Monett, Mount Vernon, Lamar and Cassville. If approved, the split would take effect in the fall of 1982, though schools from the separate conferences would continue to play each other.

In that final fall of unified Big 13 Conference football, the Cardinals had a bevy of players named to the all-conference squad. Bruce Humphrey was the only first-team member of any of the schools to be selected at three positions: quarterback, defensive back and punter. David Wood at offensive tackle, Derrick Betebenner at defensive tackle and Larry McReynolds at defensive end also earned first-team honors. The team's leading rusher, Ron Wallace, earned second-team honors, and so did Wood, at defensive tackle. Derek Johnson earned second-team honors at center, as did Tim Chaney at linebacker and Stuart Hughes at defensive back. Hughes earned honorable mention honors at defensive end.

With Carl Junction leaving the Big 13 Western Division for the Eastern Division and its smaller schools, the 1981 game between the rival Cardinals and the Bulldogs would be the last for several years. Carl Junction's unwillingness to stay in the same division – and vandalism – were cited as reasons the two teams wouldn't play in 1982.

"It was our choice," superintendent Ron Lankford told the *Sentinel*. He felt it was in the school's best interest to play Aurora instead, though he admitted the gate wouldn't exceed that of Carl Junction. Part of the problem, Lankford said, was that the rivalry between the two schools had gotten out of hand. In 1981 Webb City High School and businesses around town were spraypainted by students from Carl Junction, and Carl Junction police had squelched a counter attack by students from Webb City dubbed "The Great Pumpkin Caper." They had planned to throw something like 200 pumpkins onto Carl Junction's football field. There had been other incidents, as well. Carl Junction students had once burned the letters "CJ" onto the field at Cardinal Stadium.

"The other factor, he says, is that Carl Junction effectively said 'they didn't want to play us' when they refused to even up the two divisions within the proposed Big 14 by joining the larger schools currently known as the Big 6," the newspaper reported.

The Big 14 Conference never manifested. Instead, Carl Junction joined East Newton, Aurora, Lamar, Cassville, Seneca, Monett and Mount Vernon in forming the Big 8, and Webb City, Carthage, Neosho, McDonald County, Nevada and Joplin Memorial formed the Big 6. And the Cardinals refused to schedule the Bulldogs, which disappointed Carl Junction head coach H.B. Davis. The Bulldogs filled their non-conference games with three other schools from the new Big 6: Memorial, Carthage and Neosho. Webb City, meanwhile, filled out its schedule with four Big 8 opponents: East Newton, Mount Vernon, Aurora and Monett, and also Pittsburg.

Hutchison's second team returned six starters from the 6-3 year, along with eight other lettermen, but all but two or three of those were playing new positions. The team elected seniors Phil Roderique, Chris Gilliam, Bryan Boyd and Doug Heiniger as captains.

The Cardinals lost their first game of 1982, 6-0 at East Newton, but bounced back to beat Mount Vernon 22-6 with Ron Wallace rushing for 141 yards on 24 carries, two touchdowns and a pair of two-point conversions. In week three the Cardinals hosted Aurora, which had finished second in the state a year prior and was led by senior all-state quarterback Steve Mayfield, who had thrown for 1,659 yards and 22 touchdowns as a junior. He was the son of Jack Mayfield, a 1951 Webb City graduate who was an all-star running back for the Cardinals and earned his letter all four years in football. Jack Mayfield had married his high school sweetheart, Veva Storm, just days after graduating from Webb City. The Aurora game was delayed by more than an hour due to a severe storm with driving rain and several lightning strikes. When the teams finally kicked off, Mayfield guided the Houn' Dawgs to an 8-6 win.

After four games the Cardinals were just 1-3, though their defense had limited opponents to a total of just 36 points, an average of nine per game. The offense, though, was only averaging 8.75 points per game. They would finish with four wins and six losses, which remarkably earned them second place in the Big 6. Conference teams started the season with a combined 5-24 record, though, which explains what a down year it was.

Hutchison's final year coaching the Cardinals was 1983. Spirits were high in the offseason with the team returning 17 seniors and 15 lettermen, and the Cardinals were especially experienced on offense with Stuart Hughes coming back at quarterback and Bruce Parks and Teddy Harre returning in the backfield. They lost again to East Newton in the season opener, but rattled off three wins in a row before falling to Pittsburg and Carthage, which evened their record at 3-3. The offense had its best game in three years when the Cardinals smacked

McDonald County 41-13 to get back above .500. John Roderique, a freshman, scored a fourth-quarter touchdown on a two-yard run. Webb City added a 27-13 win against Memorial and finished the season 5-5 overall and 2-3 in the conference, which earned them a share of third place in the Big 6.

This photo of John Roderique appeared in the Webb City Sentinel after Roderique's game-winning field goal in the 1985 playoffs. Photo by Bob Foos.

17. BEGIN THE DRIVE IN '85

In the more than 100 years since Webb City High School began playing football, there have been incredible teams and entire decades marked by the school's dominance on the gridiron. There have been lousy teams, too, and decades where the Cardinals were lucky to finish with a winning season or two.

Since 1984, the Cardinals have played 381 football games and they've lost only 48 times. That's an average of 1.6 losses per season, and they almost always play more than 10 games. It's a winning percentage of 87 percent. In 30 years Webb City hasn't had a single losing season. The worst year you'll find in that span is a 5-5 season in 1998.

This run of success is more than just incredible teams and decades of dominance. In the last 30 years, Webb City football has become a spectacle to behold.

In the book *Pictorial History of Webb City, Carterville, Oronogo*, published in 2008, Patricia (Goddard) Freeman describes this spectacle. She writes of the home and away games with standing room only, of the locals setting up their lawn chairs outside Cardinal Stadium early in the day of a game to wait for the opening of the gate. During the team's playoff games and trips to the state championship, buses were chartered with seating sold out. Whenever the Cardinals traveled, opposing fans often noted they were outnumbered by those from Webb City.

"Halftime shows with the Mighty Marching Cardinal Pride Band, Color Guard and Redette Dance Team performances were spectacular and a crowd draw. The stands became a grand sea of red – at home and away. Whole neighborhoods emptied on game night. It was remarked that burglars could have an easy time of it in Webb City on Friday evenings during football season. Out-of-towners were incredulous at the game attendance. While waiting at the end of a long ticket line one year, a fan from Nevada, Missouri, looked wide-eyed at the Webb City crowd and packed parking lot and was overheard to say, "This is ONLY football!" Freeman wrote.

As Freeman notes, the modern dynasty of Cardinals football and the overwhelming support from Webb City residents can be traced back to one season: 1985. That was the year Mark McDonald, the former Tom Gosch assistant, led the program to the state playoffs for the first time in school history. Players joined together by all getting a "buzz" hair cut, and the slogan of the season was "Begin the drive in '85!"

Mark McDonald was hired prior to the 1984 season to replace Mike Hutchison, who replaced Tom Gosch and coached for three years. McDonald's first team was captained by seniors Mike Keeling, Bill Rowland, David Moore and Mike Hulderman, and had some other key seniors in Steve Thompson, Rodney Thompson, Dean Bearden and Mike Smith. Several players would earn all-conference honors. John Roderique was a first-team linebacker and Keeling was a first-team defensive back. Jeff Goddard was a second-team quarterback and defensive back, Scott Smith was a second-team defensive tackle and David Howard was a second-team nose guard.

"The most memorable game was playing Pittsburg in 1983 when they were state champs," said Hulderman, a quarterback who is now chair of the Criminal Justice Department at MSSU. "Knowing they were one of the best teams in the area, it was a challenge for us and we were excited to play them. I looked forward to playing Carthage and Neosho every year."

Goddard had transferred into the school district and McDonald expected his team to throw the ball a lot in 1984. Receivers Brad Rea and Mike Keeling were his primary weapons going in.

David Moore, the senior running back, scored a 16-yard touchdown to give McDonald a 22-16 win in his first game at the helm as the Cardinals beat East Newton to open the season.

A few weeks later the Cardinals blew out Monett 36-10 on the road in their first win at Monett since 1966. Goddard ran for two touchdowns and threw for two more. That win put them at 3-1, but back-to-back losses to Pittsburg and Carthage evened their record at 3-3.

John Roderique led the team with 13 tackles, and Willie Roderique scored on a 10-yard run to help Webb City get back in the win column in a 29-0 victory against McDonald County. They won two more games after that, but lost to Joplin Memorial and Neosho to end the year and finished with a 5-5 record.

While McDonald's first team was relatively inexperienced, the playing time paid off a year later. The 1985 team entered the season a stronger, quicker squad after an offseason in the weight room and returned 20 lettermen and 16 starters. While the Cardinals had only eight seniors in 1984, they had 23 in 1985 – almost half the team of 47 players.

"We've talked about wanting to be over .500," McDonald told the newspaper. A conference championship and playoff contention were other goals for the team.

Almost a quarter of the team's roster was related, with 10 of the players being brothers. There was John and Willie Roderique, the sons of Jenell Roderique; Kevin and Kendall Russell, the sons of Gene and Cheryl Russell; Jeff and Jack Lassiter, sons of Jack and Jeanie Lassiter; Brian and Patrick Hughes, the sons of Alan and Judy Hughes; and Jeff and Joey Goddard. Most of the brothers had played together since junior high. John Roderique was a senior linebacker, running back and placekicker; Willie played strong safety and running back. The Russells were actually twins, and both were seniors; Kevin played split end and Kendall played flanker. Jeff Lassiter, a junior, played offensive guard and defensive tackle, and sophomore Jack played nose guard and offensive guard. Brian Hughes, a senior, played linebacker, and Patrick, a sophomore, was the team's backup quarterback. As for the Goddards, Jeff, a senior and the son of Bog Goddard and Louise Stone, was the team's quarterback and free safety, while Joey, the son of Bob Goddard and Susie Lawrence, and also a senior, played center and snapped the ball to his brother.

The Cardinals got off to a quick start, blowing out their regular season-opening opponent East Newton 47-0, but Mount Vernon scored a touchdown with less than a minute left in the game in week two and handed Webb City a 12-6 defeat. In that game at Cardinal Stadium, Webb City got as close as the Mountaineers' 4-yard line with seconds left on the clock, but quarterback Jeff Goddard's pass fell incomplete on the last play of the game and the Cardinals were whistled for an ineligible receiver downfield anyway.

Webb City's 10-game schedule in 1985 included just three road games. The team headed to Aurora in week three to face a talented offensive squad, and after that would play three straight home games. They blew out the Houn' Dawgs 38-8, and pitched a shutout at home against Monett, 34-0.

After beating Seneca 38-13, the team had won three straight and wrapped up non-conference play. Goddard led the team's offensive effort with 214 passing yards against the Indians while completing 14 of 21 attempts, and he rushed for 74 yards on 10 carries. John Roderique added three touchdowns, and brother Willie Roderique scored one of his own. Goddard and Kevin Russell also added points.

Webb City began Southwest Conference play ranked first in its district and against old rival Carthage. Against the Tigers, the Cardinals didn't punt even once. A recovered fumble at the Carthage 35 set up a three-yard touchdown run by John Roderique. After a Carthage punt, the Cardinals drove 59 yards and scored when Goddard threw a 33-yard touchdown strike to Scott Smith. The duo connected for another touchdown later in the first half, and the Cardinals held Carthage scoreless in the second half of a 43-12 win. Kevin Russell led the team in receiving with five catches for 52 yards and Tony Perry tallied 39 yards on three catches. Smith had 38 yards and two touchdowns. Willie Roderique outpaced his older brother in the ground game with 83 yards on 15 rushes. Goddard completed 11 of 15 passes for 124 yards. Webb City finished the game with 381 offensive yards while limiting the Tigers to just 75, and the Cardinals gained 21 first downs to Carthage's three. It was, needless to say, a dominating win.

With homecoming on tap in week seven, Webb City was red hot. It had won four straight games and was 5-1 overall. The winning streak went to five with a 48-6 crushing of McDonald County. The Roderique brothers combined for a huge game, scoring 30 of the team's points. Willie scored three touchdowns from 23 yards, 10 yards and 30 yards, and finished with 97 rushing yards on just eight carries. Meanwhile, John intercepted a pass and returned it for a touchdown and kicked six extra points. Goddard was once again dynamic at quarterback, rushing for a 10-yard score and passing to Kevin Russell for a 26-yard touchdown. Mark Baker scored a touchdown, too.

Excitement around town was really building as the regular season entered its final weeks. The Cardinals knocked off Nevada 40-6 for their sixth straight win. They took a 19-0 lead in the first quarter after converting two Nevada turnovers and a short punt into points. Willie Roderique continued to lead the team's running game with 82 yards on 14 carries, but he was far from the only weapon on the ground. Tony Perry rushed 12 times for 81 yards and John Roderique had five runs for 23 yards. They didn't just rely on the ground game, either. Jeff Goddard completed eight passes for 116 yards with Kevin Russell catching half his throws for 60 yards. And the Webb City defense finished with five interceptions, though the defense took a hit when senior defensive back Brad Rea suffered a broken hand.

There were now just two regular-season games left, and the Cardinals were 7-1, but their biggest test all season was awaiting them in week nine: the Camdenton Lakers.

"The Webb City Cardinals, who never have made it to the state football playoffs, may have the potential this season," wrote Larry Lee, the *Sentinel*'s assistant editor. "Consider the Cardinals are ranked number one offensively among Missouri 4A schools. Coach Mark McDonald's Cards have outscored their first eight opponents 294-57. The team is ranked number one in District 6 with six straight victories under its belt. With all that going for the Cardinals, McDonald would have every right to begin getting a little excited about postseason play. But he isn't looking past tonight's game with undefeated Camdenton in Cardinal Stadium."

Indeed, the Lakers were unbeaten. And also ranked No. 1 in the state in Division 4A. Webb City wasn't yet state ranked, despite outscoring every team in 4A, but a win against Camdenton would probably get the team into the polls. Adding to the excitement surrounding the team, if Webb City could hang on to its top district ranking after games against Camdenton and Neosho, the Cardinals would host their first playoff game in school history against the second-place team from District 6. If they won that game, they'd play the winner from District 5, which likely would be Camdenton. After that, the state semifinals, and then the 4A state championship inside Busch Stadium in St. Louis.

The Camdenton game would go down as an instant classic.

John Roderique scored the team's only touchdown in the first half, a one-yard run in the second quarter. He was now the 10th-highest scorer statewide in Class 4A. Camdenton sandwiched Roderique's run with two touchdowns, a 26-yard pass and a 63-yard run, and the Lakers led 13-6 at the half.

Disaster struck in the second half. Camdenton intercepted a Jeff Goddard pass, and also a pitch, and turned both turnovers into score.

"Those were gifts," McDonald later said. "Not really gifts, but they made them on our miscues. I knew we would move the ball, but I didn't know how the kids would react."

The turnovers put the Cardinals in a 26-6 hole in the third quarter. They were taking their worst beating of the whole season. Their next four possessions would change everything.

"We just kept fighting back," McDonald said.

The defense shut Camdenton down. Kevin Russell made a key interception. Goddard threw 10- and 13-yard touchdown passes to Russell. John Roderique scored from a yard out. Scott Smith made a "super catch" on a two-point conversion, and Roderique kicked two more extra points. For the first time all night long, Webb City had a lead – 27-26. Goddard added some insurance with a one-yard run in the fourth quarter, putting the game out of reach with Webb City ahead 34-26. The win sealed a home playoff game for the Cardinals, who finally entered the state polls at No. 8.

A week later, Webb City concluded a 9-1 regular season and a Southwest Conference championship with a 34-13 throttling of Neosho. It was the team's first outright conference championship since Henry May's team won the Big 8 in 1961. This time there was no late-night bus ride around the Carthage square.

So the Cardinals were in the playoffs for the first time, and they'd get to play their first playoff game – the District 6 championship against Willard – in the friendly confines of Cardinal Stadium. Except that four inches of rain fell in the two days before the November game, and it was too much for the field at Cardinal Stadium to handle. The game was moved to Fred G. Hughes Stadium at Missouri Southern State University, where it was witnessed by 1,387 fans. It was still raining when the two teams kicked off, and the Cardinals committed three turnovers in the first quarter against the Tigers.

Willard had somehow won eight of 10 games despite averaging just 15 points per game, and Webb City's defense was allowing only 9.6 points per game. Of course, the Tigers gave up an average of only five points a game. With both teams hampered by a "deluge of water," the Cardinals limited Willard to just two first downs the whole game, both in the first half. Webb City's turnovers kept it a scoreless game early on. The team had more trouble holding onto the football than it did moving down the field; two of the fumbles came at the Willard 44- and 25-yard lines. Willard had the same trouble, fumbling twice, and Webb City's David Howard recovered both of them.

Brad Rea picked off a Willard pass and returned it 40 yards to the Willard 22-yard line late in the first quarter, though Webb City could advance only five yards in three plays. On fourth down, Jeff Goddard completed a 12-yard pass to Scott Smith at the 5-yard line. As the quarter ended, John Roderique carried the ball to within a yard of the end zone, and on the first play of the second he punched it in. His extra point made it 7-0, and the score would remain unchanged into the fourth quarter. At that point Willie Roderique rushed for 11 yards to the 1-foot line, and John punched it in again and kicked another extra point. Final score: Webb City 14, Willard 0.

"The kids just kept fighting back," McDonald told the newspaper. He promised an intense week of practice as his team prepared to travel to West Plains in the state quarterfinals. The Zizzers, who went 5-5 in the regular season, downed Camdenton 3-0 in the District 5 title game. West Plains had somehow won just one home game all season, but had not allowed a score in its previous 18 quarters of play. Whoever won the quarterfinal game would host the winner of Kansas City Center vs. St. Joseph Lafayette.

It was said the contingent of Webb City fans equaled, if not outnumbered, the West Plains home crowd. The high school chartered three buses that carried 126 fans to the game, and another five school buses carried with them 148 high school students. Many others drove the "210 miles through heavy rain with minimal visibility to the hometown of Dolly Parton's former partner, Porter Waggoner," the *Sentinel* noted.

With bad weather in the area, the worst storms stayed just outside West Plains, but it still rained most of the night, causing a muddy field. And yet the game was played fairly cleanly, with just one penalty called the entire contest, an offsides miscue against the Cardinals. It lasted less than two hours.

West Plains' defense, and the field conditions, effectively shut down Webb City's offense. In the second quarter a Jeff Goddard pass was deflected and intercepted. That came after the Zizzers had turned it over by failing to convert on a fourth-and-one at the Webb City 14, but West Plains now had first-and-goal at the Cardinal 8. Two plays later the Zizzers scored and went ahead by a touchdown, and for three quarters they kept Webb City's offense at bay; West Plains' scoreless streak went to 21 quarters.

"It altered what we tried to do, what we could do," said head coach Mark McDonald. "We had to run more straight ahead stuff than we wanted."

The Cardinals had the ball at their own 39-yard line as the fourth quarter started. Three plays later they faced a third-and-8, but finally the "Big Mac Attack" offensive unit came to life. Goddard completed his only pass for a gain all game, caught by Scott Smith, and Webb City had the ball across midfield. On the very next play Willie Roderique took a handoff on a draw play and ran 34 yards to the West Plains' 14. Goddard then kept the ball, spun around to his right and shook off a tackle to find the end zone. John Roderique's extra point tied the game at 7-7 with barely 10 minutes left in the fourth quarter.

"We had one big pass play," McDonald said. "We got it when we needed it."

He never really considered going for two and the lead.

"We felt like there was plenty of time, that we could score again," he said. "At least have the opportunity to score again."

That chance came sooner than expected. The Cardinals intercepted a deflected pass at the West Plains 39. John Roderique carried twice for 14 and four yards, respectively, but a Goddard fumble at the 20 gave the ball back to Zizzers.

They went three-and-out and punted to the Cardinals, who started at their own 38. They moved into West Plains' territory and had the ball just 39 yards from the end zone with 59 seconds on the clock; McDonald called timeout.

On first down, Goddard threw incomplete. Willie Roderique ran for 13 yards and a first down a play later. Two plays after that, the ball was at the 11 and only 16 seconds remained in the game. Webb City called another timeout.

John Roderique loosened his leg, and out came the field goal unit for the 28-yard attempt to win the game.

"It was perfect," the newspaper wrote.

And in the newspaper, a black and white photo of Roderique, in his muddy jersey and proclaiming with his finger that the Cardinals were No. 1.

It was on to the semifinals.

The semifinal game against the Kansas City Center Yellow Jackets would finally be the first playoff game ever played at Cardinal Stadium. Nearly 2,000 fans braved the windy, chilly weather. From the very beginning things went poorly for Webb City. Center returned the opening kickoff to midfield and scored two plays later. But the Cardinal defense was keeping the team in it. They recovered three fumbles and stopped the Yellow Jackets four times on fourth down. On one series Center was stopped four straight times at the 1-yard line. Brian Hughes recorded sacks in each of the first two quarters.

The team's luck began to change late in the first quarter. The Cardinals punted, but the ball was bobbled by Center's return man at his own 13 and Webb City was in business. Willie Roderique ran for two yards, then a Goddard pass for Kevin Russell was swatted away. Goddard looked for Russell again on third-and-eight but his pass to the end zone was incomplete. John Roderique stepped up and booted a 30-yard field goal to make it a 7-3 game.

Three Webb City interceptions in the game's final five minutes kept Center ahead, but barely. The Cardinals' last chance to score ended in an interception at the Center 20. Some believed Webb City's receiver had been pulled down before the ball arrived, but no flag was thrown and Webb City's 1985 season came to an end with a four-point semifinal loss. The team was limited to just 61 yards of offense.

Kansas City Center outweighed the Cardinals' offense by an average of 14 pounds for every player. The Yellow Jackets had left Kansas City on chartered buses the day before the game and practiced on the artificial turf at Fred G. Hughes Stadium – they would, after all, be playing on the turf at Busch Stadium a week later, they believed.

"The big, the bad, and the ugly came to town last Saturday," wrote Larry Lee in a *Sentinel* column.

"Yet big and bad as those Yellow Jackets were, what area football fans most will remember was their lack of good manners," he continued. "They were, in a word, ugly. Their band set the tone marching into Cardinal Stadium uniformed in villainous black. The drummers irreverently rolled halfway through the invocation. Then the band positioned itself between Webb City fans and the Redettes pom-pon squad and proceeded to try to drum Morris Day and the Time out of the stadium. Shortly after the opening kickoff, a Center assistant coach in the press box couldn't get his headset to work. He screamed at the Cardinal assistant coach, 'Mine's not working! You can't use yours! It's in the (MSHSAA rule) book! Put yours down! Who's in charge of the press box?!"

The off-putting behavior went further than that. A Center fan rearranged a Webb City sign that read "There's no stoppin' us now" to say "Here's stoppin' us now." But the ugliest display, according to Lee, came during the Cardinals' acceptance of the state semifinal trophy at midfield. The Yellow Jackets lined up in the northeast corner of the field and ran behind Webb City's players while waving "number one" fingers in the air.

Lee's column took a positive turn, as well. He had moved to Webb City halfway through the season, and commended the Cardinals for their class. He countered the complaints that sports are sometimes given too much emphasis, writing "a school needs to have spirit and pride before the students, the teachers, the administration, and ultimately the community will give a rip and go that necessary extra mile to provide the best learning environment possible. Sports is one way to foster school pride, and from what I've seen here in Webb City, the Cardinal spirit is alive and kicking."

Lee also referenced a letter Mark McDonald had received from the West Plains' coaching staff.

"In my seventeen years of coaching, I have never witnessed such a fine performance of sportsmanship and play as you displayed this past Monday night at our contest. May God bless you on your quest for the 4A state championship," wrote Ted Michael and his West Plains assistants.

There were plenty of postseason honors for the Cardinals after their 11-2 year. Named to the all-Southwest Conference first team were quarterback Jeff Goddard, guard Rob Thurlo, tackle Dusty Allen, running back Willie Roderique, punter John Roderique, and kicker John Roderique. First-team defensive honors went to end Paul Stewart, tackle Scott Smith, nose guard David Howard, linebacker John Roderique and defensive backs Jeff Goddard, Derrick Reynolds and Willie Roderique. Brian Hughes earned second-team honors for his season on defense, Smith earned second-team honors at tight end along with tackle Todd VanSlyke, guard Andy Rogers, center Joey Goddard and Tony Perry and John Roderique at running back.

John Roderique also became the school's first all-state selection. Three months later his mother, Jenell Roderique, watched as he signed a letter of intent to play linebacker for Pittsburg State University. A day later Kevin Russell signed with Missouri Southern. Roderique was recruited by Southern, Missouri Western and Central Missouri State, as well, but chose the Gorillas because he felt comfortable with their defensive system, which was similar to Webb City's. Pittsburg State coach Dennis Franchione attended the signing.

18. THE JERRY KILL YEARS

He's always said it was one of the best jobs he's ever had, maybe the funnest two years of his entire coaching career. That's saying a lot considering Jerry Kill coaches on one of the biggest stages in football, leading the Minnesota Golden Gophers into battle each fall in the mighty Big 10 conference.

Kill is 53 today, and his rapid ascension through the coaching ranks has been impressive. He's served as both defensive coordinator and offensive coordinator during two stints at Pittsburg State University, and he started his head coaching career at the college level with Saginaw Valley State in 1994. Five years later he took the job at Emporia State University, and after a brief stint with that Division II school, in the same conference as Pittsburg State, he got his first coaching job at the Division I level with Southern Illinois University. Kill coached there from 2001 to 2007, and from 2008 until 2010 he led Northern Illinois' football program. In 2011 he climbed another rung on the ladder, and he's led the Golden Gophers ever since.

But more than two decades ago Kill was just a high school coach patrolling the sidelines at Cardinal Stadium. And yet, in those two short years at Webb City, he would lead the Cardinals to heights never seen before.

Mark McDonald coached one more year after that incredible 1985 season. His 1986 Cardinals were still pretty good, but the season was riddled with injuries. Willie Roderique, the team's catalyst, missed much of the season. Scott Smith overcame an early injury to provide a boost to the team's defense, and he was named to the all-state first team. Offensive tackle Dusty Allen earned all-state second-team honors after blowing open holes for the team's backfield and protecting quarterback Patrick Hughes.

The year got off to a rocky start. The Cardinals pounded East Newton to win their first game, but Roderique broke his ankle in a 13-0 loss at Mount Vernon in week two. Several weeks later, Webb City had struggled to a 2-3 start, but its luck would begin to change after an 18-0 shutout against Carthage to get back to .500. Dan Crutcher, in a special column for the *Sentinel*, said the game was the pinnacle of the 1986 season.

"Younger fans think of the football schedule as consisting of three seasons: the warm-up games, the Southwest Conference games, and the state championship playoffs," he wrote. "Long-time fans, say those over forty years of age, see a fourth season. It consists of only one game in a year – the CARTHAGE game! If the Redbirds win only one game in a year, it is still an acceptable campaign IF that win is over Carthage."

Crutcher attributed the importance of this game to the large number of contests the schools had played against each other, and the fact that it had historically been the final game of the year, on Thanksgiving Day. Back then, the Cardinals and Tigers would play in the morning, and the Joplin Eagles and Springfield Bulldogs would play in the afternoon. A large number of people attended both games. The 1986 contest was apparently the 90th between the two rivals.

Webb City was 5-3 after wins against McDonald County and Nevada, but got blown out 49-6 against Camdenton. The Cardinals ended the regular season by beating Neosho in a shutout, giving them the conference championship and another trip to the state playoffs.

This time their playoff run would be short-lived, however. They faced Springfield Central in the first round, and with 1:11 left in the fourth quarter and the game tied at 20-20, it appeared overtime was likely on a frigid night with temperatures hovering in the 20s. The Cardinals received a boost by the return of Willie Roderique in his No. 20 jersey. He gave Webb City a 17-14 lead with seconds remaining in the fourth quarter after carrying the ball on four of seven plays. Central answered with a long drive and a touchdown to lead by three points, but Dan Burke booted a 37-yard field goal to tie the game at 20 with barely a minute to play. But on the ensuing kickoff, Central's Daren Faulkner returned the ball 80 yards for the game-winning touchdown. The Cardinals finished the season 6-5.

McDonald left with a 22-12 record in three seasons as head coach, two conference championships and two playoff appearances. Early in the summer of 1987, Webb City hired Mount Vernon head coach Tom Cox, hoping to continue the success of the mid-1980s. Cox was one of the few Webb City coaches who wasn't a Pittsburg State guy; he had graduated from Missouri Southern where he played four years of football and two years of baseball. He coached high school football at his alma mater in St. Louis for a year, then took the Mount Vernon job and coached the Mountaineers for eight seasons, six years as head coach.

"While the rivalry between Mount Vernon and Webb City is already intense, Cox feels his move across the line of fire may serve as an incentive to the Mount Vernon players, some of which are reportedly unhappy with Cox's decision. However, the fact that he is familiar with the personnel and the strengths and weaknesses of Mount Vernon will certainly work to Webb City's advantage," the newspaper wrote.

Recall it was Cox's Mountaineers who pitched a 13-0 shutout against the Cardinals a year earlier in the game Willie Roderique suffered his broken ankle. And Mount Vernon was the only team to beat the incredible 1985 Webb City squad in the regular season, 12-6 in week two.

In 1987 the Cardinals would face the four toughest teams in the Big 8 Conference, and Carthage, Neosho and Springfield Hillcrest would be tough foes within the Southwest Conference. One of those Big 8 schools would be rival Carl Junction, who the Cardinals hadn't played since 1981 after vandalism and the Big 13 split temporarily put an end to things. School officials hoped vandalism wouldn't be a problem again.

Led by Lance Gosch, the son of Tom Gosch and brother of Bret, on defense, and quarterback Patrick Hughes on offense, the Cardinals allowed only eight points total in their first three games and scored at least 26 points in five games while finishing the season with a 6-4 record. When it was over, Gosch was named a second-team all-state linebacker and a first-team all-area linebacker. Hughes was a second-team all-area defensive back, Jack Lassiter was a third-team all-area defensive lineman, and center Monty Belcher and defensive end Steve Burch were named to the all-area honorable mention team. Hughes was a first-team all-conference player at quarterback, punter and defensive back, and Gosch was a first-team all-conference player at linebacker and running back. Belcher, Burch, Lassiter and tight end Mike Leake also earned first-team conference honors, and offensive guard and defensive tackle Craig Thurlo, defensive back Monty Belcher, offensive guard Lassiter, wide receiver Brian Walker and offensive tackle Brent Pierce were second-team all-conference players.

The same year, John Roderique was playing linebacker for Pittsburg State as the Gorillas advanced to the semifinal round of NAIA Division I playoffs. He recorded 13 tackles in the semifinal game, but Pitt State lost 20-10 to Cameron University. It was the second straight year the Gorillas had lost to Cameron in the semifinals.

"Roderique started his football career when he was in the fourth grade and has continued despite a broken leg his freshman year in high school," the *Sentinel* wrote. "During high school, he played predominantly at linebacker but filled in at running back as well. 'It's always been fun,' he said. 'When it stops being fun it's time to quit.' Only a sophomore this year, Roderique has seen considerable playing time and was named defensive player-of-the-game when PSU defeated Northeastern State (Okla.) University in the playoffs. He was credited with nine tackles, two fumble recoveries, one interception and a broken pass."

The defensive coordinator for those Pittsburg State teams? Jerry Kill.

Jerry Kill recalls John Roderique as an outstanding high school football player. Kill had a good relationship with Mark McDonald, and he was the one who recruited Roderique to Pittsburg State.

"I would tell you from a personal opinion, I've coached at all levels and I think John was one of the better linebackers I've ever coached," Kill says now. "He was physically tough, smart. He had football instincts. He was a super young man and I really enjoyed coaching him. Now I'm very proud of him. I kind of think of him as an adopted son, so to speak."

Kill spent three seasons as the defensive coordinator at Pittsburg State, 1985-87, while Dennis Franchione was in the midst of his five-year stint coaching the Gorillas. It was an incredible coaching staff. Franchione had graduated from PSU and coached at Miller High School in Missouri for a year. He coached two Kansas high schools after that, became an assistant coach at Kansas State University and then was hired to be the head coach at Southwestern College in Winfield, Kansas in 1981. In two years at Southwestern he compiled a 14-4-2 record, won the Kansas Collegiate Athletic Conference title and the Sunflower Bowl. His 1982 team won nine games and had its best season in 25 years. He then spent two years as an offensive coordinator at Tennessee Tech, and was hired as Pittsburg State's head coach in 1985. In five seasons with the Gorillas, his teams went 53-6 and 37-1 in the conference. He won conference titles every season and twice was named NAIA National Coach of the Year. Franchione became head coach at Southwest Texas State in 1990, New Mexico in 1992, Texas Christian in 1998, Alabama in 2001, and Texas A&M in 2003. He coached the Aggies for five years, and has coached Texas State since 2011.

At TCU, Franchione led the Horned Frogs to their first victory in a bowl game and their first top-25 finish since the 1950s. He coached LaDainian Tomlinson, who led the nation in rushing in 1999. At Alabama, he took a team that had gone 3-8 the year before his arrival and went 7-5 in 2001 and 10-3 in 2002. Alabama offered him a 10-year, $15 million extension, but the school was slapped with NCAA sanctions resulting from violations of Mike DuBose, Franchione's predecessor. Franchione resigned and accepted the job at Texas A&M; he went 32-28 there.

In 1988, Roderique's linebacker coach was Gary Patterson, who later followed Franchione from New Mexico to TCU and became Texas Christian's new head coach in 2000 when Franchione left for Alabama. Patterson has compiled a 132-45 record at TCU, gone to 12 bowl games and finished the 2010 season 13-0 after winning the Rose Bowl. He was named 2009 Associated Press Coach of the Year.

Following the 1987 season, Kill had been working for three years as Pittsburg State's defensive coordinator. In February 1988, after turning them down twice, Tom Cox finally decided to accept the head coaching position at Ozark High School, and the Cardinals were looking for their fourth new head coach since Gosch stepped down following the 1980 season. Cox said it was a difficult decision to leave Webb City, but taking over a program in the fastest-growing county in the state was appealing.

"I think it's got a lot of potential," he told the newspaper.

Ozark had nearly double the football roster as did Webb City, and a bigger staff and a seventh-grade program. He hesitated to take the job, though, because of the players in Webb City. They were reportedly, and understandably, quite surprised to see him leave after a year. Athletics director Tom Gosch was surprised too, and disappointed, but wished Cox "all the luck in the world."

A few weeks later, on April Fools' Day, the *Sentinel* announced Webb City had made a huge hire: the Cardinals had lured Jerry Kill away from the world of college football. But it was no joke, and Kill was chosen out of a field of 31 applicants.

"We were looking for stability," Gosch said in the newspaper. "I think he (Kill) will be with us as long as he wants to be with us because I think he will be successful."

As Kill looks back on his decision to go to Webb City, he said the biggest reasons he was attracted to the job were the district administration and specifically Tom Gosch. Kill had coached Gosch's son, Lance, at Pittsburg State, and he says he had a great deal of respect for Tom.

"I knew the support that I'd have there at Webb City, and I wanted to be a head coach," he says. "I think I was 26 years old. I decided to give it a chance and it turned out to be a great time in my life."

Kill received plenty of help from coaches at Pittsburg State in getting things structured. It was, after all, his first head coaching gig. Kurt Thompson followed him over and joined the Cardinals' staff, and Bobby Campbell volunteered; he later won a state championship as the head coach at Fort Scott, (Kansas) High School.

"And then the coaching staff that was already there, they welcomed the philosophy we came in with," Kill says. "It just all fit and the kids worked hard, did what we asked them to do. I think we ran it like a small college program with a high school philosophy, so to speak, within a high school scheme. We were blessed with hard-nosed, tough kids who'd do anything. They'd run through a wall for you, and they still do that. There have been some good players come out of Webb City, there's no question about that."

Kill's teams ran the split back veer offense, just as the Cardinals do today. He learned to coach from some of the best, even before his time at Pittsburg State. He cites two good high school coaches he played for in Cheney, Kansas: Ken Diskin and Jack Thomas. After high school, he played football at Southwestern College in Winfield, Kansas, and his third year there the school hired who else but Dennis Franchione as the head coach.

"Not only did I play for him, I learned a lot of football from him," Kill says. "I had to. I wasn't a great athlete. I was an overachiever so I had to learn the game, and I paid attention during the time I played there."

He spent another semester at Southwestern playing for Charley Cowdrey, who had been a head coach at Fort Scott Community College for three years, an assistant at Missouri for eight years, and head coach at Illinois State for four years. He was another good influence on Kill. Kill got his first coaching job at

Midwest City High School in the Oklahoma City area. Mike Gundy was the team's quarterback; he's now the head coach at Oklahoma State University. At Midwest City, Kill also coached wrestling and even some girls' basketball. He and his wife lived in a trailer house and made barely more than a couple hundred dollars a month. He also worked at a grocery store and made donuts.

And by the mid '80s, Franchione was at Pittsburg State and recruited Kill to join his staff there.

"I had a pretty good game plan on how to do things," Kill says. "I had a pretty good foundation because I was influenced by a lot of good people. There's no question the influence Coach Franchione had on me during my early career was certainly critical in my development as a coach."

Another word about Pittsburg State's coaching tree. The Gorillas are, of course, one of the preeminent programs in NCAA Division II football, with four national titles since 1957, but the proud coaching history surrounding the university goes beyond the likes of Kill, Franchione, Gary Patterson and Chuck Broyles. Sam Pittman played defensive end for the Gorillas and was hired in 2013 to be the offensive line coach at the University of Arkansas. He's one of the highest-paid offensive line coaches in the nation, and he turned down an offer from Alabama to coach there. Willie Fritz coached for Pittsburg State in 1982 and was the head coach at Central Missouri for 12 years, at Sam Houston State University from 2010 to 2013, and is now at Georgia Southern. There have been plenty of others, including successful high school coaches.

"It's a deep-rooted university to turn out great coaches," Kill says. "I was fortunate in my time there that I've coached both of the coaches who have gone through Webb City at the same time, Kurt and John. Kurt was the elder statesman and John was the young freshman. Kurt had a lot to do with developing John. Webb City's been smart to keep it in the family, so to speak. Nothing's really changed. They're still running the split back veer and the same defensive scheme. They haven't changed a whole lot except the names of the head coaches. I think the philosophy, even though we may all have different personalities, hasn't changed a whole lot."

19. JERRY KILL FOR PRESIDENT

Kill was already pretty well familiar with other conference schools by the time the 1988 season rolled around. He'd been recruiting their seniors to Pittsburg State, after all. And at Webb City, he was still recruiting, but within the high school. When he took over there were just six seniors on the team, but by the time the season began he'd added a handful more. Of 16 juniors on the team, half weren't going to come out until Kill convinced them to. His first team returned only 11 lettermen and five starters. Wide receiver Michael Leake was the only all-conference player back, but Kill was expecting big things from Chance Wistrom, who had transferred in from Florida.

"I really can't tell you what to expect this year," Kill told coaches and reporters at the annual Southwest Conference fall press conference in Carthage. "I'll start eight or nine who haven't seen a football field for a long time. It could be an experience. Or a bad experience."

The Cardinals had a balanced schedule, five games at home and five on the road, and they would entertain Carl Junction, East Newton, Springfield Central, McDonald County and Neosho. A three-week slate of road games in October, at Nixa, Nevada and Carthage, would be tough. And the Cardinals were even an underdog in the season opener against Carl Junction.

Offensively Webb City expected to run the ball and the option a substantial amount of the time. Senior Keith Rogers, a 5-foot-11, 165-pound quarterback, would lead the offense.

"He's very good, very intelligent," Kill told the paper. "He's a good person to lead the team."

The team had a good running back corps, too, with senior Mike Wilson and juniors Matt Berry, Jeff Johnson and Kevin Crane. The running game would depend on the guys Kill called "the hogs," his offensive line, which was to be led by senior Chance Wistrom at tackle and senior Scott Allen. Seniors Brent Pierce and Craig Thurlo were expected to start at guards, junior Mike Collette at center, senior Scott Walker at tight end and sophomore Craig Divine backing up Walker. Seniors Mike Leake, Kelly Cleveland, Scott Drake and Eric Smith, and junior Greg Rogers would catch most of the team's passes.

Defensively the Cardinals had senior Jeff Hance, Leake and Collette at linebackers, with Walker leading the defense at inside linebacker along with Kevin Crane. Jeff Pinion was also in the mix. Senior Jason Rea and junior Adam

Spence were expected to start at defensive tackles, with Wistrom and Allen at the ends and Thurlo and sophomore Jeff Ogden providing depth at defensive end. Berry, Wilson and sophomore Brett Williams were in the defensive backfield, along with Drake and Cleveland.

Wistrom lived up to the preseason hype in the season opener, recording nine tackles and an interception at defensive end.

"I thought Chance played as well as any high school lineman I've seen," Kill told the newspaper. "He played like a man possessed."

Wistrom was one of six "players of the week" selected by Kill in the first installment of the weekly newspaper feature. It was one of many new things Kill brought to Webb City; he also encouraged Webb City youth to attend games as the "Bleacher Creatures."

The other players of the week in the Carl Junction game included Matt Berry, the junior defensive back who made eight tackles, broke up two passes and recovered a fumble. He excelled offensively, too, rushing five times for 128 yards. Junior Mike Collette was recognized at center, Keith Rogers was named "back of the week," junior Greg Rogers was named for his special teams work, especially his kicking, and sophomore Jeff Ogden was selected as the work team player of the week.

Remember, Carl Junction had been the favorite before the game, but the Cardinals out-hit the Bulldogs and were in better condition. Those factors, plus the contributions from the players of the week, led to a 27-0 Webb City win. Even the Bleacher Creatures had a hand in the win, Kill said.

"It was awesome," he told the *Sentinel*. "They excited our kids. I know they were the difference in a score or two."

The team also wore red armbands for team unity.

In week two, Kill's inexperienced Cardinals did something no other Webb City team had done in roughly a quarter of a century: win a road game at Mount Vernon. The Mountaineers jumped ahead 8-0 and recovered a Cardinals' fumble on the ensuing kickoff, but Webb City's defense held pat and the offense scored four straight touchdowns. Final score: Webb City 28, Mount Vernon 16. Kevin Crane rushed 54 yards for the team's first touchdown, and Keith Rogers threw a 23-yard scoring strike to Jeff Hance to give the team a 14-8 halftime lead. Rogers added a four-yard touchdown run in the second half, and Mike Wilson scored from 74 yards out.

With East Newton coming to Webb City in week three, Kill called on the Bleacher Creatures to double their ranks. About 200 had attended the first home game. Anyone between the ages of 5 and 13 could sign up before the game, and the group would run to its special section before kickoff.

The defense, under the direction of defensive coordinator Steve Gollhofer, was huge against East Newton. Sophomore cornerback Brett Williams intercepted three passes and junior linebacker Kevin Crane returned another pickoff for a touchdown. Kill started playing backups shortly after halftime, and when it was all over the Cardinals were 3-0 after dominating the Patriots 54-6. Kill's players of the week: Mike Wilson (11 rushes, 91 yards), Craig Thurlo (offensive lineman), Jason Rea (defensive line), Brett Williams (three interceptions, two breakups, four tackles), Gene Stanley (two special teams tackles) and Kyle Bethel (work team player).

Webb City played its best overall game through four weeks in a 33-6 win at Monett. The defense limited the Cubs to 127 rushing yards and 22 passing yards, and Webb City's special teams blocked a punt and forced two bad kicks in addition to returning a second-half kickoff to the Monett 35. Matt Berry scored a touchdown the very next play.

"I'm a little surprised how fast we've improved," Kill told the paper. "The kids worked so hard to get where we are."

With a home game against Springfield Central up next, Kill reiterated his call for more Bleacher Creatures, and continued a common theme by taking time to thank Webb City's fans.

"We really appreciate the support of the town of Webb City," he said.

When they played on the road, the Cardinals had as many fans as the home team.

"The more enthusiasm there is the better we play," he said. "They (the fans) are as much a part of it as anybody."

In week five, the winning just continued. Central returned the opening kickoff to the Webb City 25-yard line and jumped out to a 7-0 lead, which made for a nervous beginning, but Keith Rogers scored twice and Kevin Crane once to lead the Cardinals to a 20-7 win. All the scoring happened in the first half; Webb City fumbled three times in the second half and missed out on other opportunities. Kill credited coach Richard Correll with the sterling play of the team's offensive line.

Now 5-0, the Cardinals would take to the road for the third time and face their most physical opponent to date in the Nixa Eagles. It would also be the team's closest game through six weeks.

A three-yard Keith Rogers' run in the second quarter and a 33-yard field goal by Matt Berry staked the Cardinals to a 10-0 lead, but the Eagles would come back in the second half. Webb City blocked the extra point on Nixa's first touchdown, but the Eagles scored with nine minutes left in the fourth quarter to jump ahead 12-10. The Webb City offense responded with a 78-yard drive and Crane scored from a yard out for the 18-12 win.

"The team could have panicked and got shook up, but instead they took the ball all the way down, scored and won," Kill said.

"The kids showed composure, heart and confidence – that's what you look for in a good team."

Players of the week against Nixa were Keith Rogers, who Kill said was like another coach on the field; Jeff Hance and Craig Thurlo on the offensive line; Kevin Crane on the defensive line after he had 17 tackles, four for a loss and a fumble recovery in addition to 31 rushes for 141 yards offensively; freshman Mark Smith, who was named special teams player of the week a week earlier, but against Nixa was recognized for his defensive play; sophomore Craig Divine on special teams after he did a solid job on kickoff return and made three tackles in punt coverage; and sophomore Jason Ansley as the work team player of the week.

The Southwest Conference was so small that the team didn't play its first conference game until seven weeks in when it traveled to Nevada to face the 1-6 Tigers. Matt Berry scored three of the team's six touchdowns in the 39-13 win, while Keith Rogers, Kevin Crane and Jeff Johnson each added a score. Berry also ran for a two-point conversion and kicked an extra point.

So far the Cardinals had cruised through their regular season schedule, but in week eight they would face their toughest team all year – Carthage – as Webb City began three weeks of district play to finish the schedule. The Tigers were just 4-3, but Kill wasn't taking them lightly.

"It ought to be a great game," he said.

Carthage had won 14-0 in 1987, and for the Cardinals to improve to 8-0 in 1988 they would need to control the football on offense with no turnovers, control Carthage quarterback Chris Honaker and the running game, but primarily handle the adversity Kill was sure his team would face in the game.

When that Friday night arrived, the Cardinals had a secret weapon: their crowd.

"We were playing 12 men on their 11," Kill said afterwards. "Our 12th man was the crowd. They were unbelievable – I can't say enough about it!"

And the game was played at Carthage's K.E. "Doc" Baker Stadium, where the visitors' stands were overflowing. Those Webb City fans had a lot to cheer about. The team punted just twice all night, kept the vaunted Carthage running attack to only 83 yards and shut down Honaker, one of the state's best quarterbacks. What Kill said would be the team's toughest game turned into another blowout: 39-7 Webb City. But like the Springfield Central game, the Cardinals had trouble at the beginning. Carthage led 7-0 after Webb City couldn't control the opening kickoff. But Webb City's 71-yard drive and Matt Berry's 11-yard scoring run and two-point conversion made it 8-7. Seniors Jason Rea and Scott Walker blocked a punt apiece, one on the Tigers' 5-yard line in the fourth quarter.

Players of the week were Matt Berry, who by now was averaging more than 10 yards a carry and had 15 rushes for 199 yards against Carthage; Scott Drake and Kelly Cleveland on the offensive line, who each had key blocks for Berry; Chance Wistrom, on the offensive line after going up against a defender 20 to 25 pounds heavier than he was and controlling him all night; defensive lineman

Adam Spence, who made four sacks; defensive back Kevin Crane; and special teams player Mark Smith, who had four solo tackles. Berry was also selected as the Springfield area player of the week.

The win boosted Webb City's conference record to 2-0 and dropped the defending champs to 1-1. The Cardinals were also now state-ranked at No. 8. They would face McDonald County in their second district game, which was also homecoming, in week nine.

Not that it would have taken much to win over the fans with a football pedigree like Jerry Kill's in the late '80s, but after beating McDonald County 39-0, Kill was a hero in Webb City. A photograph in the Webb City newspaper summed it all up: Tim Livingston, in his Webb City letter jacket, holding a sign high above his head that read "Kill for President."

There was still one district game remaining, but the win sealed a playoff berth for the Cardinals, who would host the Wednesday night game at Cardinal Stadium. Even if it lost to Neosho, Webb City would win the district, but an outright conference championship was still up for grabs.

"We're approaching it as THE game," Kill said. "This is the most important game of our season – it's for a perfect season."

And the Cardinals were perfect; they won 32-6. Kevin Crane rushed for four touchdowns, while Chance Wistrom played his best game all season.

In a poignant column a week later, *Sentinel* editor Bob Foos reflected the community's sentiment towards this Cardinals team that had begun with so many question marks, won 10 games and gone to the state playoffs. He cited Kill's generosity in giving credit to "the young and the old bleacher creatures," for the team's success, and wrote that Kill deservedly gave 99 percent of the credit to his players, who had spent summer mornings lifting weights while everyone else in town slept. But Kill deserved credit, too, Foos wrote, especially for his recruiting.

"He scouted boys catching outfield flies on summer nights looking for potential receivers. At the same time, while making small talk behind the batter's box, he enlisted fan and parent support. He's taught the boys to be men – to always show class whether on the field, in the classroom, with family and friends. Three schools have written the school board commenting on the high quality of sportsmanship displayed by the Cardinals."

Foos gave Kill an "A plus" for his involvement with the community and his accessibility with parents, fans and media alike.

"This column was written before the playoff game Wednesday night," Foos concluded. "The outcome doesn't matter. We've had our cake. Any more wins will just be like dabbing on more icing. It's hard to imagine a greater thrill – even if we won the Show-Me Bowl – than when we clobbered Carthage. Weren't we great? Thanks Cards for a great season, those magical weeks of playoff anticipation and for letting us all feel like the winners you are."

By the time that column was out, the Cardinals had already hosted that Wednesday night playoff game, against Republic.

After 10 games of the 1988 season Webb City had outscored its opponents by an average of more than 32 points per game. The Cardinals had won by 48 points in one game, by 39 in another and had given up double-digit points in only three contests, the most being Mount Vernon's 16 in a 10-point Webb City win. But with a Wednesday night playoff game on tap at Cardinal Stadium in early November, the days of blowouts were likely over. With Republic making the trip west to Webb City, the Cardinals were back in the playoffs for the first time in two years, and only the third time in school history.

The first half was a defensive struggle. It wasn't until late in the third quarter when Republic broke the scoreless tie, blocking a Webb City punt at the Cardinals' 23-yard line. The play resulted in a safety and a 2-0 lead for the visiting Tigers with around a minute left until the fourth quarter.

Republic almost scored offensive points with its possession following the safety, but the Webb City defense kept it a one-possession game. Starting at their own 15-yard line, the Cardinals marched 85 yards in just nine plays, including six runs by Kevin Crane – one for 33 yards – and three runs by quarterback Keith Rogers, who scampered nine yards for the touchdown with 6:15 left in the game. Webb City was stopped short on a two-point try and led 6-2. The lead wouldn't stand for long.

Republic scored on its very next possession when senior running back Scooter Dipper found the end zone, but Adam Spence came up with a crucial block on the extra point to keep the Cardinals within two points at 8-6.

Webb City got the ball back at its own 41-yard line with enough time for one drive to win the game. Crane would finish the game with more than 130 rushing yards on 29 carries, and it was obvious the Cardinals would turn to him with the game on the line. The 181-pound junior carried nine times on the 12-play drive, which included a long catch by Jeff Hance.

With nine seconds on the clock, the Cardinals had the ball a foot away from the Republic goal line and faced a fourth-and-goal. It was no surprise who would be getting the football: the workhorse Crane, who plunged in for the game-winning touchdown.

"The game wasn't over until it was over," Kill said after the 12-8 win. He said the 12th man advantage had once again been a factor.

"They (the Cards) showed great character," he said. "My hat's off to our kids and to our fans."

Webb City, now 11-0, was on to the second round of the Class 4A playoffs. It would travel to Camdenton the following Monday for a 7:30 p.m. game against the Lakers, 14-7 winners over Kearney. The school announced that buses would once again be chartered for the trip.

Camdenton was the two-time defending state champion under Coach Bob Shore, but its stadium wasn't big enough to hold all the Webb City fans who drove north. Some fans stood outside the fence and others tried to squeeze underneath the bleachers. In the second quarter of the game, Camdenton officials, after some prodding by assistant superintendent Ron Lankford, it was noted, allowed fans to stand on the track so they could see.

Not that the Lakers' consecutive state championships weren't impressive enough, but Camdenton's group of seniors had compiled a 36-1-1 record. That didn't seem to phase the Cardinals much; they took an early lead when Jeff Hance intercepted a pass and ran it back for a touchdown. Camdenton, after a fumble recovery, scored to lead 7-6, and held a 13-6 lead at halftime. It remained a touchdown game until Webb City scored early in the fourth quarter. Webb City went for two points and the lead, but its conversion attempt was stopped short. The Cardinals couldn't capitalize on any of their other scoring opportunities. When it was over, Camdenton had won 20-12.

"We had a tremendous season," Kill told the *Sentinel*. "We've started something positive here at Webb City – something for the younger kids to carry on."

Though the season was over, there was already reason to look forward to 1989; both junior running backs, Matt Berry and Kevin Crane, would be back along with several others. In the newspaper, Kill dished out a season's worth of credit: to senior Mike Leake, who had returned after missing most of the year with a knee injury, but was a key factor at the end; to senior defensive end Chance Wistrom, who Richard Correll said was one of the best he had ever coached; to quarterback Keith Rogers – Kill said you judge a quarterback by the number of games he wins and 11 wasn't "too shabby." He also credited his coaching staff, athletics director Tom Gosch and the rest of the administration.

Jerry Kill runs down the sideline while Stan Wallace carries the ball in the 1989 state semifinal game at St. Joseph Lafayette.

20. THE FIRST STATE CHAMPIONSHIP

Few games in the long history of the Carl Junction/Webb City rivalry have equaled the build-up and anticipation of the opening game of the 1989 football season. It was played in Carl Junction.

The Bulldogs, 7-6 the year before, had won five of their final six games and gone to the state semifinals. The Cardinals had gone 11-1 and to the state quarterfinals. Both teams were picked to win their conferences.

"I don't know what more you'd want in a high school football game," Kill said in the paper.

Of the 100 players on Webb City's team, only 18 were returning lettermen, but seven of those were returning starters and a lot was expected of what was a young Webb City team.

Key players for Webb City were Jeff Ogden, Craig Divine, Doug Collard, Adam Spence, Allen Goddard, Marcus Herrell, Andy Booth, Gary Webster and Brad Carey on the defensive line; Kevin Crane, Jeff Johnson and Scott Gossett at inside linebackers; Mark Smith, Mike Collette, Chris Whitfield and Billy Pippen at outside linebackers; Matt Berry, Brett Williams, Jason Ansley, Greg Rogers, Dustin Storm and Stan Wallace in the defensive secondary. Mark Smith, a sophomore, led the offense at quarterback; Divine, Pippin, Whitfield, Spence and Chad Carey played tight end; Rogers, Ansley, Williams and Chad Shields were wide receivers, and the running backs were Crane, Johnson, Berry and Gossett. On the offensive line Webb City had Shawn Hansen, Booth, Ogden, Collette, Mike Calef, Kirk Philpot, Corey Johnson, Herrell and Goddard.

Kill said Smith, a 6-foot-3, 215-pound physical specimen, could handle the pressure of leading the team.

"It's very unusual to see a sophomore starting at quarterback, but Mark is a very unusual sophomore," he said.

He also called for Webb City fans to equal or surpass the number of hometown Carl Junction fans at the game.

"A lot of people will be wanting revenge on us, so we're going to have to be ready each week," Kill said.

The Bulldogs, a tough and physical team, were one of those after revenge after losing to the Cardinals 27-0 in 1988.

More than 100 kids signed up for the Bleacher Creatures on the Wednesday before the game, and on Friday at 6 p.m. Webb City fans met in the north parking lot of the high school to caravan to the game. The crowd that gathered was by far the largest ever at Bulldog Stadium with around 4,000 people in attendance. Admission was $2 for adults and a dollar for students, and Carl Junction still walked away with more than $3,000 in its share of the gate split. Two years earlier when the teams renewed their rivalry, Carl Junction had made $2,200.

The Bulldogs fumbled the ball five times in the game and the Cardinals recovered every one; Carl Junction also muffed a punt. Webb City, too, lost all of its fumbles but committed three. Already leading by two touchdowns, the Cardinals recovered their own punt at the Carl Junction 43-yard line early in the second half and scored three plays later. After recovering a Carl Junction fumble at the Bulldogs' 28 they scored again and led 28-0 before Carl Junction scored twice in the fourth quarter.

"There are people we could have beaten Friday night," said Carl Junction head coach H.B. Davis, "but not Webb City."

With the 28-14 win, Webb City was ranked No. 2 in the state, but the team suffered a big loss when senior all-state running back Kevin Crane went down with a knee injury. He didn't play in week two against Mount Vernon, but the Cardinals were still by far the better team and they won 28-0. Senior running back Matt Berry picked up the slack and was named Springfield-area player of the week after rushing 10 times for an astounding 217 yards.

Steve Gollhofer and Kurt Thompson, Webb City's defensive coaches, "did an excellent job getting the defense ready to play. The defense dominated the football game," Kill told the newspaper. The defense was led by senior Adam Spence, who helped the Cardinals limit the Mountaineers to less than 70 rushing yards.

At East Newton in week three, Webb City committed three turnovers in the first quarter but still managed to trounce the Patriots 54-7. Mark Smith, the sophomore quarterback, had a huge game, rushing for the team's first score, adding another touchdown on the ground and throwing for two more, one to sophomore tight end Jason Hamilton and one to senior receiver Chad Shields. Matt Berry and sophomore running back Stan Wallace each scored two touchdowns; Berry ran 59 yards for one.

Amazingly, East Newton finished the game with just four rushing yards and barely 100 yards through the air.

By week four Kevin Crane wasn't yet 100 percent healed, but there was a chance he would play against Monett as Webb City looked for a 4-0 start. The Cubs were 2-1 and had been shut out by Seneca the previous week, but Kill told everyone to expect a close game. He was right. Webb City took a 21-6 lead into the fourth quarter, but allowed Monett to score 16 straight points and the Cardinals found themselves trailing by a point with less than two minutes remaining in the game. It came down to a 28-yard field goal attempt by senior Eric Smith with two seconds on the clock; Smith had started the previous year as the team's student trainer, but he was by now a key player, and his field goal kick gave the Cardinals a thrilling 24-22 victory.

"He went from being a trainer and carrying tape to winning a football game," Kill said.

Webb City scored once in every quarter of the game. Senior Matt Berry rushed 21 times for 199 yards and touchdown runs of 56 and 24 yards. Mark Smith scored the other touchdown on a 25-yard run, while Smith kicked all three extra points.

"We showed excellent character and tremendous composure," Kill said. "That's what it takes to be a good team. I think our football team learned a lot at last week's game."

Now 4-0 and still ranked No. 2 in the state, the Cardinals headed east to face Springfield Central in week five, a team coached by former Webb City standout Alan Spencer. His team was no match for Webb City in 1989. In another game dominated by the defense, Webb City limited Central to just three first downs in winning 34-3, and Kevin Crane's presence was felt – especially on defense. He and fellow defensive back Scott Gossett combined for 20 tackles, many for a loss. Running backs Matt Berry and Jeff Johnson combined for 200 rushing yards.

A week later there was no doubt where the game of the week would be played – Webb City. The Cardinals were 5-0 and still ranked No. 2 while Nixa came to town with a 4-1 record and ranked ninth in the state. Webb City also had won 16 consecutive regular season games.

After a quarter the game had lived up to the hype. It was tied at 14. But for the final three quarters it wasn't even close. Mark Smith had another huge game, scoring three touchdowns – two on offensive runs, the other on a 28-yard fumble return while playing linebacker. Kevin Crane scored a 19-yard touchdown in the first quarter and caught a two-point conversion; Eric Smith kicked four extra points and rushed for a two-point conversion; Jeff Johnson scored on a 10-yard run and Matt Berry on a 14-yard run. Sophomore Stan Wallace added a nine-yard touchdown run in the fourth quarter. When it was all over Webb City left the field with a 51-20 victory.

On homecoming night the Cardinals overcame a slew of penalties – more than 100 yards' worth – and a short week of practice to blast Nevada 53-0 on a Thursday night. The offense accumulated more than 470 yards and the defense had what is quite possibly the best defensive game a Webb City football team has ever played. Nevada finished with one yard of offense – 10 passing yards and negative-nine rushing yards.

"You can't be too displeased with that," Kill said.

Matt Berry scored three touchdowns and Adam Spence hauled in a 29-yard touchdown pass from Mark Smith. David Brown, Scott Gossett and Matt Goddard also scored.

The annual rivalry game with Carthage was the biggest game of the year through week eight. The Cardinals were 7-0 and the Tigers 6-1. Just like 1988 the game marked the first of three weeks of district play, and in '88, when the Cardinals won by 32 points, the game was essentially to determine first place in the district and a playoff berth.

Kill again said the fans would be a determining factor in the game. He had received a scouting report that the Tigers were worried about the crowd support Webb City would receive.

"One of the big concerns Carthage had was coming over here with our pre-game," Kill said. "The more we have here, the more it will concern them."

The Bleacher Creatures would also play a huge role.

"I want the Bleacher Creatures to save their voices (for tonight)," Kill said. "They need to stand, cheer and rock 'n' roll all night long."

Portable bleachers were brought in to handle an expected overflow crowd.

The game itself would pit Carthage's speed versus Webb City's strength. Strength won the night. Mark Smith's 29-yard touchdown pass to Adam Spence, and Eric Smith's 24-yard field goal seconds before the break gave Webb City a 10-0 halftime lead, and Matt Berry made it 17-0 late in the third quarter before Carthage's speed finally showed up. Tigers receiver Augie Saba hauled in 34-yard and 55-yard touchdown passes in the fourth quarter and all of a sudden it was a 17-13 game. Mark Smith led a drive down the field and Spence scored the final touchdown to give Webb City a 23-13 win. The Cardinals rushed for 400 yards in their final home game of the regular season. A week later they locked up the district by scoring 41 points in the first half at McDonald County and thrashing the Mustangs 47-6. Kevin Crane returned a fumble for a touchdown and later scored a rushing touchdown; Matt Berry scored twice and so did Mark

Smith. Adam Spence also blocked a punt and scored a 22-yard touchdown. With the win Webb City would travel to Republic or Willard on a Wednesday night for the Class 4A sectional game. But even with the district championship already locked up, there was still one more regular season game at Neosho. Webb City won 48-14.

Of all the fans in attendance at the sectional game at Republic, half were from Webb City. Republic was another team out for revenge after losing 12-8 under the same circumstances a year earlier, but they wouldn't find it in 1989. Kevin Crane rushed for 150 yards on 25 carries and made several spectacular tackles – two for a loss. Matt Berry wasn't far behind, tallying 140 yards, and senior tight end Adam Spence made two catches for more than 50 yards. Mark Smith totaled 70 offensive yards and scored all three Webb City touchdowns in the 21-3 win. The Cardinals actually fumbled the ball six times and lost five.

The decisive win gave the Cardinals a chance to play another game in the friendly confines of Cardinal Stadium when they hosted Kearney in the quarterfinals. The Bulldogs had won 35-27 at Camdenton in the sectionals.

The duo of Kevin Crane and Matt Berry was unstoppable again. Crane rushed for 140 yards and Berry 125, and Jeff Johnson added 70 as the Cardinals finished with more than 350 yards rushing. Crane scored the first touchdown of the game and Berry added a 30-yard scoring run to give Webb City a 14-0 halftime lead, but the team fumbled the kickoff return to open the third quarter. On Kearney's second play of the drive, Mark Smith picked off a pass. Jason Ansley recorded another interception and that turnover set up another scoring drive. Crane rushed 56 yards for a touchdown, but a holding penalty took the points off the scoreboard. No matter, on the very next play Berry took a pitch and ran 48 yards for a touchdown. Eric Smith added a 21-yard field goal in the fourth quarter and Webb City won 24-6.

The Cardinals were now 12-0 and the win against Kearney was significant for more than the fact that it moved Webb City into the semifinals against Lafayette in St. Joseph. The win broke a school record for victories in a season. The previous record of 11 wins had been set in 1985, by the school's first playoff team. The 1988 team was the first to finish the regular season a perfect 10-0 and had tied the '85 team with 11 wins but lost in the quarterfinals.

Lafayette was 8-3 and had won 24-16 against Kansas City Center in the quarterfinals. Once again student buses, charter buses and hundreds, if not thousands, of cars would be making the trip from Webb City.

"So many people pulling for us is a lot of the reason why we're winning," Kill said.

The Cardinals left Friday morning to prepare for the 1:30 p.m. Saturday game, and most of their fans were standing in line by 10:30 Saturday morning. A few hours later they had ample reason to celebrate.

Webb City scored 28 points in the first quarter and led 35-0 by the half.

Second-string players finished out the second half of a 49-6 win. Matt Berry was a monster out of the backfield, rushing for more than 250 yards and three touchdowns, including one for 74 yards. Kevin Crane scored twice and senior Jeff Johnson added another touchdown. Adam Spence, the senior tight end, scored the first points of the game on a 30-yard pass from Mark Smith. Sophomore Stan Wallace had an 80-yard punt return for a touchdown, but it was called back for a penalty.

"Shoe-polish prophecies on their car windows, like 'Webb City will be 13-0' and 'State will be fine in '89' had come true," the *Sentinel* wrote.

Webb City was headed to the Show-Me Bowl. And instead of the four-hour drive to St. Joseph, fans would need to drive only an hour to Springfield for the championship game on the day after Thanksgiving, to be played at Briggs Stadium on the campus of what was then Southwest Missouri State University. Kickoff was slated for 3 p.m.

While the Cardinals were making their first appearance in the state championship game, it was a different story for their opponent: St. Louis Sumner. The Bulldogs had won the 4A championship in 1973 and the 5A championship in 1982 and had gone to the state semifinals in 1988. Overall, Sumner had been to the playoffs 13 times.

"We know what caliber Sumner is," said Jerry Kill. "They're a big, big football team."

The Bulldogs averaged 265 pounds on their offensive line and had a 6-foot-5, 300-pound noseguard on defense. Their only loss all year was to East St. Louis, the No. 1 high school team in the nation.

"They're very physical, but speed-wise we match up," Kill said.

Sumner was ranked fifth in the state and had beaten top-ranked Potosi 28-21 in the other semifinal. Webb City was still ranked second.

After record crowds had followed the Cardinals all season long, administrators ordered double the usual allotment of 1,000 tickets for the game, and 2,000 advance tickets were sold. That broke a state record; it was more tickets than any school of any size had ever sold in advance, breaking the previous record of 1,500. White shoe polish disappeared from store shelves before the game and appeared on the windows of cars and Webb City businesses.

On the day of the game it was sunny out and 58 degrees but windy, with gusts of 30 miles an hour. With Webb City giving up an average of 60 pounds per player, many fans around the state expected Sumner to dominate. In the first quarter it looked like it could happen. The Bulldogs drove 77 yards on 21 plays and were in position to score when senior defensive lineman Doug Collard recovered a fumble at the Webb City 3-yard line. The Cardinals didn't score, but gained momentum. Kevin Crane finally put Webb City on top with two touchdown runs in the second quarter, for six and eight yards, and the Cardinals led 13-0. Eric Smith's 23-yard field goal into the wind in the third quarter was the icing on the cake in the 16-0 win.

When it was over, Jerry Kill kept a promise to his team: if the Cardinals won the title, he'd do a dance on the field. He dropped on his back and "began kicking his feet in the air."

"The Worm," he called it. "That's the way we used to do it in Cheney, Kansas."

Friday night after the game, more than 2,000 fans waited along Webb City's Main Street for an hour. When the buses finally arrived, players were greeted with a ticker-tape parade as the town celebrated a 16-0 win and its first-ever state championship. The crowd was so large players and coaches exited the buses and walked down the street receiving handshakes and hugs. On the front page of the newspaper, a picture of Jerry Kill with a No. 1 on his hand high in the air, covered in confetti, riding on the shoulders of Denny Smith and Howard House, Jr.

Now more than two decades removed from the celebration, Jerry Kill still thinks back on that night.

"When you win a state championship and you drive the yellow school bus down Main Street, people coming out of bars with letter jackets on and you get out of the bus and they carry you all the way to the school, it just brought the whole community together," he says. "We beat a team in the state championship that athletically was tremendously gifted but it was our day on that day and I don't think anybody gave us a chance with those kids. There's nothing like winning the first one. We had a reunion not too long ago and those kids, they haven't forgotten. It's something nobody can ever take away. There's so many great memories, so many great stories, I could personally write a book on those two years."

Sixteen players were selected for all-Southwest Conference honors. Earning first-team honors on both sides of the ball were Matt Berry, Kevin Crane, Craig Divine, Jeff Ogden and Mark Smith. Mike Collette, Scott Gossett, Shawn Hansen, Eric Smith, Adam Spence and Gary Webster also earned first-team honors. Second-team honors went to Jason Ansley, Andy Booth, Doug Collard and Jeff Johnson; Collard was named to both the offensive and defensive teams. B.J. Williams and Ansley earned honorable mention selections, as well.

Kill says now he never talked before the season about the possibility it would be a special year. "Our kids just went to work," he says. "We were gifted with having a tremendous athlete in Mark Smith, who was going to be a sophomore. He had gone through his first year and he was a gifted young man. We had an outstanding backfield with Kevin Crane and Matt Berry, and Kevin was also a great linebacker and Mark played some at linebacker. We just had a group of kids who all bonded together; they enjoyed being around each other. We had the weight room open in the summertime and our kids didn't miss weightlifting. If we had to go pick them up, we picked them up. However many were on that team, they didn't miss many days. We worked hard. We ran it like a college program and those kids bought into it. I think at the end of the day they thought they were stronger, faster and tougher than everybody because of what they did in the summer time and the offseason training."

Kill describes the players as "hard-hat, lunch-pail" type individuals. It's an identity that can be traced back to Webb City's history as a hard-working mining town.

"I think you are who you are, and the town identifies with hard-working people," Kill says. "The mines, the industry, that's who those people are and the game of football is their identity. There would be people who would show up and put blankets down. They'd start rolling in at 1 in the afternoon or put their blankets down in the morning before a game and I think they still do that to this day. Football is important there. The whole school participates in it.

"It all starts with Dr. Lankford. He was a tremendous superintendent. The floors in those schools are clean and neat and nice and when all the other schools start struggling with budgets over the years, Webb City hasn't done that because of the management of the administration. They just did a tremendous job there. They took great pride in their community, great pride in their school system, all the way up from elementary on. The band – we had the biggest band. When we'd go play anybody or they'd come to our place, our kids ran out of the locker room and shoot we had the Bleacher Creatures, the band, the fans – I think teams were beat before they ever got on the field sometimes."

Not long after the state championship, Webb City football got more good news: John Roderique was selected as the Mid-America Intercollegiate Athletic Association defensive player of the year after his senior season at linebacker for Pittsburg State. A defensive leader for the Gorillas, Roderique helped Pitt State win a school-record 12 games in 1989.

And with that, Dennis Franchione left for bigger things, and the Gorillas hired Chuck Broyles as their new head coach. As he filled his staff in the months after football season, the rumors ran rampant around Webb City: would Jerry Kill be going back to Pittsburg State? One winter day, while Kill was sitting in study hall, Broyles paid him a visit and asked him to come back as the Gorillas' offensive coordinator.

On a Thursday morning in late January it became official; Kill gathered his players and broke the news. Later that afternoon he was announced as Pittsburg State's new offensive coordinator. Three days later, Franchione offered Kill another job, but he had already committed to join Broyles' staff.

"I went and talked with Ron Lankford, I talked to James Paullus and Tom Gosch," Kill said. "I can remember sitting in Ron Lankford's office and he says, 'Coach, you approached it like college football. You've done a great job here. We certainly understand the opportunity you have to go back to Pittsburg State, financially and so forth.' It was a good situation. At that time Ron kind of laughed and he said, 'I don't know if this will ever happen again for Webb City.'

I tease him all the time from this day on. He just laughs. At the time I think a lot of people thought it might never happen again and it's happened 10 times since."

Kill served as Chuck Broyle's offensive coordinator through the 1993 season, helping the Gorillas win another national championship, then went to Saginaw Valley State, on to Emporia State, then Southern Illinois, Northern Illinois and the Big 10 Conference and the University of Minnesota.

The celebration on Main Street after Webb City's first state championship. More than 2,000 fans waited for an hour for the team to arrive. Photo by Bob Foos.

Players celebrate Webb City's win over Sumner at Briggs Stadium on the campus of Southwest Missouri State University in Springfield. Photo by Bob Foos.

Jerry Kill keeps a promise to his team after the Cardinals won a state championship. Kill said if the team won he'd do a dance; he called it "the worm" and said "that's the way we used to do it in Cheney, Kansas." Photo by Bob Foos.

Denny Smith and Howard House, Jr. carry head coach Jerry Kill on their shoulders during a parade on Main Street after Webb City's first state championship in 1989. Photo by Bob Foos.

21. A SURPRISE HIRE?

With Jerry Kill's departure for Pittsburg State, Webb City football needed a new head coach, and there would be enormous shoes to fill for whoever came next. Kill had gone 25-1 in two seasons and the Cardinals had won 14 straight games and their first state championship. Kurt Thompson, Kill's hard-working assistant coach, taught science at the high school and was moved to the weight room with no promises he'd get the head coaching job. In fact, he probably didn't even want it. He spoke with athletics director Tom Gosch and the high school principal, James Paullus, about the job and said he wasn't interested in applying. Whoever followed Jerry Kill would get fired, he said, and the coach after that would have a pretty good situation. Paullus told Thompson he should at least consider the position, that it was a great opportunity, but the discussion ended there.

An assistant wrestling coach, Thompson was at the state championship meet in early spring when he got a call from Anvil Welch, the Webb City sports beat writer for *The Joplin Globe*; he congratulated Thompson on getting the head coaching job. There had been a school board meeting and the district had decided Thompson was the guy to lead the Cardinals into the 1990s.

"I never applied for the job, never interviewed for the job or anything; they just told me it was mine," Thompson recalls. "At that point you couldn't pass it up. We had great kids coming back and the culture had already been developed by Coach Kill. We just continued doing the same things."

Thompson was only 23 years old when he was hired, and he turned 24 before the first game of the 1990 season. Like Kill and so many others, he was a Pittsburg State guy. He had graduated high school in Iola, Kansas, and after playing a year of junior college football, he transferred to PSU and starred for three years, earning All-American honors as a senior linebacker, when John Roderique was a sophomore. They became close friends.

When Thompson followed Kill to Webb City, he served as defensive coordinator for the junior varsity team. At the varsity level he coached running backs and inside linebackers that first season for Kill, and his second year he coached tight ends and receivers on offense and linebackers on defense.

"I had never called an offensive play in my life until our first game against Carl Junction that year," Thompson says.

In learning to be a head coach, Thompson couldn't have studied under two better coaches than Dennis Franchione and Jerry Kill.

"I worked for as good a man as there is for two years," he says. "I played under Dennis Franchione, who has a lot different style than Coach Kill. I just showed up everyday and worked hard. That's the best thing Coach Kill taught any of us as players and assistant coaches. I still remember one of our junior high coaches saying to me – I'd run over and talk to the players in the springtime, the junior high kids – he said, 'There's no way you're going to work as many hours as Coach Kill did.' I said, 'How can you expect me not to?' The bar was set. We went through there and had a very good staff and some very good players. Good players make good coaches. I think all coaches will tell you that, or most of them will."

Kill ran the Webb City football program like a college program, watching extensive amounts of film and compiling scouting reports for the team's opponents. Nobody else was doing that in high school at the time. That's the way Thompson learned to coach – he didn't know anything different.

Jerry Kill drove an old green car when he was at Webb City and would park it in front of the pillars directly in front of the high school's main entrance. On Saturday afternoons after watching film and starting the preparations for his next opponent, Kill would sometimes ask Thompson to give him a ride home, or he'd call his wife to pick him up and ask Thompson to give him a ride the next morning. It took Thompson a while to figure out what was going on.

"He did this for a reason," Thompson says. "Hell, those people would see his car up there all night. All the townspeople thought he was spending the night up there. 'My God, Coach Kill was up there all weekend! I went by 11 o'clock at night and he was still there. I was there 7 o'clock the next morning and he was there.' They'd say, 'Does he live up there?' I'd say half the time he does. Those kids, those parents, saw it. He was there a bunch, trust me, more than anybody ever had been. We'd go before daylight so the whole city would be showing up and they thought he spent the night there half the time during the season. He worked hard and it was pretty funny; those people had no idea. They thought he stayed up there all the time."

It's funny in hindsight, but Kill's ploy worked. If he was living there half the time during the season, how could any of the players or anybody else have an excuse not to work hard?

As far as schematics go, Thompson didn't mess with what the Cardinals had had so much success with. He kept the offensive and defensive systems that Kill had installed the same. At a reunion a few years ago for the 1989 championship team, which was attended by Kill, Thompson mentioned that he was very fortunate to get the job and said he probably wasn't ready for it. Ron Lankford, Webb City's now-retired superintendent, said "We wanted one of our guys. We didn't want somebody to come in and tell us how we needed to change things because things were going the way they needed to be and we wanted to continue doing that."

As the 1990 season neared and Webb City geared up to defend its title, there were plenty of unknowns. Thompson was just 24 years old and like he said, had never called an offensive play in his life.

"It will be tough to duplicate what we did last year," he told a local newspaper. "We have the opportunity to be a pretty good football team."

As usual, the Cardinals opened the season with Carl Junction, but the rest of the schedule was quite a bit different from previous years. Instead of playing so many of the small schools from the former Big 13, like East Newton and Mount Vernon, Webb City stocked up on bigger, tough opponents like Class 5A Glendale and Kickapoo, the two best schools in Springfield, and even scheduled a game against Joplin at Missouri Southern's Fred G. Hughes Stadium.

"That was very eye opening for us," Thompson says. "But once again it made us better towards the end of the year."

Mark Smith, the stellar quarterback, was returning for his junior season, but the Cardinals lost all three running backs from a potent backfield in 1989. Thompson said six younger backs could probably fill the void. There were some other big pieces back, notably seniors Craig Divine and Jeff Ogden, who along with Smith had been all-state players the year before. Divine was a lot bigger and faster, Thompson told the newspaper, and Smith was a year smarter. Thompson also had junior Marcus Herrell, who had "done a lot of great things" in practices; senior Andy Booth, who was "a lot better than he was at this time last year"; and other starters like B.J. Williams and Jason Ansley, who along with Herrell Thompson said would stand out on defense. All six of those players would be offensive standouts, too, he said, as well as seniors Shawn Hansen and Booth.

"We didn't know what we had at that time," Thompson recalls. "We just played and went out and practiced hard. Craig Divine, Jeff Alden and B.J. Williams are three names that stuck out, captains who had played for us the prior year and started for us when we won a state championship. We had a few of those kids back. Some of them were three-year starters. We had those kids and we had some underclassmen fill in. Marcus Herrell played a lot as a sophomore in '89 when we won it. A kid named Shawn Hansen, Jason Ansley – boy, it brings back some memories.

"Mark was our workhorse offensively. Everything went through him. We got better each week, even those games we got beat. You go from playing East Newton in game two to Glendale, and that's nothing bad towards East Newton, but there's a big difference. Our kids believed in what we were doing and believed in themselves and their teammates, and that led us a long ways."

Richard Correll was the only returning varsity assistant coach; Trey Moeller and Clay Deem had moved from freshman football to the varsity staff and were joined by Jesse Wall, who had also excelled on the field for Pittsburg State and had done his student teaching at Webb City that spring.

There were other changes around the program, too, as the Cardinals hosted Carl Junction in week one; Cardinal Stadium had been revamped in the off-season, with 500 seats added to the home side and a new visitors' press box constructed. The grass had been "babied" in the offseason, and Lankford said it was the best the playing surface had been in years.

If any Webb City fans were holding their breath against the Bulldogs, their concerns were quickly eased; Webb City throttled its rivals 51-14 and Thompson got his first win.

The Cardinals threw the ball more than they had a year earlier. Smith threw touchdown passes to Divine, Williams and Ansley. With the team needing a new running back to emerge, junior Matt Goddard led the team in rushing against the Bulldogs and scored two touchdowns. Smith ran for three more.

Against Glendale in week two Webb City played a 5A school for the first time in 10 years, dating back to Webb City's brief stint in the Ozark Conference. The teams split two games then. Severe weather – heavy rain and lightning – delayed the opening kickoff for nearly an hour, and it rained throughout the game. Smith scored on a two-yard run in the first half, then threw a 30-yard pass to Williams, who ran another 30 yards to score and put Webb City up 14-12. With Glendale threatening late, Ansley picked off a pass with just 37 seconds left in the game to seal the two-point win.

The schedule didn't get any easier a week later, when the Cardinals made the short drive to Missouri Southern to play Joplin. The Cardinals were ranked first in Class 4A, while Joplin was 8th in 5A, and at least 7,000 fans packed the stadium. Those who came to root for the Cardinals didn't leave happy. Smith broke a bone in his hand late in the first quarter while making a tackle on defense; he continued to play well on defense after having his hand wrapped, but it was an injury that would sideline him for weeks. Junior Dustin Storm replaced Smith on offense, and Jason Hamilton replaced Smith at linebacker in future weeks. Against the Eagles, Webb City fumbled the ball four times and lost three of them; they would drop to 5th in the state after losing 36-7. The loss broke a 22-game regular season winning streak, dating back to 1987, and also ended Webb City's run of 16 straight wins overall.

The turnover woes continued a week later against Monett with six more fumbles, three of which were lost. But Thompson's team showed some heart, coming from behind twice to win 16-13. B.J. Williams caught a 35-yard touchdown pass from Storm, and Williams' two-point conversion put the Cards ahead. After Monett scored again in the third quarter, Storm completed a 43-yard touchdown pass to senior Billy Pippen with less than three minutes left in the game. The same duo hooked up for the two-point conversion.

Both Webb City and Kickapoo had identical 3-1 records when they played in week five, and Kickapoo had just knocked off Joplin 15-12. Things went better than the Joplin game, but not by much: Webb City lost 34-15.

The schedule was finally getting easier, though, as the Cardinals returned to some more traditional opponents. And those three games against 5A opponents had made the team much, much better. Webb City steamrolled Nevada 48-0, then Neosho 20-0. Against Carthage in district play, Smith finally returned at quarterback. Each team scored just one touchdown in the first half, which saw sluggish play from the Cardinals, but the second half was a different story. The Cardinals won 36-7 to clinch the District 10 title and another playoff berth. The district already decided, a 53-6 throttling of McDonald County ended the regular season with icing on the cake.

On a cold night in early November the Cardinals welcomed Salem to town for Thompson's first playoff game, a sectional showdown against a high-powered offense. On the second play of the game Salem's quarterback busted loose for a 63-yard touchdown, putting a scare into the home crowd. But Webb City's playmaker, Smith, led the Cardinals on a 72-yard opening drive and scored on a 1-yard run.

Salem answered immediately with a 66-yard scoring drive to lead 14-6, and almost scored again after driving to the Webb City 21-yard line, but a field goal was blocked. The Cardinals finally evened the score after a 44-yard drive and Smith's four-yard scamper. He added the two-point conversion to tie it at 14. Webb City scored again on the opening drive of the second half, marching 67 yards to take a 20-14 lead. Salem then drove to the Webb City 24, but the defense held the Tigers on a fourth-and-4.

Less than a minute into the fourth quarter, Webb City's defense again made a play fans would fondly remember – for different reasons. Junior Brad Carey earned the nickname "Wrong Way" after recovering a fumble and running toward the wrong end zone before he realized he was heading toward his own goal line. But the fumble recovery set up the winning score, Smith's fourth touchdown run of the game, and the Cardinals held on late to advance to the quarterfinals with a 26-21 win.

Four hours away at Marshall in the quarterfinals, senior running back Lynn Stanley offered his best game of the season to help Webb City win 34-21. Running back Stan Wallace was good, too, and so was Mark Smith.

"Lynn had success running the ball early and it was hard not to keep giving him the ball," Thompson told the newspaper. "The offensive line played very well after a slow start. They controlled the line of scrimmage."

Defensively, B.J. Williams had two interceptions and Smith added a third.

Webb City had now gone at least as far as the quarterfinals for three straight years, and was back in the semifinals for the second consecutive season. Not surprisingly, when all-conference teams were announced the same week, they were filled with Cardinals. Of the 17 first-team selections on offense, eight were Cardinals. Unanimous choices were senior tight end Craig Divine, senior tackle

Jeff Ogden and senior guard Andy Booth. Other first teamers were wide receiver B.J. Williams, quarterbacks Mark Smith and Dusty Storm, junior running back Stan Wallace and junior punter Brad Carey. Senior guard Shawn Hansen and junior center Marcus Herrell earned second-team honors, and senior Billy Pippin was an honorable mention selection at tight end.

It was more of the same defensively; eight of the 13 first-team players were Cardinals, with Herrell at end, Ogden on the line, Williams and junior Matt Goddard in the backfield as unanimous picks. Senior lineman Aaron Broaddus, linebackers Smith and Divine and senior back Jason Ansley were also first-team selections. Senior Kirk Philpot and junior David Cook were second-team linebackers.

Just a game away now from defending their state title at the University of Missouri football stadium, the Cardinals faced Columbia Rock Bridge in the semifinals at Cardinal Stadium. Though Rock Bridge High School had been open only since 1973, the Bruins already had two state championships (1975, 1977) and had made a total of five playoff appearances. They had gone to the sectionals a year earlier.

The 1:30 p.m. Saturday game pitted Webb City, 9-2, against 8-3 Rock Bridge, who had lost three-straight early in the season when hampered by injuries. Rock Bridge defeated St. Joe Benton 24-14 in the quarterfinals.

The Cardinals scraped together a 21-20 win in the game, coming from behind to tie the game and force overtime and eventually winning on a missed Rock Bridge extra point. A week later in Columbia, they faced St. Louis Sumner in a rematch of the 1989 title game.

Mark Smith set a Class 4A Show-Me Bowl record for the longest run from scrimmage, a 66-yard touchdown run two plays into Webb City's first possession and B.J. Williams added a two-point conversion to tie the game at 8-8 after Sumner scored quickly on a 44-yard run less than two minutes into the game. Sumner got the ball back and moved quickly into Webb City territory, getting as close as the 2-yard line before penalties pushed the ball back to the 11. On fourth-and-goal, Ogden made the stop.

After Sumner bobbled a punt early in the second quarter at its own 20, Webb City scored on another Smith run that was set up by a leaping 12-yard reception by Craig Divine. Wallace's extra point made it 15-8 Webb City. Sumner scored but missed the PAT, and later in the second quarter Goddard intercepted a pass and returned the ball 22 yards but the return was called back on a clipping penalty. On the same drive, Divine caught a pass and ran 75 yards for a touchdown, but the score was called back for another clipping penalty.

The key play of the game, according to Sumner coach Lawrence Wells, was a blocked punt recovered in the end zone that put Webb City in a 20-15 deficit. The Cardinals answered, though, again on a Smith touchdown run, but the conversion failed and Webb City held a 21-20 lead. That was the end of the scoring for the Cardinals; Sumner scored twice more and won 36-21.

"We're not going to make any excuses," Thompson said. "We got beat by a great football team. We can handle it. I'm proud of them, they're proud of themselves."

Thompson's thoughts on the game haven't changed in 20-plus years.

"We got beat by a team that was better than us," he says now. "I still remember walking out at halftime reading the stats and their two running backs each rushed for over 100 years in the first half so we were just kind of hanging on and then the head coach made a poor call on a fake punt that got us behind. That was a team that was a lot more athletic than we were and we made a heck of a game out of it for awhile."

Mark Smith looks for an opening in the defense during the 1990 home semifinal game against Columbia Rock Bridge, which Webb City won 21-20. Photo by Bob Foos.

22. THE MUD BOWL

The Cardinals learned at least two important things about their football team in 1990: Kurt Thompson could coach, and the team could win in the post-Jerry Kill era. Expectations were still high going into the fall of 1991. Webb City opened that season ranked second in the state and the Southwest Conference favorites despite returning just three starters on offense: Mark Smith, center Marcus Herrell and tailback Stan Wallace. The team's strength was its senior class. Of the 22 starters, 21 were seniors. Sumner was the preseason No. 1.

"Every year seniors step up that have been in the back row the last couple of years and take advantage of their opportunities," Thompson told the *Sentinel*.

Going into the season opener at Carl Junction, the starting offensive lineup was Herrell at center, Chris Pittman and Jason Cole at guards, Brad Carey and Kyle Jones at tackles, Chris Fetters at tight end, Zack Haddock and Jason Hamilton rotating at the other end, Matt Boyer at fullback, Stan Wallace at running back and Smith at quarterback. Five players would alternate at the flanker/receiver position, with one of Pat Capron, James Galardo or Chris Walker starting.

On defense the Cardinals' starters were Jones and Herrell at ends, Cole and Carey at tackles, Fetters and Haddock rotating at inside linebacker with Smith at the other inside backer, David Cook, Hamilton and Dustin Storm sharing the two outside linebacker spots, Capron and Wallace at cornerbacks and Matt Goddard playing free safety. Carey would also punt, Smith would kick off and Wallace would handle field goals and PATs.

There was also a new Cardinal in 1991. After players watched Louisville play in a bowl game the year before they told Thompson they liked the "tough" Cardinal logo that university used. Thompson looked into it, found he could use the same logo and put it to a vote of the team's seniors, who said they liked the Louisville Cardinal better. Webb City had actually used a different Cardinal the year before, too, but prior to that the team had used the same logo for decades. When Tom Gosch arrived in 1962 the team's helmets were Columbia blue with a red stripe down the middle and a thin white strip on each side. Later on the switch was made to helmets that were all white. Gosch eventually purchased the Cardinal helmet logos for 50 cents apiece directly from the equipment manager of the St. Louis Cardinals.

There were plenty of highlights in the season-opening 38-20 win at Carl

Junction. Senior Matt Boyer rushed 12 times for 118 yards, Marcus Herrell had 10 tackles, Smith had 15 tackles, a sack and caused a fumble in his first game at inside linebacker after moving from the outside, and Goddard blocked a punt and had an interception. Wallace rushed for a 50-yard touchdown on the first play of the game and finished with 168 yards on 11 rushes.

The Cardinals scored on their first five possession of the game, and showed some big-play potential. After 30 yards had been the team's longest run during the 1990 regular season, they broke that mark three times against the Bulldogs. After Wallace's 50-yarder, Smith had a 50-yard touchdown on the next possession, and in the second quarter Boyer scored from 77 yards out.

"It's nice to know we have some people to make the big play," Thompson said.

After his all-state selection as a junior, Smith was considered one of the best players in the state of Missouri in 1991 and as teams focused their defense on him, it was freeing up others for big runs.

In the home opener against 5A Glendale, the Cardinals broke another big play on the first play of the game. Smith threw an 80-yard touchdown pass to Jason Hamilton to give Webb City an early lead. They went on to win 19-13 with Stan Wallace scoring two touchdowns.

For the first time all season Cardinals' fans weren't thrilled with the first play of the game in week three. Webb City fumbled the kickoff and Bentonville scored four plays later. Stephen Crane blocked the extra point, and Bentonville never scored again as Webb City went to 3-0 with a 34-6 win. Herrell and Goddard each recovered a fumble, Capron and Storm each picked off a pass and Capron also caught a 50-yard touchdown.

Despite lacking some intensity against Monett in week four, the Cardinals still won 37-6. Yet again, the game's opening kickoff proved to be a key play. This time Monett fumbled and Stephen Crane recovered it at the Cubs' 20-yard line. On the very next play, Mark Smith threw a touchdown pass to Crane, who made a diving catch in the end zone. Smith's two-point conversion made it 8-0 just 31 seconds into the game. It was another huge rushing game for the Cardinals; they ran for 413 yards on 52 carries, while limiting Monett to just 98 rushing yards and 27 yards through the air. Matt Boyer tallied 153 of the rushing yards on 16 carries, and Smith ran just 10 times for 141 yards.

The schedule would get much tougher in the next few weeks. First, another game against 5A Kickapoo – on the road – and then a much-anticipated showdown with Pittsburg.

"We'll need big crowd support to help us overcome the advantage of being on the road," Thompson told the newspaper.

On a rain-soaked field, the Cardinals won easily, 28-7. The story of that Friday night had more to do with some off-the-field events than Webb City's fifth win, though. Webb City fans showed up to Kickapoo's stadium much earlier than the home crowd, and many found seats on the home side of the field. But Kickapoo administrators asked those Webb City fans to move to the small visitors bleachers "in the spirit of sportsmanship" so Chiefs fans would get a good seat for homecoming. Cardinals fans were reluctant to give up those good seats and make the trek around a muddy track to the visitors bleachers, which were hard to watch from. Many moved and watched the game standing behind the Webb City bench. The controversy went beyond seating, though. Two tires on the Webb City team buses were slashed and new tires had to be found in Springfield and brought to the stadium so the Cardinals could leave that night.

To call the Webb City/Pittsburg showdown of 1991 the game of the week would be an understatement. Webb City was ranked first in Missouri Class 4A, undefeated through five games and had gone to the state finals a year earlier. Pittsburg was ranked No. 1 in Kansas Class 5A, also 5-0, and was the Kansas defending state champion.

Roughly 7,500 fans crammed into Cardinal Stadium for the game, and even the extra bleachers set up around the track weren't enough to hold everyone. Many arrived at the stadium to get in line at noon that day, and gates didn't even open until 5:15 p.m.

Just three plays into the game the Purple Dragons struck for a 71-yard touchdown, but Webb City soon answered. The Cardinals then took a 14-7 lead, but Pittsburg answered, though a missed extra point left the Cardinals with a 14-13 lead at the half. In the second half the Cardinals scored twice and Pittsburg once as Webb City won 28-19.

"Two good football teams put on a great show," Thompson said. "That's what football is all about."

Thompson still remembers it as a special game.

"It was just a great game," he recalls. "They were a very good football program. We felt like we were there at that time. It was a huge crowd, I still remember that. I kind of get chills now thinking about it. That's unbelievable. It was just a phenomenal game. Two things I remember; there were some very good football players on the field, but two great football players: Mark Smith and a very good young man from Pittsburg named Poncho Sales. It was just a phenomenal game and those two kids were just a couple of war daddies going at it. He played linebacker and Mark played on offense."

Sales was a three-year starter for Pittsburg and an all-state honoree as a senior. He continued his career at Coffeyville Community College in 1993 and had a great career there. He made 24 tackles in a game against Garden City in 1993, tying a single-game record at the school. He finished as the school's all-time leading tackler, and signed with Wyoming University after graduating in 1995. He transferred to Pittsburg State and started in 1996 and 1997. He was an all-MIAA linebacker.

Before the game Thompson told one of his assistants that Mark Smith played big games better than any player he'd ever coached or been around. While Thompson was worried his Cardinals wouldn't be able to defend Pittsburg, he told the assistant that Smith would make some plays he had never seen before. He didn't disappoint, finishing with 121 rushing yards on 25 carries, and Stan Wallace had 14 rushes for 109 yards. Pat Capron caught two passes, including a 95-yarder for a touchdown.

"We had great respect for their program," Thompson says. "We were kind of on the flip side. Larry Garman was ending his career and I was just starting mine and he was very, very good to me. He would help me out anytime he could leading up to that game. He was very influential for me and that was neat because you know those were well-coached teams who played hard and physical and it was a hard-fought game."

After the emotional win, it was hard for the team to get too excited to play a one-win Nevada team a week later, but it was homecoming in Webb City and the Cardinals put on a good show for the home crowd, winning 48-0. Mark Smith, Stan Wallace and Matt Boyer each scored twice and Matt Goddard returned a fumble 37 yards for another touchdown. As usual, the final statistics were lopsided. Webb City rushed for 352 yards and limited the Tigers to only 66. Stan Wallace had a particularly amazing stat line: 11 rushes, 182 yards. Webb City's defense forced seven turnovers. Dustin Storm, Zack Haddock, Kyle Jones/Marcus Herrell, Nelson Daniels and Goddard recovered fumbles, and Smith and Chris Walkers made interceptions.

Webb City won a shootout against Neosho in the first round of district play, 62-28, and a win against Carthage would all but assure the Cardinals of another district championship. Carthage was 5-2 after beating McDonald County 48-6 in its district opener. Against the Wildcats, Pat Capron caught five passes from Mark Smith for five touchdowns and 126 yards. Smith completed nine of 13 passes overall for 176 yards, and added nine rushes for 118 yards, with Wallace rushing 12 times for 116 yards and Matt Boyer rushing 19 times for 104 yards. Stephen Crane and Storm each had an interception.

Against Carthage the Webb City defense pitched a shutout and the Cardinals won 35-0 to seal their fourth straight playoff appearance and sixth in seven years. Carthage was limited to 130 total yards, with 40 of them coming in the fourth quarter on one run. Dustin Storm picked off a pass to set up one touchdown, and Mark Smith had an interception of his own. Webb City's offense continued to roll, gaining 406 yards. Smith threw two passes to Chris Walker for 80 yards, rushed for 149 yards on 17 carries, Stan Wallace had 119 yards on 17 carries and Matt Boyer rushed 14 times for 61 yards.

It was 20 degrees at kickoff with a wind chill even lower.

"This is what you work all year for," Thompson told the newspaper. "Now they're getting rewards for all that hard work."

As had happened frequently in previous years, Webb City's district dominance had rendered the week 10 game against McDonald County meaningless, but the Cardinals won 49-0 anyway.

Webb City traveled to Ozark for the sectional round of the playoffs expecting to face a really good offensive team. Ozark running back Ryan Estes looked to be the biggest threat the Cardinals would face after he averaged more than 160 yards a game in the regular season, but Webb City held him to only 30 yards in what turned into a 40-7 blowout win. Senior Pat Capron intercepted a pass as the first half ended and sophomore Stephen Crane intercepted one in the third quarter, returning it 15 yards to the Ozark 42-yard line. Stan Wallace scored from 39 yards out a couple plays later. Crane later recovered a fumble in the fourth quarter and returned it 21 yards. Smith, as usual, led the way offensively with three touchdowns and 136 rushing yards. Wallace finished with 145 rushing yards and Matt Boyer had 82; each scored a touchdown.

The Cardinals returned home to face Republic in the quarterfinals, and Stan Wallace scored a 38-yard touchdown on Webb City's first possession of the game. Mark Smith scored on the team's second possession, then threw a 39-yard touchdown to Jason Hamilton on the third possession after Brad Carey recovered a fumble following a hard tackle by linebacker Dustin Storm. Stephen Crane had one rush in the game and went for an 11-yard touchdown in the third quarter. Final score: Webb City 27, Republic 7. Smith had a bruised shoulder and rushed for only 37 yards, while Wallace (25 for 148) and Boyer (17 for 101) picked up the slack. Crane and Capron each added interceptions again.

For the semifinals the Cardinals traveled back to St. Joseph Benton, which had a 10-1 record and a particularly stout defense that had allowed only 30 points in its last seven games. Webb City's defense was just as good, though, allowing 113 points all year for an average of just 9.4 per game. Almost half those points came in two games against Carl Junction and Neosho.

The field at James E. Sparks Memorial Field was covered in thick mud that Saturday in St. Joseph, which hampered a Webb City offense based on making quick cuts, and helped a Benton offense based on size and running straight up the field. The field had been covered by snow the night before, and when it was cleared there was three to six inches of mud. No yard lines were visible. The Cardinals mustered only nine total rushing yards and 32 passing yards, but their defense limited Benton to just 62 rushing yards and no passing yards. In a defensive struggle in the mud, it all came down to who could capitalize on mistakes. When the ball slipped off the punter's foot and landed inside Webb City's 20-yard line in the second quarter, Benton recovered and scored a few plays later for the first touchdown of the game. In the middle of the fourth quarter, Benton scored on an eight-yard run. Those were the only scores of the game, and Webb City's season ended at 12-1 with a 14-0 loss in the semifinals.

There had been talk of postponing the game, but Thompson declined because the field wouldn't have been any better a day later, and Missouri Western

The Webb City defense looks on during the infamous Mud Bowl game at St. Joseph Benton in the 1991 semifinals. Benton won 14-0. Photo by Bob Foos.

State College's offer to use its field wasn't acceptable to Benton officials.

"The kids work hard all year and then to have to play in those conditions, it's too bad," Thompson told the newspaper.

It was an especially tough way for the careers of Mark Smith and others to end. Seniors filled 19 of 22 starting positions that year, and ended their careers with a 47-5 record since their freshmen seasons. Their varsity record in three years was 36-4.

"We got beat in the worst game," Thompson says now. "That was the mud bowl. I've never seen anything like it. I still remember Richard Correll saying in our locker room how that was the saddest thing he ever saw because Mark Smith, the greatest player who's ever played here, is out slopping around in the mud his last game and he couldn't do anything about it. It was a heartbreaker because I think we could have beat them in a normal field situation but it was what it was."

A few months later, Smith signed with the University of Arkansas to play linebacker. When his Razorback career was finished, Smith had made 305 tackles, which ranks 14th all-time at the university. He made five tackles for a loss in a game against Alabama in 1993, which is tied for first in the school's record book. Smith also led Arkansas in total tackles for two straight seasons, 1994 and 1995. His junior campaign in 1995 saw the Webb City native record 115 tackles and force two fumbles. He was a first team All-SEC selection, and was later chosen as a linebacker on Arkansas' all-decade team encompassing 1990-1999.

He had grown up a fan of legendary Kansas City Chiefs linebacker Derrick Thomas, and when his college career was done, Smith got a chance to follow in Thomas' footsteps. He signed with the Chiefs as a free agent following the 1997 draft, and spent time on the team's practice squad.

"I hope I don't embarrass myself too much as I ask him for his autograph on the first day," Smith told the *Sentinel* that April.

Kurt Thompson, now more than two decades after Smith played his final game at Webb City, says Webb City football wouldn't be what it is today if not for the talented quarterback and linebacker.

"He is the man who got Webb City football going," Thompson says. "Jerry Kill will tell you the same thing. Mark is so humble. Grant Wistrom was a damn good player, but Mark touched the ball every play because he played quarterback. We wouldn't have won near as many games. After that '89 reunion, Jerry didn't talk Mark up too much, but afterwards we were talking and he said we wouldn't even be here without Mark. That's why we won. Without Mark it just wouldn't have happened. There would have been three years we would have been average. He was a difference maker, no question."

Kurt Thompson addresses the team during the 1992 semifinal game against Hickman Mills. Photo by Bob Foos.

23. THE 'OUTLAW CLASS'

With all those seniors graduating, leaving 19 starting positions up for grabs, the 1992 season was considered a rebuilding year. The Cardinals returned only three part-time starters on defense and one starter on offense. One bright spot was the team's junior class, which hadn't lost a game in eighth grade football, freshman football or junior varsity.

"We're excited," Thompson said. "Some of the kids have waited their turn, paid their dues and are getting their turn now. We have a lot of two-way starters who hadn't played as underclassmen."

Webb City businesses sported windows decorated with shoe-polish slogans of support written by Webb City cheerleaders, and Carl Junction's Booster Club planned a pep rally and bonfire the night before the two teams met in the season opener. Webb City's starters for that first game offensively were Jeremy Mallory at left tight end, Chris Pittman at left tackle, Dennis Burleson and Derek

Foltz alternating at left guard, Matt Bruffett at center, Aaron Kwolek at right guard, Travis Brock at right tackle, Grant Wistrom at right tight end, Brandon Eggleston, Brad Ansley and Jonathan Dawson alternating at flanker, Matt Lewis at quarterback, Ryan Eck at fullback and Stephen Crane at tailback. Brock, Wistrom, Ansley, Lewis, Eck and Crane were juniors and everyone else was a senior.

Defensively Wistrom would start at left end, Brock at left tackle, Kwolek at right tackle, Pittman and Foltz would alternate at right end, Eck and Burleson were at inside linebacker, Bruffett and Mallory at outside linebackers, Crane at free safety, Ansley, Dawson and Jason Chamness would alternate at cornerbacks.

Even though it was a rebuilding year, there were still expectations that the Cardinals could challenge for a state championship.

"We set our goal every year to win the state championship," Thompson told the newspaper. "That's the ultimate goal for our level. Whether it is reachable or not, we have high expectations.

"There is a lot of pressure on us to win – from ourselves and the community," he said. "Pressure and high expectations make me work a little harder; it makes the kids work a little harder."

Despite fumbling the ball on their first two possessions, the Cardinals still won the game against Carl Junction 57-7, with Lewis completing seven of 13 passes for 123 yards and two touchdowns in his first start at quarterback. He rushed for two more scores. But two weeks later Webb City had a losing record after falling 19-16 at Pittsburg and 33-7 at Bentonville.

"We played good people," Thompson says. "Pittsburg beat us in overtime. Going into it, as a coach you always try to be positive with your kids but deep down you have your thoughts and my thought was can we just play them tough and be competitive with them and doggone they beat us in overtime and we should have beat them. We had our chances. We went to Bentonville and just didn't play good, got it handed to us. They were very bitter about the year before; they felt like we had run the score up on them a little bit and they got after us and we didn't play very good, we didn't respond very well. We kind of decided after that game, we were playing a lot of kids on both sides and we made four or five personnel changes to get more kids on the field and that benefited us, although the first game coming back at Eldon after we'd lost two, they were the poorest team we'd played all year and we were behind 6-0 at the half. That was very frustrating as a coach. I went into the locker room and I don't think I said very many things but it was an embarrassment how we played. That kind of got us on a role. We played very good from that point on. That was a junior-dominated team with Grant, Matt Lewis, Stephen Crane, Ryan, Brad Ansley, all those kids were first-year starters as juniors. We had a whole lot of those guys."

At Pittsburg, Webb City had led 13-6, but the Purple Dragons scored with 34 seconds left in the game to tie it up and send it into overtime. Overtime in both Kansas and Missouri at that time was played in a different format. Each team had four downs to score from the 10-yard line. The Cardinals lost the coin toss and got the ball first. They couldn't score a touchdown but David Smart kicked a field goal for a 16-13 lead. On third-and-5, Pittsburg scored the winning touchdown. The loss dropped Webb City to eighth in Missouri Class 4A, and boosted Pittsburg to third in Kansas 5A.

A week later Bentonville scored one touchdown in each of the first three quarters and two in the fourth while Webb City's only TD came in the second quarter when Matt Lewis scored on a quarterback keeper from the 1-yard line.

"We need to win," Thompson said about the Eldon game in week four.

The Mustangs recovered a fumble and returned it 45 yards for a touchdown, the only score of the first half.

"I told them they worked too hard to play like they did in the first half," Thompson told the *Sentinel* about his halftime speech. "I told them they embarrassed themselves; they were a much better football team than they showed themselves to be."

In the second half the Cardinals played like the team they were, scoring two touchdowns in the third quarter and three in the fourth to win 35-6. Matt Lewis scored on a nine-yard run, Brad Ansley returned a fumble 28 yards for a touchdown, Lewis scored on an 11-yard run, Lewis threw an 18-yard touchdown to Ansley and then Wistrom caught a 47-yard touchdown pass. The second half would prove to be the turning point of the season.

The win evened Webb City's record at 2-2 and actually ended one of the worst stretches of Cardinal football in six years: they had lost three of four games dating back to the 1991 semifinals.

The Cardinals played their best game all year against Republic, winning 31-20, and finally cracked the state polls again at No. 10. They drove 80 yards on their first possession and Ryan Eck scored on the 12th play, but after the Cardinals led 14-0 late in the first half, Republic came back with a late score and then another touchdown on its first possession of the second half and suddenly things were a lot closer. Webb City then scored on three straight possessions, including a David Smart field goal, and ran away with it.

A week later the Cardinals matched up with Lebanon, who had one of the top 50 players in the nation in 6-foot-6, 270-pound lineman Mike Wehner, who would go on to play for the University of Miami. The Yellow Jackets had thrown for more than 300 yards in knocking off Camdenton earlier in the season; Camdenton was ranked third in the state.

At the same time there was more Pittsburg State news concerning Webb City. Jerry Archer, who had played along with Tom Gosch for the Gorillas from 1959 to 1962, was inducted into the Pittsburg State Athletics Hall of Fame. The multi-sport standout from Sarcoxie had been drafted by the Detroit Lions with their ninth-round pick, and he later spent 11 years as an assistant coach for the

Cardinals. Archer was the "coach" at Coach's Corner convenience store at the intersection of Zora and Range Line in Joplin until his death in 2002.

Back on the football field, the Cardinals dominated Lebanon at Cardinal Stadium with an especially good defensive performance. Webb City ran 70 offensive plays and held Lebanon to only 36 in a 17-7 win. That was the key to the game, Thompson said.

"They had a very explosive offense," he told the paper. "The way to defend an explosive offense is to keep the ball out of their hands. We controlled the ball."

The turning point was a Grant Wistrom interception in the third quarter. With the game tied, Webb City had a bad snap on a field goal attempt at the Lebanon 15 and the Yellowjackets recovered at their own 45 with momentum on their side. But on first down, Wistrom intercepted a pass and the home stands erupted. After Lewis nearly gave the ball back on a throw that was almost picked off, Stephen Crane rushed 14 yards and eight plays later Lewis ran it in for the score. Lewis' pass to Jayme Richardson for 18 yards was the only touchdown of the first half, and after the Lewis run made it 14-7, Smart's 25-yard field goal sealed it.

Thompson gave credit for the defensive game plan to assistants Trey Moeller, Jesse Wall and Tim Davied. Lewis rushed for 122 yards, and Jeremy Mallory made five tackles.

Webb City improved to 5-2 with a 47-14 blowout against Nevada, and moved up to ninth in the state polls with its first conference win. After Lewis scored a touchdown in the first quarter, Nevada actually took a 7-6 lead in the second quarter with a score on a fourth-and-7 at the Webb City 10, but Stephen Crane's 44-yard touchdown run on the next possession put the Cardinals ahead for good. After that, Lewis ran for another touchdown then threw a pair of touchdown passes to Jayme Richardson, the junior, and finally Lewis scored on an 84-yard run and Dusty Frizzell added a one-yard score.

Up next came McDonald County, who was coached by Bruce Stancell, Thompson's roommate at Pittsburg State. Thompson didn't do him any favors, and Webb City got the homecoming win 38-6. With one district win already under their belts, the Cardinals had Neosho on a Friday night and then Carthage the following Thursday; in less than a week they'd know if they were back in the playoffs. With Neosho struggling and hampered by injuries, a win was likely, meaning the Carthage game would be for all the marbles. The Tigers were currently ranked sixth in the state, and Webb City 10th.

"It's tough sometimes to get kids focused on what's at hand," Thompson said. "Our kids are mature enough to know that if they let something happen before then, we could be in trouble."

Around the same time, Chance Wistrom was selected as the 1992 Coach E.A. Markey Football Scholarship Award recipient at Central Missouri State

University after the senior defensive end, a four-year player for the Mules, ranked fourth on the team with 51 tackles, along with three fumble recoveries – one returned for a touchdown –and he led the team with 8.5 quarterback sacks. He received the award at halftime of the Mules' 17-0 win against Missouri-Rolla.

After beating Neosho 58-7, all that stood before the Cardinals and the playoffs was a really good Carthage team in week 10. Carthage was still ranked sixth in the state polls, and Webb City was eighth. The Cardinal defense stifled the Tigers all night, allowing them just four first downs, and Webb City won 13-7 to earn a playoff berth and clinch both the district and Southwest Conference titles.

"It was a big win for us," Thompson said. "We dominated them everywhere but the scoreboard."

As he looks back on it, Thompson recalls playing up the underdog role real heavy going into the game.

"They were a good team and they played us real well," he says.

On the post-season all-Southwest Conference football team, Webb City players were everywhere, as usual. First-team offensive players were Grant Wistrom at tight end, Travis Brock at tackle, Matt Bruffett at center, Matt Lewis at quarterback, David Smart at kicker and Stephen Crane as a return specialist. First-team defensive players were Brock at tackle, Wistrom at end, Ryan Eck at inside linebacker, Jeremy Mallory and Brad Ansley at linebackers and Crane at defensive back. Second-team offensive players were Jayme Richardson at tight end, Chris Pittman at tackle, Dennis Burleson and Aaron Kwolek at guards and Eck at running back. On defense, second-team players were Pittman at end, Burleson at inside linebacker and Jonathan Dawson and Jason Chamness at defensive backs. Chad Webb was an honorable mention defensive tackle.

Back in the playoffs for the fifth straight season, the Cardinals probably felt a sense of déjà-vu when they traveled to Camdenton for the sectional game. On a rainy night, the field was soggy and muddy and fog floated around the stadium, at times obscuring the far sideline; would it be the St. Joseph mud bowl game all over again? Things started off well enough. The Lakers received the opening kickoff, but sophomore Andy Reynolds recovered a fumble at the Camdenton 23 and seven plays later Matt Lewis scored and David Smart's extra point made it 7-0. Camdenton tied the game early in the second quarter. Midway through the third, the Lakers scored again and lined up in the swinging gate formation for the extra point, but the kick was no good.

Down 13-7, Webb City couldn't score on its next possession and fans began to get anxious as the Cardinals lined up to punt. Camdenton couldn't hold on to the ball, though, and Brad Ansley recovered the fumble at midfield. Nine plays later, Lewis scored from the 1 as time expired in the third quarter, and Smart's kick made it a 14-13 game. In the fourth quarter, Camdenton drove 60 yards in 16 plays and faced a fourth-and-goal from the 2 with 25 seconds left. The Lakers lined up for a field goal; the ball wobbled through the air and missed by a lot. Webb City won by a point.

The lead in the *Sentinel* story was a quote by Jeremy Mallory. "It's the greatest feeling I ever had in my life!" he said. "I want to just keep on going."

"I feel great!" Chris Pittman said while celebrating with his teammates. "All I could think about was last year at St. Joe, but I knew deep down we could pull it off."

In the locker room after the game, Thompson told his team not to let down. "Let's make a run at it. Monday at our house."

Their opponent would be Republic, who had held off Rolla 12-2 in the sectionals, and who had lost at Webb City 31-20 in the regular season. Webb City entered the game after beating Carthage in an emotional rivalry contest, and then barely hanging on by a point against Camdenton.

"I think our kids were emotionally drained after the last two games," Thompson said.

And after beating Republic pretty soundly in October, those factors combined to make for a close quarterfinal contest.

A Stephen Crane touchdown and David Smart PAT gave the Cardinals a 7-6 lead at halftime, but a 26-yard field goal put Republic ahead 9-7 later on. After a 57-yard drive made it 15-7 in favor of Republic, things were looking gloomy for the Cardinals, though the Redbirds did stop the two-point conversion.

"We knew then we could go out and tie it up with one score, and win with two," Thompson said. "We still had a lot of hope."

Covering 59 yards in five plays, Webb City got the touchdown it needed on a 1-yard run by Lewis, and tied the game on a Lewis-to-Wistrom pass in the end zone for two points. After stopping the Tigers, Crane scored on an 11-yard run and Webb City won the game 22-15. A pair of turnovers were big factors. Aaron Kwolek recovered a Republic fumble at the Webb City 15 just before the half, and after Webb City's go-ahead score, Wistrom recovered a fumble on Republic's first offensive play with two-and-a-half minutes left in the game.

"We just didn't dominate people," Thompson says now. "We played Camdenton in a driving rain storm and beat them in a very close one and then probably should have gotten beat by Republic who we beat pretty soundly earlier in the year. We had to score two touchdowns in the fourth quarter and then we got on a roll after that."

"Great speed, very explosive offense, tremendous defense," is how Thompson described the team's semifinal opponent, Hickman Mills. But the explosive offense scored only seven points against Webb City, and the "tremendous" defense allowed 35 Cardinal points in the playoff blowout at Ruskin Stadium in metro Kansas City.

Brad Ansley returned the opening kickoff 43 yards, dropping the ball initially, then picking it up and running from the Webb City 16 to the Hickman Mills

41. Lewis ended the drive with a 14-yard scoring pass to Jayme Richardson. After the Cardinals got the ball back at their own 45 but fumbled, Hickman Mills drove to the Cardinals' 5 but couldn't score on four straight attempts. Stephen Crane ran for a touchdown, then intercepted a pass and returned it for another but the play was called back for a penalty and the Cardinals had to score from the 22. Another Lewis touchdown pass put Webb City up 21-0 at the half. Lewis and Eck added one-yard runs in the second half, and the Cougars didn't score until the final minute of the game. Final score: 35-7.

"We really worked harder than they did," Brock said. "We wanted it more." He had two fumble recoveries, and Wistrom had a third.

As usual, more Webb City fans attended the game than did hometown Cougar fans.

"That has to be intimidating for their fans to see," Thompson said. "It's special to have that support.

"The win is as much for our community as our players," he added. "Our community support is tremendous, and gives our players a lift."

There wasn't even enough room for all the fans; some had to watch from their cars or stood along the fence. There would be plenty of seats in the 60,000-seat Faurot Field at the University of Missouri, though, when Webb City would face hometown Columbia Rock Bridge in the state championship on the day after Thanksgiving.

"It's a great opportunity just to go to the state championship," said Ryan Eck in the newspaper. "We didn't get the chance last year. We came out and played in the mud and proved ourselves."

Both teams would be making their third trip to the state title game. They would be facing for the first time since the 1990 semifinal in Webb City, when the Cardinals came from behind to tie the game and force overtime, then won 21-20 after Rock Bridge missed an extra point.

It was a devastating loss for the Bruins, who still hadn't forgotten. Rock Bridge senior defensive end Josh Matthews was quoted in the *Columbia Daily Tribune*, "We're glad we got a second chance at Webb City. We're not going to let what happened to us our sophomore year happen again."

And in the same story, senior Corey Bowden added, "We're thinking about getting some revenge for our sophomore year, but we're not going to underestimate them either."

Rock Bridge was the first to score in the game, but Stephen Crane blocked the point after attempt and had another big play on Webb City's ensuing drive, throwing a 79-yard halfback pass to Brad Ansley. The pass set 4A and overall playoff records. By halftime it looked like the game was pretty much decided already. The Cardinals scored 17 points in the second quarter, and after another quick score after the break it wasn't even close anymore at 24-6. That's when Rock Bridge started its comeback.

"We certainly could taste it in our mouths," senior lineman Chris Pittman told the newspaper, "but we knew they'd come back."

Rock Bridge recovered a fumble deep in Webb City territory, took over at the 4-yard line and scored. On its next possession, Rock Bridge scored again and suddenly it was a 24-21 game. But Webb City caught some breaks. The Bruins missed a 30-yard field goal in the fourth quarter, but late in the game threatened again. Rock Bridge quarterback Matt Nivens threw a pass to the end zone, likely for the win, but Stephen Crane made another huge play and intercepted the ball.

"If I had that pass to throw over, I'd definitely take it back," Nivens said after the game.

It wasn't until the Cardinals downed the ball with 20 seconds left that Thompson knew the game was over. Final: 24-21.

"It's the best defense I've run against this season," said Rock Bridge running back Jack Roach. "They were good; they deserved to win, but it hurts to lose."

Webb City had only nine first downs in the game, Rock Bridge made 15, and that wasn't the only lopsided statistic. The Bruins rushed for 202 yards and the Cardinals just 90, but Webb City threw for 156 yards and Webb City kept Rock Bridge to barely 80 through the air. Crane led the team with 57 yards on 12 carries, Eck had seven carries for 27 yards and Lewis gained six rushing yards and completed five of 11 passes for 77 yards. Burleson and Wistrom each recovered a fumble.

The state championship was the ultimate confirmation for a senior class that hadn't won a game as eighth graders and was almost as bad in freshmen football.

"They've come a long way in the last three or four years," Thompson said. "These kids have always been told they aren't very good, but it paid off for the ones that stuck it out."

The 11-man senior class consisted of Brandon Eggleston, Jason Chamness, Jason Hunter, Matt Bruffett, Aaron Kwolek, Dennis Burleson, Derek Foltz, Chris Pittman, Jonathan Dawson, Jeremy Mallory and Jim Lee.

"We're the outlaw class," Pittman said. "No one wanted us, but we just stepped it up a notch and got it done."

Thompson told the *Sentinel* the class was a good example of "the philosophy of waiting to play."

"We talk about paying your dues and putting in your time," he said. "They're very unselfish. They waited their time, and waited patiently."

Back in Webb City, the town celebrated its team's return home with lights, sirens, confetti and even a rock song, "Redbird Rock," recorded by Charlie Brown and local musicians that debuted at the victory parade. Fans waited until nearly midnight for the team to arrive. First it was the band and pep buses that were greeted by fans lining Main Street from the Dinner Bell to Bradbury Bishop Deli. Buses carrying the football team were met at the city limits by an escort of police cars and fire trucks from Webb City and Carterville.

"That was terrific," Pittman said. "I always had a dream of coming home like that."

"It makes you feel proud," Chamness said. It was his first season with the Cardinals after moving from California. "I feel very lucky," he said. "I'm honored to be part of the Cardinals."

Eggleston told the paper it didn't really dawn on him until Sunday. He had moved from Joplin to Webb City two years earlier.

"It feels great down inside," he said. "I'll remember it forever."

After all the confetti had been cleaned up there were postseason awards to hand out, and the state had taken notice of the Cardinals. Grant Wistrom was a first-team all-state defensive end. He finished the year with two interceptions, three fumble recoveries, two blocked punts and 11 sacks. He also had a big offensive year, leading the team in receiving with 31 receptions for 504 yards, and he scored two touchdowns and two extra points. Stephen Crane was a first-team all-state running back. He led the team with 207 rushes for 1,398 yards and 15 touchdowns. He had 12 catches for 199 yards, returned 12 kickoffs for 190 yards and returned 12 punts for 218 yards. He also completed the 79-yard pass in the title game. On defense he had three interceptions, a fumble recovery and two PAT blocks. Travis Brock was a first team all-state offensive lineman. David Smart was a second-team all-state kicker after making 48 of 53 extra point attempts and six of 11 field goal attempts.

Kurt Thompson was named the Class 4A Coach of the Year.

"When you're around successful programs you win awards," he said later. "I'm also fortunate to have excellent assistant coaches: Richard Correll, Trey Moeller, Tim Davied, Jesse Wall and Jason Wright; freshman coaches Brad Jerry Lewis and 'Norm' Snow; and eighth grade coaches Tim Doss and Jerry Walker."

"He's deserved this for three years and finally received it; that's the way we feel about him," said Athletics Director Steve Gollhofer.

Other team leaders included Lewis, who completed 76 of 140 passes for 1,234 yards, rushed 175 times for 883 yards and scored 20 touchdowns; Brad Ansley, who caught 23 passes for 377 yards, recovered five fumbles and intercepted five passes; and Ryan Eck, who punted 33 times for 1,050 yards.

On the year the Cardinals rushed for 3,215 yards and kept opponents to 1,427 yards. They gained 4,528 offensive yards and held opponents to 2,859.

The Joplin Globe's all-area team included Wistrom at defensive end, Brock at defensive tackle, Crane at defensive back and Smart at kicker on the first team; Lewis at quarterback and Eck at linebacker on the second team; and Matt Bruffett at center, Aaron Kwolek on the offensive line, Chris Pittman at defensive end and Jeremy Mallory at linebacker.

Wistrom and Crane were named to the *Springfield News-Leader*'s all-

Ozarks team.

At the team's athletics awards ceremony, Pittman won the most inspirational award, Crane was the most valuable offensive player and Wistrom was named both the most valuable player on defense and overall most valuable player.

There was only one thing to do next.

"Get back to work and win another," Thompson said.

24. DEFENDING THEIR TITLE

As football camp opened in the summer of 1993, Thompson said his biggest concern was making the kids hungry again, but the start of practices was a golden opportunity to mold some more championship players.

"Those great players are always going to be great players," he told the newspaper. "But we've taken that marginal player that a lot of programs would have kicked back saying, 'Oh, that kid's never going to be a player. He'll never make it.' We've made all those kids by putting them in the weight room and teaching them to work hard. By the time they're seniors, they'll be great football players."

There was a stark difference from the previous fall, when the team was replacing so many starters and wasn't expected to be great; in 1993, expectations were sky high as the talented junior class that had been key to a state championship a year earlier was now taking the field for the last season.

Thompson, especially, noticed the pressure.

"1992 was fun because a lot of people didn't expect it," he says. "1993, you had a little more pressure on you because everybody expected you to do well. I can still remember the state championship game and the press conference a comment about how, 'Now you can relax and enjoy it and have fun.' That was one of those years it was very fun. We had great kids to coach, but you had that pressure of expecting to win and you need to and that's a little different type of pressure. It was a very relaxed group. I can still remember I always wanted to be serious and on everything and I had to kind of cut back that year because those kids were very relaxed. They were very confident in what they did. As long as they went out and performed like they did, then I needed to step back and leave them alone. The kids did a great job of preparing themselves, the coaching staff did a fantastic job. That's one of those dream seasons where everything goes as planned. For the most part we stayed pretty healthy to where we didn't lose kids for a long period of time. You've got to have that unless you have a ton of depth and we didn't have that depth back then. We had some very good kids on that team, some players who had success, and you can go through that lineup and that's probably as talented a group as there's been go through there in a lot of years."

The Cardinals were ranked No. 1 in the state in the preseason poll. They were a unanimous pick to win the Southwest Conference again. Senior Stephen

Crane was back at tailback after rushing for nearly 1,400 yards, senior Matt Lewis was back at quarterback after accounting for more than 2,000 offensive yards, and senior tight end Grant Wistrom was back after leading the team in receiving. Other returning starters on offense were flanker Brad Ansley, tight end Jayme Richardson, all-state strong tackle Travis Brock and Ryan Eck at fullback. The only real question offensively was the offensive line, with three juniors and a sophomore starting, but it would be anchored by Brock, a 6-foot-2, 280-pound lineman. Chad Webb, a 225-pound junior, would start at right guard, 205-pound junior Chad Boulware would start at center, 220-pound sophomore Jonathan Shull would start at left guard and Anthony Black, a 210-pound junior, would start at left tackle.

Even with all that talent back on offense, the defense was the team's strength, with nine seniors and two juniors starting. Webb City had allowed just 100 yards rushing and 13 points a game in 1992.

"A lot of people don't want to be No. 1," Thompson said. "They don't want the pressure on them. We'll take it. The time we really want to be No. 1 is that Friday after Thanksgiving. That's when it means something."

The 1993 team was one of the most dominant teams ever at Webb City. Only twice in 14 games did the Cardinals score fewer than 40 points, and they averaged 42.6 points per game. The defense was just incredible, holding opponents scoreless eight times, and allowing only 60 points all season, an average of 4.3 points per game. It was, arguably, the best defensive team Webb City has ever had.

"And we could have had more shutouts," Thompson says. "We would play our starters and then if they scored on our young kids, they scored on our young kids. I can still remember our starters standing on the sideline getting a little frustrated when people would score on us, but that was part of it and that does nothing but help you down the road."

The Cardinals opened the season winning 41-0 at Carl Junction, and then 40-0 at home against Pittsburg. Against the Bulldogs, Webb City's defense allowed only three rushing yards on 25 carries, and three first downs in the final 30 seconds of the game. The Bulldogs finished with 33 total yards.

"I thought we played all right for our first game of the year," Thompson said.

"Coach (Jesse) Wall set a goal for us to hold them under 50 yards rushing and to shut them out," the 6-foot-5, 230-pound Wistrom said. "And that's what we did."

Webb City's offense scored touchdowns on its first six possessions, and the Bulldogs started at their own 19, 25, 19, 20 and 35 on their first five possessions. Stephen Crane scored two touchdowns and returned two punts for 48 yards before leaving with an ankle sprain, and senior Dusty Frizzell rushed five times for 31 yards in his place. Lewis ran for two touchdowns, completed five of seven passes for 133 yards and a 37-yard touchdown to Wistrom, who ran a short hitch pattern to the right side then outran three defenders to the end zone.

Pittsburg in week one had pounded Springfield Glendale with its ground attack, finishing with 325 rushing yards and averaging nearly nine yards per carry. Senior tailback Gabe Anderson scored on runs of 50, 65 and 53 yards on his first three carries of the game.

At Webb City the Purple Dragons managed just 103 rushing yards on 27 carries, and the Cardinals scored 33 points in the first half, turning two fumbles and two interceptions into 20 points. Pittsburg had entered the game as the No. 2 team in the state of Kansas.

"I knew Webb City had a good team," said Pittsburg head coach Larry Garman. "We knew coming into this game they had a good team."

Webb City's defense faced its toughest challenge of the season against Waynesville in week three and the Tigers' dangerous backfield which had just rushed for 252 yards on 40 carries in a win against third-ranked Festus. In the first half, at least, it was all Webb City. The Cardinals turned three Waynesville turnovers into three scores and led 15-0 at halftime, but Webb City's turnovers in the second half let the Tigers get back into the game.

After sophomore Shawn Mayes made an electric 30-yard punt return to the Waynesville 25-yard line, Matt Lewis scored to put Webb City ahead 22-8 with 6:15 left in the game. Waynesville quarterback Doug McFadden sprinted 38 yards for a touchdown to make it a seven-point game with 4:58 left, and after a Cardinals' fumble on their next possession, the Tigers had the ball back just 27 yards away from another touchdown. On the very next play one of Waynesville's talented running backs got a handoff up the middle, cut back to the left and scored. Suddenly the game was tied.

Webb City couldn't do much on its next series, and Ryan Eck was forced to punt from his own 25. The ball bounced into a Waynesville player's leg and the Cardinals recovered at the Tigers' 42 with 1:18 left in the game. Webb City pushed the ball down to the 25, and with nine seconds left David Smart booted a 42-yard field goal for the win. He had made a 32-yard field goal in the second quarter.

"I just wanted the game over with," Smart told the newspaper. "I didn't want the game to go to overtime. We had some bad things happen to us in overtime last year, and I didn't want that to happen again."

Up next was Eldon, which would be a test for Webb City's pass defense after the Mustangs had passed roughly 80 percent of the time in their first two games of the year. Thompson also wanted the Cardinals to amp up their running game, which was averaging only 105 yards per game after three wins. One of the problems was the ankle injury to Crane; he still wasn't 100 percent and only had 70 yards on the season. Though Crane didn't play at tailback against Eldon, Webb City finally unleashed its rushing attack to the tune of 321 yards in the

44-0 blowout on a stormy night at Cardinal Stadium. In Crane's absence, 12 different players carried the ball. Dusty Frizzell had 61 yards on 10 carries but left in the second quarter with a twisted ankle.

"We knew we were going to be walking into a hornet's nest," said Eldon coach Kevin Alewine afterwards. "They're a great football team. We tried something new, offensively, because we thought across the lines we were going to be outmanned. And, basically, we were."

Eldon tried the swinging gate formation, but retreated into its standard offensive sets after the Cardinals led 22-0. It was another absolutely dominating defensive game by Webb City. The Mustangs finished with negative eight yards rushing on 12 carries, and threw for 37 yards and two first downs. The Cardinals intercepted five passes: two by Shawn Mayes, and one each from Mark Drake, Brad Ansley and Michael Hill.

The Eldon game marked a four-game stretch where Webb City won 44-0 against the Mustangs, 47-0 against Republic, 49-7 against Lebanon and 48-0 against Nevada.

Ryan "Rhino" Eck, the senior fullback, became the first Cardinal to eclipse the 100-yard mark in the win at Republic, tallying 102 yards and three touchdown on 14 rushes in the game. Stephen Crane returned and rushed for 86 yards and two touchdowns before aggravating the ankle in the third quarter. The game was actually called with 8:27 left in the fourth quarter because of a "spectacular" thunderstorm. Republic had the ball at the Webb City 25-yard line at the time.

"I saw that lightning coming in, and I was hollering at the officials before they called it," Thompson said. "I'm not going to let my kids stand out there with lightning all around. I told them I was going to take my kids off the field, if they didn't stop it."

Republic moved the ball easily on its first possession, collecting four of its nine first downs, but Darris Lassiter picked off a pass to turn momentum in Webb City's favor.

In the Lebanon game the Cardinals faced quarterback Derek Jensen, a 6-foot-1, 190-pound senior who was being recruited by several Big Eight and Big Ten schools. But gone were the days when Webb City's players were chronically undersized compared to the opposition; against Lebanon the Cardinals were bigger by about 30 pounds per player. They scored four touchdowns before halftime in the 49-7 rout to improve their record to 6-0 and extend their winning streak to 17 games. Webb City dominated the line of scrimmage, rushing for 227 yards, throwing for 107 and scoring three times apiece on the ground and through the air.

Eck rushed 10 times for 66 yards and a touchdown, and also threw a 27-yard option pass to Ansley in the third quarter that went for a touchdown. Ansley also scored a touchdown on a punt block return. Crane returned again and scored a touchdown while rushing for 53 yards on eight carries. Lewis completed six of seven passes for 107 yards and two scores.

Webb City's defense harassed Jensen all night and kept the Yellow Jackets to just 110 offensive yards. The only Lebanon score – and 63 of its 88 passing yards – came on a dump pass from the backup quarterback against Webb City's second-string defense.

The Southwest Conference season finally began against Nevada, who was actually looking to clinch the conference title after winning its first three conference games. Nevada was led by first-year head coach Bruce Humphrey, a Webb City graduate who had played under Tom Gosch. The Cardinals got off to a slow start on homecoming night, but sent Humphrey and his Tigers back home with a 48-0 skunking despite scoring just twice in the first half. It was Webb City's 24th consecutive win in the Southwest Conference, dating back to 1987.

Matt Lewis ran for two touchdowns and threw touchdown passes to Jayme Richardson for 23 yards and to Brad Ansley for 21 yards. Crane, finally healthy, had his breakout game of the year with 112 yards on only eight carries. In the second quarter he took the ball on a counter play, busted through the hole and faked out a pair of defenders, then sprinted 59 yards down the sideline.

Webb City's defense allowed only 49 yards of total offense, including 24 rushing yards on 27 carries. Nevada fumbled eight times and lost two of them.

"They didn't have a whole lot of respect for us coming into the game," said Wistrom. "They thought they could put it to us. We just wanted to show them that you don't beat Webb City at home."

Crane had an even more spectacular performance in the first week of district play against McDonald County. He rushed 17 times, scored four touchdowns and collected 148 yards while helping the Cardinals tally 449 yards of offense, the most all season. Webb City scored four times in the first half and won 42-15. Already leading 28-0 after two quarters, on Webb City's first possession of the second half, Crane carried the ball on every play and ended it with a 26-yard score. Lewis completed seven of nine passes for 141 yards and two touchdowns, one to Ansley, who broke a tackle and ran 61 yards for the score.

On a snowy, cold field at Bob Anderson Stadium in Neosho, Webb City clinched another district championship by pounding the host Wildcats 61-0 in their best offensive performance so far, racking up 508 yards of offense including 372 yards on the ground. The Cardinals took advantage of four turnovers and already had a 41-0 lead by halftime. Crane once again led the rushing attack with three touchdowns and 168 yards on 13 carries. Two of his touchdowns came on long first-half runs and accounted for 119 of his yards. After the Neosho game, Crane had rushed for 428 yards and seven touchdowns in three games on just 38 carries, an average of more than 11 yards per carry.

Jayme Richardson had a touchdown for the fourth straight game, a 59-yarder from Lewis, who ran for two touchdowns as well. Ryan Eck ran for an 11-yard touchdown, and backup quarterback Mark Drake added a 63-yard scoring run. Shawn Mayes also returned a kick 90 yards for a touchdown to open the second half.

Through nine games, Webb City's defense, led by linemen Grant Wistrom, Travis Brock, Chad Webb and Adrian Wynne, had allowed only 115 yards per game, the lowest in the four-state area, and they gave up only 65 yards to Neosho.

A week later Webb City ended the regular season by beating Carthage 48-6. Crane scored twice, ran for 108 yards and Eck intercepted a pass and returned it 67 yards for a touchdown, then blocked a punt on Carthage's next possession that was returned by Brad Ansley 21 yards for another touchdown. Lewis threw for 101 yards and two scores

In the first round of playoff action Crane had another "best game of the season" with 179 rushing yards and two scores, marking his fifth straight game with at least 100 yards. Once again the Cardinals scored six times in the first half and beat Nevada 45-3 for the second win of the year against the Tigers. Even Grant Wistrom scored a rushing touchdown in the game.

"The offensive line played great, just like they have all year," Crane said after the game. "They just get off the ball and knock the crap out of people. It makes my job a lot easier."

Lewis threw for 73 yards and a touchdown to Brad Ansley. While the defense wasn't quite as good as it was the first time against Nevada – it allowed a field goal in the fourth quarter, after all – Ryan Eck intercepted two passes to kill Nevada drives. Dusty Frizzell recovered a fumble when Nevada had driven into Webb City territory on its first possession.

The trend of quick starts continued at Salem in the quarterfinals. The Redbirds scored on their first five possessions and led 34-0 at halftime before winning 41-0. Crane topped 100 yards again, but Lewis was the big performer on offense. He ran for three touchdowns and threw for two more. He scored on the team's first possession after taking over at the Salem 41-yard line, then ran for a 1-yard touchdown on the second possession. Later on, facing a third-and-1 at the Salem 30, Lewis was tackled for a 4-yard loss, but after a timeout he faked a handoff to Crane and passed to Wistrom on a slant route, who outran three defenders and scored. Later in the first half the Cardinals were facing a fourth-and-15 at the Salem 26. Thompson called a timeout, and when Webb City came back on to the field it lined up in the swinging gate formation with all its linemen on one side of the field and Lewis, Wistrom and another player on the opposite side. Lewis passed to Wistrom, who scored again

A week after Salem had rolled up 450 rushing yards against previously unbeaten Ozark, the Cardinals held Salem to only 79 yards.

"I never thought in my wildest dreams that we'd go in there and shut them out," Thompson said. "We were expecting to play four quarters. Our players seem to surprise us all the time."

With the arrival of the semifinals came a chance for revenge against St. Joseph Benton, the team that had ended Webb City's 1991 season and the career of the great Mark Smith on a field covered in thick mud. This time the game was at Cardinal Stadium, but the Redbirds again had trouble getting their running game going against Benton, and they reverted to trick plays in the first half to score points. They tried a run from the swinging gate formation on a third-and-8, but Ryan Eck was stuffed for no gain. With 20 seconds left in the half, Thompson called for a hook-and-ladder, a play he had added to the play book a week earlier. Matt Lewis threw to Brad Ansley on the left side, and Ansley pitched the ball to Stephen Crane who sprinted 33 yards down the sideline for a touchdown. The other score had come on a 23-yard end around run by Wistrom with 3:30 left in the first quarter.

But as the half arrived, the Cardinals had a slim lead – 12-0 – and Thompson wasn't pleased. He walked into the locker room and said something along the lines of, "Two scores and this is our last ball game. You think about that." Then he walked out and left the players to think about the message.

"I just remembered that two years prior, that's the team that had beaten us up in St. Joe and up to that point in my career that's probably the first time I've ever coached with a little bit of a grudge," Thompson says. "We had that in the back of our mind and felt like that was an opportunity we had taken away from us when they were sophomores. We probably played our kids longer than what I would have in a normal situation. Our kids just exploded. They played with a chip on their shoulder. They still remembered and we brought it up to them a lot about wanting to go out and make a statement and our kids did that. Those kids went out and played. We didn't do anything fancy. People knew what we were going to do and we just lined up and our kids believed in one another and played for their teammates."

Webb City didn't need trick plays in the second half. After Thompson's brief remarks at the half, the Cardinals came out and turned three turnovers into three touchdowns in the first nine minutes of the third quarter and went on to get their revenge in a big way, beating St. Joseph 46-0. The first touchdown came on a Lewis-to-Jayme Richardson pass, the second on a four-yard Lewis run, and the third on a Lewis-to-Ansley pass. In the fourth quarter Eck scored from three yards out, and Crane from a yard out. Crane finished with 96 yards on 23 carries, Lewis ran for 34 yards and threw for 129 yards and two scores.

While the offense had struggled for part of the game, the defense had been its usual self. Benton was held to only 71 offensive yards and four first downs in the game, and didn't reach Webb City territory until the last play of the game.

"It was a total defensive effort," Wistrom told the paper. "We just played great today. Defense wins championships and we're playing great defense right now."

"I keep telling them every week we're not going to shut everybody out,"

Thompson added. "But they keep doing it."

The state championship game a week later was another rematch, this time of the 1992 state title game against Columbia Rock Bridge, but the teams had switched roles. In 1992 Webb City had been the surprise team in the championship game, the rebuilding squad that won 10 straight games and beat a senior-dominated Bruins team that had steamrolled through the playoffs. But in 1993 Webb City was the senior-laden squad, and Rock Bridge was the team that had started slowly but gained steam in the playoffs.

"They remind me a lot of us last year," Thompson said at the time. "They had a good year and graduated most of their kids. It looks like they started a little slowly, but they've gotten better as the year has gone on."

Rock Bridge had two losses, but neither had come on the field. The Missouri State High School Activities Association had forced the Bruins to forfeit two games after they had used an ineligible player. The player, a backup, saw action on one play against Sedalia Smith-Cotton in week three, and another play against Fulton in week five. Rock Bridge appealed on the grounds that ineligible player had no effect on either game, but MSHSAA wouldn't budge.

The Bruins were a powerful running team, with nearly 4,000 yards on the ground that season, and they featured senior Jack Roach who had run for 2,104 yards and 25 touchdowns on 209 carries. Rock Bridge coach John Henage said at the time he was the best running back he'd ever coached, and Henage was in his 17th season.

Webb City's running game had accounted for 3,062 yards, with Crane rushing 138 times for 1,134 yards and Matt Lewis completing 63 passes for another 1,559 yards. Henage said the Cardinals were "big."

"I think they should be playing on Saturdays and Sundays, and we should be playing on Fridays," he said in reference to the Cardinals' offensive and defensive lines, which averaged about 230 pounds per player, nearly 40 pounds more than the Bruins.

About 5,000 Webb City fans drove to Springfield for the championship game on Black Friday, and they had plenty of reasons to celebrate. On Webb City's second possession, Grant Wistrom took an inside handoff but was stopped behind the line of scrimmage; before hitting the turf he pitched the ball to Stephen Crane, who ran 43 yards for a touchdown with just more than five minutes left in the quarter. With 1:31 left in the half, Matt Lewis threw a pass to Brad Ansley on an out pattern after the Cardinals got the ball at the Bruins' 40-yard line following an 8-yard punt. Ansley scored and Webb City held a 14-0 halftime lead.

The third quarter was largely a stalemate, but Rock Bridge finally captured some momentum late in the period when it scored on its second possession of the half, marching 67 yards and scoring on a 33-yard run to make it a 14-7 game. After that both teams exchanged punts, but Webb City finally put together a 51-yard drive over 13 plays. Facing a fourth-and-goal at the 1, Ryan Eck got the ball and punched it in to put the Cardinals ahead 20-7. The drive took more than seven minutes off the clock in the fourth quarter, and after Eck's touchdown, only 2:16 remained in the game. Rock Bridge wouldn't score again.

"It's tougher to stay on top than it is to get on top," Thompson said. "This year everybody was expecting the pressure. Everybody was expecting us to do well. To come out and answer the bell every Friday night and perform the way our players did was just unreal."

Webb City kept the Bruins' rushing game under control, allowing 165 yards and eight first downs, and Roach, the vaunted tailback, only rushed for 71 yards on 15 carries.

Two months later, Grant Wistrom, Brad Ansley and Travis Brock signed letters of intent to continue playing in college. Wistrom chose the University of Nebraska, Ansley Missouri Southern and Brock Southwest Missouri State University.

Grant Wistrom hauls in a pass through the fog during the 1992 sectional playoff game at Camdenton, which Webb City won 14-13. Photo by Bob Foos.

25. GRANT WISTROM

It would take two hands for Grant Wistrom to wear every championship ring he earned during his legendary football career. With two state championships in high school, three national championships in college and a Super Bowl win in the National Football League, Wistrom is the most decorated football player in Webb City history.

He finished his high school career with a 25-game winning streak and then won 26 straight games to start his college career at the University of Nebraska. While in high school, the Cardinals compiled a record of 48-6, and during his four years as a Cornhusker, Nebraska went 49-2. He was drafted in the first round of the 1998 NFL Draft by the St. Louis Rams and played in 132 NFL games, recording more than 400 tackles, 53 sacks and five interceptions.

But even while playing on Sunday, first for the Rams and then the Seattle Seahawks, it wasn't lost on Wistrom that his career had started in a small town in southwest Missouri, as a Webb City Cardinal. He thought about the fact often.

"Over and over again," he says now. "Over and over again. It hurt at first when I was drafted by the Rams because being a college-aged kid, I was ready to get out and see a little bit more of the world and they were the losingest team in the last decade. I got over that, and obviously winning a Super Bowl kind of eases a lot of pain, and the fact of being a Missouri kid, I went to high school in Missouri, played for the Rams, winning a Super Bowl and having your buddies still be able to come up for a game and how excited they would get for that, I was so appreciative of where I was and where I came from. It did help make me a better player because I did focus on that and I knew people from Webb City took a lot of pride in what I was doing at the time and I didn't want to let them down. I wanted to continue what I had started because you always hear, 'I'm from Webb City and I thank you for what you're doing.' I'm like, 'I just enjoy playing football and I'm glad you're a fan.' It helped keep me at the level I was at and helped propel me forward."

Wistrom's father, Ron, taught him the game of football at an early age, coaching him from the time he started playing in second grade on. Those early lessons didn't focus so much on the X's and O's, but more about the right way to play the game and how to attack life. The philosophy is simple: never take a play off, because eventually the person you're competing against will and that's when you take advantage of the opportunity.

"As a defensive end, there's 75 or 80 snaps a game you might be involved in and I know that if I play hard for every single one of them, chances are the guy I'm going against is going to take one play off," Wistrom says. "It may be a stalemate on 74 of those 75 plays, but that one play he takes off is my opportunity to create a big play. You never know when your opponent is going to let his guard down, which is why you have to keep your foot on that accelerator at all times."

Ron Wistrom coached each of his boys – Chance, Grant and Tracey – in baseball and football. They'd each say their father was the hardest coach they ever had, according to their mother, Kathy Wistrom, who wrote a book about the family titled *Mrs. Wistrom's ABC's: What I Learned Raising Three All-Americans.* She wrote that her husband was tough as a coach, but above all else, was honest and fair.

While Grant Wistrom had already made a name for himself in high school, especially as a first-team All-America selection, his reputation grew nationally while at Nebraska. As a freshman in the fall of 1994, he appeared in all 13 games and made 36 tackles with 4.5 tackles for a loss of 49 yards and 6.5 sacks for a loss of 55 yards. He recorded 11 quarterback hurries, and Wistrom was named Big Eight conference Newcomer of the Year while the Cornhuskers went undefeated and won their first national championship since 1971 by defeating the University of Miami 24-17 in the Orange Bowl.

During his sophomore season, Wistrom started all 12 games for Nebraska, which went undefeated again and won another national championship. During the season he made 44 tackles and four sacks, and led the team with 15 tackles for a loss. He hurried opposing quarterbacks 13 times. Nebraska's defense, which ranked second nationally against the run, allowed an average of only 14.5 points per game while the team averaged 53.2. Wistrom earned first-team all-Big Eight honors, and was a third-team All-America selection. Nebraska beat four ranked opponents and won the title with a 62-24 win against Florida in the Fiesta Bowl. That Cornhuskers team is considered one of the greatest in the history of college football.

In 1996, Nebraska started the season ranked No. 1 in the nation and finished 11-2 while playing in the first-ever Big 12 Championship game and then beating Virginia Tech 41-21 in the Orange Bowl.

Wistrom, then a junior, was named the Big 12 Defensive Player of the Year in the conference's first year of existence. His 75 tackles ranked third on the team and he led the Huskers with 20 tackles for a loss and 9.5 sacks. He also intercepted a pass, forced a fumble and blocked two kicks. He was a first-team All-American and a finalist for the Nagurski Trophy, awarded to the best defensive player in the country.

He was named Big 12 Defensive Player of the Year again as a senior captain in 1997, leading the vaunted Blackshirts defense again in tackles for a loss (17) and sacks (8.5), as well as forced fumbles (3).

Nebraska won its third national championship in four years, beating Tennessee 42-17 in the Orange Bowl after powering past Texas A&M 54-15 for the Big 12 title.

Once again a consensus All-American, Wistrom was also once again a finalist for the Bronko Nagurski Trophy and he received the Lombardi Award, given each year to the best lineman or linebacker.

Barely four years after helping Webb City win the 1993 Missouri state championship, Wistrom's name was etched into the Nebraska football record books. He is the career leader in tackles for loss with 58.5 for a total of 260 yards. He ranks second in career sacks with 26.5, just three behind outside linebacker Trev Alberts.

As a defensive end, Wistrom holds the Nebraska record for tackles in a game with 15, which he accomplished Nov. 29, 1996, against Colorado.
In 1998, Wistrom's No. 98 jersey was retired at Nebraska. In 2000 he was named to the Nebraska football All-Century Team, and in 2009 he was inducted into the College Football Hall of Fame.

In her book, Kathy Wistrom recalled how close Grant had come to signing with the University of Michigan, one of several major college programs who recruited her son, including Stanford and Miami. Grant returned from a campus visit to Michigan ready to sign with the Wolverines, but his parents encouraged him to take the rest of his college visits. During his visit to Nebraska, Trev Alberts, then the best player on the team, served as Grant's guide. Following Alberts' senior season in 1993, he earned the Dick Butkus Award as the nation's best linebacker, and was drafted fifth overall by the Indianapolis Colts in the 1994 draft. Alberts later worked as an analyst for ESPN's College GameDay. He was hired in 2009 as the University of Nebraska-Omaha's athletics director.

But even with someone of Alberts' stature giving Wistrom the campus tour, Grant still wanted to play for Michigan. Legendary Nebraska head coach Tom Osborne and assistant Ron Brown visited Webb City, and the family later arranged for Grant to take another visit to Nebraska, this time on their own dime, according to Kathy. Brown suggested Wistrom spend time with some of the team's players, and when Grant returned to the motel room he declared he wanted to be a Husker.

"He said he felt as if he really fit in with them," Kathy wrote. "They were more like him than the Hurricanes or Wolverines. We told him not to make a snap decision, but to go home and think about it. And one morning Grant said he had prayed about where to go, and when he got up in the morning, he knew he was supposed to be a Husker."

Of course, his football career was far from over when he was done at Nebraska. With the first pick of the 1998 NFL draft, the Indianapolis Colts selected Peyton Manning. With the fourth overall pick, the Oakland Raiders chose Heisman Trophy winner Charles Woodson. St. Louis then took Wistrom with the sixth overall pick.

The Rams had suffered through eight consecutive losing seasons and went 4-12 in Wistrom's first season. A year later, St. Louis was in the Super Bowl against the Tennessee Titans. The Rams led 23-16 late in the fourth quarter before the Titans drove to the 10-yard line with six seconds left in the game, and wide receiver Kevin Dyson was stopped a yard short of the goal line, giving Wistrom and the Rams a championship. The Webb City product made 33 tackles and six-and-a-half sacks that season and also had two interceptions.

In 2000 and 2001 Wistrom was even better, logging a total of 20 sacks and 95 tackles. He played for the Rams through the 2003 season before signing a six year, $33 million contract with the Seattle Seahawks. He made four trips to the playoffs with St. Louis and two Super Bowl appearances. He played in Seattle for three more seasons, then retired after the 2006 season.

During his nine-year professional career, Wistrom played in 132 games and started 114 of those. He finished with 53 sacks, five interceptions, eight fumble recoveries and 333 total tackles.

After all the years of football, all the accolades and awards, the championships and Super Bowls, when Wistrom reflects on his time playing football for Webb City, one of the first things that comes to mind is the parking lot outside the high school on game days.

"There's nothing like being in high school and you walk out of the school at 3 o'clock and you see a crowd lining up at the gate at 3 o'clock in the afternoon," he says. "Gates don't open till 5:30 or 6, but people are lining up at 3 o'clock and tailgating so they can get a good seat for the game. You can't put a price on how much it means to a kid, especially someone who loves football and has given so much of their time and energy to be a great football player and play on a great team. I talk about that still and what that meant to me as a player and still what that means to me to be from Webb City and to think about what that football program means to that town. It's still something that sticks with me."

Wistrom was likely a big attraction for those fans waiting in line, and there was good reason to show up early for a good seat inside the friendly – and not exactly large – confines of Cardinal Stadium with the way the Redbirds were playing in the early '90s.

Another of Wistrom's favorite memories as a Cardinal was the big showdown with Pittsburg in 1991. Both teams entered the game ranked No. 1 in their respective state with identical 5-0 records, and 7,500 fans had crammed into Cardinal Stadium to witness it. Webb City went on to win 28-19.

"There's two things I remember about that game," Wistrom says. "One is just the crowd at the game. The stands were packed on both sides, but then people were four or five deep all the way around the field. It was as much standing room only as you can get at a high school game and still be able to see the game. The other thing I remember is a hit between Mark Smith and Poncho Sales right at the goal line. He was a linebacker for Pittsburg, the best player on their team, and Mark was the best player on our team. The game was billed as a contest between those two players, and Mark hit that kid so hard. Mark was carrying the ball and just folded him like a cheap suit."

Wistrom and his brothers Chance and Tracey were each born in Joplin, but the family moved to Florida when Grant was 4. They moved back in time for Chance to start as a junior in 1988 for Jerry Kill and the Cardinals, and Grant watched a year later as his brother helped Webb City win its first state championship.

Webb City went 22-4 during Grant's freshman and sophomore seasons, advancing to the championship game and the state semifinals, but Wistrom says there wasn't an expectation that the team had to play for a state championship every year.

"Especially when we were there, to think we went out with the sole goal of winning the state championship, that just wasn't true," he says. "We had to win week one, we had to win the conference, we had to win the district and then let's worry about our first playoff game. There were a lot of little steps we had to accomplish before we got there."

After the 1991 season that ended in the semifinal loss to St. Joseph Benton, 1992 was considered a rebuilding year. A great senior class that included Mark Smith had graduated, and the Cardinals got off to a 1-2 start including a 33-7 loss against Bentonville, Arkansas.

"We got our butts kicked by Bentonville pretty badly," Wistrom recalls.

"After that we had this attitude like, 'We're not going to let this happen again.' We had worked way too hard in the offseason, we had struggled too long to get to that point. A resolve came over the team and that was the last game we lost for 25 games or so."

That season culminated in Kurt Thompson's first state championship as the team's head coach, and Grant Wistrom, like his brother Chance, participated in the rite of passage, the parade down Main Street after the title game.

"You've just accomplished everything you can at the high school level," Wistrom says. "To come back and celebrate with the fans who have been supporting you all year long, seeing that outpouring of emotion and excitement is really awesome. The Pee Wee football kids were watching those parades, now they're participating as a player in those parades. It all just continues to feed on itself."

By the time Wistrom was a senior, nobody was underestimating Webb City's football team, and he anchored one of the most dominant Cardinal defenses ever, with seven shutouts in the regular season and two in the playoffs. Wistrom says that team was the epitome of Webb City football.

"As great as that team was, very few kids were standouts as far as college athletes," he says. "I went on to play college football and a couple other kids had chances to, but it was really just a bunch of kids who had busted their butts to make themselves into the best football team they could be. That was the end product. It wasn't a result of incredible talent; there was some, but not an exorbitant amount. It was just a bunch of guys maximizing their abilities and playing together and playing for each other."

Now, more than 20 years after he played his last game for Webb City, Grant Wistrom is widely considered to be the best player ever to take the field for the Cardinals. He remains the only player in school history to earn USA Today first-team All-American honors, but Wistrom maintains he wouldn't receive all the personal accolades if not for the success of the teams he played on in high school.

"Being a good football player on a great team, you start to receive a lot more of that sort of attention," he says. "It is cool and I take pride in it, but it's all more a reflection of just how good our football teams were, just how dominant they were."

Wistrom gives a lot of credit for his career to Kurt Thompson, and says his old coach was paid far below minimum wage for the hours he put in. Wistrom now is a co-owner of CrossFit Springfield and CrossFit Springfield East, the training gyms that have become wildly popular. He spent a year as an assistant coach at Parkview High School in Springfield, where brother Chance was working as principal, and now coaches his son's youth team.

"That's about all I'm good for," he says.

In *Webb City Football: A History of Champions*, Wistrom wrote that the team's coaches instilled a belief in the players that they were the best, and the players believed that nobody worked harder than they did. He wrote that the players always believed they were going to win the game, no matter the circumstances.

His career has taken him to teams that possessed that mentality, and teams that didn't. Wistrom says he's been around programs with defeat "written on their face before they even step on the field." That mentality is also something that can change.

"It's just not because you're from Webb City you have a winning attitude," he says. "It's something that's instilled and driven in from day one that we will win, while in other places no matter what the score is, we will find a way to lose. That's a tough culture to turn around, to create that belief, but once you've got a program like Webb City's where we believe we're going to win no matter what, it's tough to turn that type of attitude around, as well."

That winning culture is one of the big reasons the Cardinals have become such a powerhouse, but it's far from the only reason. It's not a single answer, or an easy one, Wistrom says, as to why Webb City has been so good for so long. Instead, it's a lot of little things.

"It's the coaches, it's the players, it's the community, it's the parents, it's the Pee Wee program, it's the school system, it's the administrators, it's the principals, it's the teachers, it's the other students, it's everything," he says. "Everything lends to success there. There isn't one definite answer. It's a lot of little things that combine to make Webb City football what it is."

There is nothing that can compare with a high school football game in a place like Webb City, where the players take the field and play with heart and soul and for no other reason than they love the game. That's how Kathy Wistrom feels about the subject, and in her book she wrote how many of those players taking the field will never play beyond high school, and their only reward is the cheer of the crowd. Some, of course, are fortunate enough to win a state championship.

"This may sound dorky," she wrote, "but I think the first state title Grant's team won was probably just as exciting as his college championship or the Super Bowl ... watching the highlight tape of Grant's high school championship team gives me goose bumps! I can't explain it, but it's a thrill I'll never forget, and neither will the players. The entire town showed up for a parade. We had an autograph-signing session for the team, and everywhere the players went they were idolized."

Grant Wistrom's legacy is cemented at Webb City, but one would be remiss not to give brothers Chance and Tracey their credit, too. Not that anybody has forgotten. All three Wistroms will go down among the Webb City greats, and as a trio they are possibly the most prominent family to have donned the school colors, adding to the rich tradition of family members playing for the Cardinals.

Chance only played the one season, of course, after the family moved from Florida, and he helped Webb City to an 11-1 record and a playoff berth in 1988. He was a first-team all-state selection as a defensive lineman and was named a second team All American.

Kathy Wistrom wrote that her son was overlooked by the Division I schools because of his size – a 165-pound defensive end – but there were plenty of Division II schools interested and he chose Central Missouri State University after taking several college visits. On Thursday nights Ron and Kathy watched Tracey play junior high football. On Friday they watched Grant play for the high school, and on Saturdays the family would load up the car and make the drive to Warrensburg. Chance Wistrom's name is now etched into the Central record books. He is tied for third in career fumble recoveries with seven; he's tied for fourth for sacks in a season with 10, and he's tied for fifth all-time with 19 career sacks.

Tracey Wistrom, after finishing his high school career in the fall of 1996, chose to play for the University of Nebraska, but not before helping the Cardinals win the state basketball championship. According to Kathy Wistrom, a Nebraska football game is the only thing that surpasses a Webb City game, and one of the neatest experiences is the tunnel walk, where the players exit the locker room and take the field.

As a tight end for the Cornhuskers, Tracey finished his Nebraska career with 1,150 receiving yards, surpassing Junior Miller's school record of 1,045. His 58 career receptions rank 12th all time in the Husker record books. He twice earned first team all-Big 12 honors, and was a third team All-American in 2000.

26. THE MID NINETIES

The 1994 and 1995 seasons were "bad years" as Kurt Thompson puts it, and yet they were seasons a lot of teams would kill for. They were only "bad years" when compared to the success of Thompson's first four seasons, when Webb City went 48-6 with four trips to the playoffs and two straight championships with a 25-game winning streak to boot. That winning streak reached 26 games with the annual throttling of Carl Junction, 46-8, in the first game of the 1994 season, but came to an end with a 28-19 loss at Pittsburg a week later. Thompson's teams went 7-2 in 1994 and 6-3 in 1995 and didn't make the playoffs either year, ending a six-year streak of postseason football.

"Our kids did all the same things they had done the prior years; it just didn't happen," Thompson says. "People need to realize there's a fine line between winning and losing."

By late August 1994 Thompson and assistant coach Jesse Wall were still deciding who would play quarterback, the first time in five years the Cardinals had been without a quarterback in late August. Both Shawn Mayes and Mark Drake were competing for the job, and Thompson anticipated making a decision early in the week of the season opener at home against Carl Junction.

"Mark and Shawn are both good athletes," he said. "It's going to be a tough decision to make, but either one of them will do a good job."

There were other challenges facing the '94 squad, like an influx of young players without starting experience, and after that first home game against Carl Junction, the Cardinals didn't play at home again until week five. Tracey Wistrom, who was originally slated to play quarterback and defensive lineman, had also dislocated his knee and was expected to miss the first four weeks.

By the time the Bulldogs came to town, Mayes had been tabbed as the starting quarterback, leaving Drake open to play defense and do the team's kicking and punting.

"Shawn's a good leader," Thompson told the paper. "He takes charge and knows his own capabilities. Mark's playing so many other positions; it was a move that was best for the football team at this point."

Four starters returned on the offensive line: left tackle Anthony Black, left guard Jonathan Shull, right guard Chad Webb and Chad Boulware, who had played center but was now at right end. Newcomers were Andy Reynolds at left end, Craig Lankford at center and Mike Cook at right tackle. In the backfield

Webb City had Darris Lassiter, Rick Rivera and Evan Crutcher, and at flanker there was Brenten Byrd, Luke Boyer and Mark Drake.

Chad Webb and Chad Boulware would start at defensive ends; Andy Reynolds, Brad Gannaway and Evan Crutcher would play at inside linebacker; T.J. Houston and Lee Wyman were the team's outside linebackers; Mark Drake and Michael Hill were at cornerbacks and Darris Lassiter was at free safety. Gabe Gary, Mike Cook, Jonathan Shull and Anthony Black were all in the running to start at defensive tackle.

At the same time a bunch of new Cardinals were getting their first starting experience, an old great was getting his, too. Mark Smith earned his first start at strongside linebacker for the University of Arkansas in its season opener against Southern Methodist at War Memorial Stadium in Little Rock. At 6-foot-3 and 230 pounds, Smith wore No. 44.

"He plays really hard," said Arkansas linebackers coach Joe Pate. "He can be a good leader for us. We're looking forward to a very good year from Mark."

As a redshirt freshman in 1993, Smith had started in two games later in the season and played in all 11 games, recording 21 solo tackles and 41 total. He had been a backup for Shannon Wright, who died unexpectedly in the middle of the season.

According to Arkansas' preseason media guide, Smith would give himself the nickname "Bashful," and the business major's dream job would be heading an airline company. He would switch places with Derrick Thomas if he could switch places with any athlete, and he was a noted talent when it came to imitating cartoon voices.

In the 1994 season opener, five different Cardinals scored against the Bulldogs. Webb City actually trailed 8-6 before scoring six straight touchdowns to put the game away. After the loss at Pittsburg in week two, Webb City rattled off five straight wins – 22-6 at Hickman Mills, 30-23 at Coffeyville, 22-12 against Lebanon, 23-21 at Nevada and 29-16 against McDonald County. The win against Nevada was the team's first Southwest Conference game of the year, and the win against McDonald County marked the beginning of district play. In that game the Cardinals played without several starters after what was described as a "weekend drinking incident," but they survived a Mustangs' comeback to get the win. Mark Drake threw a 35-yard touchdown pass to Brenten Byrd in the first quarter, and Drake added six points on two field goals.

A capacity crowd showed up for the next district game against Neosho, a game that would likely decide who would advance to the playoffs. Neosho was undefeated and led by seniors, and won the game 21-14.

A week later, already out of the playoff picture, Webb City flattened rival Carthage 34-18 to end the 7-2 season on a high note. Mayes ran for three touchdowns, and the Cardinals finished with 447 rushing yards on 43 carries.

"We wish we were playing in the offseason but that can't happen every year," Thompson said. "It's kind of become a habit around here. People have kind of taken it for granted. There's been a lot of pressure because everyone expects them to win all the time and that's not going to happen."

The team also said goodbye to 22 seniors: Travis Hopper, Brenten Byrd, Andy Myers, Michael Hill, Mark Drake, Justin Luttrell, Brad Barton, T.J. Houston, Luke Boyer, Rick Rivera, J.J. Johnson, Chris Henson, Darris Lassiter, Craig Lankford, Troy Hulse, Anthony Black, Chad Webb, Justin Collard, Chad Boulware, Andy Reynolds, Lee Wyman and Brenton Taylor.

In 1995 Shawn Mayes was back at starting quarterback as a senior, and the Cardinals' resolve had been strengthened after a disappointing (but winning) season in 1994. The schedule was still tough, though, especially after Carl Junction had dropped Webb City as an opponent. Another Big 8 team, Seneca, agreed to play Webb City in Carl Junction's place. The Cardinals opened the season offensively with Jarred Lamb and Justin Allen at flanker, Tracey Wistrom and Chad Steele at tight end, Jonathan Shull and Matt Hakes at tackle, Kyle Foltz, Chad Rose and Aaron Goddard at guards, Josh Beecham at center, Mayes at quarterback, Evan Crutcher at fullback and Matt Mense at tailback. Defensively, Chad Rose and Mike Welch were at tackle, Jonathan Shull and Kyle Foltz were at ends, Evan Crutcher and Mark Bertrand were at inside linebackers, Scott Spence and Tracey Wistrom were at outside linebackers, Matt Mense was at safety and Shawn Mayes and Ryan Burpo were at cornerbacks.

Webb City led Seneca by eight points in the third quarter, but the Indians came back and won 21-15. Seneca later completed an undefeated season and beat Herculaneum 35-14 in the Class 3A state championship.

A week after the Seneca loss, Webb City lost 30-12 at home against Pittsburg to start the season 0-2. After that Webb City won five straight: 42-7 against Monett, 48-7 against Coffeyville, 32-6 at Lebanon, 32-12 against Nevada and 31-13 at McDonald County. Just like a year earlier, the Cardinals were 2-0 in Southwest Conference play and 1-0 in the district with a game against Neosho to likely decide who would go to the playoffs. Again, the Wildcats won. Neosho's formidable defense limited the Cardinals to 135 total yards and a shutout in the 7-0 victory. It was the first time Webb City hadn't scored in a game since the 1991 semifinals against St. Joseph Benton, the "Mud Bowl." The only score was a 1-yard run by Neosho quarterback Eric Hughes in the second quarter.

Again, just like a year earlier, Webb City ended the season on a high note by blowing Carthage out of the water, 53-20. The win gave the Cardinals a share of the conference championship with Neosho. Ryan Burpo rushed for 109 yards on 12 carries and had three touchdowns; Mayes scored twice and ran for 84 yards. Evan Crutcher added a five-yard run in the second quarter, and Mark Bertrand scored from 19 yards out in the fourth quarter.

Webb City once again said goodbye to a talented senior class: Shawn Mayes, Justin Allen, Evan Crutcher, Jared Lamb, Scott Stanko, Aaron Goddard,

Dustin Moore, Travis Passley, Jonathan Shull, Kyle Fultz, Oliver Cornell, Chad Steele, Nathan Dawson and Mike Powell.

Several players earned all-Southwest Conference honors. Selected to the first team were Jonathan Shull at defensive end, Chad Rose at defensive tackle, Tracey Wistrom at outside linebacker and tight end, Evan Crutcher at inside linebacker, Shawn Mayes at defensive back, Kyle Foltz at guard and Mike Welch at punter. Kyle Foltz, Aaron Goddard and Ryan Burpo earned second-team honors on defense, and Jonathan Shull, Josh Beecham, Shawn Mayes, Evan Crutcher, Matt Mense and Mike Welch were second-team selections on offense. Mike Welch, Mark Bertrand, Matt Hakes, Aaron Goddard, Chad Steele and Ryan Burpo also earned honorable mention honors.

A few months later, in February 1996, a former great returned to Webb City High School for a ceremony prior to a Cardinals' basketball game. John Roderique's No. 36 was formally retired at Webb City, 10 years after he had helped the Cardinals to the state semifinals.

"I like to think we got the winning tradition started," he said.

The ceremony was a chance for fans to relive Roderique's great playing career. He was a first-team all-conference linebacker, punter and kicker at Webb City, a second-team all conference running back, KSN Player of the Year, and was also selected to first team all-area, all-district and all-state teams. In 1988 he was a first team all-conference player for the Gorillas, a first-team All-American, and PSU's Most Valuable Defensive Player. In 1989 he was the MIAA Defensive Player of the Year, an Associated Press Small College All-American, a Division II All American, a *Football Gazette* All-American, a Kodak All-American and PSU's Carnie Smith Most Valuable Player award winner.

He was now an assistant coach and recruiter for Pittsburg State.

In the fall of 1996 the focus was entirely on getting back to the playoffs and trying to win another championship. It had been two years since the Cardinals made the postseason, but they returned a loaded roster. On offense, most of the skill players were back, like Tracey Wistrom, Matt Mense and Mark Bertrand. Quarterback Shawn Mayes had graduated, and Mense moved from running back to quarterback with junior Josh Chapman backing him up. Mense, a senior, had fully recovered from a knee injury suffered in 1995. Bertrand and Ryan Burpo were in the backfield, and Scott Murray, Adam Schooley and Ty Wynne would also see time in the backfield. The Cardinals also expected to throw the ball more with the 6-foot-5 Wistrom on the field, and they also had tight ends Scott Spence and Chris Bruffett, and wide receiver Austin Midcap.

Four starters returned on the offensive line: Josh Beecham, Caleb Miller, Chad Rose and Nathan Hoenshell. The other starter was Matt Hakes, with Mike Welch, Adam Collard, Philip Stotts and Andy Martinez in reserve roles.

The team's defensive unit was also expected to be strong with Rose, Stotts,

Collard and Vance Endicott on the line, Wistrom, Bertrand and Miller playing linebacker and Burpo at defensive back. Wynne, Schooley, Chapman, Richie Adkins and Cole Shewmake were competing for jobs at cornerback. Welch was likely the biggest kicker in the state at six-feet, 260 pounds. He was also a state champion golfer.

In the newspaper, Thompson said the players needed to back up their words on the field. The senior class was just freshmen when Webb City had last made the postseason.

"If these players know what it takes to be great, I haven't seen it yet in practice," he said.

The schedule was also maybe the toughest in Thompson's seven years; the season started at home against Branson, then the Cardinals went to Pittsburg before hosting Joplin, Kansas City Central and Lebanon.

"We could be 0-4 to start off the season real easily," he said.

Branson returned nine defensive starters, a quarterback, fullback and tailback, and the Pirates had gone to the playoffs in 1995 but lost to Seneca. When the game started, Branson got the ball at the 35-yard line and promptly drove the field and scored, and then Webb City failed to convert a fourth-down attempt in Branson territory on its first possession. At the start of the second quarter Branson drove the ball again into the Webb City red zone, but Adam Schooley recovered a fumble on the 17 and the Cardinals played it safe on their next drive with the ground game. Burpo, Mense and fullback Mark Bertrand each had long runs to move the ball down to the Branson 22, and then Mense scored the team's first touchdown of the season on an option keeper.

Again the Cardinals had trouble stopping the Pirates, but this time Branson moved downfield with the passing game and kicked a field goal. With less than a minute left in the half, Mense guided the team on a long drive with passes to Austin Midcap and Richie Adkins, and Thompson called timeout with 10 seconds left. Mense threw to Wistrom in the corner of the end, who made a dramatic catch, and Burpo's two-point conversion gave Webb City a 15-9 halftime lead. Burpo carried the ball on Webb City's first drive of the third quarter, which put the Cardinals up by two touchdowns, and Wynne added a seven-yard touchdown after Burpo left with leg cramps. Branson battled back, though, scoring early in the fourth quarter, but the Cardinals hung on to open the year with a 36-21 win.

The Cardinals allowed only 76 yards at Pittsburg, and won 33-13 to avenge losses to the Purple Dragons in two straight years. Webb City scored on its first three possession and led 20-0 at the half behind a seven-yard run from Bertrand, a five-yard run by Burpo and a 1-yard run by Mense. In the fourth quarter, Bruffett caught a 37-yard touchdown pass and Burpo scored from seven yards out. Mense finished with more than 100 yards on the ground.

In week three, Tracey Wistrom had a monster game as the Cardinals stunned a capacity crowd and steamrolled Joplin 41-6, and Webb City was now ranked first in the state. Wistrom caught three touchdown passes from Matt Mense and took a 53-yard reverse in for a touchdown. On defense he made three tackles for a loss and had an interception. Mike Welch boomed field goals of 31 and 47 yards, the 47-yarder coming in the final minute of the half to put the Cardinals up 28-0.

Kansas City Central came to town in week four and almost immediately things went sour for the visitors. The Eagles punted on their first possession, Tracey Wistrom blocked the kick and Webb City scored a safety when the ball went out the left side of the end zone after a scramble for it. The Cardinals got the ball at the Central 36 after the free kick, and on the first play from scrimmage Ryan Burpo scored the first of his two touchdowns. Matt Mense's two-point conversion made it 10-0 less than three minutes into the game. Burpo scored from 41 yards out on Webb City's second possession, and when Central got the ball back it fumbled on its first play. Wistrom recovered the ball and Mense scored on a three-yard run to make it 24-0. Central then gave the ball back on a 4-yard punt, and when the Cardinals came onto the field, Central had only 10 players, leaving Wistrom wide open for a 22-yard touchdown reception. With 1:17 left in the first quarter, Webb City led 31-0.

Mense connected with Wistrom for another touchdown pass, making it 38-0 before the game took a turn for the ugly with four fumbles over the course of 17 plays. Webb City led 38-6 at halftime and went on to win 51-14.

Against Lebanon, Webb City trailed 7-0 after a quarter but took a five-point lead into the half. In the second half, though, Webb City exploded for 35 points and won 47-7. Burpo ran for more than 200 yards and Mense threw for 194 yards in a balanced offensive attack. Thompson spread the offense out in the third quarter, moving Wistrom off the line, and the Cardinals covered 70 yards in six running plays, with Burpo covering the final 37 yards and scoring to make it a 19-7 game. Burpo runs and Wistrom receptions took the ball down to the Lebanon 8 later on and Mense carried down to the 2, but two illegal procedure penalties led to a third-and-goal from the 12. Thompson called timeout and called for a tight-end option play. Wistrom got the ball on a reverse, ran down the line and pitched to Burpo, who carried the ball to the 6. On fourth-and-goal, Webb City lined up in the swinging gate formation and appeared to be settling for a field goal. But before the linemen moved back to their conventional formation, Wistrom snapped the ball to Mense, who faked a run, stepped back and passed to Wistrom for the touchdown. One Mense touchdown and two by Bertrand iced the game.

For two straight years Webb City's playoff hopes had ended thanks to Neosho, and now the Cardinals had a chance for some revenge against the Wildcats after starting the season 5-0. District realignment meant the game had no outcome on the postseason, but it was still a conference match and those previous district losses hadn't been forgotten. Early on Neosho got all the breaks and held a 14-0 lead in the second quarter. Would it be three straight years of torment at the hands of Neosho? It was a touchdown game with 6:16 left in the half when Neosho lined up to punt. Thompson gambled and sent nine players after the block, and Chris Bruffett got his hand on the ball. Unfortunately the ball bounced and was caught by Neosho's Matt Despit behind the line of scrimmage, and he eluded the rest of Webb City's return team for a 60-yard touchdown. A 74-yard drive over 11 plays was capped by a short Matt Mense run to put Webb City on the scoreboard for the first time. After that the Cardinals recovered a fumble at the Wildcat 25, and with just 45 seconds left in the half Mense found Wistrom in the corner of the end zone for another touchdown. Mense plunged in for the two-point conversion to put Webb City up 15-14 at the break.

The momentum didn't carry over into the third quarter. Webb City punted on its first possession of the second half, and Neosho promptly drove to the Webb City 26-yard line. It was time for the Cardinals' defense to make some plays. Burpo tipped a pass out of the hands of a Neosho receiver at the goal line, and on a fourth-down field goal attempt Adam Schooley blasted through the line to block the kick. With the ball again, the Cardinals moved into Neosho territory before penalties backed them into a first-and-20 hole and Thompson again called for the swinging gate. Just like before, Wistrom snapped to Mense, then caught the pass for a 15-yard gain and Mense kept the ball for a first down a few players later. Burpo later scored a 1-yard touchdown. On their next possession, Bertrand scored from five yards out and Webb City led 29-14, a score it would hold for the rest of the night. Burpo rushed for 141 yards in the game.

McDonald County came to Cardinal Stadium for homecoming night, which was also the last game before district season started. In its first and only shutout of the season, Webb City won 36-0. In the first half the Mustangs tallied 85 yards of offense, and in the second half they didn't get past their own 44 (and gained only 16 yards). As usual, Wistrom hauled in the majority of Mense's passes – six for 86 yards – but Mense also spread his targets around. Burpo caught three passes, and backup quarterback Josh Chapman hauled in an 11-yard first down catch. He finished with two receptions for 19 yards. Richie Adkins was in on the action, too. On defense Mark Bertrand returned a fumble 43 yards for a touchdown, and Wistrom recovered a Mac County fumble at midfield.

And so Webb City took its 7-0 record into district play, and the new district groupings were evident from the very start when Webb City faced Harrisonville instead of a team closer to home. Harrisonville, too, was 7-0. Webb City had maintained its No. 1 ranking since the big win against Joplin, while Harrisonville had moved up in the polls to No. 3 in the state. The big match-up would be Webb City's offense, which averaged more than 400 yards and 39 points per game, against a Harrisonville defense that had allowed a total of 417 yards all season, and only 53 points. The Wildcats' defense had recorded 10 interceptions, and quarterback Matt Mense hadn't yet thrown one.

In racking up seven wins, Webb City had won by an average of 28 points, but starting with the Harrisonville game, three weeks of district play were a different story. The Cardinals won all three, but none were decided by more than 10 points.

There were 10 turnovers in the game at Harrisonville evenly split between both teams. Webb City fumbled on its second offensive play of the game, but Caleb Miller made a big stop to halt Harrisonville, which already led 7-0 after scoring on its first drive of the game. After that the teams exchanged touchdowns, and the Cardinals pulled ahead 14-13 with two minutes left in the first half; then Harrisonville punted, but the Cardinals muffed the return and the Wildcats had the ball at the Webb City 37. Two plays later, Nathan Hoenshell picked off a pass to preserve the fragile lead going into the half.

Webb City's first drive of the second half stalled and a punt was returned all the way to the Cardinals' 27. A big fourth-down stand by the Webb City defense kept the Redbirds ahead by a point, and the offense added to that with a 13-play, 71-yard drive capped by Mense's second touchdown of the game. Mike Welch added the two-point conversion to make it a 22-13 game. After that the game got sloppy again. The teams traded turnovers over the game's next five possessions, one of which was an Adam Schooley interception at midfield. With a chance to put the game away, the Cardinals fumbled again at the Wildcat 18 with barely five minutes left in the game.

A holding penalty and a four-yard loss pushed Harrisonville back to its 5. On a third-and-23, Harrisonville quarterback Willie Pruitt dropped back to pass and overthrew his target. The ball ended up in the hands of Webb City defensive back Josh Chapman, who followed the cavalry into the end zone with four minutes left to play. The Cardinals led 29-13.

Harrisonville went on a long scoring drive in the final minutes of the game to pull within a touchdown and a two-point conversion, but Ryan Burpo recovered the onside kick and Mense took a knee to end the game at 29-21.

The Cardinals were 8-0, and they controlled their own destiny – as did Nevada. The Tigers had won six straight games and were red hot when district play started, outscoring opponents 230-32 during the winning streak. The game would likely decide who would win the district, though a two-way or even three-way tie wasn't impossible, and it would almost certainly decide the Southwest Conference championship.

Midway through the first quarter, Nevada returned a kickoff 80 yards for a touchdown and went ahead 10-6 in the game at Webb City, but Nevada's defense couldn't stop the Cardinals, who scored on their first three possessions and led 20-10 at the break. Perhaps motivated at the half after only trailing by 10 points, Nevada's defense was a pumped-up bunch to start the third quarter, and it stopped Webb City on the Cardinals' first drive. Then Nevada's offense scored, becoming just the second team after Pittsburg to score points on Webb City in the third quarter. The 77-yard drive covered 12 plays and made it a 20-17 game with just more than three minutes left in the quarter.

Mense ran six times during Webb City's 11-play drive to answer, and he exploded through the line on a fourth-and-short in Nevada territory to gain 26 yards and set up a first-and-goal for Bertrand, who scored on the very next play. Nevada settled for a 30-yard field goal to keep it a one-possession game, and the Tigers tried an onside kick – it didn't travel far enough, and Tracey Wistrom scooped the ball up and ran all the way to the Nevada 33. Welch's 31-yard field goal made it 30-20 Webb City, but Nevada still had time left to throw the ball down the field. The Tigers completed two of their five attempts before Josh Chapman intercepted a pass to clinch the win.

The win clinched the district, and the Cardinals were finally back in the playoffs.

They concluded the regular season at Carthage and Thompson took on a familiar face: Jesse Wall. The former Webb City assistant was now head coach at Carthage.

"Nobody's going to fool anybody in this game," Thompson said. "It might come down to who's got the better mud tires on."

Heavy rains on the Wednesday before the game left a muddy field for both teams. Carthage was wrapping up a poor season, having won just twice, but the rivalry was enough to motivate the Tigers to play their rivals close and Webb City only won 14-7. Webb City's high-powered offense barely eclipsed 200 yards in the game, and the difference was a pair of touchdowns by Ryan Burpo. A fumble late in the game gave Carthage a chance to tie it up, but Caleb Miller made a huge fourth-down stop to cap Webb City's undefeated regular season.

With the beginning of the postseason Webb City traveled north to Kansas City to face Center. The Yellowjackets boasted three solid running backs and a huge offensive line that averaged 275 pounds, but the smaller, quicker Cardinal line dominated the game. Even so, the Cardinals trailed at the half for the first time all season, 7-6. The second half was a different story; Webb City's defense gave up only 38 yards and the Cardinals cruised to a 34-7 win.

"We played our hearts out tonight," Thompson said. "We came out and played big in the second half against a tough team."

Quarterback Matt Mense and tight end Tracey Wistrom were keys to the second-half turnaround. Mense scored three rushing touchdowns and Wistrom scored one of his own while catching all three of Mense's second-half passes for 96 yards. Mense led the second half rushing attack with 73 yards.

The Monday night quarterfinal game against Ozark would mark the last time Webb City's seniors ever played at Cardinal Stadium, and they went out with style in one of the team's most-dominant games all year, a 42-13 triumph.

"We've stepped up our play the last few weeks," said Wistrom, one of those seniors. "We just want to keep improving each week."

It was also the last time a Wistrom would play at Cardinal Stadium. While following in the footsteps of his older brothers, Chance and Grant, initially put pressure on Tracey, by 1996 it didn't affect him anymore.

"I think I'm past the pressure now," he told the newspaper. "It was tough at first, but I think I've proved myself, and people are taking notice of what I can do."

Wistrom had been a huge part of the 11-0 start, and so had quarterback Matt Mense. Mense had accounted for six touchdowns in two playoff games.

"I try not to look too much at the numbers," he said. "But there are two that I do know: no interceptions and no sacks. That means we've got a pretty good offensive line."

Every member of the offensive line was a senior: Chris Bruffett, Scott Spence, Adam Collard, Caleb Miller, Chad Rose, Josh Beecham, Nathan Hoenshell, Matt Hakes and Wistrom.

As the game started, Webb City drove into Ozark territory but turned it over on downs. Josh Chapman got it back in a hurry with yet another interception, and then he caught his first touchdown pass of the season. On first down Mense threw to Wistrom, and Thompson noticed the cornerback on Chapman immediately left to help cover the big tight end. The very next play Thompson yelled, "Catch the ball Tracey!" before the ball was snapped, and sure enough Chapman was wide open on the sideline and he scored a 34-yard touchdown.

"We hadn't put that play in all year, we hadn't even practiced it, but it was there, and Matt put the ball in where it needed to be," Thompson said.

Later in the first half Mense executed the two-minute drill and covered 44 yards with three passes. A pass to Wistrom in the end zone fell incomplete with eight seconds left in the quarter, so Webb City settled for a 23-yard field goal instead and led 17-0 after two quarters. In the third quarter, Webb City dominated. The Cardinals had done it all year long, outscoring opponents 104-14 in that quarter alone. By the time there was 8:32 left in the fourth quarter, the Cardinals led 36-0 following the second of three Ty Wynne touchdowns.

Now just one win away from returning to the state championship game – to be played at the Trans World Dome in St. Louis – Webb City traveled to Excelsior Springs to face the fourth-ranked Tigers in a semifinal battle. They had won the 1994 state championship and entered the '96 game with an 11-1 record, and hadn't yet allowed a point in the playoffs. Offensively, Excelsior Springs' go-to weapon was a 230-pound fullback, Tucker Woolsey, who would go on to become a four-year starting fullback for Northwest Missouri State University and help the Bearcats win back-to-back national championships in 1998 and 1999.

Three fumbles by Excelsior Springs and a Ryan Burpo interception kept the Cardinals in the game, but they too had turnover problems, with three in the game. From the very start it was evident this was going to be a tough game. On Webb City's first drive it took 13 plays to move the ball 37 yards, and on a third-and-six Mense was sacked for the first time all year. Following a punt, the Tigers promptly moved 81 yards in only six plays and scored when the 5-foot-9 Woolsey bowled his way 22 yards for a touchdown. He rushed three times on the drive and totaled 62 of his 119 yards.

Webb City punted on its second possession, but then so did Excelsior Springs – twice in a row, in fact. The second fumble finally led to Webb City points on a 14-yard Mense run. He kept the ball again on a two-point try but came up a half yard short. At the half the game was still gridlocked, but Excelsior Springs led 7-6.

Things didn't start much better after the half. A bad snap on a punt gave the ball to Excelsior Springs just 30 yards from the end zone. But on fourth and short, quarterback Matt Sullivan was tackled for a loss by Adam Schooley. Webb City finally had some momentum, and it drove all the way to the Tigers' 3-yard line before fumbling.

On Excelsior Springs' next possession Burpo blocked a punt and the Cardinals had the ball in the red zone again. After an incomplete pass on third-and-10, a field goal put them ahead 9-7.

Caleb Miller recovered a fumble and Thompson reached into his bag of tricks to give his offense a boost. Mense handed off to Wistrom on a reverse, and he pitched the ball to Burpo, who evaded a group of defenders and gained 30 yards. The drive stalled, though, and a 35-yard field goal was wide right; it remained a 9-7 game.

The clock winding down, Excelsior Springs had time for one last drive. The Tigers started at their own 20 and over the next two-plus minutes moved the ball into Webb City territory. With 39 seconds left in the game, Excelsior Springs put the game in the hands of Woolsey. He broke through the defense and scored on a 14-yard run. Final score: Excelsior Springs 14, Webb City 9. The 12-1 season was over.

"If any group I've coached deserved to go to a championship, it was this one," Thompson said after the game. "They have been more focused than any team I've ever had."

It was a shocking loss, and the players took it especially hard. Even today Thompson remembers the post-game mood.

"That group was a lot like the '93 team," he says. "A very close senior group, very good players. It meant a whole lot to them. The kids played hard; a lot of them had been two-year starters and some of them three-year starters. Things went as planned until we got beat by a very good football team in Excelsior Springs. We probably played the state championship game that day. We played very well; they scored in the last couple minutes of the game to beat us. That's a state championship-caliber football team. Those kids struggled. I remember in the locker room they were broken hearted. I remember walking out and all those senior kids, they were just sitting in the locker room and didn't want to come out. That's the first time I've ever gone out and talked to six or eight dads and told them to go in and talk to their sons. It really hurt those kids. It meant a whole lot to them. Some were younger siblings, like Grant's little brother Tracey. They were kids who were waiting for their time and it just didn't happen for them. They had a great season, a great year; they just knew they were going to win a state championship. They just thought it was going to happen. Not that they didn't work at it. They worked their tails off, but they got their hearts broken by a good football team that day."

A week later Excelsior Springs pounded Camdenton 36-15 in the championship game.

It was the first time in five years Webb City had ended the season with a loss.

A little more than two months later, Tracey Wistrom followed in his brother Grant's footsteps and signed with the University of Nebraska to play tight end. He chose the Cornhuskers over Northwestern University and Kansas State. At the same time, Nathan Hoenshell signed with the University of Missouri-Rolla.

The semifinal loss would also be Kurt Thompson's last game at Webb City. As the school year drew to a close, Thompson announced he was leaving to become an assistant coach at Coffeyville Community College where he would coach the defensive secondary.

"This is an opportunity for me to get my feet wet coaching college football," he told the paper. "This was too good to pass up. I hope this will open some doors for me."

Thompson left a legacy of success on the field – he compiled a 74-12 record in seven seasons – and several of his 12 assistant coaches went on to contribute to education in the Webb City area. Trey Moeller went on to become athletics director and assistant principal at Webb City; Clay Deem served on the Carl Junction school board and in the admissions office at Missouri Southern; Jesse Wall, a "football guru" according to Thompson, took over at Carthage and later coached at Joplin, in Oklahoma and at Carl Junction.

Thompson told the newspaper one of his most vivid memories was the first offensive series in his first game as a head coach.

"I was so nervous, I wasn't exactly sure what plays to call," he said.

Thompson spent one season at Coffeyville, and later coached at Kickapoo and Republic. He coached his last game for Republic in 2012, finishing that season with a 5-6 record. In his seven seasons at Webb City, he won two state championships and played for a third, and went to the semifinals twice while making the playoffs five times. That success was a factor in his decision to leave.

"A little bit that played into it was whether you can keep that going, I'm not going to lie," he says. "I always wanted to scratch that itch of coaching at the collegiate level and I had that opportunity. Hindsight being like it is, it wasn't very smart. John and I were good friends, we talked all the time, and before that time we had talked about how we oughta just switch jobs for a year to see what it would be like for both of us. He was the guy I think was going to be the person if he wanted the job. He and I talked at length going into it. I don't think he talked to anybody, but I think he had as much weighing on my decision. It would affect him as much as anyone. I decided to make that jump. Hindsight is 20-20. I left a great place and did not realize what type of program was there and was going to continue. We had no idea about that. John since then has had some opportunities and when it comes down to it you'd be silly to leave. I said don't ever do it. Think about it but it'd have to be something really sweet before you'd get out of that now. It just felt like that was the right time for me to do that."

What Jerry Kill started in 1988 and 1989, Kurt Thompson built and grew throughout the 1990s. If the 1985 team and then Kill's excellent two seasons put Webb City football on the map, Thompson made sure it stayed there. Of course, the question people always ask is what exactly makes Webb City so good? It's a question Thompson still is asked all the time, and he doesn't know how to answer. It's not a simple answer, either.

"Just a lot of tradition," he says. "A lot of kids who work their tails off. I still think there's not a coaching staff that does a better job preparing their kids than they do. I firmly believe that. You go watch them practice. We tried to do it when I was there and it's only gotten better because the numbers have gotten better. We tried to run it like a college program, as far as training our athletes and practicing like that, trying to maximize your time. And at that time we were closer to it than anybody else. The game's changed quite a bit. When Coach Kill got there in '89 nobody had a summer weight lifting program. He had them all come in and had them all lifting. The first two or three years of my career that's one of the reasons we were winning. We were lifting all summer and had a weightlifting class in school and a lot of schools weren't doing that and our kids were much stronger and they believed in themselves. We were much more physical because of that. We would put them through hell in the summer time. We'd have two and a half weeks of two-a-day practices and those were tough. Those kids came out of that and they were ready for school to start so they could back off of practice time. There's just a lot of tradition. They've had some darn good high school football players go through there. Anybody can coach a great player. If you can make that average kid into a good player, make a below average kid into an average player, just elevate them a little bit, I think they do that as well as anybody. There's a system they believe in and those kids know that system; it's ingrained in them. They know what to expect every day at practice, they know what to expect scheme-wise offensively and defensively. They know what to do, and John's been patient to line up and just run the football at people and most people don't do that anymore because it's not the in thing to do. He's stuck with it and won a lot of games doing that."

That system ingrained in the players, the veer offense, is often credited as a major factor. For the fan in the bleachers it looks like a simple system that's hard to stop, but Thompson says it's not as simple as it looks.

"You can watch Webb play and think they're running the same play over and over, but it may be blocked differently each time they run it," he says. "It's very difficult to defend. You've got to have discipline to do it. I think one of the reasons they flourish so much now offensively is everybody's in the spread offense so they have one week, about three practice days, to prepare to defend that. You can't do that. People have a tendency to be able to defend what they're doing and how many people are running that offense? So they don't have a clue and if the coaches do, they get out there and practice and try to teach their kids and then things are OK for a little while but on third-and-one when they don't do what they're supposed to do defensively that's when you break a big play and score touchdowns."

Webb City is also known for making smart adjustments at the half. Countless times in the last two decades an opponent will play the Cardinals close for two quarters and then Webb City turns the second half into a blowout. Whether it's because those other teams worked themselves up into a frenzy and were emotionally drained by the half or because the Cardinals made the right adjustments, or both, it's hard to argue with the results. Recall that Thompson's final team outscored opponents by 100 points in the third quarter. At the time he didn't think he was making many adjustments in the locker room, but after being exposed to other coaches and programs he realizes he was.

"Our kids understood what we were doing and we would come in and make subtle adjustments at halftime," he says. "We're going to block it differently. That's all I ever knew. I still remember we used to watch a lot of video and we didn't attack schemes as much as individuals. We would watch a person. Whether we wanted to run to the right or left, and in our offense we had enough flexibility to do it. At halftime maybe not making scheme adjustments but kids saying, 'Coach we need to run at 75, he's not as good as 52 on the other side,' so scheme-wise we would flip our offensive line. Our kids understood what we were wanting, so they'd come in at halftime and give us information. It may not have been a scheme thing, but 'We need to run at this guy, Coach; he's not very good' or 'We're really wearing him out; he's about to give up.' That's what we really tried to attack."

There's another reason the Cardinals are so good, especially at home, and it's impossible to quantify. The fact that Webb City has become such a dominant program and often seems destined to win a game gets into the heads of opposing teams. Often, players feel like they're going to lose the game before they even take the field. Thompson has an interesting perspective on this phenomenon, having experienced its benefits on the home sideline but also how hard it is to overcome from the other side. When he coached at Republic he led his teams into Cardinal Stadium and he said it's a big factor.

"Your kids don't think they can win when they go there," he says. "That's the advantage. It's the darndest thing I don't know how to get over it. I don't understand it, but getting 16-, 17-, 18-year-old kids to get over that mental block is something different."

Thompson has become lifelong friends with many of his former players. He still talks to Mark Smith every few weeks.

"I've been pallbearers at funerals and best mans in players' weddings that I coached," he said. "That's a unique situation. Just a lot of good people and probably some of those kids appreciate it more now than what they did back then. It was a great place to be at that time and still is. Coach Kill has told me every time I've been around him that it's the best job he ever had. He's said that in clinics where I've listened to him speak. I remember one time Mark McDonald, Coach Roderique, me and Coach Kill were sitting talking and Coach Kill was giving us hell saying we were the stupid ones because we left there and John's the only one smart enough to stay.

Within a week of Thompson's announcement that he was leaving for Coffeyville, it was already common knowledge in Webb City that the job had been offered to John Roderique and that he had accepted. The school board made it official at its May meeting.

Andrew Shull, left, and Philip Stotts, right, celebrate a Webb City win during the 1997 championship season. Photo by Bob Foos.

27. JOHN RODERIQUE'S FIRST CHAMPIONSHIP

Richie Adkins was a junior during the semifinal season of 1996 and a senior during John Roderique's inaugural season at the helm. That '96 team is one of the best teams that never won a title, he says.

"We went up to Excelsior Springs and had some tough luck up there, but that was a really, really good football team my junior year," he says. "I don't know if it's a forgotten team just because it didn't win a state championship, but there was a lot of talent on that team, a lot of really good players. That was a really tough loss; I'll never forget that one and I'm sure those seniors who were a year older than me haven't forgotten it, either."

Adkins moved to Webb City when he was in the fourth grade. A wide receiver and corner, he remembers Kurt Thompson as a hard-nosed coach but a fun one to play for. You always knew Thompson had your back, he says, and it was Thompson who convinced Adkins as a young high school player that he could be a decent player for the Cardinals.

"He was a real good motivator," he said. "I think that same year, that junior year, was a tough loss for him too. I know he'd put a lot of time into that team and a lot of time in with those seniors."

With Thompson's departure, and the graduation of Tracey Wistrom and the rest of his talented senior class, there were once again big question marks surrounding the football program in the summer and fall of 1997. Roderique had never been a head coach, and whether he would be any good remained to be seen; all Adkins and his teammates knew was that they'd just lost a great one. They didn't really know much at all about Roderique, in fact.

"We knew who he was just because he's from Webb City and was on some good teams at Webb City," Adkins says. "We knew who he was and where he came from, but that was about it. We knew we were losing a good coach in Coach Thompson, and at that point there were a lot of people unsure about what the future might hold. Turns out it was a pretty good thing."

When Thompson replaced Jerry Kill in 1990, he tried to keep as many things as he could the same for an easy transition, and it paid off with a 10-3 season and a state championship appearance. Roderique did the same. Adkins says that was a big help. The conditioning program was already in place, the offensive and defensive systems were already in place; Roderique added a few things he'd picked up in college and tweaked some details on offense and defense. There was a learning curve, but it wasn't like a new coach bringing in a new system.

"The system didn't really change, it was just a few terminology things we had to pick up on," Adkins says.

The 1997 Cardinals weren't supposed to be very good. There were only a handful of players returning who had seen any kind of playing time on Friday nights, and Adkins still remembers the annual *Pigskin Preview* magazine picking Webb City to go 5-5.

"The team in 1996 was a team that didn't win a state championship, but we probably should have," Adkins says. "The next year nobody had a lot of expectations for us. It was different than any other team they've probably had."

The players didn't know what to expect either. They knew it was a pretty good team and they knew they had a pretty good quarterback in senior Josh Chapman, but he had only been a backup to that point. They also knew they were better than a 5-5 team, and the magazine's somewhat dim outlook was motivation.

"That did motivate us a little bit," Adkins says. "We don't put much stock into what those say all the time, but when we have higher expectations than that and we knew we could be a better football team than that. I can understand why because we had at the time a lot of no-name guys people hadn't heard of because they hadn't played very much, but at the same time we practiced and played behind some really good players and were able to go against them every day. I think that really helped us for the next year."

It wasn't until the team won its first two games of the season, at Branson and against Pittsburg, that everyone started feeling really good about the team.

During the preseason jamboree at Monett, Chapman stood out both for his legs and for his arm. Behind him, running backs Ty Wynne and Adam Schooley were ready for their shots. Wynne had rushed for 239 yards as a sophomore. Depth was a problem, though, and the Cardinals had many players going both ways. The team was especially thin on the offensive line, but it featured four senior starters: Bryan Bard, a 6-foot-1, 210-pounder at strong tackler; Ray Bryant, a 190-pound strong guard; James Renfro, a 235-pound quick guard; and 205-pound quick tackle Andy Martinez. Juniors Andrew Shull, at tight end; Phillip Beecham, at center; and Josh Pollock and senior Levi Herrin, at tight end; rounded out the line. Adkins got the start at wide receiver. On defense, Shull started at left end, senior Kelson Hombs at left tackle, Martinez at right tackle and senior Philip Stotts at right end. Outside linebackers were Herrin and Wynne, with senior Ray Bryant and junior Tyson Adams at inside linebacker. Chapman and Adkins started at cornerback, Schooley at strong safety. Stotts and Cole Shewmake were the kickers, and Wynne and Brandon Yost the punters.

At Branson in week one, the Cardinals went for 475 yards of total offense and stymied the Pirates all night, allowing only 89 yards and two first downs. Though Branson turned two turnovers into two scores, Webb City won 28-14. Wynne and Chapman had excellent games; Wynne rushed for 134 yards – gaining 49 yards on one run alone – and caught passes for 69 and 33 yards. Chapman had a 53-yard touchdown on an option keeper, darting up the left sideline and cutting back in front of two tacklers. But it was fullback Adam Schooley who Roderique said was the player of the game. He ran for 103 yards and made good blocks all night long. Defensively, Ray Bryant led the team with eight tackles and an interception. Wynne also had six stops and an interception, and Andrew Shull and Kelson Hombs made seven tackles each.

The Pittsburg game was another battle between highly-ranked teams. Even after losing a really good senior class and a head coach, and despite local media picking the Cardinals as a .500 team, they were ranked first in Missouri Class 4A. The Purple Dragons were ranked third in Kansas 5A. It was Roderique's first home game as a head coach; the last time he'd been on the field at Cardinal Stadium it was a 7-3 loss in the 1985 semifinals that ended his high school playing career.

The defense had another stellar game against Pittsburg, stopping the Purple Dragons five times on fourth down, and Webb City won 21-0. It could have been worse, but the Cardinals fumbled into the end zone in the first half. A week later they blasted Joplin 33-7, and everyone was starting to buy in. Chapman scored a 58-yard touchdown and Wynne threw a 62-yard touchdown pass to Adkins. Wynne also returned a kickoff for a touchdown and returned an interception for a score. The big plays put the Cardinals ahead 26-7 after they'd run only seven offensive plays.

The game at Missouri Southern's Fred G. Hughes Stadium marked the end of a two-year agreement for the teams to play, and there was doubt they would play again in the near future. Joplin wanted to keep the game at Missouri Southern, but Webb City didn't want to give up a home game.

"It's nice to be home, and there's a mystique at Cardinal Stadium," superintendent Ron Lankford told the newspaper. "We're 52-3 there over the past 10 years, and we don't want to play a home game off that field."

Security was also a factor. Lankford shared concerns about "extraneous things" at the contest.

"In this game, the kids are up a little more than the usual game," he said.

As it turns out, the two schools haven't played since.

At home against Kansas City Central a week later, the Cardinals were outscored 20-7 in the second half. Fortunately they already led 26-0 after the first two quarters and Webb City improved to 4-0 with the 33-20 win. At that point in the season Roderique said his team needed to improve three little things: offense, defense and the kicking game. The defense once again allowed 20 points, but it had certainly improved in a 43-20 win at Lebanon. Webb City allowed just 60 rushing yards, an average of two yards per carry, and tallied six sacks in the game.

"(Assistant coach Tim) Davied did an outstanding job calling that game," Roderique said afterwards. "I don't know if we've ever had that many in a game before."

Cole Shewmake was a perfect 5-for-5 on extra point attempts, and Philip Stotts scored a two-point conversion on a pitch play out of the swinging gate formation.

When Neosho came to town a week later, the conference season had finally begun, and the series that probably stood out the most was a red zone stand by Webb City's backup defense. The Wildcats had the ball at the Cardinals' 10-yard line and two incomplete passes and a pair of short running plays were all they could get. It preserved a shutout in Webb City's 29-point win. Webb City led 22-0 at halftime after its starting defense allowed only one first down, but the Cardinals could only convert one of five Neosho fumbles into a touchdown.

Through that point in the season the defensive line of Andrew Shull, Kelson Hombs, Andy Martinez and Philip Stotts had combined for eight sacks, 14 quarterback hurries and 14 tackles for a loss. They were a big reason the Cardinals were 6-0, and in the secondary Chapman and Richie Adkins each had three interceptions through seven games. The offensive playmakers were doing their part, too. Against McDonald County, Josh Chapman passed to Andrew Shull for a 74-yard touchdown on the team's first offensive play of the game. Chapman threw the ball well all night, completing five of nine passes for 147 yards and four touchdowns. He also ran for 91 yards on nine carries and scored a touchdown. Ty Wynne continued to lead the team in rushing. His 176 yards against the Mustangs brought his season total to 765 yards. Webb City amassed an astounding 586 yards of offense against McDonald County.

District play brought another highly-anticipated match-up with Harrisonville, ranked fourth in the state and undefeated. The Wildcats, coming off a 54-3 trouncing of Kearney, were looking to avenge the 1996 loss to the Cardinals by a touchdown. Their defense had allowed a total of 25 points in seven games.

On a night where several big plays went the Cardinals' way, perhaps the biggest was a fourth-and-goal at the Webb City 1-yard line. Harrisonville quarterback John Ortiz tried to sneak into the end zone, but Kelson Hombs and Tyson Adams stuffed him and Webb City went into the half with a 14-0 lead. On the game's opening kickoff, Stotts recovered a fumble at the Harrisonville 39. A few plays later, on fourth-and-six, Chapman passed to tight end Levi Herrin, who made a spectacular diving catch at the 15 to keep the drive going, and four plays later Wynne scored.

A long Harrisonville drive later in the half ended with a fumble, and on the very next play Chapman passed to Wynne for a 37-yard run. A play later, Schooley scored a 37-yard touchdown.

In the second half Ortiz was knocked out of the game and Chapman scrambled for a 33-yard touchdown. The Cardinals won 26-0.

The game that stands out to Adkins more than any other that season is the second district game at Nevada. Both teams were 8-0 and battling for a Southwest Conference and district championship, and a packed house at Tiger Stadium witnessed the Cardinals' closest game of the season.

"There was a huge crowd everywhere and it was by far the biggest game of the season," Adkins says. "The most intense game that I've been a part of."

And Adkins played a huge role in the game's outcome.

Nevada had rolled through the regular season by steamrolling opponents, running right over them. Webb City hoped to counter with speed. A 95-yard drive right before the half was the difference. Chapman completed a 22-yard pass to Ty Wynne to move the ball away from Webb City's end zone on the drive, then hit Adam Schooley over the middle for a 24-yard gain. Chapman spiked the ball to stop the clock, then lofted a 35-yard pass to Adkins for the touchdown.

The 7-0 lead stood in the second half, and the defense added two points in the fourth quarter. Brandon Yost pinned the Tigers at their 1 with a nice punt, and three plays later Andrew Shull busted through the line and sacked the Nevada quarterback for a safety. Nevada managed only 125 yards of offense in the game, and Webb City had sealed a district title with the 9-0 shutout, its third scoreless game in four weeks, and fourth shutout of the season.

"This has been a nice transition for me," Roderique told the newspaper on the eve of playoff football. "The biggest advantage has been the coaching staff. Not only do they work hard, but they're fun to be around, and everything has been good so far."

One statistic jumped out to him: Webb City's 40 takeaways, which he said was the single biggest factor in the 9-0 start. They were evenly split between 20 interceptions and 20 fumble recoveries. Adkins had six interceptions, including one that effectively ended the Nevada game.

That week also marked Grant Wistrom's final game at Memorial Stadium in Lincoln. In the nationally-televised game, Wistrom forced three fumbles, recovering one of them, and recorded three sacks and nine solo tackles. He was named Big 12 player of the week.

Webb City took a 10-0 record into the sectional round of the playoffs after thrashing Carthage 35-7 to end the regular season. The Raymore-Peculiar Panthers came to town, and silenced all the cowbells on the Webb City side of the field after going ahead 9-7 early in the second quarter. The rest of the first half, though, the bells rang frequently. Webb City scored 20 unanswered points and led 27-9 at halftime.

"At first, I thought it would be one of those games where whoever had the ball last would win," Roderique said. "But we got some breaks and opened a little lead."

Wynne's kickoff return into Ray-Pec territory sparked the big run. Chapman passed to Chase Emery for a 20-yard gain, then pump-faked the same play and hit Adkins, who was wide open for a big gain to the Ray-Pec 1. Chapman scored on the next play and Webb City never trailed again in the 45-15 win. The Panthers fumbled on the ensuing kickoff and the ball was recovered by Adam Minard at the Ray-Pec 35. Chapman connected with Adkins again, this time for a touchdown. Late in the second quarter Chapman came up with the first of his two interceptions in the game. On fourth-and-three at the Panther 39, Chapman passed to Wynne for 28 yards. With 20 seconds left in the half and a fourth-and-goal at the 4, Chapman passed to Adkins again for a touchdown. Finally Webb City fans could breathe more easily after a tenuous start to the game. The Panthers put together drives of nine and 11 plays in taking their lead. Wynne's 12-yard touchdown made it 7-3 Webb City before Ray-Pec drove again.

When Webb City's first drive of the second half stalled, Cole Shewmake booted the team's first field goal of the year, but after another Panthers score it was just a 30-15 game. Colby Southward later blocked a punt in Panther territory, and Schooley scored on a 13-yard run. Later on, Levi Herrin and Chapman added interceptions and Chapman scored from seven yards out. Turnovers plagued Ray-Pec the entire second half. At one point Schooley stripped the ball from a receiver and Herrin recovered in the end zone for a touchback.

The Cardinals traveled to Ozark for the quarterfinals, knowing that a victory would mean a home semifinal game at Cardinal Stadium. Chapman had largely been the face of the offense all season, and he was priority No. 1 for the Ozark defense. Roderique said Ozark seemed to have two plans in the game: take Chapman out of the running game, and take Chapman out of the game. Of course, there were still two other options in the option offense: fullback Adam Schooley and tailback Ty Wynne. Wynne rushed for 138 yards on 16 attempts and scored twice, and Schooley rushed 26 times for 100 yards.

"With the option, the defense dictates where we run the ball," Roderique said. "We just really executed well.

"When you run the option, the quarterback should expect to get hit, and they were hitting hard Monday," he added.

Chapman did throw the ball with some success. He threw touchdown passes to both Adkins and Herrin

The defense also played a great game. In the first quarter Ozark gained only one yard of offense and both Chapman and Herrin intercepted passes. On special teams, Brandon Yost faked a punt and ran for a first down at midfield; the Cardinals went on to score on the drive to take a 14-0 lead. Ozark tied the game in the second quarter, but the Cardinals ended the half with two long drives and led 28-14 at the half. Two long drives to open the second half effectively put the game away, and if they didn't, Chapman's interception at the goal line did. Webb City won 35-14.

Gates at Cardinal Stadium opened at noon a week later for the 1:30 kickoff against Savannah. The Cardinals were in the final four for the eighth time in 13 seasons. But an ominous sight greeted Webb City fans that Saturday; the Savages wore the same colors, black and gold, as Excelsior Springs had in the semifinals a year earlier. And the weather was similar, too; foggy and cool.

"And it was also the same score at halftime, 7-6," Chapman told the newspaper afterwards.

Only because of Richie Adkins' 7-yard touchdown reception was the game that close.

Neither team scored in the third quarter, and fans were getting even more nervous. In the fourth quarter, Chapman batted down a Savannah pass on a fourth down, and the Cardinals had the ball. Two first downs put the Cardinals at midfield with a first-and-10, but two plays later they faced a third-and-9. Chapman passed to Wynne, who was wide open in the middle of the field, for a 35-yard gain. A clipping call brought the ball back some, but it was still a first down. On a third-and-15, Wynne was big again, gaining 21 yards. On another third down, Chapman passed to Levi Herrin down to the goal line.

Down to the final five minutes and five seconds of the fourth quarter, Webb City faced a fourth-and-goal at the 1-yard line. Roderique called a timeout to discuss the team's options.

"I asked the seniors what they wanted to do, and they wanted to go for it," he said. "It was an easy decision, because if we don't score, that's close enough, the defense could score a safety, get a turnover or get the ball back with good field position."

The Cardinals came onto the field and lined up in the I-formation, a different look than the usual veer offensive set. Wynne got the handoff and powered it in to give the Cardinals a 12-7 lead.

Savannah got the ball back at its own 30. On a third-and-3, Philip Stotts sacked the Savages' quarterback, but officials ruled the quarterback's desperation toss was legal, and an incompletion. On the next play, Wynne picked off an Eric Miller pass and returned it to the Webb City 23. Six players later he scored on an eight-yard run, and Cardinals fans could finally breath a sigh of relief. Schooley ended the game with another interception of Miller, and he returned it to the Cardinals' bench, where he was mobbed by his teammates as he held the ball high in the air. Webb City won 19-7.

"They were hurting out there," Martinez said. "After the game, (Miller) came up and told me his chest was still hurting from a hit I gave him early in the game."

It was on to the championship in St. Louis.

When Webb City and North County met at the Trans World Dome in St. Louis, it was the second time that year the two schools had met for a championship. The North County Raiders had defeated the Cardinals for the baseball championship that June in Columbia.

"But this game is a little more exciting than baseball," said Adam Schooley, the senior running back and safety who had also played baseball.

Webb City had ended the regular season ranked first in the state, and North County ended as the No. 2 team. The Raiders threw the ball more than anybody Webb City had played that season; most of their 343 yards in the semifinals came through the air. The Cardinals had plenty of defensive firepower, though. Chapman had 10 interceptions, and Adkins had six. As a team, starters had 29 interceptions on the year. And don't forget the defensive line of Philip Stotts, Andy Martinez, Kelson Hombs and Andrew Shull, which had combined for 43 tackles for a loss, 13 sacks, five forced fumbles, seven fumble recoveries and 21 hurries.

Offensively, Chapman led the team; he had thrown for nearly 1,300 yards and 16 touchdowns and rushed for more than 1,200 yards and 21 touchdowns.

The game didn't start well, though. Fifteen seconds in, Webb City already trailed 7-0 after the Raiders scored on their first play from scrimmage, a 73-yard touchdown pass.

"I didn't say anything to them after the play, but they didn't panic," Roderique said.

"I remember going into that game we were thinking, 'Are we good enough? Can we do this?' Because we knew we were facing a really good team," Adkins says. "It was a pretty good wakeup call, and it made us all nervous when they scored on the first play of the game."

But Webb City moved the ball with ease. The Cardinals answered the quick score with a drive down to the North County 33 before turning it over. After a North County punt, Webb City once again drove into Raiders territory and turned the ball over again. The big break came on a high snap with North County punting; the Cardinals recovered at the Raiders' 22-yard line to start the second quarter, and Chapman scored two plays later to tie the game.

Webb City's defense flexed some muscle; North County gained only one yard on its next possession, and then the Cardinals drove down and scored again on another Chapman run. The big play on that drive was a 35-yard pass to Ty Wynne on a third-and-6. Kicker Cole Shewmake added two field goals in the second quarter, and the Cardinals led 20-7 at halftime. The first was a 28-yarder with 41 seconds left in the half, and on the ensuing kickoff North County fumbled the squib kick, setting up Shewmake's 34-yard field goal with two seconds on the clock.

Ty Wynne's kickoff return to the 42 gave the team great field position to start the second half and three plays later Chapman added his third touchdown of the game, a 51-yard run. On Webb City's next possession, Wynne took a handoff on a third-and-24 and ran to his right; before he was tackled he threw a perfect pass to Richie Adkins for a 33-yard gain. Another turnover gave the ball back, though.

Chapman scored his fourth touchdown on a 47-yard run to end the third quarter; in that quarter alone he rushed for 94 yards and two scores.

Early in the fourth quarter, Ray Bryant intercepted a pass in the red zone and the Cardinals marched all the way to the North County 11 before committing their fourth turnover of the game. Once again the Raiders were forced to punt after Webb City's defense held tough, and for the second time the snap went over the punter's head. This time it went out the back of the end zone for a safety. After the free kick, the Cardinals scored again on a 1-yard Philip Stotts run. North County added a 49-yard touchdown pass in the final 10 seconds of the game, when Webb City substitutions left only 10 players on the field, and the Cardinals won 44-14.

"I can't give enough credit to the playoffs and coaches," Roderique said. "I felt like we could beat anybody, because we just improved every week.

"I just appreciate the chance to coach, and the players and coaches have been great to work with all year. The seniors have really come a long way."

Chapman deserved a lot of the credit for his career game. He set two Class 4A Show-Me Bowl records. His four rushing touchdowns broke the previous record of three set by Mark Smith in the 1990 game, and Chapman's 262 yards were 54 better than the previous record set in 1986. Only eight players in all classes had rushed for four touchdowns in the title game. Perhaps his most impressive run was on an option keeper in the third quarter when he broke three or four tackles and then lowered his shoulder and bulldozed over the safety for his fourth touchdown.

Shewmake's two field goals tied a Show-Me Bowl record, and Ray Bryant and Levi Herrin each tied the record for interceptions with one apiece. As a team, the Cardinals offense set a record and became the first team ever to total more than 500 yards in the game; they rushed for 366. The 7.9 yards per play average was another 4A record.

After the game, Webb City fans hurried back to town ahead of the team and gathered on Main Street on a rainy night. It was pouring when the team buses turned onto Main Street with a police car and fire truck escort, but the town celebrated anyway. After all, this was better than a 5-5 season.

Before the state championship game the *Sentinel* had poked fun at the preseason predictions. While many around town had said it in whispered conversations, editor Bob Foos wrote, only sportscaster Jay Radzavicz had the "audacity" to put it in print.

"Here's what he said in KOAM-TV's *Pigskin Preview*," Foos wrote. "'Several constants will remain this fall in Webb City. The stands at Cardinal Stadium will be packed, and the players will continue with the tradition of playing emotional and fundamentally sound football. However, don't expect this young group to contend for a state championship this fall. A .500 season will be an accomplishment that the Cardinals can be proud of.'"

When it was obvious Radzavicz was wrong, he ran sprints at practice with the players to make up for it.

And Webb City had its fourth state championship.

Josh Chapman went on to play quarterback at Missouri Southern and had a record-breaking career. He finished with 3,233 rushing yards and 5,368 passing yards and broke the career record for total yards with 8,801. He was an All-American in 2002.

Andrew Shull went on to star on the defensive line at Kansas State. He started five of the Wildcats' final six games as a redshirt sophomore in 2001, then led the team in sacks in 2002 and 2003. He's tied for second all-time at Kansas State with three sacks in a game. He did that twice, both times against Baylor. His 10 sacks in 2002 rank 10th all time for the Wildcats, and his 20 career sacks rank sixth all-time. His junior and senior seasons were some of the best for Kansas State football. The Wildcats went 11-2 in 2002 and were ranked sixth in the nation in the coaches' poll and seventh in the Associated Press poll. They beat Arizona State 34-27 in the Holiday Bowl. In 2003 the Wildcats finished 11-4 and won the Big 12 championship in thrilling fashion by beating No. 1 Oklahoma 35-7 at Arrowhead Stadium in Kansas City. Shull, wearing No. 98, made five tackles in the game, three tackles for a loss and recorded a sack.

Kansas State lost by a touchdown to Ohio State in the Fiesta Bowl. It was the school's first-ever BCS appearance.

The Pittsburg State University coaching tree has been well established, but it's likely fewer people are aware of all the success Webb City players and assistants have had later on as head coaches. There was Jesse Wall, of course, who spent time as a Kurt Thompson assistant and then went to Carthage, Joplin and Carl Junction. Another great example is Richie Adkins, who is now coaching football at Jasper High School the way he learned to play it at Webb City and at Pittsburg State.

In 2010 and 2011 the Jasper Eagles won a total of one game and lost 17 others. Adkins was hired prior to the 2012 season, and in his rookie season the Eagles lost their first five games and six of their first seven. But after the 1-6 start Jasper finished the year with three wins in four games and went to the playoffs. The 2013 season was even better; Jasper went 11-1 and made a trip to the playoffs. In two seasons Adkins turned Jasper from the team everybody wanted to the play into the team everyone dreaded. The Eagles went 9-2 in 2014.

Adkins moved to Webb City with his family when he was in fourth grade, and he was a junior during the 1996 season. After finishing his high school career with a stellar 1997 season he walked on at Pittsburg State as a wide receiver. In 2005 he came to Jasper as an assistant coach and spent three years there before returning to the Gorillas as a graduate assistant for one year. In 2009 he started a three-year run as an assistant on John Roderique's staff before taking the head coaching job at Jasper.

Considering Webb City and Pittsburg State are really the only two programs he's been involved with, most of what he does at Jasper comes from that background.

"Especially from Webb City," he says. "When I was there practicing and then there as a coach, I see how they set up practice and how they prepare for a game during the week and that's really what I've translated over here, the preparation. Prepare our kids better than the other kids on Friday night if possible so our kids can just go out and play. That's really what I've taken from both sides. How to prepare the kids each week."

Serving as Webb City's special teams coordinator was especially hopeful for the now-head coach.

"That's been big even today with helping me with organization and practice schedules and those kinds of things because there's a lot of organization that goes into special teams, especially at a bigger school."

He also coached tight ends and defensive backs during his time with the Cardinals.

As for that age-old question: what makes Webb City so good? Adkins says it's about expectations.

"Every time the kids show up, whether it be weights in the summertime or practice in the summer and during the regular season, however long they're there, whether it be two hours, an hour, they give everything they've got every time. They don't always ask them to be there as many hours or as many days of the week as some other programs but when they are there they are expected to work as hard as they can and they do. They know their expectations and they know if they don't meet those expectations there's another guy who will and there's somebody who will play in front of them. I think back to when I was a senior and we won the state championship; people didn't think we were going to be very good, but we had a lot of guys who had worked hard for four years and gone against some really good players in practice and then when it's their turn they're out there to play and they're good players. There's a lot of kids there who are practicing every day against some really good players. You might not know who they are, but the next year it'll be their turn and when it's their turn they're going to give it everything they've got because a lot of the times it's only one year they get the shot and when they get their shot they don't want to be the group or the kids who didn't win it."

28. THE NEW MILLENNIUM

That age old question: what makes Webb City so good? It's obvious there are a multitude of factors involved in the success of the last 30 years, from tradition to work ethic to some incredibly gifted athletes. It's the fact that it can never be said that a Webb City team was not well prepared for an opponent. But it's also the team's weight program, the coaching, the mentality of everyone involved. And those are just a few right answers.

Kyle Mense had one of the best vantage points of anyone to see and experience firsthand the Cardinals' success: on the field, under center. As a two-year starter at quarterback, Mense helped Webb City to its first state championship of the new millennium in 2000, his senior year.

"You grow up in Webb City and that's all you hear about is the high school football team and how they won a state championship or how good they're going to be," he says. "You want to be a part of that. Look at the turnout. You have kids who aren't athletic who come out to play football because they want to be on the football team. Pretty much every who wants to play football does. It's growing up seeing the program, the winning and you want to be a part of that and you've got that drive and if you don't have that drive you don't make the team, you won't play. You have to give it everything you've got to be able to play."

One of the biggest reasons the Cardinals are so good, according to Mense, is obvious, though sometimes overlooked: the veer offense. While other high school teams have changed their offensive philosophies, have gone to the spread offense and other flashy systems, since 1988 Webb City's bread and butter has been the veer. While systems such as the spread offense rely on finding a great quarterback with a good arm and multiple receivers who can catch the football reliably, the veer offense is assignment football.

"I'm just a believer that the veer in high school is a very tough offense to stop because of the way it's blocked," Mense says. "You need a guy who makes the right reads, and as far as your offensive linemen go, there's a lot of double teams and it shouldn't be that hard to block. You're not asking guys to do single blocks; they're doing double blocks because they don't block the defensive end on the outside veer, they do a double block and scrape off to a linebacker. You should be getting three or four yards every play."

Ever since Jerry Kill was hired, the split-back veer has been a staple at

Webb City. Laurie Shaffer, then the assistant editor for the *Sentinel*, broke the system down for readers in a feature piece in 1990.

"What looks to the casual observer like just a clash of muscle on the field every Friday night is every bit as much a contest of minds," Shaffer wrote.

At its most basic, the veer offense is this: three linemen on either side of the center, the quarterback behind center with two running backs split behind him, and a flanker split out wide on one side of the field, behind the line of scrimmage.

"You have to dedicate yourself to being good at something, and we want to run," Thompson told Shaffer. "It's more demoralizing as a defensive player if somebody runs over and over you."

There are several advantages of the system. Offensive linemen don't have to be enormous players due to those double teams, which is a good thing considering Webb City's century-plus tradition of undersized but speedy players. The offense can attack quickly anywhere along the line of scrimmage, or even outside. The veer formation looks simple, but a variety of plays can be run from it: the option, which in itself can be several different plays to several different players; misdirection plays; power plays and passing plays. Another advantage is the defense's pursuit, or lack thereof; because defenders must be disciplined to stop the option, they often get a late break in pursuing the football, which leads to more big plays. The veer offense is also fairly simple, at least from a basic standpoint, and with constant repetition the system can be mastered. The offensive game plan doesn't change much from week to week. Also, as was the case in 1990 and is still the case now, few teams run the veer offense, which means few teams can defend it well.

One of the most frequent offensive plays the Cardinals ran in 1990, and in the years since, is the inside veer, which Kurt Thompson often called on first down. The quarterback must make two quick reads, and one of three different backs will get the ball. Against a 5-2 defense, with two ends, two tackles and a nose guard, the center and guard double team the nose guard, the offensive tackle blocks the defensive tackle and then chips off to a linebacker, and the defensive end is left unblocked as the tight end pulls outside to block the strong safety. The quarterback takes the snap and steps back with his right foot if the play is to the right side, and his first decision is whether to give the ball to the dive back, who runs straight ahead and could have quite a hole to run through if the nose guard, tackle and linebacker have been blocked effectively. If the other defensive tackle moves up field, the hole will be there, but if he moves down the line of scrimmage and into the path of the running back, the quarterback pulls the ball and moves down the line of scrimmage. The quarterback's second read is the defensive end: if he moves up field to take the other split back, the quarterback keeps the ball and cuts up field off tackle. If the defensive end plays the quarterback, he pitches the ball to the running back, who has plenty of room to run if everyone else has blocked their assignment correctly.

It's a simple offense, at least in terms of philosophy, but the execution, the scheming involved, can be much more intricate and detail-oriented than many realize. And the offense, though philosophically the same, can change year to year.

"It's not something that's just, 'This is what it is and it's always that,'" John Roderique says. "It changes from year to year, and I think a big part of it is utilizing our personnel. We do things that are to the strength of our kids, but we keep them in the same framework. The 2012 season was an example where we got into the shotgun and pistol offense, some no huddle stuff, three-back shotgun, some different things. With our backs and quarterback, we could utilize all that by being a little more diverse offensively. We could pound it at people. We play a team like Har-Ber and we don't want to let them have too many chances with the football, so we want to sustain the ball for long drives and keep it away from them. Against Har-Ber in 2012 we didn't get in the shotgun one time that game because we wanted to keep the ball on the line of scrimmage and we wanted to run all of the phases of our triple option against them. There's other games where we may want to throw it a little more. A lot of it depends on who we're playing and their abilities or how they defend us. A lot of those things will fluctuate. We always want to be able to establish the run and try to control the game with our offense and our running game. That's a basic."

Roderique calls the plays on offense most of the time, at least the ones that work, he says with a grin. Really, not much has changed since he took over in 1997. He's subtracted here and tweaked some things there. The offense is, however, much more advanced now than it's ever been. One of the team's best plays now is the outside veer, a triple option play, but it may block the play three different ways depending on what the defense shows or the situation.

"We have the ability now to do those things, run one play and block it two or three different ways," Roderique says. "We can do that with much of our offense and the running game that we didn't do back in '97. I think a big component you look at from teams back then to teams now is the overall team speed. I think it's better now than it's ever been in the history of Webb City football. I look back at 2000, 2001 and some of those years, we played several guys both ways. We played seven or eight guys on both sides of the football. Right now we started 22 different guys in 2012. That's what neat, I think, is the overall level of our play at every position is much higher than it's ever been."

This is where the program's weight training and offseason workouts come in to play, and also the increasing turnout over the years. In Roderique's first season, roughly 55 or 60 players came out for the team. Now those numbers are as high as 85 players.

In 1999 Kyle Mense stepped into the starting quarterback role after Webb

City's worst season since the early 1980s. When you're used to winning state championships, just playing .500 football is devastating, and the Cardinals were actually 3-5 in 1998 before winning 37-20 at Neosho and then edging Nevada 6-0 in overtime to end the season. In 1999, the Cardinals were back on track, though. They started the year 5-0 and while scoring more than 28 points only once in those first five games, the defense allowed only 18 points in the first four games. But after the quick start, Mense broke his leg and Web City was blown out 42-7 at Camdenton, the eventual state champions. The Cardinals came back to blow out both Kansas City Central and McDonald County, by 55 points and 47 points, respectively, and they finished the year with an 8-2 record but missed the playoffs again. It was a season marked by several key injuries. In addition to Mense, starting tight end and inside linebacker B.J. Scofield broke his leg, and starting wide receiver Ryan McFarland broke his neck – in the same game. McFarland's injury occurred when he made a tackle, and after a few minutes he got to his feet and walked to the sideline. After the game he even went to the homecoming dance for pictures, but as the pain grew worse he finally went to the hospital. The injury ended his playing career. He later spent eight seasons as an assistant coach at Webb City, and was hired as the head coach at Riverton, Kansas before the 2014 season.

In the days and weeks leading up to the season opener against Branson in 2000, John Roderique was adamant the team was destined for great things, even as the Cardinals worked tirelessly in 100-plus temperatures. The team returned

Ryan McFarland, right, broke his neck while making a tackle during the 1999 season. Photo by Bob Foos.

four of its offensive linemen, and the entire backfield – Mense at quarterback and running backs Nathan Copher and Chris Taylor. The defense looked thin on the line early on, but did return senior Josh Belcher and had a solid corps of linebackers with Scofield and Justin Smith back at inside linebackers.

"Last year was disappointing because we weren't in the playoffs," Roderique said. "This year we hope it's different."

Mense says there was pressure on the team to go back to the playoffs after the two-year drought, and he especially felt it; his older brother, Matt, had quarterbacked the 1996 team that suffered the devastating five-point loss at Excelsior Springs in the semifinals.

"He never got a state championship ring and I didn't want that to happen to me," Mense says. "I was thinking maybe there was a Mense curse. We had a pretty good class behind us, the junior class my senior year, and they had always been pretty successful in football. My class wasn't that great in junior high; we were OK, just not great. We had a lot of returning starters because a lot of us played as juniors. We knew we were going to be pretty good. I don't know if we thought we were going to be state championship good because we got smoked by Camdenton the year before, but we thought we were going to be pretty good and we thought we had a chance to win it."

In the first three games of the 2000 season, Webb City didn't exactly look like a championship contender. The Cardinals edged Branson 6-0 in week one, then won 19-7 at Pittsburg and 25-16 at Rogers. Quality wins, sure, but not terribly convincing, either. The team felt fortunate to have beaten Branson in a game that raised some concerns, namely fumbles and an inability to find the end zone. There were highlights; Chris Taylor made 10 tackles, half of them solo; Scofield had four solo tackles and eight total; Adam Spieker had four solo tackles and Johnny Wynne had a nice punt return. Mense scored the game's only touchdown.

There were more problems in the win at Pittsburg, and Roderique said things "could have been better." While both teams were plagued by turnovers, the Cards finally put the game out of reach in the third quarter after Joseph Fuller recovered a bobbled punt to give the offense good field position. Joe Smith's high-stepping touchdown up the middle, his third of the game, capped the drive. Grant McDonald ended one Pittsburg scoring threat with an interception in the end zone in the first half, which ended with Webb City clinging to a 13-7 lead.

"It was just a slow start offensively," Mense recalls. "We took a little while to get our blocking down and adjust to game speed. Offense is a little harder to get used to at the beginning of the year. Branson, they were just a bunch of quick guys and it was hard to get around the corners on them."

One of the games that really stood out to Mense is the Pittsburg win, and not for a good reason. He played, as he describes it, a "terrible" first half.

"I don't know what my deal was; something was in my head that game," he says. "I fumbled a snap and lost it early on, and next time we got the ball I was probably 25 yards downfield and I glanced over to see if Nathan (Copher) was there and as I glanced the safety came a little faster than I thought and he put his helmet right on the ball and I lost it. I think I made a couple wrong reads; I don't know where my head was at. At one point we lined up to punt and I called cover 2 instead of cover 1 – cover 2 means we're faking it and the ball comes to me and I just stand there thinking, 'Why'd you snap it to me? I must have just said cover 2.' And then I ran the wrong way on top of that. I didn't even follow the blockers or I would have gotten a first down."

Roderique wasn't happy.

"I took my time getting over to the sideline, I'm not going to lie," Mense says. "By the time I got over there he was already done yelling at Chaz Mayes, our deep snapper. He was just waiting there, fuming, hands on his hips, headset off, just waiting for me to come over. I don't remember exactly what he said but it was something along the lines of, 'What is wrong with you? You better get your head in the game. You want to sit on the bench all night? I'll put you there.'"

The Cardinals moved up in the polls to No. 4 in the state after the victory.

The week three game at Rogers was lopsided in several statistical categories. Rogers tallied 21 first downs to Webb City's 6, and threw for 244 yards compared to Webb City's 55. And, while the Cardinals struggled to make extra points, Rogers tacked on a 46-yard field goal. But on the ground, it was all Webb City. The Cardinals rushed for 268 yards and held Rogers to 131. By halftime it was 19-0 Webb City, and a fumble near the goal line took away what could have been a four-touchdown lead. In the second half, the Mounties scored 16-straight, including the 46-yard field goal into the wind in the fourth quarter. After a big defensive stop in the fourth quarter, Chris Taylor romped 45 yards for a touchdown with 1:15 left in the game to end it.

As the Cardinals eyed a 4-0 start to the year, the met the undefeated Seneca Indians for the first time since 1995. The Indians were coached by former Webb City and Central Missouri State player Chance Wistrom. When his team took the field, the players ran through a banner hoisted by cheerleaders that read "Shuffle the Cards." The Cardinals had the better hand.

"Everything went right for us in that game," Roderique said. "The team played hard all night."

Mense redeemed himself for the first half at Pittsburg with three rushing touchdowns and a pair of key completions, and Garrett Taylor, Joe Smith, Johnny Wynne and Nathan Copher each scored touchdowns in the 49-0 romp. Chris Taylor rushed for 138 of the team's 366 yards on the ground, and place kicker Landon Dobbs was perfect in seven extra-point attempts while Ryan DeMoss boomed his kickoffs.

If the team officially declared itself a contender in the blowout at Seneca, it reinforced that notion a week later against Nevada at Cardinal Stadium. Almost immediately the visiting Tigers fumbled, and Chris Taylor scored to make it a 6-0 game. On Nevada's second possession, it fumbled again and then was flagged for roughing the passer when the Cardinals took over. The very next play, Kyle Mense hit Grant McDonald for a touchdown and then Nathan Copher scored the two-point conversion to make it 14-0 barely four minutes in. Those early mistakes set the tone for the rest of the night.

Copher scored again in the first quarter, and Landon Dobbs' kick made it 21-0, and Taylor's second touchdown made it 27-0 as the first quarter drew to a close. In the second quarter, Taylor added a 33-yard touchdown at the 11:34 mark, and Copher scored on a 44-yard run a few minutes later. In the final three minutes of the half, Joseph Fuller scored from two yards out and it was a 48-0 game at halftime. Roderique was already taking his starters out of the game before the half.

On homecoming night Webb City welcomed Saint Thomas Aquinas, a school from Overland Park, Kansas that was only in its 13th year of existence. In their first 12 seasons, the Saints had gone to the playoffs six times.

"We know we're going to probably run into a buzz saw when we get to Webb City, but we'll be ready," head coach Kevin Kopecky told the newspaper. "We need and want to play teams like that ... we have high expectations."

It was a bitter cold night, and for once many fans decided to leave shortly after the game started, but they didn't go far – most retreated to their cars to listen on the radio. On Webb City's first possession it fumbled, but Chris Taylor came up with a huge interception at the Cardinals' 7-yard line to keep it a scoreless game. After a Webb City punt, the Saints marched into the red zone again and went ahead 3-0 on a field goal. After yet another Webb City punt, Aquinas tried some trickery with a halfback pass, but Taylor read it from the start and picked off another pass, this time near midfield. Still, the Cardinals couldn't get anything going offensively. They tried to keep their next drive going on fourth down but came up short, and after pulling off a fake punt a few plays later, the Saints had the ball inside Webb City territory early in the second quarter. They later fumbled at the 45.

For once Webb City moved the ball, but the offense was stymied again when Aquinas came up with an interception at its own 4, and after the Saints tacked on another field goal the Cardinals trailed 6-0 at halftime on homecoming night.

A determined team came out of the locker room for the second half, and got perhaps some more motivation when a Saints player allegedly tried to kick B.J. Scofield's head into the home stands. Finally, in the fourth quarter, the team broke through. The Cardinals marched to the Aquinas 10, and Grant McDonald made a spectacular catch in the end zone on a halfback pass from Taylor with 11:31 to play, and Dobbs' extra point made it a 7-6 game. After that, the defense held, and the Cardinals won by a point.

"Remember, guys, it's a win, but there was a very fine line there – a very fine line. Remember that next week's a new game," Roderique told his players when it was over.

The following Friday night at Glendale that fine line had become a 19-point margin of victory as Webb City won 26-7. A long Chris Taylor punt returned sparked the Cardinals in the first quarter, and on the ensuing drive Mense threw a 14-yard touchdown pass to Justin Thurston. After Nathan Copher returned an interception into Glendale territory, Joe Smith rushed six yards for a touchdown and the 12-0 lead. In the third quarter Mense threw a bullet to Copher for another touchdown and a 19-0 lead. Still leading by 12 early in the fourth quarter, Grant McDonald's interception kept the Falcons at bay, and then Mense hit Scofield for a 5-yard touchdown. Final score: 26-7.

It was already time for district play, and the week eight game at Neosho was a huge one. Webb City was 7-0 going into Class 4A District 12 action, and Neosho was 6-1. Carthage and McDonald County, the only other teams in the district, each had losing records, so whoever won the battle between the Cardinals and Wildcats would likely go to the playoffs. The game would also decide the Southwest Conference. Webb City, Neosho and Mac County were each 1-0 in conference play.

On a personal level it was an opportunity to avenge the loss to Neosho a year earlier, when Webb City was 7-1 and headed to a playoff berth before the 5-3 Wildcats spoiled those plans and earned the playoff berth themselves. But in 2000, the Cardinals didn't have to wait long for revenge, not when Chris Taylor took the opening kickoff and returned it 91 yards down the sideline for a quick touchdown. A two-point conversion made it an 8-0 game just seconds in, and when it was all over the Redbirds came home with a 57-12 win and control of the district and conference races.

Nathan Copher's 6-yard touchdown capped an 81-yard opening drive for the Cardinals, and then Mense threw a 27-yard pass to Scofield, who ran an additional 38 yards to make it 22-0 in the first quarter. On one possession in the second quarter Webb City was penalized more than 45 yards, but the team settled down and Taylor's 14-yard touchdown made it 29-0. It was 29-8 at halftime. Taylor's next touchdown made it a 36-8 game. Neosho eventually pulled with 36-22 but Mense's 1-yard touchdown in the fourth quarter gave the team some breathing room, and after Garrett Taylor intercepted a pass, Mense kept the ball on three straight plays before scoring from the 27. The scoring ended when Josh Holden, a defensive lineman, recovered a fumble and returned it all the way down the field for a touchdown. Final score: 57-22.

In the second week of district play the Cardinals fumbled the ball to open the game and the Mustangs took an early lead, but Webb City came back to win 45-18, and with Neosho's win against Carthage on the same night, the Cardinals were officially playoff-bound again. Chris Taylor scored from 11 yards and Kyle Mense scored from the 8 in the first quarter, and Taylor added another touchdown in the second quarter before the Mustangs managed to score again. Mac County scored first in the second half, too, but Nathan Copher scored a touchdown in the third quarter and Dobbs kicked a field goal; in the fourth quarter Copher returned an interception 51 yards for a touchdown, and Mense scored from the 27.

The final game of the regular season, against Carthage, meant nothing, and while some wondered if it was worth risking injury right before the playoffs, Roderique was adamant the game meant something.

"Someone told me the other day that we don't really have anything to play for in the game," he said beforehand. "But we do – we have a 10-0 season compared to a 9-1 season to play for. And it's what we'll always have, even if this thing doesn't go any further."

Webb City won 35-0, and a confident bunch of Cardinals were excited to be back in the playoffs.

"Especially once we got going midseason, we were feeling pretty confident every game we went into," Mense says now. "Even when we got into the playoffs we still weren't ranked No. 1 and we had to play Ozark, who was ranked No. 1, and we thought we were going to win. We thought we would."

The Cardinals were ranked third when they hosted top-ranked Ozark in the sectional, and from the very beginning proved they were the better team. Webb City moved 56 yards on its first possession and scored on a 1-yard Mense run, and Landon Dobbs' 30-yard field goal made it 10-0 in the second quarter. Just before the half the Cardinals' running game struck again, and it was a 17-0 game after two quarters. After Ozark cut the lead to 11 points in the third quarter, Joe Smith capped a long, clock-burning drive with a 5-yard touchdown to make it a 24-6 game. In the fourth quarter, with Ozark trying desperately to make a game of it, junior linebacker Garrett Taylor picked off a pass and returned it for a touchdown, and Webb City won the game 31-6.

"We lost to a great football team tonight," said Ozark head coach Phil Montgomery. "They responded to our challenge, and showed us just how good they really are. They showed a lot of class, and they deserved to win."

"Tonight I want you to put a grin on your face," Roderique told the team at midfield. "I will, because you deserve it. So go home and get some rest. You've got to come in here next week and be ready to play."

In the quarterfinals Webb City faced a tall order with Camdenton coming to town. The Lakers were defending state champions, had won 24 of 25 games and had trounced the Cardinals by 35 points in 1999. This year would be much different, and B.J. Scofield would make a season-defining play. Webb City kicked off to start the game and promptly stopped Camdenton on its first two plays. On third down the Lakers looked to throw the ball and their quarterback –

a fairly cocky player – rolled out in the backfield. As the quarterback looked for a receiver to get open down the field, Scofield was shadowing him as he drifted toward the sideline. Scofield finally decided to go after him and sprinted toward the sideline; right when he got there the quarterback lofted a prayer down the field and at the exact same time Scofield absolutely drilled him. The quarterback sailed through the air, through the players standing on the sideline and his helmet flew over the track in the air.

"He knocked his helmet off," Mense says. "You could see it on film; he just lays there. B.J. gets up all excited and starts running back. I was standing on the other side and I actually watched it happen. I didn't watch where the ball went; I saw his helmet fly through the air. On film you can see it; he just gets up, doesn't even get his helmet and he just goes and sits on the bench and puts his head down. He came back in the game, but you could tell he was done. You could see it in his eyes."

What followed was a statement win for the Redbirds. They started at the Camdenton 48 on their first possession, and Chris Taylor sprinted down the sideline on first down for the game's opening score. On their second drive Nathan Copher and Taylor moved the ball on the ground, and Mense and Scofield connected through the air for a touchdown. It was 14-0 at halftime. Taylor's 3-yard scoring run capped Webb City's first possession of the third quarter, and Copher's run from the 3 made it 28-0. In the fourth quarter, Taylor threw a halfback-option pass to Justin Thurston for the team's fifth touchdown, and then Joe Smith intercepted a pass and returned it 75 yards for another score. Webb City won 42-0.

Mense says his best performance of the season came just before halftime at Park Hill in the semifinals. Junior running back Joe Smith's 7-yard touchdown run finished off a 73-yard scoring drive in the first quarter, and Smith's 4-yard touchdown run in the second quarter made it a 14-0 game. Copher intercepted a pass with 1:15 left in the first half on the Trojans' side of midfield, and on came Mense to guide the two-minute offense.

"For some reason we weren't relaying plays in with the receivers, so we ran all the way down and I was just sprinting back and forth from sideline to huddle, sideline to huddle non-stop getting plays and taking them back in. We ended up scoring right before half with a couple seconds left on the clock. We were smoking them that whole first half. We were working them pretty well."

Mense's touchdown pass to Thurston made it 21-0 at halftime, and those last six points would prove invaluable in the second half. The Trojans recovered a questionable fumble early in the third quarter and then scored on a 67-yard run, but Webb City came back with an 11-yard reverse run by sophomore Johnny Wynne to make it 28-7. Park Hill converted on fourth down on its next drive, gaining 48 yards on a long pass down to the Webb City 1, and a short run the next play made it 28-13 with 4:10 left in the third. Then, after a Webb City fumble, the Trojans scored again to pull within 28-19. Park Hill had scored 12 unanswered points in less than 15 seconds. Mense finally broke through with a 3-yard score to make it 35-19, but with 6:38 still to go in the game, Park Hill scored again and converted the two-point conversion; it was 35-27.

The Trojans got the ball back with 3:15 left to play, but needed to go 86 yards. They moved the ball at will, covering more than 76 yards and had the ball inside the Webb City 10 in the game's final moments. Finally, though, the Cardinals dug deep and came up with a huge stop. They won the game by eight points and were headed back to St. Louis for the championship, where they would face the McCluer North Stars at 3:15 p.m. Saturday inside the Trans World Dome.

The Stars were an especially arrogant team, and had defeated Washington 28-16 in the semifinals.

"We can do anything we want," McCluer North quarterback Daryle Jones told reporters after the win.

Mense remembers watching film on Jones and the Stars, and even then the Cardinals could tell McCluer North wasn't a very disciplined team.

"The only reason they got there is because they were more athletic probably than the other teams they played," Mense says. "You go in against a team like that and we're so structured in the way we block and everything. We've got everything assigned and who we read off of and who we're keying on. Those guys aren't really ready for stuff like that. They're more of a backyard football team the way they play. They're there more for athleticism and show. Their quarterback the whole time in pregame was dancing and trying to psych us out. The whole time we were laughing and thinking, 'OK, just wait 'till the game begins.' He was real athletic, probably more athletic than 99 percent of our team, but they had no structure or discipline so I really didn't think it was going to be that tough of a game. The east side was always the weaker side of the state, anyway."

When the game started, the Cardinals marched 80 yards with runs from Nathan Copher and Chris Taylor, and Taylor scored on a 37-yard run. The game was pretty well over already.

"Once we put up a real quick score on them they were pretty deflated," Mense says. "They pretty much hung it up."

After Joe Smith recovered a fumble at the 35, Mense threw a touchdown pass to Justin Thurston to make it 14-0 early in the second quarter.

"They started getting pretty tense after that first score," Taylor told the newspaper. "After that second TD they got really tense so we kinda keyed on that."

Later on, B.J. Scofield waylaid a return man, causing a fumble that was recovered by Johnny Wynne, and three players after that Taylor scored a 6-yard touchdown. After stopping the Stars on downs, Webb City got the ball at its own 43-yard line with 1:20 left in the half. It moved the ball into McCluer territory, but with 55 seconds left in the half the punting unit came onto the field. As

Mense made his way to the sideline, he saw something and called timeout. On the sideline he convinced Roderique to go for it on fourth down. Taylor got the ball, the first down and a 48-yard touchdown. It was 28-0 at halftime.

"That's something Kyle and the rest of the guys out there do real well," Roderique said. "It makes your job a lot easier when you've got leaders like that on the field."

In the third quarter the defense kept the Stars to only 32 yards of offense, and Dan Stanley's 64-yard punt buried McCluer at its own 3. The Stars' frustrations mounted, and at one point in the fourth quarter Jason Pruitt was flagged for offensive pass interference on two consecutive plays, and then ejected after punching Nathan Copher in the face mask.

With six minutes left in the game, Mense threw a touchdown strike to Justin Smith to make it 34-0, just a point shy of instituting the mercy clock, but later in the fourth quarter things got even worse for the Stars. Webb City's defense had pushed them back from their own 25 to the 16 and then Justin Smith unleashed a huge hit on Jones, the quarterback, and the ball flew into the hands of Josh Belcher at the 20. Garrett Taylor scored a few plays later, and Webb City won 41-0.

"All year long we've worked to get here," Roderique said in his postgame press conference. "But you know, it's really a bittersweet deal. This is one of the last times we're all going to be together as a team, and it really tugs at my heart."

"Our offensive line has been pulling it out for us all season," Mense said after the game. "The coaches letting us play (Roderique, Richard Correll, Dusty Allen, Aaron Hafner, Darrell Hicks, Brandon Funk, Bryce Darnell, and Brenten Byrd)...Ryan (McFarland) and the rest of the guy supporting us on the sidelines are just as important to this team as anyone...we all won this together."

The team arrived back on Main Street in Webb City at 1 a.m. that night, where a hoard of adoring fans awaited.

"It's a good feeling," Mense says now. "I guess I should say I love football, but I hate the practice and especially when you get into the playoffs and you go all the way to a state championship, it's just four or five more weeks of practice and it wears you thin because you do the same thing over and over and over. Practice is pretty daunting for a long time, but then you get up there and you're really excited, pretty nervous, your stomach gets all twisted and you play the game. Our game, fortunately, was over in the first quarter and I don't even think I played the second half, maybe one series. It was really relieving. I just sat there and enjoyed it. They let me carry the trophy out of the bus and it's pretty exciting. There are a lot of people out there, a lot of people you don't know but it's great we have fans that actually come and support us, not just parents."

The motto of that season was "Hold the Rope," and this explanation hung all season in the weight room:

"Every year a professional football team wins the world championship. Every year a college team wins the national title. Every year a high school team in each classification wins a state title. All of these teams have one thing in common. No matter how tough it became throughout their season, they did one thing...they held the rope. What is holding the rope? Imagine you are hanging from the edge of a cliff with a drop of 500 feet. The only thing between you and a fall to your death is a rope, with the person of your choice at the other end. Who do you know has the guts to pull you to safety? Who do you know that will let the rope burn their hands and not let go? How many people do you know who are going to withstand the burning pain and watch blood drip from their hands for you? If you can name two people that is not good enough because those two people might not be around. The next time your team is together, look around and ask yourself, 'Who can I trust to hold the rope? Who is going to let their hands bleed for me?' When you can look at every member of your team and say to yourself that they all would hold the rope, then your team is destined to win a lot of football games. You see, the teams that hold the rope when the going gets tough are 'winners.' When you are down by two touchdowns and thoroughly exhausted, yell at your teammates to 'hold the rope, let it burn, but don't let go.' Every year there are winners and losers in every sport. Every year the winners hold the rope. You do not have to be the best team on the field to win the game. If you play with poise and do what your coaches ask of you, and most of all hold the rope, you will be successful. No matter what sport you play, in order to win, you must have commitment to the team. If you are supposed to run four sprint laps don't cheat. Give it your all. Once you start letting up at practice or start missing workouts you've killed the team because you did not hold the rope. Don't let your team down...you have to HOLD THE ROPE!"

Three seniors were awarded all-state honors when the season was over: Robbie Gordon, a 6-foot-1, 270-pound two-year starter at offensive tackle; B.J. Scofield, a 6-foot-1, 195-pound three-year starter at inside linebacker; and Dan Stanley, for two years the team's punter, and who averaged 56.3 yards on three punts in the title game. Junior running back Chris Taylor was named to the all-state second team after rushing for more than 1,800 yards (he had more than 1,400 yards as a sophomore). Roderique, for the second time, was named 4A Coach of the Year.

After rushing for more than 3,200 yards his sophomore and junior seasons, senior running back Chris Taylor was the focal point of the Webb City offense in 2001. Six of the team's 15 seniors were chosen as team captains: wide receiver and defensive back Grant McDonald, running back and outside linebacker Joe Smith, tight end and middle linebacker Justin Smith, running back and defensive back Chris Taylor, quarterback and outside linebacker Garrett Taylor and offensive and defensive lineman Tyler White.

There were major holes on the defense, with Nathan Copher, B.J. Scofield and Josh Belcher gone from a unit that had posted six shutouts in 14 games, including two in the playoffs. Offensively, White was the anchor on the line at center in his third year as a starter, and Smith had three years of experience at tight end. For the first time in years the Cardinals had two quarterbacks to choose from: Garrett Taylor, who was recovering from offseason knee surgery, and wide receiver Johnny Wynne, who saw time there in the offseason.

Special teams were another question mark after the team had lost Dan Stanley, a two-year all-state punter; Landon Dobbs, an all-conference kicker; and Chaz Mayes, a three-year starter at long snapper.

A lot of the questions surrounding the team were answered in the season's first game, at Branson, when Webb City pounded the Pirates 43-8. At one point in the first quarter a high snap led to great field position for the Pirates, who got the ball at the Webb City 25-yard line, but the team's defense stuffed Branson on four straight plays. On the ensuing drive, Chris Taylor took a pitch and ran 84 yards for the first touchdown of the season. He later added a 60-yard punt return for a touchdown to make it a 14-0 game midway through the first quarter. Joe Smith got in on the action before the quarter was over, scoring on a 21-yard run, and as the second quarter began, Taylor scored from 32 yards out and the Cardinals led 33-0 at halftime.

Senior quarterback Garrett Taylor added a 45-yard touchdown run in the second half to put the mercy clock in place, and Casey Eichelberger ended the scoring with a 20-yard field goal.

The 2001 home opener was against Pittsburg, which had finished second in the state the prior year and had returned more than a dozen starters. The Purple Dragons featured Dylan Meier at quarterback, who later started at quarterback for Kansas State University.

Pittsburg took a 14-10 lead in the second half as the Cardinals had a hard time stopping the Purple Dragons on the ground and through the air, but with less than two minutes left in the third quarter the momentum shifted. Tyler White stripped the ball and Adam Spieker recovered it on the Webb City 42-yard line. On first down, Garrett Taylor threw a pass to Grant McDonald on the sideline and McDonald scored. That made it a 17-14 game. Eichelberger's early field goal had started the Cardinals off with a 3-0 lead and he'd nailed both extra points. He kicked another PAT after Chris Taylor returned a punt for a touchdown to make it 24-14. Bryan Strausbaugh intercepted a Meier pass in the fourth quarter, and as storms approached and the wind grew colder, the Cardinals ran out the clock until the officials finally called the game with 2:03 remaining. It started pouring about five minutes later.

Everybody expected visiting Rogers, Arkansas to throw the ball all over the field in the week three game, but instead it was the Cardinals who showed off their passing attack. Garrett Taylor completed 10 of 11 passes and threw four touchdowns, and Chris Taylor showed off his baseball arm by completing a halfback pass in the third quarter. Garrett Taylor completed passes to Bryan Strausbaugh, Grant McDonald and Johnny Wynne – all receivers – and also to tight end Justin Smith and running back Joe Smith. Chris Taylor, for the third straight game, returned a punt for a touchdown and when Webb City's offense finally lined up for the first time Garrett Taylor threw a 12-yard touchdown to Justin Smith. McDonald caught a 21-yard touchdown pass on the team's second possession, which was set up by Chris Taylor's halfback pass to Wynne. Webb City led 21-0 after a quarter. With 56 seconds left in the half, Wynne caught a 51-yard touchdown pass and Webb City held a 29-7 lead.

In the second half, Chris Taylor scored on a 9-yard run, then picked off a pass at midfield to set up a Garrett Taylor-to-Wynne touchdown pass. And, capping the scoring, Chris Taylor added a long touchdown run for good measure. He finished the game with two interceptions on defense, while Wynne and McDonald also picked off passes. Webb City won 50-7.

For the second time of the year Webb City took to the road in week four, and Seneca is always a tough place to play. It's a small, intimate stadium and the Indians were still guided by former Webb City great Chance Wistrom. In 2001, though, it wasn't much of a game. The Cardinals scored five touchdowns in the first half and led 35-0 by the break. Garrett Taylor completed eight passes for 114 yards. Chris Taylor broke a 64-yard touchdown run down the sideline for the first points of the game, and he scored the team's final points, too, with a 60-yard score in the third quarter after Grant McDonald's interception.

Two touchdowns came directly from the Webb City defense. Middle linebacker Justin Smith intercepted a first quarter pass and returned it 32 yards for the team's second touchdown, and Drew Frazier later recovered a fumble in the end zone. Chris Taylor returned a punt 34 yards to the Seneca 9-yard line, and tight end Dustin Moreland caught a 4-yard touchdown from Garrett Taylor. Webb City was now 4-0 after winning 44-7.

The Southwest Conference season opened a week later at Nevada, and it proved a perfect opportunity for some younger Cardinals to see the field; it was another blowout. Frank DeLozier, Ryan DeMoss and Jeremy Smart combined for a 79-yard drive late in the game, and Donny McDowell fell on the football in the end zone for the team's final points in the 52-0 win. Chris Taylor was a monster on the ground, rushing seven times for 175 yards and three touchdowns – all in the first half. His first score came after Johnny Wynne blocked a punt and recovered it at the 9. Joe Smith added two touchdowns of his own, and DeMoss scored one. Casey Eichelberger was perfect on all seven PAT kicks and he also booted a 40-yard field goal. Overall, Webb City tallied 454 rushing yards and 516 total yards.

The Cardinals were now 5-0, and had allowed a total of 14 points in three games while scoring 146, but as the team took to the road for the third straight week, the schedule was much, much tougher. The game at Jefferson City, a 5A school and historically one of the best programs in Missouri, would pit the Jays' size against the Cardinals' speed. Jefferson City was also the third-largest high school in the state, and had a depth advantage, too. The school's 10 state championships was also a record at that time.

Despite being the top-ranked school in 4A, the Cardinals went into the game as underdogs.

"We're just asking our kids to play their best," John Roderique said. "They don't have anything to lose. They're not expected to win."

It was a playoff atmosphere in Jefferson City, and a soggy field tended to favor Jefferson City's style of play, so Roderique knew it was important to score first. His defense held the Jays to nine yards on their first drive, and when the Cardinals got the ball for the first time they drove 65 yards in five plays and took a 7-0 lead. Garrett Taylor rushed for 17 yards and then 7 more; he threw an 18-yard pass to Bryan Strausbaugh, then Joe Smith took the ball 13 yards and into the red zone. Chris Taylor scored from the 17.

In a game in which the Jays were held to fewer than 100 yards rushing, their only score came on defense, and it was a murky call. Backed into his own end zone, Garrett Taylor dropped back to pass and started to throw the ball when he was hit. Jefferson City recovered the ball, and officials ruled it a fumble and a touchdown.

With Jefferson City blitzing most of the time, Garrett Taylor completed three quick passes on the team's next possession, and then tight end Justin Smith cleared the way for Joe Smith with a great block on a 32-yard touchdown. Webb City led 14-6 in the fourth quarter, but the Jays recovered a fumble at midfield and had one of their best chances of the game to tie it up. But on the very next play, Chris Taylor intercepted a pass. The Cardinals ran four minutes off the clock, then sent Eichelberger out for a 41-yard field goal. His kick was blocked, but the Jays were flagged for running into the kicker, and Eichelberger tried again from 31 yards and nailed it. The Cardinals had knocked off the legendary Jays, 17-6.

Finally back on their home field in week seven, which was also homecoming night and the final game before district play, the Cardinals played a complete game against Glendale. They scored on their first three possessions to lead 21-0 after a quarter, and the lead grew to 35-0 in the second quarter. Nearly a week after the game the rumor was that Glendale's coaching staff was still disputing a phenomenal touchdown grab by Grant McDonald – the first touchdown of the game – saying the ball bounced before he caught it. Roderique told the *Sentinel* he had the video evidence to prove it didn't.

The team's second touchdown started with Adam Spieker forcing a fumble, which was recovered by Justin Smith. That set up a reverse, with Garrett Taylor handing off to Johnny Wynne, and tight end Dustin Moreland made a key block to pave the way for Wynne's 16-yard scoring run. On the team's third possession, Justin Smith caught a long pass from Garrett Taylor and Joe Smith gained 30 yards on one carry. Justin Smith caught the 2-yard touchdown.

The Falcons made only five first downs in the game, and gained a mere 83 yards on offense. Webb City's offense rushed for 353 yards and added 64 more through the air.

Chris Taylor scored a touchdown on the team's fourth scoring drive, and after that backups Frank DeLozier and Ryan DeMoss added touchdowns. DeMoss' run was a 61-yarder. After the 42-7 win, the Cardinals were 7-0 and on a roll as the district slate of Neosho at home, McDonald County on the road and Carthage at home awaited. And those three district opponents had combined to win just eight games all season.

Chris Taylor had already compiled 812 rushing yards despite carrying the ball just 65 times. Normally the team's primary rusher would already have 100 carries, but with all the lopsided wins, reserves had seen the field more than usual. Five different players had at least 150 yards already.

The game against Neosho was one of the most lopsided all season. The Cardinals scored the first six times they had the ball, led 43-0 at halftime and cruised to a 50-6 win. Assistant Mike Smith said the team was reminded before the game that Neosho had been responsible for one of just two losses suffered by the current senior class. Despite the high-scoring output, the team's offensive statistics weren't as gaudy as one might expect. Webb City had tremendous field position, starting drives in the first half at the Neosho 45, Neosho 19, Neosho 32, Neosho 28, Neosho 29 and Neosho 49. Another drive started at the 50. The Cardinals scored 29 points in the first quarter; Chris Taylor had a 27-yard run, and scored again after Garrett Taylor intercepted a pass at the 19. After a blocked punt was recovered by Dustin Moreland at the 32, Joe Smith caught a 28-yard touchdown pass. Justin Smith's fumble recovery set up a 7-yard touchdown grab by Strausbaugh, his first of the season.

After Adam Spieker sacked the quarterback on a third down early in the second quarter, Chris Taylor scored his third touchdown of the game, and Joe Smith's touchdown run made it 43-0 at halftime.

By the time district play was over, the Cardinals had outscored their opponents 164-25, adding a 58-7 win against McDonald County and a 56-12 thrashing of Carthage in what was a meaningless game for postseason contention. Against McDonald County, which was Roderique's 50th career win, Chris Taylor scored five touchdowns. The first came after a Bryan Strausbaugh interception that he returned to the 20. At one point it was just a 14-7 game after McDonald County's first and only score, but on the very next play, Garrett Taylor threw a 55-yard pass down the middle to Johnny Wynne. Another score came on a 55-yard run by Garrett Taylor. Webb City rushed for 440 yards in the game, with 197 of those coming from Chris Taylor alone.

A week later, though, Taylor was done for the season after breaking his arm in the sectional game at Nixa, and "find a way to win" became the team's new motto. Roderique said Taylor was the team's best football player, its leader, its "main guy." He finished the year with 1,146 yards and 20 touchdowns on 91 carries, and had scored a total of 146 points in 10 games.

Nixa led 8-0 as the first quarter ended, and Taylor stayed on the field after a 6-yard run. He didn't want to leave his teammates, but team physician David Black eventually took him away to have surgery.

"They played inspired from that time on," Roderique told the newspaper. "He means so much to our football team. There were not very many dry eyes in the locker room."

With Chris Taylor's season done, second-leading rusher Joe Smith became the go-to guy in the backfield. He scored the team's first four touchdowns at Nixa and added a fifth on a 12-yard reception. Ryan DeMoss scored on a 32-yard run, as well. Webb City won the game 42-8.

The Cardinals were back on the road for the quarterfinals at Camdenton, and for once this game came down to the fourth quarter. Garrett Taylor's touchdown after the Cardinals recovered a fumble at the Lakers' 24-yard line was the first score of the game, but a blocked punt set up Camdenton's answering touchdown. It remained a 7-7 game into the fourth quarter.

Ryan DeMoss and Frank DeLozier each had to step up in this game; not only was Chris Taylor done for the season, but Joe Smith had sprained an ankle and couldn't play. It was still a 7-7 game with 4:27 left in the fourth when DeMoss had runs of 15 and 16 yards to set up a 4-yard score by DeLozier. After four straight incompletions by Camdenton, DeMoss ran 30 yards for another touchdown; Webb City won 21-7 to return home for the semifinals.

Around the same time, with his season already over, Chris Taylor made it official and signed with the University of Arkansas to play baseball.

Each of the players wore a No. 30 decal to honor Taylor during the semifinal game against Park Hill. Earlier in the season, Park Hill's leading running backs, Jason Agee and Jonathan Cooper, told a *Kansas City Star* reporter that the hits they'd received from Webb City's "corn-fed boys" were the hardest hits they'd ever received. It had been a close game – 35-27 – when the teams met in the 2000 semifinals.

The Trojans took an early 3-0 lead, but on a first-and-15, Garrett Taylor shocked the crowd by hitting Grant McDonald for a big 56-yard touchdown pass. Webb City's third possession of the game was one of the turning points. The Cardinals were lined up to punt, but a penalty was called on the Park Hill nose guard for saying "hut, hut" during the cadence. Then, a second flag was thrown on a Trojan assistant, who was heard to swear while complaining about the initial penalty. That was enough for a first down, and two plays later DeMoss scored a 53-yard run and the Cardinals took a 14-3 halftime lead.

Park Hill recovered a fumble and made it a 14-10 game early in the third, but DeLozier answered with a 40-yard run to start Webb City's ensuing drive. A few plays later, he scored from the 1. But Park Hill answered again, and it was a 21-17 game for all of nine seconds before a facemask penalty on the kickoff started the Cardinals at their own 42, and Joe Smith, on first down, rushed 58 yards for the score. Casey Eichelberger added a 32-yard field goal following a Park Hill fumble, and the game ended 31-17.

In the Show-Me Bowl, Webb City would face the Washington High School Blue Jays, who felt they were the ones who should have played the Cardinals in St. Louis a year earlier. The Cardinals left early on Friday morning and practiced at Sullivan High School before attending the Class 5A championship game that night and then watching film. Their game was set for 3:15 p.m. Saturday. It would be another record-breaking performance.

Garrett Taylor was nearly perfect. He completed five of eight passes for 105 yards, and rushed for 109 yards. Ryan DeMoss led the team with 125 rushing yards, and the Cardinals would have set a record for most rushing yards in the title game except for a 12-yard loss, which left them with 375 in the game. They finished with 480 yards of total offense. The 17 rushing first downs was a 4A state record that had stood since 1987, and the team's average yards per play – 8.57 – broke the previous record of 7.9 that had been set by the 1997 Cardinals.

Defensively, the Cardinals allowed just one third-down conversion in seven attempts, while Webb City's offense converted seven of nine third-down plays. The Blue Jays also couldn't convert a single fourth-down attempt, and they went for it three times.

On the second play of the game, Johnny Wynne took a reverse and rushed 62 yards, and then DeMoss scored from the 6. On the team's third possession, Garrett Taylor scored a 48-yard touchdown to make it 14-0. In the second, Joe Smith caught a 41-yard touchdown pass, then Justin Smith hauled in a 6-yard touchdown. Casey Eichelberger tacked on a 23-yard field goal and the team led 31-0 at halftime.

In the third quarter, Matt Beaver forced a fumble that was recovered by Ryan Belcher, and DeMoss scored his second touchdown of the game shortly after. Bryan Strausbaugh came up with an interception on Washington's next possession, and Garrett Taylor scored his second rushing touchdown of the game, which ended in a 45-0 shutout. It was Webb City's second straight shutout in the state championship game.

Before the game, Grant Wistrom had spoken to the team and encouraged them to think about someone they wanted to play for. It was an obvious choice: Chris Taylor.

"We all love Chris Taylor," Justin Smith told the newspaper. He said the injury had "lit a fire underneath everyone."

"We were defeated by a very good team," Blue Jays head coach Jeff Duncan said in the postgame press conference. "They make you play perfect. When you get the ball, you feel you have to play perfect."

In the interview room, Roderique was joined by Garrett Taylor, Tyler White and Justin Smith.

"No. 22 (Smith) is probably the smartest player I've ever coached in my life," Roderique said. He said it was normal for Smith, a tight end and defensive back, to suggest plays while standing on the field."

The senior class, in its three years of varsity football, had gone 36-2 with 10 shutouts, including three in the playoffs. In 2001 the Cardinals allowed double-digit points just twice.

"Our defense has probably been underrated all year," Roderique said. He credited Mike Smith.

It was Webb City's sixth state championship, and for the second time the Cardinals had won back-to-back titles.

Andrew Stanley on the field at the Edward Jones Dome in St. Louis after Webb City lost to Clayton 27-26 in overtime in the 2004 state championship game. Stanley became just the fourth running back in state history to rush for more than 200 yards in a championship game. Photo by Bob Foos.

29. A TITLE DROUGHT

After winning consecutive state championships in 2000 and 2001, Webb City's winning streak stood at 29 games, and the streak grew to 30 with a convincing 61-16 win against Branson in the first week of the 2002 campaign. In week two, the streak ended when the Cardinals lost by a touchdown at Bentonville, Arkansas. Webb City lost one more game that regular season but went back to the playoffs and back to the semifinals for a third straight year. That was as far as the team went in 2002, though, and the season marked the start of the longest championship drought since Jerry Kill and Mark Smith brought home the first title in 1989.

Webb City has been to the playoffs every single year of the new millennium, and has won eight championships in the century's first 13 seasons. The Cardinals' record since 2000: 180 wins, 12 losses. From 2002 through the 2005 seasons, the Cardinals went 41-9 but didn't bring home a championship trophy. They went to the semifinals in 2002 and 2003, lost by a point in the 2004 championship game, and lost by a touchdown in the 2005 quarterfinals. As is the case with nearly every single season that didn't end in a celebratory parade down Main Street, most other schools would gladly have taken those years for themselves, but when it takes more than two hands to count all the championship rings, seasons that don't add another to the collection can be overlooked by some.

The 2002 season was the "year of the unknown" for Webb City football. Roderique told the newspaper that not knowing his own team made him nervous, but the team's defense had dominated Carl Junction, Monett and Willard in the annual jamboree, allowing just one score. Aaron Davied was a highlight at inside linebacker and defensive tackles Ryan Belcher and Adam Spieker were dominant. Johnny Wynne made his presence known at free safety with some big hits. Ryan DeMoss and Seth Houston ran hard on offense, but turnovers and penalties plagued the Cardinals on that side of the ball.

After starting the 2002 season with the win against Branson and the loss at Bentonville, the team hit its stride in the next four games. Webb City beat Kansas City Ruskin by 40 points, Nevada by 32 and then shut out Kansas City Westport 56-0. On the road at Pittsburg, the Cardinals won 38-9 to improve to 5-1 before the team lost its first home game in three years, 42-28 against Columbia Hickman. They finished the regular season 8-2 after beating Neosho, McDonald County and Carthage, and then blew out Republic 55-14 in the sectional game. On the road at Jefferson City Helias in the quarterfinals, fans were treated to a classic.

The teams went to overtime tied at 21. Webb City got the first possession and had to settle for a field goal by Casey Eichelberger to take a 24-21 lead. A touchdown for Helias would win it. Immediately the Crusaders, who had gouged Webb City through the air during regulation, completed a pass to the Webb City 3-yard line. It looked like the game was over; Jefferson City had four downs to gain three yards.

"It doesn't get any more challenging than that," Roderique said afterward. Nine times out of 10, a team in that situation will score, he said. Even he couldn't help but think the game was over. But, remember that old cliché. It's not over till it's over.

"We say that on defense," Roderique said. "It ain't over till the ball crosses the goal line."

Jefferson City fullback Dan Brenneke gained a yard on first down. Quarterback Kyle Shimmens gained another yard on second down. On third down, Brenneke was stuffed at the line of scrimmage. Fourth down, one yard to go. Shimmens took the snap and headed to his right; Roderique thought the Crusaders might pass. Outside linebacker Ryan DeMoss honed in on Shimmens, with linebacker Travis Wallace following from the middle. The quarterback kept the ball and dove for the goal line, where he collided with both Webb City linebackers, and he might have scored if not for free safety Johnny Wynne, who finished him off. Shimmens' helmet crossed the goal line; the ball did not.

"It was one of the most exciting finishes that I've had here," Roderique said.

Wynne, at quarterback, led the team with 122 rushing yards, and Seth Houston ran for 68 yards and three touchdowns. Other players with key contributions were sophomore Bryce Allen and senior Travis Wallace. Allen, who hadn't seen much varsity time, replaced Drew Gollhofer at center after Gollhofer suffered a high ankle sprain; Allen's job was to block linebacker Tom Koenigsfeld, Helias' best player. Wallace went in at linebacker for Coty Bryant, who injured his hand. He was big in the effort to keep the Crusaders out of the end zone in overtime.

In the semifinals the team hosted Kearney, who had outscored its playoff opponents 143-0. The Cardinals scored three touchdowns, but lost the game 35-21.

Webb City lost 18 players from that 10-3 squad, and they were replaced by 18 seniors and 26 juniors in 2003. The annual jamboree, held in Willard that season, was the final tune-up before the Cardinals opened against Branson, and as usual there were positives and negatives in the scrimmage.

"Overall, I was not say, disappointed, but I was not pleased," Roderique was quoted as saying. "I think our kids had good effort, but we did not play very smart both offensively and defensively. I thought we didn't do a great job scheme-wise. We had some kids who had some good individual performances. There were some positives."

The team's new quarterback was junior Brayden Drake, who as a backup to Johnny Wynne in 2002 had completed one of five passes – it went 62 yards for a touchdown. The backfield consisted of junior Andrew Stanley and senior Landon Taylor at running backs. Stanley rushed for 569 yards as a sophomore and scored 10 touchdowns, and Taylor had gained 143 yards a season before. Vince Warbinton started at wide receiver. The offensive line was anchored by senior Ryan Belcher at right guard. He was joined by Bryce Allen at center, Eric Bearden at right tackle, Justin Parish at left guard, Johnnie Jacks at left tackle and Matt Bickett and Cody Gordon at tight end.

Only three starters returned on defense, among them Belcher at tackle who had recorded 26 solo tackles and assisted on 54 others in 2002. On the defensive line, Parish was at the other tackle position and Bearden and Allen were at ends. Chris Endicott and Jared Schweitzer were at inside linebackers and Jake Cooke and Taylor were at outside linebackers. In the defensive backfield, the Cardinals had Drake and Jared Minard, with Warbinton at free safety.

Webb City once again opened the year with a thrashing of Branson, and the only loss in the first half of the regular season was a 31-24 setback at Ridgeway that took four overtimes to decide. Back-to-back losses to Pittsburg and Columbia Hickman left the Cardinals just 4-3 entering district play, but after beating Neosho 56-0, McDonald County 19-7 and Carthage 42-0 the team once again had momentum heading into the postseason. A 35-6 win at Hillcrest in the sectional gave them more steam, and after getting past Nixa 29-15, they hosted Kearney once more for a semifinal rematch.

This one was even worse than the first. The Cardinals turned the ball over on five straight possessions in the first half and lost 43-0. It was the worst defeat at Cardinal Stadium in recent memory.

"We were outmatched a little bit today," John Roderique said after the game. "When you turn the ball over time after time, bad things are going to happen to you. (Kearney) is as good as any team in the state."

Kearney won state championships each year after beating the Redbirds in the semifinals.

In the fall of 2004, the Cardinals were hungry for a return to the dome in St. Louis. They had a ton of depth entering that season, and Roderique hoped his players hadn't forgotten the loss to Kearney.

"I hope it is still somewhere in their bellies," he said in August. "We don't talk about (the loss) much in practice. Just like we didn't talk about winning state titles when we did that a few years ago. This is a new season. The chemistry of this team is different. The players are different. Our hope as a football team is that we will play better than we did a year ago."

With Brayden Drake back under center as a senior, Roderique planned to open the offense up and throw the ball more. In limited time in 2003 after nursing an injury, Drake had completed 24 of 47 passes for about 53 yards a game and a total of 10 touchdowns. He rushed for 315 yards. Backing him up in 2004 was senior Jake Cooke. Behind Drake the Cardinals had senior Andrew Stanley at fullback and junior Marty Rodgers at tailback. Stanley rushed 133 times in 2003 for seven touchdowns and 727 yards.

"Andrew is the power runner," Roderique said.

Rodgers was used mainly as a return specialist his sophomore year, but in 14 carries he had gained 75 yards. He averaged better than 20 yards per kick return.

"Marty is a pure playmaker," Roderique said. "He is someone who you want to put the ball in their hands."

The backfield was even deeper, too. Eddie Helton, Michael Bickett, Caleb Sigars, Jacob Perry and Brandon Berry were ready to spell either Stanley or Rodgers if needed. In front of the whole group, the offensive line featured three returning starters and some newcomers with big potential. Seniors Eric Bearden and Johnnie Jacks were back; Bearden at 6-foot-1, 235 pounds and Jacks at 5-11, 225. Senior Bryce Allen, who was all of six feet tall and 200 pounds, returned at center. Three newcomers vied for playing time at guard: 5-foot-9, 225-pound Joseph Mahaffey; 5-10, 205-pound Brent Bertelsen and 6-1, 260-pound Richard Moore.

Five seniors led the team's receiving corps, including Vince Warbinton.

"Vince can flat out run," Roderique said. "He is thin, but has that great speed."

Scott Taylor and newcomer Eric Clark, the baseball team's centerfielder, were also in the mix, along with Josh Martin and Josh Stoner.

The defensive unit was led by returning end Bearden and linebacker Endicott. The rest of the line included D.J. Midcap, Moore, Jacks, Allen and sophomore Nick Sanders. Cooke, Jared Schweitzer, Robert Norvell and Berry were at linebacker. Rodgers returned at free safety, as did cornerbacks Taylor and Warbinton. Stone, Drake, Travis Hilburn, Sigars and Bickett could also see time.

On special teams, Will McDaniel returned as the team's kicker. Endicott was the team's punter, and Alec French the long snapper. The overall squad featured 70 players in grades 10 through 12.

The 2004 Cardinals were dominant from the very start; it was the best team since the 2001 champions. Webb City beat Willard 49-6 in week one, then Republic 55-7, and Jefferson City 34-17. Against Nevada in the first conference game, the Cardinals won 70-6. They beat Columbia Rock Bridge by 35 points in another tough non-conference match up, and then won 29-14 a week later at Pittsburg. After an open week, district play began with the team handling Neosho 33-13, dismantling McDonald County 56-0, and cruising at Carthage 49-14. Back to the playoffs.

Ozark was no match in the sectional game, which the Cardinals won 41-6. They beat their old nemesis, Camdenton, 20-12 in the quarterfinals. There would be no rematch with Kearney in the semifinals, though. The Bulldogs hadn't even made the playoffs. In their place, Webb City hosted St. Joseph-Benton in Roderique's 100th game as head coach. He went in with an 85-14 record, and didn't even realize the milestone until he received an email from *Sentinel* editor Bob Foos.

"Bob mentioned this to me and I guess this is a special game," he told the newspaper. "I can't believe time has gone so fast. When you get into this situation in the playoffs, our fifth year in the semifinals, this will be a difficult game to lose. We are so close to being (at state) and realizing our dreams that we have worked for all year long."

For the 12th time that season, the defense didn't allow more than 14 points. In fact, Benton scored only eight points as the Cardinals punched their ticket to St. Louis with a 42-8 victory. The game was tied at 8 in the second quarter before the team scored three times in less than three minutes. Stanley carried the ball 15 times for 107 yards and three touchdowns. When it was over, Will McDaniel and his teammates quietly carried a Gatorade cooler up to Roderique and drenched him in freezing cold water.

"Whoo, that's cold," he shouted. "Who did that?"

In the 2004 title game the Cardinals faced the Clayton Greyhounds and their senior quarterback and defensive back Jairus Byrd. Byrd went into the game with 25 touchdowns, 1,240 rushing yards on 131 carries, 785 passing yards and 10 touchdowns. He'd even caught six passes for 125 yards, and was second on the team in tackles to go along with six interceptions and two fumble recoveries.

"I think (Byrd) is making me lose sleep," Roderique said before the game. "He is a heck of a player. He is without a doubt the best player we will have played against this year. It will be a challenge to defend him."

Byrd lived up to all the hype and then some in the title game. The Greyhounds were the first team to score, meaning the Cardinals trailed in a state championship game for the first time since 1997, but after Andrew Stanley returned an interception for a touchdown, Webb City pulled ahead 13-6. Not long after, Byrd threw a 54-yard bomb for a touchdown and the game was tied at 13 at halftime.

On their first drive of the second half, Webb City had a first-and-10 at the Clayton 18-yard line but couldn't convert on fourth down. Later on the Cardinals went ahead 20-13, and had a chance to put the game away in the fourth quarter after a missed Clayton field goal, but the team went three-and-out and punted. Clayton tied the game on its ensuing drive.

Webb City had two more chances to tie the game at the end of regulation. One drive ended with a fumble in Clayton territory. The team's final drive in regulation got as far as the Greyhound 43 but ended in another turnover. The game went to overtime and each team had a chance to score from the 25-yard line.

Clayton scored a touchdown, an 18-yard pass from Byrd to Torrey Tate on a fourth-and-4. With the point after, the Greyhounds led 27-20. Out came Webb City's offense. On a fourth-and-5, Brayden Drake scrambled for five yards and a first down. On a fourth-and-6, he scrambled to his right and scored, making it a 27-26 game. The Cardinals could force another overtime with an extra point, or win the game with a two-point conversion. Roderique decided to go for the win.

Stanley got the ball, saw an opening and plunged toward the goal line. Byrd closed quickly, and tackled Stanley less than a yard away from the end zone. The Cardinals lost the game.

"Wow, there at the end, if you score then it was a great play, and if you don't score it was a bad call," Roderique said. "I will take the credit for the poor call. We missed some opportunities today. We were in that situation at the end of the game, and I will take all the credit for it."

Stanley had a heck of a game, becoming just the fourth running back to surpass 200 yards rushing at state. He finished with 219 yards on 25 carries and scored two touchdowns to go along with his interception return.

"I was the first one who said go for it," Stanley said. "Coach looked right at us and said, 'It's up to you guys.' I was the first one to say go for it. I didn't call my own number though.

"I saw the hole and there was just one linebacker, and I make a living on one-on-ones with a linebacker," he added.

It was Clayton's first state championship.

"I think I need to take a deep breath," Clayton head coach Mike Musick said. "That was the most unbelievable football game I have ever seen. We played some great teams, MICDS and Holt, but this game was just awesome. Our kids played their guts out. That (Webb City) is an outstanding football team. That is the best football team we have ever played."

Jairus Byrd, of course, went on to play for the Oregon Ducks, where he was an all-Pac 10 first-team selection as a junior in 2008. He was a second-round selection by the Buffalo Bills in the 2009 NFL Draft and went on to become a three-time Pro Bowl selection. He signed a six-year, $56 million contract with the New Orleans Saints in 2014.

And Brayden Drake went on to a stellar baseball career. He signed with Missouri State after leading Webb City to the 2005 state championship. He was a two-time all-state honoree, and finished in the top 10 in several categories at Missouri State. His No. 5 jersey – the same number he wore for the Bears, too – was retired at Webb City in 2010 after he was an All-American third baseman as a senior in college. He was drafted by the San Diego Padres in the 12th round of the 2009 June Amateur Draft.

The football team that took the field at Willard for the first game of 2005 looked substantially different. Marty Rodgers, now a senior, was back at tailback, and a trio of other seniors – Michael Bickett, Jacob Perry and Caleb Sigars – were also quite capable of handling the team's rushing duties. Junior Collin Howard was slated to start at quarterback, but broke his collarbone in the jamboree and was forced to miss several games. In his place, the team was confident in junior Bradley Workman, whose main target was senior receiver Alex Talbott. Senior Clayton Arft and junior Marcus Ozbun also had good hands. Other than Rodgers, though, the only other returning starter was senior tight end and linebacker Cody Gordon. Senior Brayton Rand started at tight end and linebacker, as well.

On the offensive line, junior Zeke Tarrant started at center, senior Cody Hulsey and junior Brett Stewart at guards, and junior Cody Johnson and senior Richard Moore at tackles.

John Roderique felt especially good about the team's defense.

"We've got some physical kids," he said. "They'll fly around and hit you."

On the defensive line were Moore and Johnson at tackles, and sophomore Eric Thomason and junior Nick Sanders at ends. Rand and senior Eddie Helton were at outside linebackers, Berry and Gordon at linebackers, Bickett and Talbott in the defensive backfield, and Rodgers was back to hold down the free safety position.

After four games it was clear just how good the team was defensively. Webb City outscored Willard, Republic and Jefferson City at home, and Nevada on the road, by a total of 164 points and hadn't allowed a single point. Willard (61-0), Republic (48-0) and Nevada (41-0) were especially lopsided, and against a good Jeff City team the Cardinals won 14-0. Columbia Rock Bridge, in week five, played Webb City within a touchdown, but the Redbirds went to 5-0 with a 22-14 win.

In the 11-game season – the team had another open date – Webb City recorded seven shutouts. They allowed a total of 48 points, winning by an average score of 39-5, in the regular season alone. In the first two district games against Neosho and McDonald County, the combined score was 105-6. And after a close 35-28 home win against Carthage, it was back to the playoffs. Again.

Just like in 2004, Ozark was Webb City's sectional opponent, and it was once again a blowout. For the sixth time in 18 seasons, the Cardinals met the Camdenton Lakers a week later. The defense kept Camdenton off the scoreboard on its first three possessions; on the second two, the Cardinals' held twice when the Lakers needed a yard for a first down in Webb City territory. Rodgers tipped a long pass away, and Rand followed with a sack.

With Collin Howard by now back under center, he scored the game's first points on a 68-yard run on the first play of the second quarter. But the Lakers came back with a 67-yard drive. Later, after Cody Gordon pinned the Lakers at their own 5-yard line with a punt, they ate more than four minutes from the clock and drove 95 yards to pull ahead 14-7.

The third quarter began with Howard completing a 23-yard pass to Talbott, but the team punted. On Camdenton's ensuing possession, Eddie Hilton intercepted a pass to set his team up just 39 yards away from the end zone.

Rodgers and Michael Bickett each gained 10 yards on runs, then Howard completed an 11-yard pass to Rand. Rodgers took the ball the final yard to tie the game after Shane VanStavern's extra point.

Camdenton scored after starting at its own 40 when a squib kick bounced of a Laker, and held a lead midway through the fourth quarter. Webb City, for once a victim of the field position game, got the ball at its own 4 with six minutes left in the game. The team mounted a good try. Rodgers and Howard each ran for first downs. Center Eric Thomason was there to catch the ball when it popped out of Howard's arms at one point. After a Howard sack, he completed a third-down pass to give the team new life, then Bickett gained six yards. An illegal procedure penalty backed them up to their own 45, and with time winding down, an incomplete pass ended any hopes of a comeback. The 2005 season ended with a 21-14 loss to Camdenton in the quarterfinals.

Quarterback Brayden Drake celebrates a touchdown in the 2003 quarterfinal playoff game at Nixa. Webb City won 29-15. Photo by Bob Foos.

Marty Rodgers hurdles a Republic defender during the second game of the 2005 season, which the Cardinals won 48-0. Photo by Bob Foos.

After nearly 40 years, the old Cardinal Stadium was torn down following the 2006 season. Photo by Bob Foos.

30. CARDINAL STADIUM IS REBUILT

A season-opening contest against Kickapoo was just one of a few substantial changes to Webb City's schedule in 2006. The Carthage game had moved up to week two, instead of the last game of the regular season, and the Cardinals were scheduled to end the season at Carl Junction. It would be the first time the two schools had played since 1994.

That year also marked the final season of play in "old" Cardinal Stadium, which just two years shy of 40 years old was slated to be torn down and rebuilt bigger and better.

Webb City was once again in the state title hunt despite not having won a championship in five years, but with all the talent on the field in 2006, it was a good year to end the drought. Collin Howard was back at quarterback for the preseason top-ranked school in Class 4, and so were most of the offensive linemen. It would be hard to replace Marty Rodgers in the backfield, who had joined Jerry Kill's Salukis at Southern Illinois University and was already competing for a starting job, but in his place Steven Cook and Trevor Davis started with David Ebbs, Trey Laveroni, Zac Anderson and Nick Shember in the mix as well. The line consisted of Emilio Quezada, Kyle Ogden, Eric Thomason, Chase Philpot and Cody Johnson, with Jake Cockrell at tight end. Shane VanStavern was the team's kicker.

The Cardinals still planned to run the ball, but they also had an incredible group of wide receivers. Landon Zerkel and Alan Pink started, and Brad Workman, Bryce Griffin, Chance Sossamon and Nick Pace would also see plenty of time.

Defensively, the starters on the line were Nick Sanders, Brett Stewart, Eric Thomason and Cody Johnson; at linebacker the starters were Zac Anderson, David Ebbs, Jeff Stoner and Trevor Davis; and in the backfield Landon Zerkel was joined by Bryce Griffin and Brad Workman.

Zerkel, who went on to a great career at Missouri Southern, says there really wasn't any urgency to get back to St. Louis and win another ring that year.

"Maybe the coaches feel pressure, but that year we had a special group of guys that had grown up around each other since kindergarten," he says. "I was friends with a lot of guys who were seniors and all the guys my age. It was exciting going into it, and you could tell during the summer workouts leading up to when school started that we had a chance to do something special so it was really exciting."

The team threw the ball more in 2006, "by far" Zerkel says, though in that season opener against Kickapoo Howard threw the ball just four times. He completed three of them for 119 yards and Zerkel caught two of those for 112 yards. One was a 92-yard bomb for a touchdown. Chance Sossamon had a 35-yard reception, and Steven Cook caught one pass for seven yards.

Defensively, Zerkel added a 15-yard fumble return for a touchdown after David Ebbs knocked the ball loose, and add in touchdowns by Cook and Trevor Davis and a 30-yard VanStavern field goal, as well as a safety, and the Cardinals led Kickapoo 33-7 at halftime. They had other chances to score, but with John Roderique's old friend Kurt Thomspon on the other sideline, they didn't push it. After all, in addition to both playing linebacker for Pittsburg State in 1987, their wives were both in the Alpha Gamma Delta sorority, and Kurt stood up for John at his wedding.

Mack Kyle, the sophomore backup quarterback, ran the offense the entire second half. Cook was the team's leading rusher despite gaining just 42 yards. Others getting the ball were Davis (31 yards), Kyle (28), Preston Choate (22), Alan Pink (20), Nick Shember (13) and Zac Anderson (9). Both Kyle and Mac McIlvaine recovered fumbles, and Brad Workman intercepted a pass. Kyle also returned two kicks for a total of 65 yards.

In week two the Cardinals tangled with the Tigers and their talented sophomore quarterback Trey Derryberry. It was Carthage running back Caleb Sanders, though, who scored all three of the team's touchdowns in Webb City's 35-21 win. Derryberry's 67-yard completion to Stephen Poston set up Sanders' second touchdown of the game in the third quarter, which brought the Tigers to within 28-14. But Webb City's running game was still too much for Carthage to handle.

The first score was set up by two Howard-to-Zerkel passes and came on a 15-yard run by Davis. Cook scored on an 8-yard run in the second quarter, then Howard scored on a 5-yard run. In the third, Cook punched it in from the 2, and at the start of the fourth quarter the offense went on a 13-play drive that ate six minutes from the clock. Davis eventually scored on a 2-yard run. Already, the Cardinals were throwing the ball more, as well. Howard completed 10 of 15 passes for 74 yards. Zerkel caught three passes for 36 yards, Cook had a 17-yard reception and Caleb Powell had one grab for 21 yards. Howard also led the rushing attack with 115 yards on 12 carries. Davis gained 93 yards and Cook ran for 74. Nick Sanders recorded two sacks for a total of 15 yards in the game, and David Ebbs had a sack for a 7-yard loss.

The passing game became an even bigger weapon in the team's 27-0 win at Nixa in week three. After two straight rushes for no gain against Nixa's big defensive line, Collin Howard completed passes of 22, 22, 13, 15 and 10 yards to four different receivers. He threw a 24-yard touchdown pass to Brad Workman and rushed for three more – two from the 1-yard line and one for 24 yards. Howard finished with 112 rushing yards and threw for 156. Workman was the leading receiver, with five catches for 77 yards.

The defense wasn't bad, either. It buckled down after Nixa dropped an early touchdown pass and allowed only five first downs before the Eagles recorded three on their final possession of the game, which ended with Webb City stopping them twice at the 1-yard line. The Cardinals forced two turnovers and seven three-and-outs.

Roderique won his 100th game at Webb City a week later, another dominating performance where his Cardinals won 42-0 against Ozark.

"That was a complete game right there, if I've ever seen one," he told the team afterwards.

It was a 7-0 after a quarter behind Steven Cook's 3-yard touchdown, then early in the second quarter, with the Cardinals' defense on the field, Landon Zerkel went up to defend a pass to Ozark receiver Tyler Oakley. Both players caught the ball and fell to the ground wrestling for possession; Oakley emerged from the scrap and signaled "first down" with his arm, but Zerkel was lying on the ground in pain.

"It was a cheap shot," Zerkel told the newspaper. And Oakley, charged with taunting, was ejected from the game.

Mack Kyle then followed with an interception and a 40-yard Collin Howard touchdown. On Ozark's next possession, Jeff Stoner recovered a fumble and when the Webb City offense was held on a third-and-20, Ozark made the mistake of accepting a holding penalty to make it third-and-15 for the Cardinals. Howard ran for 21 yards, then Trevor Davis scored from the 1.

Still in the second quarter senior Blake Bearden intercepted a pass and returned it to the Ozark 24 to set up Howard's only touchdown pass of the game, to senior tight end Jacob Cockrell. After the break Davis capped a 72-yard drive with a 2-yard score, and Ozark answered with a lengthy drive all the way to the Webb City 31, but the Cardinals held on fourth-and-9. Mack Kyle added a 7-yard touchdown run in the fourth quarter.

In week five the Cardinals hosted a Nevada team that had just allowed 41 points in the first quarter to Carthage; Webb City didn't score that many, but improved to 5-0 with a 35-point win. Howard completed 11 of 14 passes for 207 yards and Mack Kyle completed his one pass for 13 yards. That brought the team's passing completion percentage to 57 percent for the season – 36 of 63 with just two interceptions.

"That's a big stat," Roderique told the paper. "If we could get above 60 percent, that would be fantastic."

Howard threw touchdown passes to Jacob Cockrell and Chance Sossamon, and two other touchdown passes to Zerkel and Alan Pink were called back due to penalties. On the ground, Steven Cook ran for two scores and Howard, Kyle and Trevor Davis each added one. Seven different runners combined for 185 yards.

The big quarter was the second; Zerkel and Nick Sanders each recovered fumbles and Webb City exploded for 28 points to lead 42-0 at the half. They won 49-14.

One of the first big tests of the 2006 season came in week six when the Cardinals crossed state lines to take on a 4-1 Pittsburg team. The Cardinals were actually scoreless in the first quarter, and they trailed 14-7 late in the first half with Pittsburg threatening to score again. Collin Howard was put in on defense to help defend against the Purple Dragons' passing attack and he came up with a big interception to end the scoring threat. Then, with just two minutes left in the second quarter, Howard led the Cardinals on a 90-yard drive and scored with eight seconds left to tie the game at 14.

The momentum didn't last in the third quarter; Webb City fumbled on its first possession and then turned it over again on an interception on its second drive. But a Zerkel interception started to change things. He picked off a Ty Siam pass and then lateraled the ball to Howard as he was being tackled. Howard took it all the way to the Pittsburg 46.

"I wasn't really expecting the ball, but I did yell pitch," Howard said after the game.

Not long after, Howard threw a 21-yard touchdown pass to Zerkel. Howard added a 43-yard rushing score on the team's next possession, making it 28-14. Pittsburg made things close in the fourth quarter, though, marching 77 yards and pulling to within a touchdown before Howard recovered an onside kick with 4:50 left. Webb City won 28-14.

Howard once again proved to be a dynamic force on offense, rushing for 122 of the team's 202 rushing yards on just 12 carries and completing 11 of 18 passes for 156 yards. Zerkel caught nine passes for 132 yards and scored twice.

Homecoming King Trevor Davis rushed for more than 100 yards and scored a pair of touchdowns in a 42-0 trouncing of St. Charles West that moved Webb City's record to 7-0. The team scored three touchdowns in each half. Howard completed 12 of 19 passes for 168 yards and Zerkel caught five balls for 70. Marcus Ozbun had three receptions for 40 yards and Workman added 45 yards on two receptions. Davis led a rushing attack that gained 230 yards with 106 of his own on 15 carries and Howard rushed seven times for 42 yards. St. Charles West, meanwhile, didn't even eclipse 100 yards of total offense. Workman picked off two of their passing attempts.

With the district slate beginning with McDonald County, the Cardinals prepared to say goodbye to beloved Cardinal Stadium. The Mac County game was the last scheduled game to be played in the stadium before the nearly 40-year-old concrete structure was demolished for aluminum seating for 4,000. The Cardinals, to that point, had won six state championships and a district title 16 of the previous 21 years since it opened. The school invited the 1969 football team – the first to play in the stadium – as special guests for the game, and about 25 were expected to attend.

The stadium received a fond and appropriate farewell. Though the game started rather uncharacteristically, with the Mustangs going 71 yards and scoring on their opening drive, Trevor Davis' 11-yard score on the last play of the first quarter tied the game at 7, and after that Cards ran away with it. They hung 30 points on the board in the second quarter: Howard scored on a 60-yard run, David Ebbs returned an interception 30 yards, Davis scored from the 11, the defense added a safety and then Mack Kyle returned the ensuing free kick 66 yards for a touchdown.

In the second half, Shane VanStavern kicked a 31-yard field goal, Jacob Cockrell caught a 67-yard touchdown pass and then Seth Helton and Chris Stoner each added fourth quarter touchdowns. The team won 60-7.

"That was awesome," Cockrell said after of his long touchdown catch. "That was my best memory in this stadium."

After dominating wins against Neosho (35-7) and Carl Junction (47-12), Webb City headed to the playoffs having won seven straight district titles. Against Neosho the Cardinals led 14-0 at the half after a 7-yard Trevor Davis touchdown and an 11-yard touchdown reception by Caleb Powell. In the second half, Davis scored from 15 yards and Steven Cook from the 4, then Howard added a 1-yard run in the fourth quarter. Davis finished that game with 130 yards on 12 carries.

Howard, on a 17-yard run, and Davis, on a 7-yard run, staked the Cardinals to a 14-0 lead after a quarter at Carl Junction, and the lead grew to 35 points by halftime after a touchdown catch by Zerkel, a 3-yard Cook run and a 31-yard Howard touchdown. Davis added a 10-yard run in the third and Marcus Ozbun hauled in a 19-yard touchdown in the fourth.

The best play from those two games came in the contest at Carl Junction. Landon Zerkel, running a streak route down the Bulldogs' sideline, hauled in a 71-yard touchdown catch with just one hand. Zerkel, who now lives in Carl Junction, says that's the one play that always comes to mind when he thinks back to his high school career.

"That was by far the luckiest catch of my life," he says. "I joke around with my buddies in Carl Junction now, but you never forget it because things went perfect. Nine out of 10 times I would have dropped that ball."

That was also the game in which both schools renewed their longstanding but dormant football rivalry. There was still a big rivalry in basketball, but Zerkel says it was fun to be a part of its renewal on the gridiron.

"One team I wish we got to play is Joplin," he says. "That never happened."

Joplin and Webb City haven't played since 1997, when the Cardinals won 33-7. A game against the Eagles would have been especially meaningful for Zerkel, whose father Kenny starred for Parkwood High School and won a pair of state championships in the 1980s.

"My dad used to get some flak for moving over to Webb City because his Joplin buddies wanted all their kids to play together," Zerkel says. "We moved over my kindergarten year and built a house by the airport by my grandparents. We had a Joplin number with a Webb City address, so we could have gone to either school but my mom wanted us to go to Webb."

Kenny Zerkel played free safety for the Bears and after redshirting a year at Missouri Southern went on to play free safety for what was then Missouri-Rolla.

"Being compared to my dad is what I wanted," Zerkel says. "That was the biggest thing for me. I wore No. 7 for him. Free safety was more my focus in high school until I realized I could play receiver in college. I just tried to imitate what he did and the stories I heard about him. It's great to go out there and make your dad proud and that was always a priority of mine."

Third-ranked Carthage, now playing in a different district, had also won and was in the playoffs as well, setting up a marquee postseason match-up against the two rivals. And Carthage's offense, after scoring more points against Webb City than anybody else but Pittsburg, had gotten even better; the Tigers had thrashed Hillcrest 55-12 a week earlier.

The game was Webb City's 53rd postseason appearance, and the Cardinals entered with a 43-9 record in those games. The sectional contest was also played in Webb City, meaning Cardinal Stadium was the site of at least one more game. As many as 6,000 fans showed up on a particularly warm fall night. Carthage opened the game with a 73-yard scoring drive capped by a Caleb Sanders touchdown, but Howard's 41-yard touchdown game made it a 7-6 game after a quarter. Webb City went ahead following Zerkel's interception in the end zone when Ozbun caught a 42-yard pass and was tackled 2-yards shy of the end zone;

David Ebbs punched it in. That made it a 12-7 game after a failed two-point try, and late in the half Carthage quarterback Trey Derryberry led his team into the red zone and another Sanders run made it 13-12 Carthage.

With barely a minute left in the half, Chance Sossamon caught the kickoff on the run and returned it to the Webb City 36. Howard then completed passes to Ozbun, Brad Workman, Ozbun and Ozbun again. Ebbs carried the ball the final seven yards, and Jacob Cockrell's two-point catch gave the Cardinals a 20-13 halftime lead.

In the third quarter Webb City returned the opening kickoff into the red zone and Howard scored the touchdown to make it 26-13. Zerkel picked off another Carthage pass to set up a Howard-to-Ozbun pass for 44 yards and a 34-13 lead. Carthage pulled within two touchdowns, but in the fourth quarter Mack Kyle scored and Webb City added a 40-yard field goal from Shane VanStavern to win 44-20.

It was a breakout game for Ozbun, who had battled a foot injury throughout the season.

"And in my opinion he was probably the best receiver," Zerkel says. "He was a great route runner, great hands; it's crazy he didn't get much playing time. We were stacked. Between me, Alan Pink and Sossamon, the shortest guy was 6-foot-4. Collin, he could throw the ball, and Coach Roderique took advantage of that."

In another sectional game, Nixa faced off with Union, which was ranked fourth in the state and had outscored its district opponents 169-21. But Nixa dismantled Union and won 56-14, meaning there would indeed be one last game at Cardinal Stadium. If Union had won, the Cardinals would have gone on the road.

The Eagles went 99 yards on their opening drive in the quarterfinal game, ending on a 47-yard touchdown pass, but the Cardinals answered with 20 points in the first half. Two of those came on Mack Kyle runs, for 11 and 5 yards, and Howard threw a 24-yard pass to Brad Workman.

After the half, Nixa drove all the way to the Cardinals' 11-yard line, but Bryce Griffin intercepted a pass in the end zone on fourth-and-5. Three possessions later, Howard found Zerkel for a 41-yard gain, then Howard ran 14 yards to set up a first and goal at the 9. Howard lobbed a pass to Zerkel, who bobbled the ball but came down with a touchdown. After a Nixa three-and-out, the Cardinals finished off the Eagles with a methodical drive featuring runs from David Ebbs, Trevor Davis and Kyle. Davis finished it off with a 1-yard score. Webb City won 35-7.

Zerkel finished with three receptions for 81 yards, a touchdown and a two-point conversion.

"Every one is the same," he told the paper, "just taking it one game at a time."

"It was exciting to play in the last game in that stadium, especially with the way it ended," said Jacob Cockrell, a senior captain.

The day after the game, Webb City's school board selected Southern Bleachers to build the replacement seating in the new stadium. The home side seating was slated to cost $866,000, and another $70,000 for band bleachers at the stadium's southwest corner. The home stands would run from goal line to goal line and go 26 rows high; enough seating for 4,052 people. The existing aluminum bleachers on the home side of the field would become the new visitors' seats.

Zerkel says now that the team didn't realize until late in the year they might win another championship.

"Our coaches were big on us taking it game to game," he says. "It didn't matter who we were playing, what their record was. We knew we were going to get everybody's best game. Once we got going in the playoffs, Lee's Summit West was in the back of our mind when the playoffs started. We'd heard a lot of stories about them. We got up to that game and we knew we were up for a battle."

Webb City went on the road for the semifinal game featuring the top-ranked Cardinals and second-ranked Lee's Summit West Titans, who drilled St. Joseph Benton 28-3 in the quarterfinals to keep their undefeated season rolling.

It was another of those games that lived up to the hype. Only 16 points were scored by both teams. Webb City's lone touchdown came with 2:27 left in a scoreless first half after the Titans had fumbled on their own 43. Junior Zach Anderson, noted for some big plays on defense all year, made his biggest stop early in the fourth quarter with Webb City clinging to a touchdown lead. Lee's Summit West was driving deep into Cardinal territory and faced a second-and-1 at the 16. Anderson drilled running back Aaron Palmer for a 3-yard loss, and two players later the Titans came up a yard short on a fourth-and-2.

"We did what we were asked to do," Anderson said. "We got big turnovers. We did it!"

The Cardinals then put the game away with a 23-yard field goal with less than five minutes to play. The Titans didn't score until the last play of the game, and Webb City won 10-6.

"I've never seen a more dominating defensive game," Roderique said after. "The defense came up big ... what a great job."

Howard, uncharacteristically, threw three interceptions in the game, but got back one with a defensive interception of his own. Lineman Brett Stewart recovered a fumble. Howard completed five passes for 81 yards, the longest for 26 yards to tight end Jacob Cockrell, which was a key play on the scoring drive ending in the field goal. Trevor Davis led with 94 rushing yards.

In Webb City's ninth state title appearance it faced an unfamiliar opponent: the unranked Hannibal Pirates. Roderique told the *Sentinel* he saw similarities between the two teams, with the Pirates appearing to be "a lot like us," he said. "Not flashy or fancy. Tough-nosed, hard-working overachievers. They've beaten some very good teams, especially Farmington and Parkway North."

Before the game in the locker room inside the dome in St. Louis, you could feel the energy.

"You could tell where everybody's minds were at," Zerkel says. "I don't know if Hannibal had an off day, but I think the credit is due to our coaching staff. We had a great game plan and we executed it pretty well.

"It was just one of those games. We clicked on all cylinders. We didn't even throw the ball much. Our running backs and offensive line had one of their best games. On defense I'm back at free safety and I can't even get up and make a tackle because our defense played its best game."

Needless to say, it all ended in a convincing win by Webb City: 26-0. The Cardinals scored in every quarter and allowed only 231 yards to Hannibal. David Ebbs, a senior, was especially active on defense, making 13 tackles including a sack and four tackles for a loss.

"We did what we were supposed to do," he said.

Offensively, the Cardinals set the tone on their very first drive. Trevor Davis scored with 7:39 left in the first quarter. Howard added a 53-yard touchdown in the second quarter.

"I've always dreamed of having one of those," he said, staring at the championship trophy after the game.

He added another touchdown in the third quarter. A rare trick play later in the game was the game's biggest play. On a first down, Brad Workman threw just his second pass all year and connected with Jake Cockrell for a 60-yard touchdown.

"I have always wanted to win a state championship ever since I first put on a set of football pads," Cockrell said. "There was no better way to end my high school career."

Hannibal missed three field goal attempts, and when it drove to the Webb City 3, Ebbs picked up the sack. On a fourth-and-4, Mack Kyle and Ebbs made the stop at the 1.

"There is no better feeling than shutting them out at the state championship game," Ebbs said.

"Oh man, growing up you always want to be a part of that state championship team," Zerkel says now. "With the chemistry we had, it's like you could taste it all season. But we had a good group of seniors that led us one game at a time and our coaches were the same way. Being at Webb City and being at Missouri Southern and playing, our preparation at Webb City was the same if not tougher and more intense. That's a lot of credit to our coaches and our senior leadership. It's crazy how much time everyone puts into it. You're not forced to be there. You want to be there because the end result is getting to St. Louis and getting that ring."

After the game, a five-hour bus ride still awaited the Cardinals.

"Webb City still rides buses everywhere, won't take a charter," Zerkel says. "I guess it's funny now, but it was probably the best thing for us. It kept us all humble. We got in the bus after the game and you knew you had five and a half hours in a yellow school bus and everybody winded down. As soon as we turned on Main you could see everybody's eyes light up. It's one of the most impressive things I've ever been a part of. Everybody out there that late. It's something I'll never forget."

The Cardinals lost a ton of offense from the championship team of 2006. The biggest loss was Collin Howard, who had completed 97 passes for 1,794 yards and 15 touchdowns, and rushed 155 times for 1,103 yards and 19 touchdowns. Also gone were running backs Trevor Davis and Stephen Cook. Davis had tallied 947 yards and scored 16 times, and Cook had rushed for 591 yards and eight touchdowns. David Ebbs, too, had graduated after rushing for 155 yards and three touchdowns.

Brad Workman and Jake Cockrell were the biggest losses among receivers and tight ends. Workman had caught 14 passes for 246 yards, and Cockrell six passes for 186 yards and two touchdowns.

There were some big performers back on that side of the ball, however. Mack Kyle, as a sophomore in 2006, had completed both of his passes for a total of 48 yards, and he had rushed for more than 300 yards and five touchdowns. He was the only rusher back who had accounted for more than 100 yards. The team also had several talented receivers back. Zerkel was a senior in 2007; he had caught 39 passes for 790 yards as a junior. Chance Sossamon was back after his 138-yard season, Alan Pink was back after gaining 110 yards, and Marcus Ozbun was back after hauling in 11 passes for 223 yards and two touchdowns.

Defensively it was more of the same. Jeff Stoner graduated after leading the team with 110 tackles in '06. So did Nick Sanders, who made 86 tackles; Brett Stewart, who had 50 tackles; Ebbs, who had 92 tackles; and Bobby Perryman, who made 41 stops. Sanders led the team with five sacks, Ebbs had three and Stoner two. Howard and Workman had combined for five interceptions and a fumble recovery.

Returning in 2007 were players like Landon Zerkel, who recorded 82 tackles as a junior; Mack Kyle, who had 55 tackles; and Zac Anderson, who had 58. Zerkel had two interceptions and a fumble recovery, too.

As a junior, Mack Kyle emerged as the offensive leader as the Cardinals tried for another repeat in 2007. That season he completed 63 percent of his passes and threw for 1,524 yards and 18 interceptions; on the ground he led the team with 134 rushes, 970 yards and 14 touchdowns. Zerkel was, as expected, his main target. He caught 41 passes for 766 yards and 10 touchdowns, and senior Alan Pink gained 408 yards and scored four times. A senior, Caleb Powell, had 101 yards receiving and two scores, and junior Austin Lepper had 189 yards and one score.

Webb City finished the year with 2,804 rushing yards spread between 10 different players. Andrew Smith was the team's second-leading rusher with 691 yards and nine touchdowns; Zac Anderson had 426 yards and three touchdowns; Seth Helton had 351 yards and three scores and a young sophomore, Braxton Baker, scored three touchdowns and rushed for 206 yards.

Senior defensive lineman Chase Philpot picked up the slack on that side of the ball, finishing the year with 75 tackles and four sacks. Senior linebacker Levi Jones had 70 tackles, Zerkel had 56, Chris Stoner had 53 and Adam Williams made 58.

Going into 2007, uncertainty was a word used frequently. Only four players returned who had started in 2006, and they filled just seven positions. Chase Philpot and Eric Thomason returned on the offensive line, Zerkel returned at receiver and Caleb Powell was back at tight end. The other starters as the season began were Andrew Smith and Zac Anderson at running backs, Parker Graham, Jake Weiss and Preston Walker on the line, Adam Williams at tight end, Alan Pink at receiver and Shane VanStavern at kicker.

Defensively, Zerkel was back at free safety and Philpot and Thomason were back on the line. Walker would also start on the line, Powell at defensive end, and at linebacker the Cardinals had Chris Stoner, Anderson and Jordan Hickman. Seth Reynolds started in the backfield, and Nick Pace was the punter.

The fall of 2007 also marked the senior season of Webb City great Adam Spieker, who was starting at center for the Missouri Tigers during one of the school's greatest seasons. The 6-foot-3, 305-pound Spieker touched the ball virtually every offensive play for Missouri's no-huddle, shotgun offense guided by Chase Daniel, who is now the backup quarterback for the Kansas City Chiefs. At Webb City Spieker had won two state championships, and he chose Missouri to continue his career over Kansas State, Kansas and Arkansas. At Missouri he went on to break the school record for consecutive starts, 48.

"I love Adam, he's one of my better friends on the offensive line, and he's an unbelievable player," Daniel told the *Sentinel* after the Tigers' 10th win in 11 games. "I mean, he's by far I think the best center in the nation. He's up for the Rimington Trophy and all that cool stuff."

Spieker, like Webb City greats Grant Wistrom and Mark Smith before him, played in some of the country's most legendary stadiums and atmospheres.

"I like playing at Texas A&M and Ole Miss, anywhere there's a lot of people," he said. "Nebraska's always fun. I like being in enemy territory, it's kind of fun just being there."

Back in Webb City, the regular season went smoothly as usual in 2007. The Cardinals shut out Kickapoo (27-0) and Nixa (26-0) and held Pittsburg, St.

Charles West, Neosho and Carl Junction to seven points or less. Only Carthage (44-25) and Ozark (36-22) scored more than 13 points. Of course, the season would end on the field at K.E. Baker Stadium in the sectionals with Carthage's thrilling last-second field goal to pull off a remarkable 23-22 upset. Webb City finished the year 10-1.

Randon Coffee, a Webb City senior, had covered his high school team for the *Sentinel* for two years, and after that season-ending loss, he summed up his feelings on the program in an eloquent column.

"Players from Webb City carry a certain stereotype with them as the ones who think they are better than everyone else," he wrote. "In fact, this is as far from the truth as any score prediction.

"Eric Thomason gets nervous before every game no matter the opponent. Chase Philpot would never talk about the team that they would play two weeks down the road. Almost every quote received from a player on the team was like this, 'We've got to work harder,' or 'We need to get ready for next week.' Mack Kyle praised his offensive line every chance he got by saying, 'They open up the holes.' Landon Zerkel never failed to mention every facet of the team before talking about his stellar performances.

"For almost all 17 men graduating this year, Nov. 7 was the final time they get a pep-talk before taking the field," he added. "The final time they hit people and run before thousands of adoring fans. The final time people see their name in a program. The final time they are able to live out their childhood dreams under the lights.

"Their names will soon be forgotten among many fans, just like last year and the years before that. They have played together through grade school, and every year they have given themselves to play the game. Some only got to watch and didn't get to experience it first hand. Others were out there gasping for air, wishing they could be on the bench so they could catch their breath.

"In the most heart-wrenching game most have ever witnessed, these careers ended."

Despite the way it ended, those players still look back at that season with fond memories. Zerkel says it was an amazing year, one of the best he's been a part of.

"The Carthage loss, hat's off to them," he says. "Trey Derryberry, what an amazing athlete he is. Stephen Poston made a great kick. I was almost able to block the kick. It was just one of those things that didn't work out. I played college football with Stephen for a few years. Most of those guys I'm friends with now. The better team got the win that night. It was one of the best games of my career, defensively and offensively."

Mack Kyle completed five passes for 116 yards – all to Zerkel. Kyle had actually been playing with a torn labrum for two games and the injury was causing him a lot of pain in the Carthage game.

"He went to the sideline and told Coach Roderique he didn't want to throw the ball anymore," Zerkel remembers. "They scored a late touchdown and then Mack runs a 50- or 60-yard touchdown. He's one of the best athletes I've ever been around, but I'll never forget seeing him run all the way down."

When it came time for Zerkel to choose a college, he first elected to play for Jerry Kill at Southern Illinois. But when Kill was hired at Northern Illinois, Zerkel had another decision to make. He had a chance to play basketball, too, and it came down to Pittsburg State, Missouri Southern and Drury for that sport. For football it was Pittsburg State or Southern. With Collin Howard already a Lion and the team running a spread offense, he decided to don the green and gold. His grandparents are big Lionbackers there, but they told him they would have put on the crimson and gold if he'd gone to Pittsburg State.

"It was awesome, but it was tough going through," Zerkel says of his career in college. "I had three different position coaches at receiver, two offensive coordinators and three different offenses. It was ups and downs. I enjoyed all my time there. I was a part of another brotherhood in football like Webb City has. It was fun and good to go out on a winning season with coach (Daryl) Daye. That was a high point."

Zerkel finished his career with his name in the MSSU record books. He ranks third all-time in receiving yardage in a season with 1,047 yards in 2011. Only Rod Smith had better seasons, and he's the career leader in receptions, receiving yards and touchdown catches for the Denver Broncos. Zerkel's 759 yards in 2010 are tied for ninth on the list.

Zerkel ranks second all-time, again behind Smith, in career receiving yardage at Southern, with 2,866 yards. Smith finished with 3,122 yards. And it all started at Webb City.

As for the question that everybody likes to ask, Zerkel, like many others, says it's a combination of so many things that makes the Cardinals so good.

"They start kids young here in Pee Wee football," he says. "You get these kids so excited and they start playing football and they're wearing their jerseys to the games. The way the parents raise their kids; I don't think any parent is too crazy about it but they bring their kids to the game and they see the guys walking down the hill and they want to be a part of that. That brotherhood that football offers. Hands down the easiest answer I can give would be our coaching staff. From Coach Roderique, from any person who has come and helped but doesn't get paid; all these guys have put in huge time and effort. They're all there for the best interest of the kids. Our coaches are the backbone of Webb City football. It was some of the best years of your life. Growing up in that community, man, it's just fun to go back every once in awhile and catch a game. Another good thing, I got to play in that stadium. We won a state championship the last year we had the old stadium. And playing on that turf the first year of the new one was one of the highlights of my career as well."

Landon Zerkel lies on the field at Carthage stunned after the Tigers' last-second win in the 2007 sectionals. Photo by Bob Foos.

The marching band performs at halftime of a game at the new Cardinal Stadium, which opened in 2007. Photo by Bob Foos.

31. BACK TO THE TITLE GAME

The worst way to end a season if you're Webb City is with a loss to Carthage, but as the 2008 campaign rolled around the Cardinals found themselves in danger of losing a game to start the season for the first time since 1995.

To start the 2008 season Webb City faced one of its toughest road games in ages – at Harrisonville. The Wildcats had won 41 straight games and three straight titles in Class 3 before making the jump to Class 4. Harrisonville returned eight defensive starters, but the Cardinals weren't exactly rebuilding, either.

Mack Kyle returned at quarterback. His favorite receivers from 2007, Landon Zerkel and Alan Pink, had graduated, but junior Boo Rodgers was ready to shine and presented the team with a dangerous downfield threat. He was joined in the receiving corps by junior Chris Hance, sophomore Austin Daniel and senior Jerry Workman. The backfield featured senior Seth Helton and junior Braxton Baker. The offensive line had Hunter Luna, Parker Graham, Andrew Kolb and Steven Rice; Adam Williams and Austin Lepper were at tight ends and Jake Brasfield was the team's kicker.

Graham, a senior, anchored what was another great Webb City offensive line. The team rushed for 4,271 yards that season and 63 touchdowns, and after he graduated the following spring, Graham signed with Oklahoma State University. He played in three games as a redshirt freshman in 2010 and started five games at right tackle, including the Fiesta Bowl as a sophomore. Graham started all 13 games as a junior, 11 at left tackle and two at right tackle; he was named the team's offensive line MVP in games against Texas Christian University and Oklahoma. In Graham's final season, 2013, he started the first five games at left tackle and then moved to the right side for the final eight games. He was named a first-team all-Big 12 player by both the conference coaches and the Associated Press. Between 2011 and 2013 the Cowboys went a combined 30-9. The 6-foot-7, 315-pounder later signed with the Baltimore Ravens, becoming yet another Webb City player to take a crack at the National Football League.

Back in 2008, several players went both ways for the Cardinals. Rodgers, the younger brother of Marty Rodgers, started in the defensive backfield along with Workman; Kyle and Williams started at linebacker and Lepper, Luna and Rice started on the defensive line. Other defensive starters were Dacota Cortez on the line, Ryan Powell at linebacker and Rian Teal and Seth Kelly in the backfield.

Braxton Baker made a huge statement in his first game starting at running back when the Cardinals played at Harrisonville. He rushed 20 times, scored four touchdowns and finished with 145 yards. It was a thrilling game, tied at 14 at the half, and after Austin Lepper recovered a fumble at the Harrisonville 19-yard line with eight minutes left in the third quarter, Baker scored a 2-yard touchdown to make it a 21-14 game with less than four minutes to go in the quarter.

"It was all the line," Baker said after the game. "I have faith in my line, I trust them. They got off the ball hard."

But Harrisonville returned the ensuing kickoff 69 yards to the Cardinals' 21. After a holding penalty and three straight stops, Harrisonville faced a fourth down from the 24 and lined up for a field goal. Instead, the ball was snapped to the holder, who threw a pass to the corner of the end zone for a game-tying touchdown.

After the teams traded punts, Harrisonville came up with a turnover at its own 43 with less than 11 minutes left in the game. The Wildcats drove to the Webb City 37 but were stopped on a fourth-and-1. Two players later, Mack Kyle gained 23 yards on the ground and a personal foul call moved the ball to the Harrisonville 27. After a 3-yard gain, Baker scored from the 24 at the 5:44 mark to make it a 27-21 Webb City lead.

Harrisonville got the ball and drove to its own 41 in four players, but fumbled a pass at the 39 that was recovered by Adam Williams. It looked like the game was over. It wasn't – yet. The Cardinals fumbled in the red zone with less than a minute on the clock, and Harrisonville had one last shot from its own 16. On first down, quarterback Sam Cooper threw a 41-yard pass down the sideline. The Wildcats looked to the air again, but this time the pass was tipped and senior Seth Kelly caught it for an interception.

"We got a little nervous there at the end," Kelly said, "but we've got a good offense, and I just knew every time we got them the ball they'd do their thing.

"I just saw the ball go up in the air and I was like, 'oh wow' and I grabbed it and covered it up."

Kyle threw for 90 yards and rushed for 51. Boo Rodgers caught two passes for 79 yards, including one for 50. Defensively, Seth Helton had a sack for a 10-yard loss and Rodgers and Williams each made nine tackles, along with eight from senior Ryan Powell.

Week two was another thrilling game. Webb City opened its home slate against Rogers, Arkansas, and just like the Harrisonville game it wasn't decided until the fourth quarter. Baker had another huge game with two touchdowns and 150 yards on 25 carries, and though Seth Helton rushed for only 40 yards in the game, three of his 12 carries went for touchdowns. The last one came with 3:27

left in the fourth quarter and put the Cardinals ahead 36-33.

On the second play of the game an interception was returned for a touchdown, and after Rogers scored on its second possession the Mountaineers led 14-0. Baker's first touchdown came late in the first quarter to make it a 14-7 game, and on the ensuing kickoff the Cardinals caught Rogers snoozing with a surprise onside attempt, which was recovered by junior Bart Starkey at the Rogers' 41. Seven players later, Helton scored to tie the game. Each team scored in the second quarter, but Rogers struck with less than a minute in the half to take a 27-21 lead into the break and its starting running back already had 97 yards on six carries.

A 2-yard Helton run in the third quarter put the Cardinals ahead by a point, but Rogers pulled ahead 33-28 after a touchdown and a failed two-point try. Webb City got the ball back at its own 29 and turned to the running game. Thirteen players later, Helton scored the winning touchdown on a 9-yard run with 3:27 to go. The two-point conversion was good. Still, it wasn't over. The Mountaineers returned the following kickoff all the way to the Cardinals' 40. Two incompletions and an offensive pass interference penalty backed them up, but a 15-yard pass gave Rogers a fourth-and-10. The Mountaineers lined up with five wide receivers and their quarterback kept the ball and scrambled through an opening. He came up inches short. Michael Tibbs, who rushed for 97 yards in the first half, gained only 22 in the second.

"I think we came out, went up 14-0 and maybe got a big head," Tibbs said. "They did that surprise onsides kick and that really gave them the momentum. In the second half, we thought because they have like eight guys going both ways we'd be in a little bit better shape than them, but they beat us, and we made a lot of mistakes we shouldn't have made."

The third-ranked Cardinals, having won by a combined nine points while starting 2-0, finally got some breathing room against Willard in week three at Cardinal Stadium. The visiting Tigers actually finished the first quarter with negative-1 yards of total offense, while Webb City's average starting position that quarter was the Willard 28-yard line. The Tigers punted three times in the first 12 minutes – from their own 25, 1 and 12 – and then fumbled on their first possession of the second quarter. Webb City won 42-14.

Braxton Baker scored two touchdowns in the first quarter, and Mack Kyle threw a 5-yard touchdown pass to Austin Lepper early in the second quarter. After that came the Willard fumble, and four players later it was a 29-0 Webb City lead after Kyle threw a 9-yard touchdown to Rodgers. Only a long punt return gave Willard a chance to score in the first half; it was 29-7 at halftime. Baker, once again, led the team in rushing with 127 yards and two scores. He had eight touchdowns through three games. Helton gained five yards and scored once; senior Brandon Williams had one 39-yard carry; junior Jeremiah Box rushed for 31 yards and a touchdown; senior Tyler Laughlin rushed for 10 yards, sophomore Madison Johnson rushed for 8 yards and sophomore Scott Roderique gained 11 yards.

"To me that's very important," Roderique said of the playing time for younger Cardinals. "It's always been my philosophy that when you get an opportunity to get those young guys in you take it. The best thing is our older guys understand that. Our older guys are mature enough and are team-oriented."

The week four home game against Ozark started off as another blowout but turned into something entirely different. The Cardinals led 20-0 after a quarter, and had limited Ozark's 6-foot-5, 210-pound quarterback Jordan Nuckolls to just 3-of-5 passing for 3 yards. But when the game was over, Nuckolls had completed 36 of his 58 attempts for 402 yards and two touchdowns. The Cardinals hung on, though, for a 41-26 win.

"We came out thinking that one of their weaknesses was probably the pass defense," Ozark's quarterback said. "They've got some big boys up front so we thought with our speed we could maybe use that as an advantage and try to find some windows. Fifty-eight times? You never plan on throwing 58 times but it was working the whole night."

By halftime it was a 28-17 game. With barely a minute left in the third quarter it was still an 11-point Webb City lead, but after an Ozark punt bounced off the foot of the Cardinals' return man the Tigers were in business at the 13. They scored, and Webb City's lead was down to five points.

It was still a 28-23 game when Ozark was pinned at its own 8 after a Webb City punt, and the Tigers soon fumbled at the 11 to give the Cardinals excellent field position with 9:44 left to play. Mack Kyle's 8-yard touchdown run made it 34-23. Boo Rodgers then intercepted a pass with five minutes left to play after the Tigers got the ball at midfield, but Ozark came back later with a 10-play drive and a field goal to make it 34-26 with 1:50 on the clock. Ozark lined up for an onside kick, which Webb City recovered, and three players later Kyle scored on a 25-yard run. Kyle finished with 104 passing yards and 70 rushing yards for four total touchdowns. Baker rushed for 187 yards and a touchdown and Box had three carries for 23 yards and a score. Helton rushed for 41 yards. Baker also caught two passes for 36 yards, and Brandon Williams, Rodgers and Adam Williams each caught passes.

Only once in the first four games had Webb City won by more than 15 points, but in the Cardinals' next eight games they never allowed more than 14 points. They beat Nixa by three touchdowns, won at Neosho by 13 points, then really gained steam and beat Branson by 20 points, Carthage by 28, Nevada by 45 and Carl Junction by 36 on the Thursday night before Halloween. They followed those wins up with a 34-0 win against Branson and a 35-8 win against Neosho in a postseason rematch.

The Nixa game, which Webb City won 28-7, was actually tied at 7-7 after two quarters. But Webb City opened the third quarter with a seven-minute,

15-play drive and a 3-yard Baker touchdown run to pull ahead. Baker carried the ball seven times on the drive and caught an 11-yard pass. The Cardinals held onto the ball for nearly 10 of 12 minutes in the third quarter and Nixa went three-and-out on its only possession.

"The first half we kept our defense on the field, and we really wanted to score on that first drive in the second half," said Austin Lepper. "We took about seven minutes off the clock. It changed the momentum of the game."

Lepper caught a 19-yard touchdown on the first play of the fourth quarter, and after a big punt return by Boo Rodgers, Baker scored his second touchdown. In the first half the Eagles had run 12 more plays than Webb City, but in the third and fourth quarters the Cardinals ran 33 plays and Nixa just 15. Kyle threw for 112 yards and a touchdown in the game and rushed for 43 yards; Baker rushed for 89 yards and two scores and Helton had 30 yards. Austin Daniel, the sophomore receiver, caught two passes for 41 yards and junior Chris Hance, Baker, and junior Cody Thompson each had a catch. Lepper had two for 37 and a score.

Rodgers also made his presence felt on defense with five solo tackles and 10 total. Helton had an 8-yard sack.

The Neosho game was another fairly close one, tied after three quarters, but Mack Kyle had a huge game for the Cardinals, who won 27-14. Kyle threw for 127 yards and one touchdown and rushed for 33 yards and two more scores. A pair of fourth-quarter touchdowns was the difference; the first a 54-yard strike from Kyle to Rodgers down the visitors' sideline. Fans also got good news when word circulated that No. 1 Carthage was losing in Branson.

Neosho head coach Shawn Flannigan lamented the fact that his team hadn't taken full advantage of some uncharacteristic Webb City turnovers. The Wildcats got the ball at the Webb City 38-yard line and 27 after second-half turnovers but scored only once and missed a field goal.

"It was huge," Flannigan said. "I told the guys after the game we created two turnovers on Webb and that just does not happen. And we didn't get much out of it."

Baker had 119 rushing yards and Daniel caught three passes for 46 yards.

The week seven game against Branson was a huge one. Webb City was still ranked third in the state and was 6-0 and 4-0 in the conference. Branson, after toppling Carthage, was seventh in the polls and also 6-0 and 3-0. The huge Branson crowd that made the drive to Webb City was quickly disappointed on that Friday night. The Pirates went three-and-out on their first possession, then Seth Helton put the Cardinals ahead with a 5-yard run. It wasn't long before Rodgers intercepted a pass and returned it 40 yards for a touchdown, then Austin Lepper hauled in touchdown passes of 22 yards and 10 yards to give the Cardinals a 27-0 lead with 8:12 left in the second quarter.

After Branson's first touchdown, Kyle scored one of his own, and Webb City won 34-14.

The Cardinals returned to the field at K.E. "Doc" Baker Stadium in Carthage where their season had ended not 12 months earlier for the first district game of 2008. Carthage, which had been ranked first in the state before losing to Branson, had the dangerous senior Trey Derryberry back at quarterback guiding the Tigers' spread offense. The best defensive strategy, Roderique said, would be to keep his team's offense on the field.

"I'm dreaming of 18- to 20-play drives that chew up seven minutes off the clock," he told the *Sentinel*.

The Cardinals needed just eight plays to score on their first possession of the game, which ended with a 6-yard Mack Kyle touchdown. The Tigers quickly answered with an 80-yard touchdown pass from Derryberry, but Braxton Baker followed with a 24-yard score and Kyle's 21-yard touchdown made it 21-7. The quarterback's best run came with 1:15 left in the first half, a 56-yard scamper down the visitors' sideline after faking a handoff; he stiff-armed one defender out of the way. That made it a 28-7 game at the half.

Webb City ran 23 plays in the first quarter and Carthage ran only six. While the Cardinals were scoring four times in their first five possessions, Carthage punted three times and turned the ball over once in the first half. Carthage had only four possessions in the second half; it punted, failed to convert on fourth down, fumbled to Austin Lepper and finally drove to the Webb City 10 as time expired. Baker, meanwhile, added a 19-yard score for the Cardinals, who won 35-7.

Derryberry threw for 348 yards, but the potent Carthage offense gained only 24 rushing yards. Kyle rushed for 128 yards and three touchdowns of his own, and Braxton Baker scored twice and rushed for 214 yards, averaging 8.9 yards per touch. Seth Helton averaged nearly eight yards on seven carries. Parker Graham, Steven Rice and Austin Lepper each recorded sacks for a total of 26 yards lost, and sophomore Scott Roderique led the defense with nine stops.

"Braxton Baker was alive and well tonight," Carthage head coach Jon Guidie said after the game. "He did a great job. That kid's tough. He's hard to bring down. He gets most of his yards after contact. We didn't do a very good job of wrapping him up."

And there was actually some doubt about Baker's status for the game after an injury the week before.

"At quarterback we played really well," Roderique said. "Braxton Baker playing, we really didn't know how he was going to be because he really hadn't gone full speed all week. He's just one of those kids that's tougher than like 99.9 percent of the people in the world. A lot of guys wouldn't have been able to play."

The win all but assured Webb City of yet another district title; Nevada was just 3-5 and had already beaten Carl Junction, the other team in the district. Neither team posed much of a challenge.

Nevada was first on the plate for the Cardinals, who used an aerial attack to win by 45 points, 59-14. Patrick Drake completed all four of his passes for 86 yards and a touchdown and Mack Kyle was 4-of-7 for 60 yards and a pair of touchdowns.

"It felt great," Drake said after. "We didn't think we'd win by 45. We wanted to win, but we didn't think it was going to be like this."

Webb City had nine possessions in the first half and scored seven times, once on a 34-yard field goal by Jake Brasfield. It was a 45-7 game at halftime. Kyle rushed three times for 65 yards and a touchdown; Helton ran three times for 42 yards and a touchdown; Baker had nine carries for 120 yards and a touchdown, and senior Tyler Laughlin rushed eight times for 83 yards. Five different receivers caught passes: one each for Brandon Williams, Austin Daniel and Austin Lepper; two for Adam Williams and three for Boo Rodgers. Daniel's catch was a 39-yard touchdown.

"It was awesome," Daniel said. "We came out and we were a little bit scared at first because we didn't have that good of a week in practice, but we came out and played great for senior night."

On defense, Lepper had a sack and Jerry Workman and Rodgers each had interceptions.

The district finale at Carl Junction was a little sloppier, with the Cardinals turning the ball over four times, but they rushed for 342 yards and six scores in winning 40-14 to improve to 10-0. Carl Junction punted on its first six possessions, and on the seventh Patrick Drake picked off a pass. Helton, in the first quarter, scored on runs of 52 yards and 1 yard and after a bad snap on a punt attempt set up the Cardinals just two yards away from the end zone, Braxton Baker made it a 20-0 game.

Carl Junction returned an interception for a touchdown to pull within 13 points, but on Webb City's ensuing possession Roderique elected to go for it on a fourth-and-5 at the Cardinal 45 and Helton gained seven yards. A few plays later, Baker scored from the 28.

"I think there are certain things you have to do and you need to do and I think that was one of those points," Roderique said. "If we were going to be a good football team we need to get a first down right there."

The win came against a Bulldog team coached by Bret Gosch, the former Webb City player and son of Tom Gosch.

"Webb City's a good football team, but I was very happy with the way my team came out and played for four quarters," he said. "They didn't lay down and they just kept fighting. Webb City made opportunities of our mistakes and we didn't make opportunities of theirs.

"Webb City's well-coached," he added. "They're a good ball club. They're used to winning."

Baker rushed for 143 yards and two touchdowns, Helton for 81 yards and two touchdowns and Kyle scored once and had 52 rushing yards. Jerry Workman caught two passes and Austin Daniel and Austin Lepper had one catch apiece. Drake and Kyle each intercepted passes.

The first two playoff games, against Branson and Neosho, were equally as lopsided. Severe weather forced a 30-minute delay during the Branson game at Cardinal Stadium, and when play resumed the Cardinals rolled over the Pirates 34-0. The Pirates punted after three plays to start the game, giving Webb City great field possession at the Branson 47-yard line; the Cardinals ran three plays and had the ball at the 35 when lightning and thunder got a little too close for comfort.

When the teams came back onto the field, Braxton Baker needed three carries to go the final 35 yards and score. Branson punted three more times in the first half and finally managed to pin the Cardinals at their own 5 with 3:32 left in the second. Eleven plays later they had the ball at the 2 with barely a second on the clock and a 13-0 lead. Helton got the call and was met at the goal line by a wall of defenders, but with a strong second effort the ball crossed the goal line and after a two-point conversion it was already a three-touchdown game after two quarters.

In the second half, Jeremiah Box scored and Kyle added a 41-yard touchdown run. Webb City finished the game with 23 first downs and Branson only four.

"It's our first shutout of the year," said Helton, who had a sack for a 10-yard loss. "To come out and do it in the playoffs against a team that is a very good, physical team, I feel good about our defense."

Kyle and Baker rushed for 128 and 139 yards, respectively, each scoring a touchdown, but it was Helton who led the team with two touchdowns and 50 yards.

After just beating Neosho by 13 points during the regular season, Webb City demonstrated a clearly-improved defense and offense in a 35-8 win against the Wildcats in the sectional for the team's 12th win. It was only a 14-0 game at halftime, though, with Webb City taking the lead on a 1-yard Helton score and a 33-yarder from Kyle. Baker busted through an arm tackle to score a 57-yard touchdown in the third quarter, then Kyle threw a 24-yard touchdown pass to Helton to make it 27-0. Junior Jeremiah Box tacked on the final touchdown, a 6-yard run in the third quarter.

In the two regular season games against Branson and Neosho, Webb City allowed a total of 27 points and won by an average of 17; in the playoffs against those two teams the Cardinals allowed eight points and won by an average of 30.5.

The quarterfinal game against Bolivar was a little closer. It was also Webb City's third straight playoff game at home. The Cardinals led 28-7 at halftime, but Bolivar cut that lead to two touchdowns going into the fourth quarter. Webb

City went on to win 41-21.

Bolivar came into the game after knocking off undefeated and second-ranked Union. Like Harrisonville, 2008 was Bolivar's first season in Class 4 after a nice run in Class 3.

Baker scored three touchdowns in the first half and Webb City finished with 326 rushing yards on a cold, blustery afternoon in Webb City. After Bolivar cut it to 28-14 in the third quarter, Seth Helton answered with a 2-yard run early in the fourth to put the game out of reach. Helton added another score with 6:53 left that made it a 41-14 game.

"On the field it was just a good hard-fought high school football game," Bolivar head coach Lance Roweton said. "This opened our eyes a little bit as to what Class 4 state champion-caliber football is all about. We aspire to be at Webb City's level and hopefully in the future we can face these guys again."

Webb City finally took to the road for a semifinal showdown with Kearney, which had thwarted the Redbirds' championship ambitions in 2002 and 2003. The Bulldogs, through 13 games, had never trailed in a game in 2008. Kearney was allowing just 60 rushing yards per game. In the quarterfinals, the Bulldogs shut down Sedalia Smith-Cotton's 2,000-plus-yard rusher Solomon Watkins, who gained a season-low 72 yards. Earlier, the Bulldogs had limited one of the state's all-time greatest running backs, Fort Osage's Dalton Krysa, to 66 yards.

"Defense wins championships," wrote *Kearney Journal* sports writer Chris Geinosky in a point-counterpoint column that appeared in both his newspaper and the *Sentinel*. "That old adage should be put to the test this weekend when points could be hard to come by."

Indeed, defense does win championships. But it was Webb City's championship defense that shut down Kearney in a bruising 14-7 semifinal win.

"I talked to the team before the game about just finding a way," Roderique said. "Against a team like this, they don't have any weaknesses, you just have to find a way, whatever that way may be. I think that's the way the game went today."

It took a huge defensive effort from Boo Rodgers, who blocked two field goals and intercepted a pass. The first came with Webb City trailing 7-0 and Kearney at the Cardinals' 1. Rodgers came slicing in from the edge and blocked the field goal with 20 seconds left in the first half.

The third quarter was all Webb City. Kearney punted on its first possession, then junior Jeremiah Box tied the game with a 2-yard touchdown.

"It was Boo's field goal block," Box said. "Him blocking built up huge momentum."

After another Kearney punt, Webb City was in business at its own 40. Eight plays later Braxton Baker scored the winning touchdown. Rodgers' second block was early in the fourth quarter after the Bulldogs had driven to the 12. The Bulldogs got another chance after Webb City punted with 6:17 left in the game; they drove all the way to the Webb City 12 but were stopped on a fourth-and-3.

Then with 24 seconds left, Kearney coaxed another punt out of the Cardinals and got the ball at its own 42. The Bulldogs moved to the Webb City 39 with a pass, but after two incompletions Rodgers came up with his interception to end it.

"We thought we could take over in the second half, and a credit to their line, they just stayed tough, and we weren't able to do like we normally do in the second half," Kearney coach Greg Jones said. "We just pound people, and we weren't able to do that."

Baker was held to 86 yards and Kyle to 66 on the ground. Box came into the game after Helton fractured his hand and rushed for 28 yards and a touchdown.

"He just sits on the sideline and waits his turn," Roderique said of Box. "Tremendous job for him to step into that role just like Dacota Cortez stepped in for Hunter Luna, who couldn't go because of a knee injury. Then Justin Jacks played for him in the second half."

Rodgers led the team with 11 tackles. Scott Roderique and Steven Rice each made one tackle for a loss, and Austin Lepper had two. Adam Williams also had an interception.

As usual, Webb City would celebrate Thanksgiving weekend in St. Louis and hope for a fifth title in 12 years and an eighth overall as the Cardinals tangled with 12-1 Jefferson City Helias.

"I don't expect anything different out of them," said Helias coach Chris Hentges the week before. "They've got a great program and great success. Coach Roderique does a great job and they're going to do what they're going to do. They're going to run that option and play that tough four front defense. That's the mark of a good team; they do what they do and they do it year in and year out."

The 2008 state title game goes down as arguably the most thrilling in Webb City history and one of the more exciting championship games in Missouri high school history. As *Sentinel* Editor Bob Foos wrote, "In Webb City's eight-win, two-loss Show-Me Bowl history, there have been shutouts, blowouts and a too-close one. But 2008's will be remembered as the back-and-forth one."

Helias took a 7-0 lead, but the Cardinals stormed back to go ahead 21-7 late in the first half. The Crusaders struck again and trailed by just one touchdown at the break, and in the third quarter scored on two straight possessions to pull ahead 27-21. Back came Webb City to tie the game and then go ahead by six points.

"Sacks, an interception and back-to-back blocked point-after kicks added to the uncertainty of the outcome," Foos wrote.

And midway through the fourth quarter, the Crusaders led 34-33 before the Cardinals, with a signature clock-eating drive, retook the lead 41-34. There was still time left for Helias to score and decide whether to go for the tie or the win, but Webb City's Seth Kelly came up with a monster interception to seal his team's eighth championship.

"They talk about momentum in football," John Roderique told the newspaper. "It was like a roller coaster ride today."

To start the game Webb City went three-and-out on its first two possessions. Senior defensive end Steven Rice came up with a 9-yard sack to stall Helias on its opening drive, but the Crusaders scored in just two players on their second possession – a 49-yard passing touchdown. After Helias missed a field goal, quarterback Mack Kyle completed his first pass, but the play was called back due to a penalty. He rushed for five yards back to the 20-yard line, then lofted a pass to Boo Rodgers near the sideline at the 40. Rodgers leaped and caught the pass above the Helias defender, then raced to the end zone for the tying 80-yard touchdown.

Webb City's defense staked the team to good field position on two straight possessions, and Kyle's completions to the 6-foot-3 tight end Austin Lepper keyed the scoring. Lepper's first grab went for 37 yards to the 3-yard line, and his next was a 15-yard catch down to the 1. Jeremiah Box punched the ball into the end zone both times, making it a 21-7 game. Helias, though, drove 80 yards in the final five minutes to make it a 21-14.

Helias scored on a third-and-9 at the Webb City 32 to tie the game in the third quarter, and an interception returned to the Webb City 27 set up the go-ahead score, but linebacker Seth Helton blocked the point after. Webb City now trailed by six and started at its own 13. Kyle rushed for 10 yards on a third-and-9, and then on the first play of the fourth quarter Kyle threw a 32-yard touchdown pass to Austin Daniel. The game was tied after Webb City's PAT was also blocked.

Senior defensive tackle Dacota Cortez sacked the Helias quarterback for a two-yard loss on first down, then Lepper came up with a 12-yard sack to force the Crusaders to punt from their own end zone. Rodgers caught the punt at midfield, then Kyle threw a 24-yard pass to Lepper, Braxton Baker rushed for 6 yards and Kyle scored from the 15; he was stopped short on a two-point try, and Webb City led 33-27.

Helias gained 56 yards on the second play of its ensuing possession and eventually scored to take the one-point lead with about six minutes left in the game. That's when the Cardinals answered with a 10-play drive featuring runs by Kyle, Baker and Box as the team's offensive line took over the line of scrimmage. Box's two-point run made it a 41-34 game.

Helias started its final drive at the 15 with 2:28 on the clock. But with 51 seconds left, Seth Kelly came up with the huge interception to ice it.

For the first time all year the Cardinals threw for more than 200 yards. Kyle completed seven of 10 passes for 214 yards and two scores, and he added 119 yards on 20 carries on the ground, while Baker rushed for 84 yards to finish the season with 2,002 yards and a 7.5-yard-per-carry average. He scored 23 touchdowns.

Kyle finished his senior season with 1,210 passing yards and 1,059 rushing yards and 26 total touchdowns. Helton rushed for more than 500 yards and scored 14 touchdowns, and Box rushed for 297 yards and seven scores. Rodgers led the team with 401 receiving yards and Daniel had 285 yards; each scored three times. Lepper had 248 yards and four touchdowns.

Three different players made at least 70 tackles. Rodgers led the team with 78 tackles, senior linebacker Ryan Powell had 72 and senior linebacker Adam Williams had 74. Helton, senior Steven Rice and Lepper each had six sacks. Rodgers had four interceptions, Kelly had three and Kyle and senior defensive back Rian Teal each had two. Lepper recovered four fumbles.

32. AN OLD NEMESIS

Much has been said about Webb City's "team-first" mentality. Those in the backfield always give credit to the guys blocking in front of them, and those who get no credit often deserve it the most. The selfless play of so many at Webb City is a trademark of the program. It's also true, however, that the Cardinals have had some tremendously gifted athletes and some incredible individual performances.

In the decade-plus since Webb City opened the new millennium with consecutive state titles, fans have watched many of those Cardinals with a special talent on the field. The list includes running backs like Chris Taylor and Marty Rodgers, receivers like Landon Zerkel and quarterbacks like Mack Kyle; linemen like Adam Spieker and Parker Graham and many, many others.

Running back Braxton Baker became the latest "great" Webb City player as a senior in 2009 when he followed up his 2,000-yard campaign with another 1,600 yards and 23 touchdowns. He was a force to be reckoned with out of the backfield and helped lead the team to another semifinal appearance in a season with double-digit wins.

Linemen Hunter Luna and Andrew Kolb had been key for Webb City's state title run in 2008, and both were back in 2009, though Luna was recovering from a knee surgery and wasn't ready when the team hosted Harrisonville. Kolb, an offensive starter in 2008, went both ways in 2009. Senior Patrick Drake, the younger brother of former quarterback Brayden Drake, stepped in at quarterback and had Boo Rodgers and Austin Daniel back as weapons down the field. Drake was more comfortable throwing the ball than running it. In addition to Braxton Baker, Jeremiah Box was also returning in an all-senior backfield. On the offensive line, in addition to the senior Kolb, senior Kolby Wakefield, junior Zach Gibson and sophomore Clayton Temaat opened the year, with juniors Philip Donna and Nathan Price at tight ends.

Defensively, Donna, Kolb and sophomore Trey Tripp were on the line, with juniors Nathan Ervin, Christian Hoffman, Scott Roderique and Collin Sigars, and senior Bart Starkey at linebackers; Rodgers and seniors Chris Hance and Jake Mullen were in the backfield. Prior to the season opener, Roderique pointed to a change in the team's base defense: from a four-man front to a three-man front. The 3-5 defense would allow more skilled players to get onto the field.

"It's geared toward stopping the run and pass, with more flexibility than the four-man front," he told the newspaper.

Handling kickoffs was junior Chase Capron, and freshman Alex Easley would kick PATs and field goals. Donna would punt.

The program's participation numbers continued to grow. In addition to 85 players on the varsity and junior varsity roster, Webb City had a whopping 50 freshmen out for the team.

Webb City manhandled Harrisonville 33-7 to open the season. Patrick Drake scored on an 81-yard run on the very first offensive play. Two Braxton Baker touchdowns and some "Easley done" extra points made it a 21-0 game a minute into the second quarter. Sophomore linebacker Breckin Williams returned an interception 80 yards for a touchdown to make it 27-0, and junior lineman Jordan Abercrombie added a big sack defensively to keep it a four-touchdown game at halftime. In the second half, junior Maddy Johnson returned a kickoff for a touchdown, and Harrisonville didn't score until the 3:37 mark in the fourth quarter.

At Rogers, Arkansas in week two, Webb City trailed 14-6 at halftime before Baker took the first handoff of the second half 80 yards for a touchdown as part of a 27-point scoring burst for the Cardinals in the third quarter. They won 46-27.

"Most people think I probably go in there and chew them out," John Roderique said of his halftime speech. "I just said, 'Hey guys, if they're better than us and they prove it on the field, then so be it.' I didn't feel like we put our best foot forward in the first half, didn't think we showed them anything about what we're all about and what we're capable of. I just told them I think we can play a lot better than that."

In the third quarter alone Webb City racked up 293 rushing yards. Baker had 201 yards on 12 carries in the 12-minute span, and Jeremiah Box rushed seven times for 82 yards.

"He said we needed to pick it up at halftime," Baker said of his coach's halftime talk. "He told us to be patient, be confident and we'd pick it up.

"Our line, we're not real big but we're real quick and we're physical," he added. "We get off the ball hard and we hit people in the mouth."

Hoffman led the defense with seven tackles and sophomore Jarvis Jones and Rodgers each intercepted a pass. Donna had two sacks.

Webb City went to 3-0 with a 56-7 win at Willard, and 4-0 with a 42-7 win at Ozark. In late September, on the same night the school recognized the 1989 championship team, the Cardinals doubled up Nixa 42-21. A 28-21 win against Neosho was the closest game of the regular season; after that they won 49-7 at Branson, 35-14 against Carthage, 48-15 at Nevada and then 54-0 against Carl Junction to complete another perfect district slate.

In the playoffs Webb City won rematches at home against Branson (40-21) and Carthage (41-14), then went to Bolivar and won 42-20 to earn another semifinal berth.

The Cardinals had won 28 straight games, but at Cardinal Stadium they faced an old postseason nemesis: the Kearney Bulldogs, who had won two of three playoff games against Webb City since 2002.

Kearney jumped out to a 10-0 lead in the first quarter before Braxton Baker scored a 77-yard touchdown on the first play of the second quarter; he finished the game with 173 yards on 21 carries. But Kearney quarterback Shane Hartzler threw for 177 yards on just seven attempts, and the Bulldogs took a 17-7 lead late in the half following a 90-plus yard drive. Patrick Drake answered with a touchdown with 41 seconds left that capped a 78-yard drive, and it was a 17-13 Kearney lead at halftime.

Kearney opened the third quarter with an 80-yard scoring drive to lead 24-13, and after a Webb City punt, the Bulldogs scored on a 40-yard run. Trailing 31-13, junior Scott Roderique came in at quarterback after Drake was injured, and he led a drive to the Kearney 9 but Webb City came away with no points. The Cardinals drove to the 15 in the fourth quarter, but fumbled the ball. Kearney went on to win 38-13.

"Our kids battled," John Roderique said. "There were several times we could have checked it in, but they battled."

Drake provided another strong quarterback performance for Webb City in 2009; he threw for 1,261 yards and 13 touchdowns and rushed for 11 scores and 843 yards. Box rushed for 604 yards and eight touchdowns that season, Maddy Johnson scored nine times and rushed for 402 yards, and Jamison Cady, a sophomore, had 435 yards and five touchdowns. Junior Austin Daniel hauled in 654 receiving yards and scored seven times. Boo Rodgers also had seven receiving touchdowns and 318 yards.

Defensively, linebacker Christian Hoffman had 103 total tackles, and Bart Starkey had 82. Junior Nathan Ervin had 87 stops and junior Collin Sigars made 62 tackles. Andrew Kolb and Philip Donna each made six sacks that season, and Ervin and Hunter Luna had three apiece. Chris Hance had eight interceptions and Breckin Williams and Scott Roderique each had five. Ervin recovered three fumbles.

The front page of the Webb City Sentinel proclaimed the good news after the team's 35-8 rout of Harrisonville in the 2010 semifinals.

33. THE STREAK BEGINS

Only a handful of players returned on each side of the ball for Webb City's football team in 2010, but several players who hadn't necessarily started the year before were more than ready for their time. One of those players was lineman Zac Gibson, who John Roderique said could have been a starter in 2009.

"Now he is," he told the *Sentinel*. "Hopefully he'll thrive in that role. The exciting part is seeing how kids respond."

The team had an especially strong group of seniors. Scott Roderique was ready to replace Patrick Drake at quarterback, and was also especially strong on defense. In the backfield, senior Slade Byford was at fullback and the Cardinals also had junior Jamison Cady, senior Christian Hoffman and sophomore Phoenix

Johnson in addition to outstanding senior Maddy Johnson. The team's receiving corps was among the team's biggest strengths, with senior Austin Daniel, junior Jarvis Jones and senior Tyler Busby. Seniors Nathan Price, Hayden Hickam, Philip Donna and Jeremy West were at tight end. On the line, junior Carson Powell was at center, juniors Gage Belcher and Clayton Temaat at guards and senior Jordan Abercrombie and Gibson at tackles.

On the other side of the ball there was junior Cade Higginbotham at nose guard and Donna and senior Trey Tripp on the line; inside linebackers were senior Nathan Ervin and Hoffman, and junior Wyatt Johnson, with Byford and senior Collin Sigars on the outside. Daniel and senior Andrew Pisechko were at corners. Senior Chase Capron returned to kick off, and so did sophomore Alex Easley for the extra points and field goals. Senior Hayden Hickam was the team's punter.

The loss of Braxton Baker was a huge one, though. Baker had rushed for more than 3,600 yards his last two seasons, another of the program's great running backs. But in his place, Webb City had another stellar running back in senior Maddy Johnson. As a junior in 2009, Johnson had rushed for 402 yards and nine touchdowns, but was used primarily as a dangerous kick returner. He had returned 14 kicks for 464 yards, an average of more than 33 yards per return; he had returned 18 punts for 197 yards.

Johnson was one of those spectacular athletes. He had good genes, too. His mother, Wendy, originally from England, had qualified for the Olympics as a teenager.

"If she had just had a little bit of support and money, she could have been an Olympic athlete," Johnson says now. "Not a lot of people know that. She didn't have shoes and she ran barefoot and beat everybody pretty good. We're proud of her and it's just awesome that she could do that over there and we can make her proud as well, you know. We always say we get the quickness from my dad and the speed from my mom."

Wendy did a little bit of everything, according to Johnson. Field jumps, 100-meter dash, 200, maybe some pole vault. She held a 100-meter dash record for a decade.

Johnson's father, Gary "Cat" Johnson, is among the greatest athletes ever to come out of the Joplin area. He won two state basketball championships while playing point guard for Joplin Memorial High School in 1977 and 1978, and in 2001 was inducted into the Joplin Sports Hall of Fame. In 1978 he scored a school-record 50 points in the quarterfinals of the state playoffs, and finished his high school career leading the Eagles in points per game with 20, as well as assists and steals. He held school records in all three categories.

Johnson was selected to the United States High School All-Star Team and named captain. In college, he played for Oral Roberts University and was drafted by the New Jersey Nets before playing professional basketball in England.

Despite being known for basketball, Cat Johnson actually played football early on in high school. Ironically, it was football that his sons Maddy and Phoenix excelled in at Webb City. And just like their father is considered perhaps the greatest basketball player in Joplin high school history, the Johnson brothers are among the greatest running backs in Webb City history.

"I've heard that a couple times," Cat Johnson says. "They've done very well."

The brothers rushed for a combined 6,047 yards and 102 touchdowns between 2008 and 2012. As a senior in 2010, Maddy rushed for 1,800 yards and 31 touchdowns. He averaged 10.9 yards per carry. For his career he scored 40 touchdowns and rushed for 2,231 yards. Phoenix, in 2010, scored five touchdowns and gained 418 yards. After his brother graduated, Phoenix rushed for 1,920 yards and 33 touchdowns in 2011, and another 1,478 yards and 24 touchdowns in 2012.

Cat Johnson played for a year with an NBA farm club and then went to England for eight years, where he met his wife.

"She was a track star," he says. "That's where Maddy gets his speed from. She held the 100-meter dash record for about 10 years in Leicester, England."

Just how fast was Maddy in high school? He once was clocked running a 4.37-second 40-yard dash as a senior.

"That's what the high school coaches clocked me at, and that was the fastest I ever ran and I stopped on that day," Maddy says. "We called it a day after we got under 4.4. We were pretty excited about it."

When the family returned from England, they decided to move to Webb City when Maddy was going into the fourth grade. There would be no Johnson dynasty at Joplin.

"I knew it would be difficult for them to do anything at Joplin," their father says. "At that time sports weren't that great and it was just one high school. When I was growing up we had two different schools so we had two kids playing. Joplin went to one high school, and I think the sports kind of went downhill after that. They met some kids growing up in day care they liked, so we decided to go to Webb City. We had no idea it was going to turn out like it did, but it turned out well. When I got back I had no visions where I wanted them to go."

Maddy says he's never wished he could have followed in his dad's legendary footsteps at Joplin. Everything happens for a reason, he says.

"We moved over to Webb City and I had all my friends over there," he says. "It was a real good fit, I think. Stayed out of trouble, had good friends, good families over there and good coaches. I was really led in the right direction at Webb and that really helped with the success I've had over the years because of the guidance and education I got from Webb. I think everything happens for a reason.

"We really loved basketball. We loved that. That's our passion, that's our sport because he brought us up playing basketball at a young age. When you get to a certain school and they have a certain system you feel like you have to adjust to that system and do the best you can. You don't want to disappoint anybody. I feel like my brother and I, we have the talent some of the teams needed and we didn't want to let our team down. My dad, he's proud of what we've done. It's a different route than he expected us to take, but he's proud of us where we're at now and how far we've come. It's different than basketball, but we still did our thing and did the best we could at that level."

People say the brothers are the complete opposites in terms of their strengths on the football field. Phoenix is a bigger, stronger back who's more aggressive and physical, Maddy says, while he is a smaller, faster, shiftier back.

"He has a little bit more of our mom's attitude and I have a little more of my dad," he says. "It's kind of cool how we both have our differences, but we're still brothers and successful at it, too."

Another difference is the amount of playing time each saw at Webb City. Maddy, because he came up a year behind the stellar Braxton Baker, was the team's featured running back for only one season – 2010. But Phoenix, who is two years younger, got the starting nod for two years after Maddy graduated.

"I didn't get to play as much throughout my high school career," Maddy says. "I did a little return stuff my sophomore year, a little more my junior year and got a few opportunities at running back. My senior year, it was just a great year. It was fun. I had a great time with my linemen. I used to take them out to eat before the games that week. We bonded a lot. It was awesome seeing everybody from when we started back in third or fourth grade coming up together and making that varsity appearance. It was just a great time; I'll never forget that year."

What's really impressive about Johnson's 1,800 yards and 31 touchdowns in 2010 is the fact that the team was so dominant that year that starters rarely played into the second half. One time Maddy and teammate Christian Hoffman – who both play football at Missouri State University now, along with Phoenix – added up the total number of quarters they'd played that season. It equated to about eight games, and Webb City played 15 that season. The Cardinals averaged 42.8 points per game in the regular season, and a point more in the playoffs.

In the 2010 season opener against Ozark, a 31-7 win, Johnson rushed eight times for 88 yards and two touchdowns. Webb City led just 14-7 at halftime behind touchdown runs by Scott Roderique and Johnson, but big defensive plays in the third quarter turned things around. Phoenix Johnson, a sophomore linebacker, recovered a fumble on Ozark's first drive of the third, setting up his brother's second touchdown run. On Ozark's first play after that, junior cornerback Jarvis Jones took the ball away from a receiver to give the Cardinals possession at the Ozark 31. Jamison Cady scored a few plays later, and Alex Easley booted a 24-

yard field goal in the fourth quarter. While Cady's 22 yards and a touchdown and Roderique's 79 rushing yards and a score were big, the highlight for Cardinals' fans that game was Johnson's speed.

"Maddy's a different kid this year than he was last year, and I think a lot of it has to do with confidence," John Roderique said after the game. "He's a lot more confident player and when you look at him he's more physical, faster and stronger. He's a kid that is a product of a lot of hard work. He's put in a lot of hard work."

Scott Roderique also threw for 69 yards, with Austin Daniel, Nathan Price, Jarvis Jones and Maddy Johnson each catching a pass. Meanwhile, three players had double-digit tackles: seniors Trey Tripp and Nathan Ervin with 11 each, and Hoffman with 12. Jones, Rupert Williams and Wyatt Johnson each recovered a fumble.

The passing game opened up even more in a 66-0 win against Willard a week later.

Scott Roderique completed five of seven passes for 93 yards and a touchdown to Austin Daniel, who had six catches for 93 yards. Roderique also rushed four times for 76 yards. Junior Breckin Williams completed all three of his passes for 28 yards, and he rushed for 67 yards on two carries. The running game was led by Maddy Johnson, of course, who tallied 128 yards and two touchdowns on six carries – an average of 21.3 yards per carry. Ten different players got carries and Webb City rushed for 418 yards in the game. Williams, sophomore John Roderique, junior Jamison Cady and senior Slade Byford each scored touchdowns. Junior Gage Belcher and senior Philip Donna each had sacks; Williams picked off a pass and Scott Roderique, Ervin and Hoffman came up with fumble recoveries.

When the game was over, Willard head coach Brock Roweton had one thing to say.

"I want to make sure that everyone knows Webb City is good," he said. "I want that to be my quote."

Webb City had won the opening toss and deferred to the second half, then lined up and recovered a surprise onside kick. Johnson took a pitch and raced 49 yards untouched to the end zone on Webb City's first play. The offense actually ran the wrong play.

"We called a different play and maybe we ran it wrong or whatever, but you don't anticipate scoring on the first play of the game, it just kind of happens," Roderique said.

He didn't know the kickoff team was going for the surprise onside attempt, either.

"The kickoff team probably knew, but it wasn't discussed between everybody," he said. "Those things are usually planned but not to where everybody knows about it."

Webb City used six quarterbacks and more than a dozen offensive linemen in the game. One of those was sophomore John Roderique, the coach's son, who scored on a 4-yard run late.

Hardly anybody from Branson made the drive to Webb City for the teams' week three game; probably they knew what was coming. Collin Sigars picked off a tipped pass in Webb City territory early on, and after Branson played the Cardinals tough to start the game, it was a 28-0 Webb City lead at halftime behind touchdowns from Jamison Cady and Slade Byford, as well as two touchdowns by Maddy Johnson.

The Cardinals won 42-13. Hoffman once again led a stout defense with 10 tackles. In addition to Sigars' interception, Jarvis Jones and Nathan Ervin each came up with picks, and sophomore Dalton Humphrey recovered a loose ball. Through three games, opponents had scored 20 points.

"I think a big thing we're all doing well is swarming to the ball, and we're all hungry for the ball," Sigars said. "It feels pretty good. We just have to keep rolling and do what we do best. We've got to take it one game at a time."

Scott Roderique threw another touchdown pass and Maddy Johnson averaged more than 14 yards per carry again – 156 yards and two scores on 11 touches. Byford had 65 yards, Breckin Williams scored once on the ground, and Cady had 23 yards and a touchdown. Austin Daniel caught two passes for 33 yards and a touchdown; Jones, Cady and senior Hayden Hickam each had catches, too.

"We expected a hard game," Hunter Luna said. "It feels great, but we're not worried about being 3-0; we're worried about our ultimate goal, a state championship at the end of the season."

That talented group of receivers continued to emerge against Neosho, when the Cardinals went on the road and won 48-6 to improve to 4-0. Scott Roderique was 3-for-5 with 124 yards and a touchdown, and Breckin Williams completed two of three passes for 48 yards. Austin Daniel got most of the targets, catching four passes for 158 yards and a touchdown, and Jarvis Jones had a 14-yard reception. All of those passing yards came in the first half.

As usual, Webb City did most of its damage on the ground. Maddy Johnson averaged 15 yards per carry and had 167 yards and two touchdowns; Slade Byford rushed for two touchdowns and 98 yards, and Phoenix Johnson rushed 11 times for 108 yards and a touchdown. Even Christian Hoffman got in on the action, with a 1-yard touchdown.

Hunter Luna got things rolling when he ended Neosho's first drive by drilling the Wildcat quarterback, forcing the ball loose and recovering it at the 21. That set up the Hoffman score.

"You just learn that you've got to play the game at a higher level," Nixa coach Rich Rehagen said after Webb City's 35-14 win in late September. "As the games get bigger you've got to play at a higher level."

Maddy Johnson had scoring runs of 33 and 66 yards in the first quarter of that game. On the first, he busted through the line and broke a tackle, then spun off another defender and sprinted north to the end zone. After Nathan Price caught a 14-yard touchdown strike from Scott Roderique, it was 21-0 at halftime. Roderique added another touchdown on the ground, as did Slade Byford, and Maddy Johnson finished with 150 yards. Collin Sigars had 10 tackles and Christian Hoffman 11; the only other player close was sophomore Dalton Humphrey, who had nine stops. Both Hoffman and senior Trey Tripp recorded sacks, and Austin Daniel came up with an interception.

During a 41-6 win against Republic the week after, Maddy Johnson had his most prolific rushing performance of the season. He finished the game with 219 yards and four touchdowns; he carried the ball only 10 times. That's an average of nearly 22 yards per carry. Hoffman scored on the ground and Scott Roderique threw a touchdown pass to Daniel, who added four more catches to his numbers. Hunter Luna recorded a sack on defense, Breckin Williams had an interception and sophomore Jose Speer recovered a fumble.

It was homecoming night at Cardinal Stadium and for the first time in a few weeks the team got off to a quick start. The defense made two stops for a loss, including Luna's sack on third down, on Republic's first possession. Johnson's first touchdown was a 49-yard run, and after the Williams interception, he scored from the 34. He added touchdowns of 44 yards and then 40 yards later in the game.

"How many yards?" Roderique asked after the game. "Really? Wow. I wouldn't have guessed he had 219 yards. Pretty amazing. His ability to break tackles or shake off tackles and his balance is pretty special. He's got a pretty good spin move, he's just pretty impressive. Outstanding, I guess, is how you'd describe it."

"I like the spin move right now," Johnson said. "That's probably my favorite, just spinning and getting off quick."

Now 6-0, Webb City had won each game by at least three touchdowns, but its next two games would be the closest two of the whole season. Both were on the road; the first at St. Thomas Aquinas, a private school in the Kansas City area, and the second at Carthage.

Led by quarterback Richard Davila, who had 18 total touchdowns through five games, the Saints were averaging 44 points per game and allowing just 14.

Webb City held a 21-6 lead with less than two minutes left in the first half after both Johnson brothers had scored and Scott Roderique had thrown a 28-yard touchdown to Austin Daniel. But with 12 seconds left in the half, Davila threw a 55-yard touchdown and converted the two-point attempt to make it a 21-14 game at the break.

With 5:38 left in the third, Aquinas hit its third field goal of the game and the Cardinal lead had shrunk to four points. Remarkably, it was a 50-yard make by kicker Jonathan Pyle. He added a fourth, this time for 29 yards, and all of a sudden it was a one-point game. Webb City got the ball at its own 25, its momentum gone in front of a raucous homecoming crowd. Roderique and Jamison Cady carried the ball 10 yards, but two players later the team faced a third-and-long after a fumble. Roderique stepped up and threw a 19-yard strike to Daniel on the sideline, then Phoenix Johnson had runs of six and 12 yards. At that point, Webb City turned to Maddy Johnson, who took a pitch at the 31, put a defender on the ground with a brutal juke step, and rushed down to the 2-yard line. He scored a play later.

"That was big," John Roderique said. "That was obviously the difference in the football game."

The Saints came marching to midfield in response, but Daniel intercepted the ball at his own 23. But in the final four minutes of the game, Davila rushed for a first down on a fourth-and-1, then scored. His two-point conversion pass fell incomplete, though, leaving Webb City with a slim 28-26 advantage. Christian Hoffman, a defensive leader all season, took a handoff and rushed 27 yards for a touchdown in the final minute, putting the Redbirds up 34-26, but when the extra point was blocked, the Saints still had 48 seconds to work with. On second down, however, Breckin Williams intercepted a pass and returned it to the 10.

"That's what you want," Williams said. "They get a chance to come back and tie it and just to shoot down their dreams like that, it's an amazing feeling."

Up next came another huge showdown with Carthage. The teams had last met in the 2009 sectionals, when Webb City beat the Tigers for the second time that season. In 2010, each team entered the game at K.E. Baker Stadium 7-0 overall and 6-0 in conference play. While Kearney was ranked first in the state and Bolivar third, Webb City sat in second place and Carthage in fourth. Each team featured a premier rusher: Carthage's Brian Poston, who had 1,200 yards and 21 touchdowns, and Webb City's Maddy Johnson, who had 1,000 yards and 16 scores.

"There's a lot on the line," senior Hunter Luna said after practice the day before. "This game may decide whether or not we have home field advantage. This game will decide conference, this game will decide districts. This will be a big game for us. They're a good team and it's going to be a battle."

"Two heavyweights going at it," Carthage's head coach Jon Guidie said. "It'll be a big-time atmosphere."

"I think both communities really support their team very, very well," John Roderique said. "Both places have great crowds for home games and both communities show up and support. When you've got two communities like this playing a game like this, it really adds to the excitement and the enthusiasm. As we told our guys, tomorrow night's one of the nights where you're not going to have to do a whole lot to get yourself excited. They're going to be fired up."

Six times that night a team went for it on fourth down. Webb City converted once in three tries, and scored a touchdown the very next play. Carthage converted once in three tries, and scored a touchdown two plays later. Maybe the biggest fourth down play all night, though, was on Carthage's first possession, when senior linebacker Collin Sigars blocked a punt and ran it into the end zone. It was the difference in a 21-13 Webb City win.

A 19-yard Scott Roderique pass to Jarvis Jones and a 27-yard Jamison Cady run helped Webb City advance to the Carthage 4, where the Cardinals faced a fourth-and-3. Maddy Johnson got the ball, but was stopped for no gain. Later, Carthage gave the ball to its feature back, Poston, on a fourth-and-inches play at the Tigers' 41; he was stopped inches short, and Webb City had excellent field position. The Johnson brothers each carried the ball as the Cardinals moved 10 yards, but soon found themselves a foot short on another fourth-down play. This time the quarterback Roderique kept the ball on a sneak and got a yard, then threw a 30-yard touchdown pass over the middle to Jones on the very next play. Roderique added a two-point try after Easley's extra point had earlier been blocked. But with 1:18 left in the half, Carthage capped a 77-yard drive that featured its fourth-down conversion with a touchdown to go into the locker room trailing just 14-7.

Carthage, with Poston doing most of the work, drove to the Webb City 20 as the third quarter came to a close, but faced a fourth-and-11. Scott Roderique, who was also a superb defender, came off the end on a blitz and drilled the quarterback for a 10-yard sack. The hit shifted momentum back in favor of Webb City, who promptly drove 69 yards and scored on a Cady run to lead 21-7 in the fourth quarter. After Carthage scored two minutes later, Webb City just ran the clock out.

Webb City's final two games of district play and the regular season were blowouts: a 55-7 win against McDonald County, and then a 55-0 win at Carl Junction, now coached by former Webb City assistant Jesse Wall.

Scott Roderique threw two touchdown passes against the Mustangs, while each of Phoenix Johnson, Byford, junior Marcus Kyle, Maddy Johnson and Cady scored touchdowns. Austin Daniel had 68 yards receiving and both touchdown receptions. He added another interception to his resume, too.

In the Carl Junction game, Roderique completed all seven passes for 101 yards and a touchdown to Daniel, and Roderique scored two times on the ground. Phoenix Johnson scored twice, as well. Sophomores Jeremy Mann and Jose Speer, and Trey Tripp, the senior, each had sacks. Junior Brent Greek had two interceptions, and senior Andrew Pisechko came up with one.

The only question after the regional playoff game against Bolivar was whether it had been Webb City's most complete game of the season. The Cardinals, who won 48-13 against the Liberators, scored 41 points in the first half, including touchdowns on their first five possessions. On the sixth, they took a knee and led 41-0 at halftime.

"We knew on defense we had to come out and stop the running game so they'd have to throw the ball, and we did that pretty well," Austin Daniel said. The Liberators threw two interceptions, both to Daniel; he took the first at the Webb City 10 and returned it 90 yards for the team's third touchdown.

Christian Hoffman had another 10-tackle night, and he, Hunter Luna and Philip Donna each had tackles for a loss. Luna's was a six-yard sack.

Daniel and Donna each caught touchdown passes; Daniel's for 39 yards and Donna's for 9. Maddy Johnson had another four-touchdown night, and 104 rushing yards. Scott Roderique rushed for 106 yards.

In the sectionals the Cardinals traveled to Jefferson City to face Helias, who had finished as a state runner-up the past two years.

Leading 14-7 in the third quarter, Webb City suffered a blow when Scott Roderique left the game with a foot injury. Breckin Williams replaced him at quarterback, and the coaching staff called for two straight passing plays. The second was an 80-yard touchdown pass to Austin Daniel, making it 21-7. Helias pulled within 21-14 late in the third, but Webb City went ahead 35-14 and won the game 35-21. Williams finished the night with 111 passing yards and two touchdowns, both to Daniel, who had five catches for 128 yards. Maddy Johnson scored three times and rushed for 148 of Webb City's 334 yards.

Sophomore Dalton Humphrey had a sack for an 18-yard loss, and senior Nathan Ervin led the team with 10 tackles. Philip Donna added a sack for a 10-yard loss.

The 14-point win at Helias was the closest game in five playoff contests. After that, Webb City blasted Union 42-7, and Austin Daniel tormented the Wildcats all afternoon. He caught a 45-yard touchdown pass from Breckin Williams that made it a 14-0 game, and intercepted a pass with a minute left in a first half that ended with the Cardinals holding a five-touchdown lead. He picked off another pass on Union's opening drive of the third quarter, then hauled in a 66-yard touchdown catch.

Webb City's offense didn't skip a beat with Williams at quarterback. He completed seven of nine passes for 229 yards, and Daniel had four catches for 161 yards. Yet again, Maddy Johnson scored three touchdowns. Dalton Humphrey had one of his best games all season on defense, picking up three sacks, and sophomore Jose Speer added two more. Junior Nick Lovejoy recovered a fumble.

All season long fans around the state had expected a semifinal rematch between Webb City and Kearney, but the same Harrisonville team that the Cardinals had defeated to open the 2008 and 2009 seasons had pulled off a minor upset in beating Kearney 14-10 in the quarterfinals. Harrisonville had won three titles in seven years, at one point appearing in five straight championship games.

The worst possible way to start a game off against a 12-1 Harrisonville team – on the road – would be turnovers on your first two possessions. That's exactly what happened to the Cardinals, but their defense kept the game scoreless for a quarter, Maddy Johnson scored and they took a 21-0 lead into the fourth quarter.

An Austin Daniel interception early in the game stalled one Harrisonville drive; Hunter Luna had a 14-yard sack on another. Webb City led 28-0 late in the fourth quarter before the Wildcats finally scored at the 2:33 mark. They went for the onside kick, but Phoenix Johnson caught the ball on a sprint and took it straight into the end zone. Webb City won 35-8.

While Scott Roderique hadn't yet recovered enough to play, Williams had another stellar game, throwing for 145 yards. Maddy Johnson's game consisted of 131 yards and four touchdowns, and Daniel had five catches for 118 yards, including two spectacular diving catches in the first half. The first came on a second-and-8 and moved the ball from the 17 to the 49. Five plays later, the other moved the ball from the 37 to the 11.

"Thank goodness we've got Austin Daniel on our team," John Roderique said. "What a player he is. He was the difference maker out there today, in the first half just keeping us in it and giving us a chance to put seven points on the board."

Webb City, 14-0, was all set to face an 11-3 Warrenton Warriors team for the Class 4 MSHSAA Show-Me Bowl. The Cardinals had all but sealed their ninth championship in the first quarter, when they scored 35 points. That broke the existing Show-Me Bowl record for points in a quarter of 32, which, coincidentally, was set in the 1991 Sumner/Benton title game ... the week after Benton escaped with a win against Webb City in the infamous mud bowl.

The Cardinals scored 49 points by halftime, which tied a championship game record, and the team finished with 56 points, which tied for fourth most all time. They won, of course, 56-7.

Only a few minutes after the final whistle, John Roderique sat in the interview room at the Edward Jones Dome telling a story. He recalled watching youth football players practice after his high school squad had finished for the day, and giving his brother Will, who was active with the youth program, some advice.

"I said the best thing you can do is instill a love for the game," Roderique told the assembled reporters.

Many of those same players helped Webb City blast Warrenton that same day.

"It's pretty emotional for me to see these guys," he said. "I remember I used to just get the greatest thrill watching those guys play when they were little, just practicing. They will tell you they didn't beat everybody those times. They just developed that love for the game to where they can get to this point."

Will's son – John's nephew – Scott Roderique, the senior quarterback, sat right beside his uncle in the interview room.

"We're just guys that have been dreaming about this all our lives and to get here is incredible," he said.

The game featured all the usual ways Webb City had won that season. Roderique returned at quarterback and threw two touchdown passes, both to Austin Daniel. He rushed for one more. Maddy Johnson scored two first-half touchdowns on the ground, and even returned a punt 50 yards for another. Phoenix Johnson even added a defensive score when he intercepted a pitch and ran it into the end zone. And those all came in the first two quarters.

Jamison Cady led all Cardinals with 73 rushing yards, and Johnson had 66 on just eight carries. Byford ran for 53 yards and a touchdown. Junior Keaton Teal (nine yards), sophomore Cooper Smith (eight), Williams (seven), sophomore John Roderique (five) and freshman Trey Parra (four) also got in on the action. Junior Richard Peoples even completed the only pass he threw that day for 50 yards. Daniel had 52 receiving yards, senior Hayden Hickam caught the 50-yarder, and senior Nathan Price had a 10-yard catch.

Nate Brown and Jose Speer each had sacks.

"We won a state title our sophomore year," Daniel said. "It was a pretty special thing to us, but none of us really felt like we did as much as the others. To win it our senior year, it felt like it was our turn to lead and show everyone else what it's like, and I feel like we did that."

"Webb City's always been about tradition," said Christian Hoffman. "We've had a couple of great senior classes come through here. To hear Coach Rod tell us that we have been one of the best senior classes, it really means a lot to us. I'm just glad to leave a legacy and show these underclassmen what they can work up to and accomplish when they are seniors, too."

Their coach admitted he knew "a long time ago" that this particular senior class would be good.

"I'll admit it now," he said. "Don't want to tell them that too soon and get them big-headed. It's a special group. My nephew's the quarterback and some of these guys have been around for so long. I just feel truly blessed."

Scott Roderique finished that season with 946 passing yards and 14 touchdowns. Williams threw four touchdowns and 595 yards. Maddy Johnson, of course, rushed for 1,800 yards and 31 touchdowns, and Phoenix had five touchdowns and 418 yards. Scott Roderique rushed for 701 yards and four touchdowns; Byford had 452 yards and six touchdowns; Cady had 591 yards and five touchdowns; Hoffman had 162 yards and four touchdowns, and Williams had 220 yards and three touchdowns. Cooper Smith, John Roderique and Marcus Kyle each scored once.

Austin Daniel turned in one of the best seasons for a Webb City receiver ever. He caught 51 passes for 1,103 yards and 13 touchdowns. Jarvis Jones had 186 yards and a touchdown, Nathan Price had 91 yards and a touchdown, and Donna had the 9-yard touchdown.

On defense, Phoenix Johnson had 36 tackles, including four for a loss;

Andrew Pisechko had 24 tackles; Daniel had 38; Williams had 54; Jones had 22 and one for a loss; Humphrey had 60 and six for a loss; Sigars had 68 and two for a loss; Ervin had 96 and one for a loss; Hoffman had 109 and three for a loss; Luna had 29 and one for a loss; Cade Higginbotham had 36 and one for a loss; Donna had 44 and two for a loss; Wyatt Johnson had 26; and Trey Tripp had 51 and one for a loss.

Humphrey finished with nine sacks, Speer and Luna each had four, Donna had three and Tripp had two. Daniel had seven interceptions, Williams three and Brent Greek two. Hoffman recovered two fumbles.

Special teams were another strong point. Chase Capron, the senior kicker, put the ball in the end zone about half the time he kicked off, with 51 touchbacks in 103 kickoffs. He averaged 32 yards on three punts, and Donna averaged 38 yards on 20. Alex Easley was the team's third-leading scorer, with 87 points off extra points and field goals. On PAT attempts he was 81-88, and he was a perfect 2-2 on field goals.

Nine members of the team earned all-state honors when the Missouri Football Coaches Association announced its selections. On the first-team offense: Roderique at quarterback, Johnson at running back, Daniel at receiver, and Jordan Abercrombie on the line. The first-team defense included Luna and Donna on the line, Hoffman at linebacker and Williams in the secondary.

John Roderique was chosen as the Class 4 Coach of the year, and Maddy Johnson was named the Class 4 Offensive Player of the Year.

"I didn't really try and play like them but I always looked up to Marty Rodgers and all the running backs who played at Webb City," Maddy Johnson says now. "Chris Taylor, and some of the greatest who put up 2,000 yards a year. It was awesome just trying to put myself in that category with them, and when people tell me I'm in that category it really makes me feel good and makes me think that all the hard work paid off and was worth it. There are quite a few others, too, I looked up to. I really think that helped out a lot. I know there are other players younger than me playing who looked up to me and want to do better than me. I think that's awesome. I continue to talk to them and push them and try to do the best I can so they can be the best they can at Webb.

"I really think I've been blessed with awesome opportunities and I'm happy to say that hard work really pays off and the system at Webb ... you grow up as a man there, you mature and you learn a lot of life lessons. I think it was a great experience while I was there and I'll never forget any of the moments there, the community's support. I can't think my parents enough for pushing me through everything and the continued support they give me day in and day out."

Webb city players, including quarterback Breckin Williams, center, celebrate winning the program's 10th state championship in 2011. Photo by Bob Foos.

34. THE TENTH TITLE

After the 2010 season, Webb City had amassed an 89-4 record since the start of the 2004 season. After losing to Kearney in the 2009 semifinals, the Cardinals had won roughly one third of what would eventually become a 46-game winning streak that would hike that remarkable record since 2004 to 120-4. The 2011 and 2012 seasons were among the most dominant ever for Webb City teams.

Breckin Williams took over as the quarterback in 2011 and threw for 1,457 yards and 16 touchdowns as a senior. The son of B.J. Williams, who had played on the first-ever championship team in 1989, he also rushed for 893 yards and 14 touchdowns. And he was just the team's third-leading rusher.

Phoenix Johnson, of course, was the premier back after the graduation of his brother, Maddy. He averaged more than nine yards per carry his junior season, with 1,920 total yards and 33 touchdowns. Jamison Cady, now a senior, ran for

1,239 yards and 14 touchdowns. John Roderique, the junior quarterback, threw for two touchdowns and ran for three more in limited time, and junior Cooper Smith, senior Austin Sanders, sophomore Kyle Baldassarre, sophomore Trey Parra, senior Rupert Williams and junior Kohl Slaughter each scored rushing touchdowns.

Jarvis Jones, as a senior, replaced Austin Daniel as the go-to receiver. He caught 30 passes and had seven touchdowns and 712 receiving yards, averaging nearly 24 yards per catch. Impressively, 10 players caught a total of 85 passes and averaged 18.5 yards per catch. Slaughter caught 23 passes for 368 yards and five touchdowns; junior Jalen Vaden had four touchdowns and 268 yards; Johnson even had 99 yards and two touchdowns through the air.

With the graduation of Christian Hoffman, junior Nate Brown took over as the team's leading linebacker in 2011. He had 56 solo tackles, five tackles for a loss and 93 total. Keaton Teal, a senior, had eight tackles for a loss and 47 overall. Other big performers on that side of the ball were senior Brent Greek (31 tackles), senior Klay James (33), junior Todd Fowler (55), senior Cade Higginbotham (33), senior Clayton Temaat (35), junior Logan Williams (67) and senior Wyatt Johnson (65).

Juniors Dalton Humphrey and Jose Speer were monsters, combining for nine sacks. Speer, a defensive end, had 40 tackles and seven for a loss. Humphrey, an inside linebacker, had six for a loss and 88 total. Teal and senior Nick Lovejoy, a lineman, each had two sacks. Junior cornerback Austin White had five interceptions; James, another cornerback, had three; and Brown, Greek and Logan Williams had two apiece. Williams also recovered two fumbles that season, with Webb City forcing 28 total turnovers.

Alex Easley assumed the kickoff duties and had 22 touchbacks in 61 tries. He also ranked second on the team in scoring with 95 points, and had the best season in Webb City history as a kicker. He made 83 of 85 PAT attempts, a 97.6 percent mark, and was four of five on field goals with a long of 35 yards.

Team captains that season were Carson Powell, Clayton Temaat, Breckin Williams and Jarvis Jones, each a senior. With so many skill players returning, the only real questions were who would start on the offensive line for the opener against Ozark. The lineup for that game was Powell and senior Gage Belcher at guards, Temaat at center and Lovejoy and sophomore Jordan Green at tackles.

Interestingly, before the 2011 season began Webb City's streak of 71 consecutive regular season wins was tied for the longest in Missouri history with Jefferson City, who won 71 straight between 1958 and 1966. With the 38-14 win against Ozark, the record was officially Webb City's.

"It's pretty special, there is no question about that," John Roderique said after the game. "There has been a lot of great players come through this place and a lot of great teams."

Before Webb City beat Willard 41-0 in week two, Tigers' coach Brock

Roweton hoped his team would have a different mindset than previous years.

"We need to be excited about the opportunity to play the best team in the state, maybe in any class," he told the *Sentinel*. "As an athlete, you should cherish the moment when you get to test yourself against people like that, and we get that opportunity."

If his players did, it didn't particularly help. Through two games Webb City had nine takeaways, and the Willard win was reportedly the team's 17th straight game without allowing a first-quarter touchdown. In 2011, the Cardinals rarely allowed a touchdown in any quarter.

There were the 14 points scored by Ozark, and in week three Branson put up 16 in losing 50-16. But through the season's first seven games, Webb City's defense had three shutouts and had allowed seven points each to Neosho (37-7) and Nixa (41-7). The other two shutouts came in a 42-0 win at Republic, and a 35-0 win against St. Thomas Aquinas at Cardinal Stadium. In rolling to a 7-0 start, Webb City won on average 40-6.

The team added three more takeaways against Branson, giving defensive back Austin White three in three games. Against Neosho in week four, Webb City had no scoring drive longer than five plays. The Nixa game was supposed to be a good one; Webb City, of course, was ranked first in Class 4, and Nixa had climbed to ninth in the Class 5 poll.

A week later, the Cardinals traveled to Republic to face Kurt Thompson and his Tigers. It turned into Webb City's best-rushing game of the season to that point, starting with Phoenix Johnson's 92-yard touchdown, and the team finished with 378 rushing yards.

For homecoming, St. Thomas Aquinas traveled to Webb City and John Roderique told the newspaper he liked the challenge of playing against a fairly unfamiliar team.

"It's refreshing to play against a team like this, a team we don't know a whole lot about," he said. "I always enjoy breaking down film. It's a challenge to figure out on film what exactly they are trying to do, and how to figure out what we need to do based on how they are lined up."

This year the game wasn't as thrilling as it was in 2010; Webb City won 35-0, its second straight shutout. The Cardinals allowed only 94 yards of offense. And with the win, the game many in southwest Missouri had been awaiting had finally arrived: Webb City vs. Carthage.

"I keep hearing they are down, they're not as big or as physical, but when you watch film it does not look like they have lost much to me," Carthage coach Jon Guidie told the *Sentinel*. "They are still very capable of doing the things they like to do. They will get after you a little bit up front and in the skill positions. They are as good as they have ever been in my opinion."

In a close first half the Cardinals trailed for the first time that season, 6-0 at the end of the first quarter. By halftime it was a one-point lead, Webb City 10,

Carthage 9, but the Cardinals scored on all five second-half possessions and won 41-17. After a 56-19 win at McDonald County and a 48-7 home triumph against Carl Junction, the Cardinals completed their eighth straight undefeated regular season. It marked the team's 12th straight district title. They led 34-0 at halftime of the Carl Junction game, and scored 28 in the first quarter against McDonald County.

It took a three-touchdown barrage in the second quarter to beat Bolivar 35-21 in the first game of the playoffs. Playing in a hard rain and strong wind (a half inch of rain during the game, reportedly), Bolivar recovered a late onside kick and drove into Webb City territory when, on a fourth-and-12, juniors Jose Speer and Dalton Humphrey ended the Liberators' season with a sack.

Against Jefferson City Helias in the sectional, the Cardinal offense exploded for 63 points in a 63-21 win. Breckin Williams threw for 182 yards and two touchdowns, and ran for 140 yards and two more scores. Phoenix Johnson had three touchdowns and 136 yards; Jamison Cady had 157 yards, and John Roderique and Rupert Williams each scored, too. Jalen Vaden had three catches for 75 yards and a touchdown, and Johnson also caught a 26-yard touchdown pass.

Webb City, now into the quarterfinals, came up against a huge threat in Springfield Hillcrest; specifically wide receiver Dorial Green-Beckham, the top high school recruit in the nation and the first to top 6,000 yards in his career, who had played a big role in the Hornets' 11-1 start. He later signed with the University of Missouri. Because of Green-Beckham, Hillcrest's season-opening game against Seneca was televised on ESPN.

"The big talk of course is Dorial Green-Beckham," John Roderique said. "Dorial is one of the best high school football players in the country right now. He is tremendously talented, a very gifted athlete. He's big, he's strong, he's fast."

"Webb City is the class team in Class 4," Green-Beckham told Chris Mazzocco of the *Sentinel*. "I don't know if there is a better program in the state of Missouri."

Green-Beckham came into the game with 2,176 receiving yards and 24 touchdowns, but the Cardinals shut him down. He finished with seven catches and 57 yards. No touchdowns. It was another shutout, Webb City winning 49-0. The Cardinals didn't even complete a pass in the game, instead rushing for all of 478 yards and seven touchdowns. Jamison Cady, incredibly, scored five touchdowns and rushed only 12 times. Phoenix Johnson scored another among his 163 yards, and sophomore Trey Parra had one too.

The Webb City secondary not only shut down the best wide receiver in the nation, it came up with three interceptions and a fumble recovery. Jarvis Jones, Austin White and Wyatt Johnson intercepted passes, and Logan Williams recovered the fumble. Hillcrest actually had negative rushing yards and amassed only 96 total yards.

As many good feelings as that win inspired among fans, those feelings likely disappeared in the first half of the team's semifinal game at Savannah. The Cardinals found themselves trailing by 17 points at halftime, then scored 21 unanswered points in the second half. Still, with 5:52 left in the game they trailed by three points. Quarterback Breckin Williams led his team onto the field and reportedly said, "This is the season!" in the huddle. "This makes or breaks everything. And once I said that you could see in their eyes we were taking it," he said later.

Williams led a game-winning drive that took all but four seconds of the time remaining, and ended with a 1-yard touchdown run by Phoenix Johnson; Webb City won 28-24.

"My grandpa took me in 2001 to see the Cardinals win it, now 10 years later I'm going as a senior," running back Jamison Cady said before his team headed back to St. Louis to face MICDS in the Class 4 title game. Both teams were 14-0 going in. Josh Smith, the Mary Institute and Country Day School head coach, was honest with his players that week, telling them in practice they'll never see the veer offense the way Webb City runs it.

"I've never seen a team so disciplined, where their bad plays are three and four yards," he told the newspaper. "We have to get them off schedule, away from third-and-2 and third-and-1. And when we do get them in third-and-long situations, we need to execute and get off the field."

The game would prove to be another of those back-and-forth championship classics. Webb City averaged 11.9 yards per rush in what turned into a shootout, breaking another Show-Me Bowl record.

"There were over a thousand yards in that game, I never would have thought that," John Roderique said after the game in the championship press conference. "I never would have thought we would have given up 42 either and had an opportunity to win. Sometimes you just have to roll with it."

Webb City rushed for 478 yards in the game, second behind only the 1973 Priory team (501) in Show-Me Bowl yardage. After gaining 190 yards in the semifinal, Phoenix Johnson added 192 yards against MICDS in just 18 carries.

It all started with an interception. That led to the Rams scoring in nine plays to jump out to an early lead, but Cady answered with an 11-yard score to tie the game for the first of five times. He finished with 144 yards. MICDS went ahead 14-7 on the first of five touchdown passes, but Rupert Williams returned the ensuing kick 58 yards to set up a 31-yard Williams touchdown run. It was tied at 14 after Alex Easley's extra point; he finished with eight PATs in the game, tying a Show-Me Bowl record.

The Cardinals then recovered a pooch kick and went ahead 21-14 on another Williams run, but back came the Rams with another touchdown pass to tie it up at 21. Late in the first half, Johnson broke free for a 42-yard run and then scored from the 6 to make it a 28-21 game. MICDS promptly drove to the Webb

City 11 when it ran into a fourth-and-8 situation. Johnson, playing defense, as well, brought heavy pressure into the backfield and forced an incomplete pass. It remained a 28-21 Webb City lead at halftime.

The Rams, with their first possession of the second half, tied the game again on another touchdown pass, but Williams completed his only pass of the day, a 25-yard touchdown to tight end Kohl Slaughter, and the Cardinals led 35-28. A big defensive stand forced the Rams to punt for the first time all game, and Johnson raced into the backfield and blocked the kick, giving his team possession at the 31. Four plays later, Williams found the end zone again, and the Cardinals took a 42-28 lead into the fourth quarter.

MICDS mounted a 79-yard drive over 15 plays to score again, then recovered an onside kick. Another passing touchdown tied the game at 42 with 4:09 left.

"I got a little bit nervous when it got to be 42-all," Roderique recalled. "We told our kids we have to go score after they tied the ballgame up."

Less than a minute later, Williams broke loose on a 76-yard touchdown run to make it a 49-42 game with 3:23 remaining. The defense came up with another huge stop, forcing an incompletion on fourth down, and Johnson added a 67-yard touchdown on the very next play to seal the team's 10th title.

"I have seen Coach Roderique in a clinic before and the message I got leaving that clinic was you can never be right defensively if they run it the right way, and that is exactly what they did today," Josh Smith said about Webb City's veer offense.

"It's like a train coming down the tracks," MICDS linebacker Michael Scherer said.

According to *Sentinel* beat writer Chris Mazzocco, it was a performance for the record books by Webb City. The team won 56-42, and its 56 points was tied for third all time in the Show-Me Bowl. The 98 total points scored in the game broke the previous record. Webb City's eight touchdowns ranked third all time, the eight extra points were tied for first, as were the seven rushing touchdowns. The 1,041 total yards by both teams was a new record, and Webb City's 10.2 yards per play average was second. The 11.9 yards per carry was a new record, and the 478 rushing yards was second.

MICDS had its share, too. Its 538 yards of offense was third, 28 first downs was second, 19 passing first downs was a new record, and 10 third-down conversions was tied for second. The team's 46 passing attempts was second, its 36 completions was a new record, its .782 completion percentage was second, its 415 passing yards was second and its five touchdown passes tied for third.

Richard Correll coaches the team's linemen at a practice. Photo by Bob Foos.

35. RICHARD CORRELL

Someone once told Richard Correll a decade or more ago that Webb City's run of success would be coming to an end.

The Cardinals wouldn't be able to maintain their level of play, not while graduating 20 seniors a year.

"That's not going to continue to happen," they told him. "You're going to have a run of success for three, four, five years and just like everybody else the talent level is going to go down and your program is going to suffer."

Well, it hasn't happened yet.

"Don't ever get the idea you're irreplaceable at whatever level you are, assistant or head coach," Correll says. "It's not necessarily you; the credit should go to the kids and I think Webb City coaches understand that. They themselves are not the show, it's the kids who are the show. Good players make good coaches. If a kid's got talent and he's got the willingness to do it, then as a coach you can coach that and you can help that kid develop. If they haven't got the talent and they're not willing to put forth the effort, I don't care how good a coach you are you're not going to be successful. Hat's off to the kids. That's where the credit should go. The kids that come into the program, they don't want to be the group of kids that winds up with what they would consider a poor record so they're going to work hard and they see the older guys work hard and are successful."

When Richard Correll retired after the 2011 state championship, he ended a 40-plus year career as a football coach at Webb City. He started in the fall of 1968 as the junior high head coach and coached the freshmen team for several years prior to joining the varsity staff in the late 1970s. In the decades since, Correll has been a consistent presence on the staff through a handful of different head coaches.

Originally from Oklahoma, Correll took a position as a junior high science teacher – his first teaching job – and school officials wanted to know if he could coach. He never left.

"I liked the school district," he says. "I was satisfied with what I was doing and I wasn't necessarily looking for greener grass, I guess."

Correll has always coached Webb City's offensive line, and he's coached some of the program's greats during his career. The list of best players he's coached includes names like Adam Spieker, who started at center for four years at the University of Missouri.

"He was a great player but he was a great defensive player and he was a great offensive player and so as a result he stayed on the field all the time," Correll says. "Adam was very, very good, very, very strong, had a lot of flexibility. He was a very good offensive lineman."

Another of the best players Correll has coached is Parker Graham, who started five games as a sophomore at Oklahoma State University, and every game as a junior and senior. He spent time in training camp with the Baltimore Ravens in 2014.

"He was a very good offensive lineman," Correll says.

Correll says Cody Johnson, who was a senior during the 2006 championship season, was another of the greats he coached. Johnson earned all-state honors as a defensive lineman that season, and went on to star as an offensive lineman at Northwest Missouri State University. He started all 15 games for the Bearcats as a redshirt sophomore, and by the time he was a senior in 2011 he was named to the Don Hansen All-America team as a first-string guard.

"I'm probably doing some injustice to a lot of them because I won't mention all of them, but those are some that come to mind," Correll says. "One of the things I kind of feel bad about is we've had, over the years, a lot of really, really good high school football players who weren't quite big enough to play college football. We've had a lot of very good offensive linemen who were as good as any you'd find anywhere, but they didn't have the size to play college football."

According to Correll, the continuity within Webb City's football program is a major reason for its success. Coaches could go on strike, he says, and players could walk down to the practice field and conduct practice about as well as if the coaches were there. Since Jerry Kill arrived in 1988 Webb City has employed the same offensive scheme and basically the same defensive scheme, now for more than 20 years, Correll says.

"Previous to that, when Coach Gosch was the coach we ran the split back veer and when Mark McDonald was there in the mid '80s we ran the split back veer. With the exception of a couple or three years with Mike Hutchison in the early '80s when we ran a wing-T, we've been running the split back veer since I started coaching football. The kids are familiar with the system and they have confidence in it. Nowadays a lot of the reason that it's a successful scheme is because nobody else runs it."

As an offensive line coach, Correll made sure he convinced the players that the Cardinals could line up and run the football against anybody they played, and that they would dominate the line of scrimmage. If you ask them what they want to do, they want to run the football. With few teams utilizing the split back veer, few teams are familiar with it, and when it comes time to play Webb City, an opposing school only has basically two days to prepare for it.

"Your scout team can't run it like Webb runs it," he says, "not with the timing and so forth so you don't get a really good look. When you're playing option football, the defense has got to be very disciplined. You've got certain things on defense you've got to do and if you try to do something else then somebody's going to get burned. If I'm the linebacker and my job is to take a quarterback and instead I'm trying to tackle a running back when I don't know if he's got the ball or not, well if somebody screws up it's a touchdown. It's very hard to mimic Webb's offense in a couple days with a bunch of scout team kids and so as a result kids don't get a good look at it. I truly believe that's one of the big reasons for Webb's success, along with the kids, is the fact that we're running something that I guess is called old man football. I've heard it called that before."

With Correll's retirement following the 2011 season, and Rich Adkins' move to the head coaching position at Jasper High School, a nearly decade-long run with virtually no turnover in the core varsity coaching staff came to an end.

That lack of turnover has been another hallmark of Webb City's program; the coaches who do leave generally either retire or leave to become a head coach elsewhere. The staff, in recent years, has included Aaron Davied, Andrew Doennig, Drew Gollhofer, Stephen Gollhofer, Darrell Hicks, Nathan Hulstine, Dennis Kimzey, Shaun Kloer, Grant McDonald, Gary Pendergraft, Scott Quinly, Corey Roy, Logan Walker, Travis West, B.J. Williams, Ryan McFarland and Nathan Price.

"I guess it's because I'm so nice to them," John Roderique says tongue-in-cheek. "Honestly, coaches want to have ownership. They want to have some ownership in what they do. I do think it would be a difficult job if you never got credit for anything as an assistant coach. I can't help that the head coach is the one who gets more credit probably when things go well. I always try to acknowledge our coaches and give them credit. When we talk about coaching, we're talking about not just one guy – we're talking about how a staff works together. Guys enjoy coaching in the environment we're in. Everybody enjoys having a role and having a significant role. I always tell our coaches that everybody is the head coach of their position, so everybody is going to make decisions on personnel.

"Coach Hicks has been here the longest of that crew," Roderique says. "It seems like we've always had several guys I felt could be head coaches. I've always felt very blessed with the staff I've had."

"I've worked for a lot of good coaches," Correll says. "I've learned a lot from all the different coaches I've coached with over the years. It was an enjoyable thing."

Correll again insists the credit should go to the players.

"As coaches, we never made a tackle or blocked anybody, but they've done all of it," he says. "I always felt like I was not a person who had a very strong ego. I never felt like I was trying to get glory for what I did. I had no aspirations to be a head coach, didn't want to put up with all the other distractions that go along with that. I was content to do what I did."

36. UNDEFEATED AGAIN

An overflow crowd at Bulldog Stadium witnessed Webb City hike its regular-season winning streak to 82 games and its overall winning streak to 31 when the teams opened the 2012 season at Carl Junction.

Webb City, as usual, had plenty of new athletes on the field in starting roles, and as usual, they went out and played great games. John Roderique – the coach's son – stepped in at quarterback and threw for 195 yards in the game, completing six of eight passes, and he rushed four times for 97 yards. At running back, Cooper Smith – son of defensive coordinator Mike Smith – rushed eight times and gained 140 yards.

The Cardinals won the game 45-3 and both Roderique and Smith got off to a great start in what was a special season for their fathers.

"There's no question," the elder Roderique later says. "I've always felt very fortunate and blessed with the players here and the things they go through, the hard work they put in. I've always felt that way. Always felt we had special guys. They always give a lot of effort and play hard. This year I'd be lying if I said it didn't have extra meaning, having your son playing, especially with him having such a vital role in our season, playing one of the most important positions on the field. Complete fulfillment. I feel very good, very blessed. I'm very excited for him. I feel just as good about Coach Smith having a son on the team, too. We've been here so long coaching together. Having those two boys get the opportunity to do what they did, it doesn't get any better than that for a football coach."

Of course, 2012 was another undefeated season for the Cardinals, their third-consecutive state championship. John Roderique – the quarterback – had a fantastic season, completing 64 percent of his passes and throwing for 1,670 yards, 20 touchdowns and just four interceptions. He finished the year with a quarterback rating of 133. He accounted for 36 total touchdowns, scoring 16 more on the ground while rushing for 780 yards and averaging 9.9 yards per carry.

Cooper Smith was the team's second-leading rusher, scoring 19 touchdowns and rushing for 1,106 yards on 141 carries. He also completed the only pass he threw that season, a 49-yard touchdown. The Cardinals averaged more than 300 rushing yards per game and scored 73 touchdowns on the ground. And running behind another strong offensive line, backs averaged 7.74 yards per rush.

The team was a senior-laden one, with Roderique and Smith both in their final seasons with the Redbirds, along with Phoenix Johnson, who followed up his superb 2011 season with 24 touchdowns and 1,478 yards, averaging 8.9 yards per touch. Kyle Baldassarre, Trey Parra and Tyler Davison, future starters in the backfield, rushed for 289, 364 and 207 yards that season.

Tight end Kohl Slaughter, standing 6-foot-3 and 215 pounds, was Roderique's favorite target, catching more than a third of the team's passes for 858 yards and 10 scores. He averaged nearly 24 yards per reception. He was a senior, and so was receiver Jalen Vaden, who had 29 receptions and four touchdowns while amassing 492 receiving yards.

Inside linebacker Dalton Humphrey, a senior, recorded more solo tackles (56) than assisted (52) while recording a team-high 108 stops, including nine for a loss. Not far behind him were senior defensive back Logan Williams, who made 85 tackles and three for a loss, and senior defensive end Jose Speer, who finished with 83 tackles and seven for a loss. Todd Fowler, another senior linebacker, added 75 tackles and four for a loss, and Nate Brown, a senior outside linebacker, had 71 and three. The Cardinals recorded 45 tackles for a loss and 22 sacks. Speer led the team with six sacks, Brown had four and Easton Carver, a junior defensive tackle, had three.

Webb City also added 30 takeaways, an average of two per game. Kiante Hardin, just a sophomore, led the team with seven picks, while Fowler and senior cornerback Austin White had two apiece. Twelve different players recovered a fumble, but only senior Landon Baker recorded two. Phoenix Johnson returned one recovery for 63 yards, and Brayden Goff, a senior, returned his lone interception for 43 yards. Hardin averaged 22 yards per interception return – 154 total yards.

On special teams it was another solid year with senior Alex Easley booting 82 of 87 extra point attempts and five of seven field goal attempts, including a long of 45 yards. He scored 97 points that year, and averaged 6.5 points per game.

As the Cardinals started the season with the romp at Carl Junction, Dalton Humphrey (15) and Logan Williams (12) combined for 27 tackles, including 18 solo stops; Todd Fowler and junior Cooper Strasser each recorded a sack, and sophomore Tayler Arterburn and junior Joseph Jones each recovered fumbles.

In the week two win against Springdale, Arkansas Har-Ber, roughly 10 percent of the team's tackles went for a loss, with Humphrey and Speer each making two tackles behind the line of scrimmage. Speer added a sack, and Austin White and Kiante Hardin each had interceptions in the 30-15 win.

It was another solid effort by John Roderique at quarterback, with 127 yards and a touchdown on just four completions. Phoenix Johnson caught a 64-yard touchdown pass and ran for two more touchdowns and 137 yards; Cooper Smith added a score and 101 yards.

Carthage managed to hang 20 points on the board in week three, but Webb City scored 67 in another rout. This time Roderique threw a 32-yard touchdown to Phoenix Johnson, and Kohl Slaughter caught another one. Roderique also ran for two touchdowns on the ground, and Johnson, Mason Williams, Trey Parra and Devin Pickett each scored once. No one individual topped the 100-yard mark, but the team rushed for 310 yards and built a 48-6 halftime lead.

Kiante Hardin picked off two passes in that game, returning them for a combined 62 yards, and Todd Fowler added a third.

After beating Republic 48-7 to improve to 4-0, Nixa managed to score 21 points against the Cardinals in Webb City's 49-21 win in week five. It was the most any team would score against the Redbirds all year, including the playoffs. The Cardinals recorded five interceptions in the Republic game, one each by Fowler, Humphrey, Hardin, Williams and Brown. Against Nixa, Roderique threw for 176 yards and two touchdowns. Cooper Smith threw his only pass of the year, a 49-yard touchdown. Jalen Vaden had a breakout game with seven catches, two scores and 150 yards. Slaughter also caught a touchdown pass.

After that, Webb City allowed just 7 points in its final four regular season games. It shut out Willard 45-0 in week six, Neosho 55-0 in week seven, and Branson 42-0 in week nine. The Cardinals added a win against Ozark, 28-7. Roderique threw three touchdown passes in the Willard game and rushed for a fourth. Johnson and Smith combined for five of the team's seven rushing touchdowns in the homecoming win against Neosho, and Slaughter added 100 yards on just three catches. He caught a 41-yard touchdown against Ozark, a game in which both Fowler (13) and Speer (10) recorded double digit tackles. In the Branson win the Cardinals scored six times on the ground – once every four carries – with Johnson scored twice and Roderique, Parra, Logan Cloyd and Smith once each.

When district play started, a winless West Plains team came to Webb City, which proceeded to hang 38 points in the first quarter alone in a 45-7 victory. Four touchdowns came on the ground – Johnson rushed for 145 yards and two, and Baldassarre (55) and Smith (97) also found the end zone. Cooper Strasser caught a 7-yard touchdown, and Slaughter caught one for 30. Junior Alex Lane had a sack, and sophomore Lakin Milner picked off a pass. Alex Easley scored nine points on a 37-yard field goal and a perfect 6-6 for PATs.

It was almost an identical score a week later against Republic, though it was just 14-7 after the first quarter. Twenty unanswered points in the second quarter and two touchdowns in the third turned it into a 48-7 final. Roderique threw scoring passes to Johnson and Slaughter, Johnson scored twice on rushes and Cooper Smith led the team with 108 yards. He, Cloyd and Roderique also scored. The defense feasted on turnovers all night; Fowler, Humphrey, Hardin, Williams and Brown each intercepted a pass.

The November 5 matchup at Cardinal Stadium was a good one – top-ranked

Webb City, undefeated, against fourth-ranked Springfield Hillcrest, which had won 10 of 11 games. The District 4 title was on the line. The Cardinals went out and won in, as Anvil Welch wrote in *The Globe*, "emphatic fashion," throttling the Hornets 55-10, allowing just a field goal in the first quarter and a touchdown in the second and giving up well fewer than 200 yards of offense. In contrast, the Cardinals rushed for 401 yards and eight touchdowns – three each from Johnson (13 carries, 163 yards) and Smith (7 for 62), and single scores from Roderique (8 for 121) and Tyler Davison.

On the same day, Sullivan had won 32-17 against St. Clair, and the third-ranked Eagles came to town a week later for the quarterfinals. The game marked Sullivan's eighth playoff appearance, and *The Globe* reported it had finished as a state runner-up behind Joplin Memorial in the 1976 playoffs.

In the battle of unbeatens, Webb City emerged unscathed, thanks in large part to the team's special teams play. Nate Brown, an all-state defensive player in 2011, blocked a 40-yard field goal attempt and a punt in the second quarter, setting up two touchdowns as Webb City built a 28-0 lead before the half.

The blocked field goal led to a touchdown merely seconds later, when Phoenix Johnson returned it 77 yards for a touchdown. The punt was recovered by Dalton Humphrey near the red zone, setting up a Cooper Smith touchdown run. The teams traded scores in the second half and Webb City advanced with a 35-6 win. John Roderique was perfect through the air, completing all three attempts for a total of 78 yards, including a 33-yard strike to Slaughter for a touchdown. Phoenix Johnson only tallied 39 yards, but did score, Roderique added another touchdown and Cooper Smith, who led with 81 yards, added a third. Both Humphrey and Logan Williams finished the game with 11 tackles.

In the semifinals against St. Mary's, the Cardinals took to the road, incredibly for just the first time in eight weeks, and they really aired it out in this one. Roderique threw a season-high 18 times, completing 15 of those and throwing three touchdowns, one each to Jalen Vaden, senior Jake Kent and Slaughter. Again, nobody rushed for 100 yards; Smith led the team with 89 yards and scored three big touchdowns. The other came from Trey Parra. Humphrey, once again, made 10 tackles; Austin White had a fumble recovery and an interception, and Landon Baker recovered a second fumble. Webb City won 47-7.

The Class 4 Show-Me Bowl Championship Game featured two very familiar opponents: Webb City and Jefferson City Helias. The two squads had played four times in the playoffs in 10 years and the Cardinals had won every time. There was the 24-21 overtime win in the 2002 quarterfinals, the 41-34 shootout in the 2008 title game, the 35-21 triumph in the 2010 sectionals, and a 63-21 blowout in the 2011 sectional. This marked the fourth playoff game in five years between the two.

It was over by halftime. The Cardinals struck for three touchdowns in the first quarter and led 35-7 after two quarters. They tacked on another pair in the second half and won 49-14.

It was a standout game for every one of the team's seniors. John Roderique completed six of eight passes for 105 yards and a touchdown; he rushed seven times for 105 yards and three scores. Phoenix Johnson had 11 carries, scored once, and tallied 144 yards, a 13-yard-per-carry average. Cooper Smith added 68 yards on 16 carries with one touchdown. Kohl Slaughter had two catches, one touchdown, and 62 yards; Smith had a 5-yard reception and Johnson one for 14.

Defensively, senior Kyler Crane had three tackles, Taylor Coleman had two, Austin White two, Todd Fowler six and one for a loss, Breck Mitchell one, Logan Sperry one, Jose Speer three, Casey Craig one, and Nate Brown seven.

Alex Easley kicked off eight times – seven were touchbacks. He nailed all seven extra point attempts.

"I'm always asked about Webb City football wherever I go," said State Rep. Charlie Davis at the team's postseason awards banquet. "I tell people that there is not a school district that people are more involved than the Webb City School District. This community is a team and there is no place in the state with more pride in their team than what we have right here."

There was one disappointment, though. JC Chevere, who had recently released a song titled "Webb City Anthem," had to cancel his scheduled appearance at the banquet due to an illness. He planned to later conduct a video shoot for the song.

"The song is one of those cool things that have come out of all of this," Roderique, the coach, told *The Joplin Globe*. "We're looking forward to having him here eventually."

The Cardinals had won 45 straight games, and 90 consecutive in the regular season.

Taylor Arterburn sacks Carl Junction quarterback Dustin Satterlee during the 2013 district championship at Cardinal Stadium. Photo by Brennan Stebbins.

37. THE 'QUAD SQUAD'

Twenty minutes before kickoff, fans are streaming eastward on Stadium Drive, and the intersection of Stadium and Madison becomes the busiest intersection in town. Cars line either side of Madison, parked in the grass, and to the north of the stadium, the parking lot of Sacred Heart Catholic Church is filled to capacity, with many more cars parked on the grass.

Fans lined up at the north gate pause as the marching band performs the national anthem, and everyone in and around the stadium turns to face a Webb City fire truck, its ladder extended to its full reach with the U.S. flag waving at the very top and a white Webb City Cardinals flag hanging underneath it.

Ten minutes before kickoff, it's still 91 degrees, and the stands are filling up as the band and flag girls ready for their pre-game performance. The stands on the home side are mostly red, dotted with white and blue, while the visitor bleachers are covered in red and white specks. The band opens with the fight song, and fans clap and cheer along, shouting "C-A-R-D-S Cards!"

Carl Junction, the visiting team, enters the south gate with just more than eight minutes left on the clock countdown. The Bulldogs are dressed in all white uniforms, their helmets red with the mascot depicted in a gray decal. Further south, Webb City players, wearing their traditional red tops, Columbia blue pants and white helmets, start their walk down the hill from the locker room.

The band continues playing. "Eat 'em up, eat 'em up, Go Big Red!"

Seven minutes and 24 seconds before kickoff, the Bulldogs run onto the field as their fans cheer loudly from across the stadium. On the home side, Webb City fans grow louder with anticipation as their team nears the south gate, and cow bells begin ringing.

The announcer, Bruce VonderHaar, presents the starters. At defensive lineman, a senior, No. 81, Alex Lane. A senior, No. 59, a defensive lineman, Trenton Moeller. At defensive tackle, a junior, No. 56, Connor Badgley. At defensive tackle, a junior, No. 70, Tayler Arterburn. At linebacker, a senior, No. 14, Trevor Price. At linebacker, a senior, No. 30, Carson Johnson. At outside linebacker, a senior, No. 3, Hunter Rhea. At outside linebacker, a junior, No. 9, Lakin Milner. At free safety, a junior, No. 5, Kiante Hardin. At defensive back, a junior, No. 18, Maquel Harbin. At defensive back, a junior, No. 4, Trent Parra.

"And the rest of the 2013 football Cardinals!"

The team sprints onto the field, bursting down a makeshift tunnel of band members and through a banner hoisted by the cheerleaders.

A nice breeze picks up from the south, and the sky is a clear, Columbia blue.

Webb City's team captains walk to midfield, from left: Kyle Baldassarre, a senior running back; Rhea; James Fowler, a senior offensive lineman; and Trey Parra, a senior running back. Two minutes, 38 seconds before the opening kick of the 2013 season.

On the sideline, junior quarterback Devin Pickett and Trent Parra, a junior receiver, throw footballs with junior quarterback Tyson Roderique and junior receiver Kiante Hardin. Pickett then takes practice snaps from Jordan Green, a 6-foot-2, 270-pound offensive lineman.

The Cardinals win the toss, and defer until the second half. The Bulldogs want the ball and opt to receive.

Seth Rogers, Webb City's senior kicker, places the football on the tee and waits for the whistle. He stands seven yards behind the ball, looking north, while the other 10 members of the kicking team take three-point stances. The crowd reaches a crescendo, the whistle blows, and Rogers sends a kick deep into the northern sky.

On the first play of the 2013 season, Matt Magee catches the ball at the 3-yard-line, and...the Carl Junction senior runs 97 yards untouched for a touchdown. Just 13 seconds into its first game and already Webb City trails 7-0.

Then Baldassarre drops the ensuing kick from Carl Junction, before recovering and returning the ball to the 37, where the Cardinals will run their first offensive play of the new season. On first down, Webb City gives a nod to tradition, running the split-back veer and handing the ball to Baldassarre, who gains four yards. After no gain on second down, Pickett throws to Hardin on the home sideline and the Cardinals gain 21 yards, setting up a first down at the Carl Junction 38.

But there's a fumble during a handoff.

Carl Junction gets the ball not quite two minutes into the game, looking to add to a touchdown lead against its biggest rival. But after an eight-yard gain on first down, the Webb City defense flexes some muscle and stops the Bulldogs for losses of two and three yards. Webb City gets the ball back at its own 24.

Things don't go much better this time. Pickett is sacked on second down, and a delay-of-game penalty on third down puts the Cardinals in a big hole. They punt after three plays. Later, Roderique says he wasn't surprised at the slow start.

"Maybe if it was 10 years ago, if I was younger and new at this," he says. "You scratch your head and it's like, how'd that happen? But you've got a kicker out there who kicks it right to the guy. A new kicker. Really, we haven't had to cover a lot of kickoffs over the last few years. It's just going to take some getting through. I wasn't real surprised that offensively we struggled a little bit earlier. It is what it is. You've got so many new guys out there in important positions, the skill positions, and we know how important linemen are. We weren't real happy but you can't get too upset, you've just got to work through it. I guess that's where as you coach for awhile you become more understanding to those things and the possibilities of those things happening."

Still, the defense keeps Carl Junction at bay early. The Bulldogs start at their own 22 and rush for nine yards on first down and five more on second down before losing two yards and throwing a pair of incomplete passes. Heavy pressure on quarterback Dustin Satterlee helps on a third-and-12.

Webb City starts at its own 48. Pickett passes to senior tight end Joseph Jones, a 6-foot-2, 215-pound target, for a 34-yard gain, then Baldassarre rushes for a two-yard gain, then for three more before Pickett throws a seven-yard touchdown pass to junior receiver Maquel Harbin on third down.

With one minute, 35 seconds left in the first quarter, senior Nathan Gooch's extra point ties the game at seven.

Carl Junction is pinned deep on its next possession, starting at its own 13, and a first-down penalty moves the ball back to the six-and-a-half yard line. Keynan Scheurich is met at the line on first down for no gain, and Satterlee connects with Magee for a 13-yard gain, but another Carl Junction penalty moves the ball back to the 10. Scheurich is stopped again for no gain. Then, on third-and-13, Satterlee's pass is intercepted at the 20 by senior defensive back Roosevelt Edwards, who returns it to the 9. Four plays later, Gooch nails a 26-

yard field goal that gives Webb City a 10-7 lead with 9:39 left in the half.

And the crowd chants: "C-A-R-D-S Cards!" It won't be long before they chant again.

Carl Junction starts its next possession at the 15, and disaster strikes on first down when Satterlee fumbles. Hunter Rhea, a senior outside linebacker, jumps on the ball at the 1, the ball squirts into the end zone and Rhea falls on it again for another touchdown that puts the Cardinals ahead 17-7 with 9:26 left in the first half.

The fight song plays again.

By the time the first half is over, Webb City leads 24-7, and is well on its way to its 91st consecutive regular-season win and its 46th win in a row overall. The Cardinals have scored 52 points after three quarters and lead by 29; they go on to win 52-29 with underclassmen playing most of the second half.

The Cardinals have plenty of holes to fill after winning three championships in a row. They lost their top three wide receivers to graduation, a tight end, both running backs and the quarterback. Most of them were key players for at least the last two years, and some of them for three. On the bright side, however, Webb City returns several offensive linemen in 2013, like Cooper Strasser, a senior tight end who's 6-foot-2 and 210 pounds. There's Jordan Green, a 6-foot-2 senior weighing 270 pounds, and senior Tony Carranco, who stands 6-foot and weighs 275 pounds, as well as senior James Fowler, a 6-foot, 220-pounder.

Roderique says the team has had some "pretty good" linemen over the years, and that's of course an understatement. Parker Graham is the most recent example of what has historically been a strength of the Cardinals. A 2009 graduate, Graham was an all-district, all-conference, all-area and all-state offensive lineman who signed with Oklahoma State out of high school. He redshirted in 2009, played in three games in 2010, started five games in 2011 and then started every game in 2012 and 2013 while standing 6-foot-7, 315 pounds.

So, yes, the Cardinals have had some pretty good linemen over the years, and the offensive lines at Webb City have been a big part of the team's run-first mentality. With four seniors back on the line in 2013, it's no surprise the team rushes for 321 yards against Carl Junction and averages 7.8 yards per carry.

Baldassarre and Trey Parra, both seniors, are the feature running backs, and both get their first career starts in the week one win against Carl Junction. Baldassarre is 5-foot-11, 175 pounds, and Parra is an inch shorter, same weight. They have impressive debuts, combining for 255 yards and two touchdowns. Baldassarre rushes 15 times for 135 yards, an average of nine yards per carry, and Parra rushes 10 times for 120 yards, averaging 12 yards per touch.

"Kyle and Trey are guys who are going to start at Webb City in most years," Roderique says. "Those two are pretty good players. We felt that way going into the season, and we feel even better about them now. Those two guys are like veterans. Trey played a lot last year, and Kyle, he's just a success story. He started getting better here a couple years ago, working hard, and now he's a good player."

Pickett is the team's new quarterback, replacing the coach's son, John, Jr., and though he's limited to negative yardage on the ground against Carl Junction, he has a stellar passing performance against the Bulldogs, completing nine of 10 passes for 178 yards and three touchdowns. Junior Maquel Harbin and Hardin each catch three of his passes, and Hardin gains 81 yards and scores two touchdowns, while Harbin tallies 47 yards and a score. Senior Joseph Jones catches one pass for 34 yards, and senior Kolten Potts makes two grabs for 16 yards.

"Devin, he got the ball out of his hands pretty well," Roderique says. "They were giving us a lot of cushion at times so we were able to throw the ball. We had three touchdown passes, which nobody probably expected that. He does throw the ball well. We've got to distribute it. And we've got to get more production from our quarterback in the run game. That's a big part of our offense. We were really pleased with 178 yards passing."

Defensively it's not a great first game for the Cardinals. Satterlee completes 23 of 33 passes for 271 yards and two touchdowns, and Carl Junction rushes for 139 yards. Webb City does come up with three interceptions in the game, with Harbin and junior Lakin Milner each making picks in addition to Edwards. Seventeen different players make tackles in the game, indicative of how many players Webb City gets into the game in the second half.

There are only two regular starters back from last season on this side of the ball: Hardin and junior Tayler Arterburn, a 6-foot-1, 240-pound lineman. They combine for four of Webb City's 43 tackles against Carl Junction. Three more players, seniors Alex Lane and Easton Carver, along with junior Drake Humphrey, started at different times in 2012, but all will be regular starters for the first time this season. Lane, a 6-foot-1, 185-pound defensive lineman, makes four tackles in the game, and Carver, a 5-foot-11, 190-pound lineman, has a sack for a one-yard loss. Humphrey is a 6-foot-1, 235-pound lineman.

While senior Trevor Price, a 5-foot-11, 200-pound linebacker, leads the team with six tackles and makes one tackle for a loss, the Cardinals do receive big contributions from several underclassmen in the game. Junior defensive back Cameron Tournear makes four stops, junior defensive back Austin Carter has five tackles, junior outside linebacker Lakin Milner has three tackles. Sophomore linebacker Calem Nutting has three tackles, and is one of four sophomores to record stops in the game.

Despite returning just four offensive starters and two on defense, when the preseason rankings are sent out on August 27, few are surprised to see Webb City atop the Class 4 poll and receiving all 15 first-place votes. The rankings are compiled weekly by a 15-member panel of sportswriters and broadcasters. Jefferson City Helias is ranked second after going 10-5 in 2012, and familiar foes

Harrisonville and Bolivar are ranked third and fourth, respectively.

Roderique, sitting in his office in the weight room a few days after the win, is quick to say he doesn't put much stock in the polls, and doesn't really care what they say. Still, it's impressive the amount of respect shown to a Webb City team with so many new faces in key positions, and when the week two rankings come out September 2, the Cardinals are still the unanimous best team in the state.

"I guess people don't let us use the term rebuild around here," Roderique says. "We've never talked about that. We've got a lot of young guys playing. It is what it is. Our players have a high expectation. They expect a lot of themselves, they expect a lot of our coaches, and we expect a lot of our players. That's where it starts for us. That's just kind of how the program has been. We always try to take it one week at a time, one game at a time, one play at a time. It's hard to say where this team will be, but hopefully as a young team starting the season with so many new faces in those particular spots, we've got a chance hopefully by the end to be a better team than we are now. You've got to have some luck as far as injuries and those kinds of things. We feel decent after week one. We've got a huge challenge ahead of us this week obviously."

Indeed they do; the Cardinals' next game will be at Har-Ber.

In 2012, with the remnants of Hurricane Isaac threatening southwest Missouri in week two of the football season, Webb City opened its home schedule against Springdale Har-Ber on Aug. 31. Har-Ber, the 2009 Class 7A state champion in Arkansas, entered the game ranked fourth in the state by Hooten's Arkansas Football, and a 14-point favorite, according to the website, despite the game being Har-Ber's first of the year.

Webb City, on the other hand, had throttled Carl Junction on the road 44-3 a week earlier, and had a 91-game regular season winning streak on the line. The Cardinals, of course, were ranked No. 1 in Missouri Class 4.

The game was hyped in a big way, and rightfully so. Roderique, speaking to beat writer Anvil Welch of *The Joplin Globe*, said Har-Ber had "tremendous talent" and it would take a "monumental effort" for the Cardinals to get a win. Instead, Webb City made it look easy, taking a 21-0 lead into the half and winning 30-15. Only once the rest of the season did Webb City score fewer points.

This year, though, will be different. It's not Webb City that enters as the senior-laden team, but Har-Ber, who has 44 seniors and will start 10 of them on offense and nine of them on defense. The game is not Webb City's home opener, but Har-Ber's. Webb City, as in 2012, is a unanimous No. 1 in Missouri Class 4; Har-Ber is ranked even higher than last year, considered by both the *Democrat-Gazette* and *Athlon Sports* to be the top team in the state of Arkansas. Hooten's is more cautious in its pick this year, ranking the Wildcats fourth in the state and taking Har-Ber by a point.

"We're really flipping roles; last year they had a lot of new faces out there and this year we do," Roderique says the week of the game. "They're a big school in the state of Arkansas. They're well-regarded in their class and conference. They've got some Division 1 players. They're just a really big, physical, talented group. I remember when we talked about this game, coach (Chris Wood) said they would be returning a lot in 2013, and they certainly do have a lot who played last year. Their quarterback's back, a running back, they've got some linemen. On their defensive line, they've got the Frazier kid and he's a top-five defensive lineman in the country. A five-star recruit is what they say. They're just real talented. And they're big. They're massive up front. Their three down linemen are going to average 280 or 290 pounds. That'll be the biggest challenge for us offensively, just trying to move the football against those big kids. Offensively they like to run the ball out of the spread, but they're also a team – we found out last year in the second half – they can throw it too. They have some very capable receivers. You've got to be well-balanced on both sides of the ball. They're well-coached from the standpoint that they're going to adjust to what you do, how you align. They're going to make adjustments."

He tells Welch the Wildcats are bigger, stronger and probably faster. And the Frazier Roderique speaks of is 6-foot-3, 325-pound Joshua Frazier, who's rated the 10th-best defensive tackle in the country. When the season's over, he will have offers from 11 Division 1 schools and some of the biggest programs in college football – Florida State, Georgia, Missouri, Nebraska, Notre Dame, Southern California, Texas A&M, Auburn and Arkansas. In the end, he signs with Alabama. And, as Roderique says, Frazier isn't the only big-time player that Har-Ber has at its disposal. There's also Jake Hall, a 6-foot-5, 239-pound defensive end who will later commit to Arkansas. Offensive tackle Isaac Johnson signs with Tulsa.

The question everyone asks all week is if this is the game where Webb City's streak is snapped. It's also unknown how the Cardinals would react to finally losing a game. After all, the team's seniors were still in junior high when the team last lost a game. And that was in the state semifinals in 2009. Maybe Roderique asks himself the same questions, wonders how the team would react. But in his office, days before the Cardinals load onto a bus and make the hour-plus drive south into Arkansas, he downplays the game. It's not a make or break game for his team by any means, he says, and like he told the players, it doesn't count any more than last week's game against Carl Junction.

"It's a pre-conference game," he says. "It just happens to be against a pretty good opponent. From that standpoint, when you have to prepare knowing you're going to face a really, really good team and what they're capable of, it makes you step up your practices. You've got to practice harder, prepare a little bit better. I always think about playing a team like this in terms of if you get the opportunity to play in the playoffs, you may or may not face a team as good as this team. The biggest thing we're looking for is our kids to go down and compete and play hard. The outcome is not near as important to us as it is probably to a lot of people because it's a process. As you always tell your kids, each week you want to make steps towards getting better and that's what we want to do this week."

The stands on the home side of Jarrell Williams Bulldog Stadium are nearly 80 yards long, with separate bleacher sections on either end, and it's not nearly enough to hold the crowd that turns out on the first Friday evening of September in Springdale, Arkansas. The stadium includes a two-story press box and a large scoreboard with a video screen. It's a very intimate atmosphere, with stands coming to within a few yards of the sidelines, and it's made all the more intimate by the standing-room-only crowd that crams inside.

Only a few minutes before kickoff, the line for tickets is nearly 100 yards long on the sidewalk out front, and fans grow restless when they hear the announcer introduce the teams.

"Ranked No. 1 in the state of Arkansas and led by senior quarterback Kyle Pianalto, here are your Springdale Har-Ber Wildcats!"

Webb City strikes first in the game, thanks in part to a personal foul on Har-Ber. Trey Parra gains 10 yards on a third-and-16 from the Har-Ber 29-yard line, and the Cardinals are whistled for holding on the play, but the personal foul call sets up a third-and-short at the 14. Devin Pickett fakes a handoff and breaks several tackles before he's tackled into the end zone for the first touchdown of the game, giving the Cardinals a 7-0 lead after Nathan Gooch nails the extra point.

The lead doesn't stand for long, though. Har-Ber takes less than three minutes to move 77 yards on its next possession, which includes conversions on third and fourth down. A 48-yard pass down the sideline puts the Wildcats in the red zone, and senior Matt Garrison plunges in from two yards out to tie the game with 3:21 left in the first quarter.

The Cardinals get the ball back at their own 20 after a touchback, but immediately have trouble holding onto the football. Pickett fumbles on a first-down carry, but it's recovered by James Fowler for a 15-yard gain. Two plays later, a fumbled snap is recovered by Jonas White at the 26. On second and long, Pickett pitches the ball to Parra, who makes a nice cutback inside a Har-Ber defender and rolls down to the Wildcat 8. It takes three more plays, but finally Parra scores from two yards out, and Webb City leads 14-7 at the end of the first quarter.

Almost immediately Har-Ber threatens to score again; another long pass from Pianalto moves the ball from the Wildcat 34 to the Webb City 10. The Cardinal defense stops a running attempt for no gain on first down, then gives up four yards on second down. Pianalto drops back to pass on third and goal, and Webb City junior Trent Parra is waiting two yards deep in the end zone. He picks the pass off and runs down the Webb City sideline, untouched, for a 102-yard touchdown, putting the Cardinals up 21-7 with 10:37 left in the half.

Again, Har-Ber moves almost at will, and again, the Webb City defense bends but doesn't break. The Wildcats start at their own 28 and quickly move into Cardinals territory. Pianalto throws to the end zone once more, and this time his pass is batted by Maquel Harbin into the arms of Kiante Hardin, who settles for a touchback to give the Cardinals the ball at their own 20.

They brush off a false start penalty on first down, and three plays later have the ball at their own 35. Pickett drops back to pass and throws to Hardin, who leaps in front of Har-Ber's Holden Thornton, a senior cornerback, takes the ball away and lands on the turf, maintains his balance and races to the end zone for Webb City's fourth score of the game.

It's now 28-7 with 6:42 left in the half and what was touted as the game of the week now looks like another Webb City blowout. Har-Ber does tack on another score with 4:22 left to play, and the Wildcats force Webb City to punt with less than three minutes remaining. The Wildcats get great field position, two yards inside the 50, and Pianalto rushes on a third-and-five for 31 yards to the Webb City 12. He runs it again on first down but fumbles just shy of the goal line. Hardin recovers it at the 2, and the Cardinals go into the locker room leading by two touchdowns at the half.

Webb City's opening drive of the second half is its best possession of the game. The Cardinals start at their own 20 and play their style of football: they run it right at the Wildcats. Trey Parra gains five yards, Pickett runs for nine, Kyle Baldassarre rushes for nine, then one more. Pickett crosses midfield with a 15-yard gain, then Trey Parra tallies 24 yards and the Cardinals are in the red zone. Pickett keeps the ball for 15 yards to the 2, and an offsides penalty moves the ball a yard closer for Baldassarre, who punches it in with 7:46 on the clock. Gooch, as usual, is automatic on the PAT and the Cardinals lead 35-14. Again it appears as if the rout is on. It's the last time Webb City will score in the game.

Pianalto has another pass nearly intercepted on Har-Ber's next possession, but he lucks out this time and the Wildcats mix the run and pass in driving 72 yards. Garrison gets the ball at the Webb City 35 and sprints down the home sideline with 5:15 left in the quarter; it's now 35-21.

Webb City starts its next possession on its own 43, and in two plays the Cardinals are in Wildcat territory. Pickett fumbles on third down from the Har-Ber 48, but the ball bounces back to him and he takes it around the edge for an 11-yard gain. But on the ensuing first down, his pass is intercepted at the Wildcat 13.

Webb City's offensive linemen trot off the field and gather on the bench. "Hey, we're finally moving the ball on them," one of them says. "We can run it any time we want."

Chris Wood rolls the dice with Har-Ber facing a fourth-and-1 at its own 22 and the gamble pays off: a nine-yard pass. A few minutes later, the Wildcats get a big run from Pianalto, who takes it all the way to the Webb City 7. An illegal procedure penalty backs the Wildcats up five yards, but then Pianalto passes to Camden Scott in the back of the end zone, and Webb City's lead is all of a sudden down to just a touchdown.

The Cardinals can't get any momentum back after the Har-Ber score. They punt from their own 26 early in the fourth quarter, and the ball is returned all the way to the Webb City 29. The Wildcats go for it again on fourth down, this time needing eight yards, and Pianalto finds Scott again for another touchdown to tie the game at 35 with 10:32 remaining.

Webb City tries to reset itself, starting with the ball on the 20, and the Cardinals start a solid drive. Baldassarre rushes for 15 yards, then for three more; Pickett gains six, then Baldassarre gets three yards to the 47. But the Cardinals fumble on the fifth play of the drive and the Wildcats recover inside Webb City territory. The place goes wild, and Har-Ber is even flagged for excessive celebration, which backs the ball up to its own 42. Then, on first down, Pianalto passes to Gus Vitt for a big gain to the Webb City 7. The quarterback takes it to the 1 on the next play, then punches it in on second down and Webb City trails 42-35 with 7:47 left in the game.

The Cardinals run three plays and move the ball just six yards. They punt again.

Har-Ber gets possession at its own 20 with 5:28 on the clock. This time the Wildcats are content to keep the ball on the ground, and they gain small chunks of yards each play. On third-and-1 with fewer than four minutes remaining, Pianalto gets three yards. On third-and-3 with 2:20 on the clock, Pianalto gets 10 yards. The quarterback carries the ball seven times during the 12-play drive, and Har-Ber has a first-and-goal when Pianalto finally takes a knee.

Final score: Har-Ber 42, Webb City 35. And that's how the streak ends.

Har-Ber players sprint onto the field jumping and hollering. John Roderique jogs onto the field, looking for his counterpart. He shakes hands with Chris Wood as students burst from the stands, flooding the artificial turf. One Wildcat player picks up a cheerleader and spins her around on the field. Webb City's players gather in the far end zone.

Considering Har-Ber entered the game a favorite, and is ranked by many as the best program in the state of Arkansas, the reaction of its fans and players is, perhaps, surprising. Afterwards, Wood says the reaction is because of Har-Ber's respect for Webb City.

"What Coach Roderique's done and that town and that program and that winning streak and the success they had and we went up there last year and they embarrassed us," he says, still standing in the midst of a jovial crowd on the field. "Coach Roderique schooled me in every facet as a head coach and

I learned a lot from it. We just wanted to compete better. We wanted to give a better effort tonight. Whenever you come in against a program like Webb and they've got that streak on the line, that's something to go for but it's more out of the respect for their program and who they are."

Wood's message to his team after the game draws from his previous experiences as an assistant for Gus Malzahn, who won a national championship with Auburn. Wood was Malzahn's offensive coordinator at Shiloh Christian, taking over as head coach when Malzahn took the job at Springdale High School. Wood won a state title with the Saints before joining Malzahn in Springdale, and was part of another state title team in 2005. He won a third state title in 2009 after taking over for rival Springdale Har-Ber.

"I just told them about being resilient," he says. "I told them I'm proud of them, to enjoy it and then start getting ready for Rock Bridge. The biggest thing is I was on a staff with Coach Malzahn and Coach (Kevin) Johnson (Malzahn's defensive coordinator at Shiloh and Springdale) and we went down to Junction City and we were down 24 and we were down at the half when the lights went out at Junction City. And I just told our boys, 'I've been in this situation before and I've seen this. Just stay the course, have faith and I've seen coaches and players do it before; we've just got to keep grinding.' I'm proud of them for never quitting and fighting until the end."

The game Wood is referencing is legendary in Arkansas football: the 1999 state semifinals, where No. 1 Shiloh Christian trailed No. 3 Junction City 24-0, and then 51-35 at the half. The Saints came back and won 70-64.

On the other end of the field, the mood is a subdued one as Roderique speaks quietly to his players in the end zone. Parents and fans are lined up around the huddle. When he's done, he speaks to a small assemblage of reporters, telling them the Cardinals were doing a good job offensively, but Har-Ber's size finally wore his team out.

"I mean, Josh Frazier was a difference in the second half," he says. "I really thought he was. There were some critical plays he made in the second half that were really tough."

And Pianalto was tough, too. Roderique says it certainly wasn't his first rodeo.

"He knew what to do with the football. Did a great job."

Striking a confident tone, Roderique says his message to the players was the same as it always is.

"This game, it's one game," he says. "It means about the same as what last week's does. It's a game. It's the last game heading into our conference play. Maybe we've made too much about it or people have made too much about it, but it's just one game. Obviously a really good opponent and a really good team, a highly-regarded team. I told them, 'Tomorrow's a new day and we'll regroup.' We'll learn from our mistakes and hopefully we'll be a week better next week."

Losing a three-touchdown lead is painful enough, but snapping a 91-game regular season winning streak in the process is on a whole other level. Still, if there were any risk of a letdown from Webb City in week three of the 2013 season, the team that takes the field at Cardinal Stadium in blue jerseys with white trim should be enough motivation as Webb City officially opens the conference slate against its old rival, Carthage.

Sept. 13 is the first time in a decade fans have filled Webb City's stadium to see their team play the week after a loss. Remember, every loss in that span was in the win-or-go-home Missouri playoffs.

Still, the Cardinals are in fine shape for another title run, and they're still putting up eye-popping statistics. Through two games, Devin Pickett has completed 11 of 13 passing attempts through two games for 256 yards, four touchdowns and just one interception. At Har-Ber, he went 9-of-10 for 178 yards and three scores. He's completed passes to five different receivers; Kiante Hardin has four catches for 146 yards. Three of those receptions are for touchdowns.

The bread-and-butter running game has been just as efficient. The Cardinals have already rushed for 618 yards this season, and they've done it in just 83 carries, an average of more than seven yards per attempt. Webb City has run a total of 96 plays, and they've tallied 874 offensive yards. That averages out to almost a first down on every play.

If there is cause for concern, however, it's with Webb City's defensive numbers. The Cardinals were gouged through the air and on the ground at Har-Ber. Wildcat quarterback Kyle Pianalto completed 14 of 27 passes for 288 yards and ran for another 191 while Har-Ber racked up 369 rushing yards. Add in the stats from the Carl Junction game, and Webb City has allowed 508 rushing yards in two games, an average of 6.4 yards per carry. The Cardinals have given up 559 passing yards. Turnovers have been the key. The Webb City secondary has recorded five interceptions in two games.

Carthage comes to town, also with a .500 record, and like the Cardinals, the Tigers have put up big offensive numbers. Quarterback Gabe Franklin has thrown for at least 275 yards each game, and the Tigers average more than 500 yards per game in total offense. But, unlike the Webb City defense, which has just been unspectacular, the Carthage defense has been downright lousy, giving up 96 points in two games. And the Tigers enter week three with a turnover margin of negative-five after turning the ball over three times in a 63-32 loss to Carl Junction.

The focus all week is on Webb City, and how it will respond after a rare loss.

"They don't look like they've dropped off a whole lot to me," Carthage head coach Jon Guidie says. "We watched them on film versus Har-Ber and I think they're probably better up front than they were a year ago. They have three starters back from last year and all three of those kids are better. They control the line of scrimmage. They have a very good running game, and they mix in play action with it. Up front they're as good as they've ever been. People say they're down, but we haven't seen much of that on film. They still have athletes who can run, they still have athletes who can catch. Defensively they're very athletic. They run to the ball very well."

A year ago, during the 2012 season, the Tigers led 6-0 after a quarter at Webb City and trailed by only a point, 10-9, at halftime before going on to lose 41-17. A big reason the game was so close for two quarters was Carthage's ability to establish a running game, and Guidie says that's a key in beating the Cardinals.

"You've got to establish a running game on those guys early and you've got to be able to run the football to have any success against them," he says. "We came out and ran the football. We had some 12-, 13- and 14-play drives in the first half and converted a few fourth downs. If you can establish a running game against these guys, that's what you want. You can't turn the ball over or it will get away from you really fast. They're very opportunistic."

Despite the loss, Webb City is still far and away the top-ranked team in the state football poll, garnering 12 of 15 first-place votes. Harrisonville gets the other three and is ranked second, and Jefferson City Helias is ranked third, also with a 1-1 record.

"It's been a normal work week," John Roderique tells *The Joplin Globe*. "We've been preparing for Carthage, of course. We are trying to tackle better and simply make plays – normal stuff. The main focus this time of the season is to improve each week."

Friday night finally rolls around and it's a fairly subdued atmosphere at Cardinal Stadium. Webb City takes the opening kick, runs eight plays and then punts inside Carthage territory. Immediately, though, it's clear that the Cardinals' defense has improved. On Carthage's first four possessions of the game, it punts three times and fails to convert on fourth down. One of the punts is almost blocked. The Tigers have a fifth possession but they run just three plays before the half ends and head to the locker room trailing by three touchdowns. In that first half, Carthage runs 22 offensive plays. Six of them end up in a net loss of yardage and two more go for no gain; the Tigers gain just 74 yards of total offense.

It's a different story for the Cardinals. After punting on its first possession, Webb City starts its next one at the Carthage 4-yard line after Kiante Hardin returns a punt 55 yards. Trey Parra rushes to the 1 on first down, then Devin Pickett takes a quick snap and sneaks in for the touchdown with 5:29 left in the first quarter. Webb City goes 58 yards on its next possession in six plays: four rushes and two passing plays to Maquel Harbin. His first catch goes for 10 yards, and his second is for 24 yards, putting the ball at the Carthage 2. Kyle Baldassarre punches it in from there. He scores again with 5:28 remaining in the half, capping a nine-play, 74-yard drive. Pickett connects with a wide open Roosevelt Edwards for a touchdown on the second play of the drive, but it's called back because of an illegal block.

The second half is more of the same, on both sides of the ball. Webb City's defense continues to stymie Carthage on every possession; the Tigers run three plays and punt, then three more plays and a punt. Their third possession of the second half is their best of the game, moving 57 yards to score in eight plays. But by now there's less than nine minutes left in the game and Webb City's defensive regulars are watching from the sideline. Webb City even intercepts a pass on the drive, but is flagged for interference.

Parra scores from 24 yards out to make it a 28-0 game midway through the third, and after the Cardinals tip a Carthage punt, they get the ball just 36 yards from the goal line. Baldassarre scores on a nine-yard run, making it 35-0 after three quarters. Parra adds the final score, a 44-yard run that answers the Carthage touchdown in the fourth quarter, and the Cardinals cruise to a 42-7 victory. It's the start of a new winning streak.

"We thought maybe we'd come out and run the football, but give them credit," Guidie says after the game. "They stayed in their four-man front most of the night. Those guys up front are pretty good. We couldn't get any rhythm established offensively. Those guys are big and they're athletic over there and they do a good job."

Parra finishes the game with 136 yards and two touchdowns on 14 carries, while Baldassarre scores three times and tallies 80 yards on 18 carries. The Cardinals gain 231 of their 332 yards on the ground. The passing game is still very efficient, too. Pickett completes three of six passes for 42 yards, but Tyson Roderique, John's youngest son, enters the game and completes five of six attempts for 70 yards. Roosevelt Edwards and Maquel Harbin do most of the damage in the receiving corps, combining for five catches and 98 yards.

Baldassarre says the team's confidence wasn't really shaken after the Har-Ber loss, and the big win against Carthage only helps to build it.

"Our goal's ahead of us," he says. "We're just looking forward to next week."

It's a business-like win for the Cardinals, and that's exactly what Roderique says on the field after it's over. In fact, he wants to see the team get more excited.

"That's one thing I talked about to the kids, be more enthusiastic," he says. "We've got to get our whole sideline more excited. I don't know if our kids weren't really sure about how to feel after last week or what, but certainly we've got to play with a great deal more enthusiasm and excitement."

The Webb City defense, which flexes its muscle for the first time all year, also does it with help from more players. Sixteen Cardinals recorded tackles in the Har-Ber game, but 22 do it against Carthage, led by Steven Moore's nine stops and Hunter Rhea's two tackles for a loss. Roderique says a goal was to play more kids.

Roderique wishes he'd done a better job playing more kids on the offensive side of things, and while he says he feels good about the team's offensive performance, he still wants to see a higher percentage on quarterback reads.

"Tyson got his feet a little bit wetter this week in the heat of battle," he says. "The speed of the game is so much faster. Devin is getting better. It's just a matter of getting the time and the experience. That's the biggest thing, getting that game experience because you can't put a price on the game experience. It's just not like practice. Our two backs we're getting a lot out of. They've been outstanding, Trey and Kyle. Those two guys are tough, hard-nosed, they can both run and they're both quick. We'd like to get a few more kids in the ballgame though."

It's homecoming week at Webb City High School as week four of the 2013 season rolls around in mid September. The Cardinals once again have a winning record, and a winning streak, after a 35-point throttling of rival Carthage in week three.

Arriving in town Friday afternoon is another team with a winning record in Republic, though the Tigers' 2-1 mark feels a little less convincing than Webb City's. The main concern for John Roderique is the Republic running game, which has accrued big numbers so far this season. The Tigers rushed for 379 yards in a season-opening 40-0 win at Springfield Central, and gained 288 of their 390 yards on the ground against Ozark in week three, a 49-27 loss in the Central Ozarks Large Division opener.

Republic's first-year head coach Wes Beachler tells the paper he hopes the Cardinals aren't on their 'A' game. "We're in an entirely different situation than Webb City. We hope to play as well as we possibly can. We'll have our hands full trying to play our best game."

The Cardinals are disciplined, well-coached and classy, he says. "It's the way high school football should be."

There's a light breeze and the temperature is in the 60s when 7 o'clock arrives on Friday night. The Cardinals take the field in their standard red jerseys, Columbia blue pants and white helmets. Republic wears its road white jerseys with black letters and orange trim, black pants and bright orange helmets. Webb City wins the toss and, electing to defer until the second half, lines up to kick off.

The opening kick, and Webb City's stellar coverage, pins the Tigers at their own 12-yard line. They run six plays, all of them on the ground, and get as far as the 29 before punting, and the Cardinals get the ball at the Republic 48 for their first possession of the game. Trey Parra gains eight yards on first down and nine more on second down. After throwing an incomplete pass, quarterback Devin Pickett runs for a 10-yard gain. After four more plays, Parra scores from two yards out to give Webb City a 7-0 lead with 5:39 left in the quarter. The drive takes three minutes.

The Cardinals pin the Tigers again on the next kickoff, this time at the 19, and Republic gains only four yards on three plays before it is forced to punt again. But instead of getting the punt away, this time junior Cameron Tournear, a 5-foot-9, 165-pound outside linebacker, blocks the kick and the Cardinals get the ball at the Republic 7. Pickett passes to Kiante Hardin on first down and just like that it's a 14-0 game.

After another Republic three-and-out and punt, Webb City gets the ball back with its worst field position of the game – its own 40-yard line. This time it takes just six plays to score, with help from a 40-yard Parra run, and Pickett rushes for a three-yard touchdown that makes it a three-touchdown game less than a minute into the second quarter. The homecoming festivities have already begun.

Tournear blocks another punt in the game, which is all but over by halftime. Tyson Roderique enters at quarterback and scores on a 20-yard run in the second quarter to give the Cardinals a 28-0 lead at the break. Pickett throws a 20-yard scoring pass to Hardin early in the third quarter, and Andrew Greek, the sophomore placeholder, passes to tight end Cooper Strasser for a two-point conversion to launch the running clock with 9:05 left in the period.

The courtesy clock doesn't last long, though. Republic's vaunted running game finally gains some ground and Jace DuVall scores on a 51-yard rush to cut the Webb City lead to 30 points. But later in the quarter, junior running back Tyler Davison enters the game and scores on a three-yard run, capping a 55-yard drive, and the Cardinals go up 43-6. Senior Logan Cloyd adds one more score for Webb City, a four-yard run in the fourth quarter, and the Cardinals get their second conference win by a 43-point margin, 49-6.

"We played very well in all three phases – offense, defense and the kicking game," Roderique says afterward. "We did a lot of good things. It was our most complete game to date."

It's also another extremely efficient performance from Webb City, which rushes for 292 yards and passes for 80 while limiting Republic to a season-low 154 yards on the ground and just 38 through the air. Webb City tallies 22 first downs and limits Republic to 8, but scores so fast it possesses the ball for nearly a minute less than the Tigers. Pickett's quarterback rating is a sterling 152 as he completes six of seven passes for 66 yards and two scores, and he rushes for a third touchdown among his nine carries. Roderique scores twice on the ground in 11 carries. The game is also a great example of the team's depth. No one rushes for more than 67 yards (Parra, on six carries), and nobody gets more than 11 carries, but six different Cardinals are handed the ball, and each of them runs at least four times. Five different players make receptions: Baldassarre, Parra, Hardin, junior Maquel Harbin and senior Kolten Potts.

As far as the defense goes, five players make tackles for a loss: Harbin, junior Royce Clark, sophomore Calem Nutting, junior Trent Parra and senior Easton Carver. Nobody makes more than four tackles, but 21 different players have stops.

"It was a fun time," Tournear says. "There's nothing like it."

The thing that stands out the most to the coaching staff about Webb City's throttling of Republic on homecoming is the kicking game. Two blocked punts and a third returned inside the 5 led to nearly half of the team's 49 points. The only hiccup is a missed extra point attempt, but the Cardinals tacked on a two-point conversion. The week after the game, Roderique sits in his office again and cites statistics that say if you score two non-offensive touchdowns in a game you'll win 90-some percent of the time. The Cardinals didn't score a defensive or special teams touchdown against Republic, but the special teams and defense did lead to some incredible field position. Good field position has been a hallmark of Webb City's championship teams. Four games into the 2013 season, the Cardinals have rushed for 300 yards in a game just once and thrown for 100 yards just twice. Sure, "only" 300 yards on the ground is a luxury most teams will never have, but considering the Cardinals are averaging 44.5 points, four rushing touchdowns and nearly seven yards per carry, it goes to show just how efficient and refined the team's running attack has become and how many times the offense has a short field. Of course, the Cardinals also haven't rushed for fewer than 231 yards in a game so far, either.

"The field position is huge," he says. "You go back to last week; we started one drive inside the 5, we started one around the 10, then we had another inside the 25. Those were directly related to the kicking game. The thing about last week's game is we played well and then you see the stats and we didn't put up very big numbers. This year is probably not a very big stat team. I don't see us being a huge stat team. That's one of those things we never really concerned ourselves with and our kids are really unselfish about that. Statistically, the bottom line is we want to do what we can to win. At this point in time our starters have played more in the first four ballgames than they did last year. The bottom line is we're sitting in the same place we wished to be after what happened in week two. The thing we're really doing is improving. That's what I'm really excited about, the improvement we're seeing from our kids each week."

Trey Parra and Kyle Baldassarre are strikingly similar running backs, and the staff has used them interchangeably so far. They're both quick, fast, and pound-for-pound really strong for their size. Roderique has a tough time explaining the differences between the two.

"Hopefully I'll have a better answer in a few more weeks because they look real similar to me and that's neat to have in our offense, two guys who are really similar, because a defense can't really focus on one of them. And they both do most things equally well."

The Cardinals have also remained remarkably efficient through the air. Devin Pickett has completed 20 of 26 passes, and Tyson Roderique has completed six of eight. They don't throw the ball much, but they make the most of it when they do. Roderique says the quarterbacks don't necessarily have big, strong arms, and the team doesn't want to waste downs through the air, so the coaching staff is guarded on using the pass.

"I think Devin's done a really nice job of getting the ball in the right places, reading some coverages and making good throws and making good decisions in the passing game," he says. "If that's not a top strength for you then we're going to still use it, obviously, but we're trying not to use it too much. I think if you don't use it as much it's there more when you do need it. That's been our philosophy. Also, we've got to be able to loosen people up and back them off a little bit and utilize some of the talents we've got with Kiante and Maquel."

Three players have scored at least 30 points through four games, and kicker Nathan Gooch, a six-foot, 220-pound senior, is the team's fourth-leading scorer with 26 points. And he's only kicked one field goal. On the season, Gooch has made 24 of 25 extra point attempts.

"We're really proud of him," Roderique says. "A lot of times kids are real nervous, especially kickers sometimes, but he's pretty calm and a cool and collected kind of kid. He's kicking with a lot of confidence right now back there."

Though a senior, it's Gooch's first season as the team's kicker; another nod to the strength of Webb City's special teams, and especially, kicking game. He replaces Alex Easley, the left-footed, all-state, four-year starter for the Cardinals who helped win three championships and signed with Northwest Missouri State University after graduating after the 2012 season. For four seasons Easley banged nearly every kickoff over the head of the opponent's return man for a touchback, and, as Webb City fans will fondly remember, his extra points were "Easley done."

"We're just getting lucky," Roderique says. "We coach a little bit but we're just getting lucky. Good kids."

With the sterling PAT percentage, Gooch has filled a pair of very big shoes – speaking metaphorically. His predecessor is considered one of the greatest kickers in school history. Roderique also points out that Easley probably played in more football games – 59 – than anybody else in the state.

"I can't think of a kid who would have played more games than Alex Easley in high school history," Roderique says. "He wore something like No. 60 that first year in 2009. He's definitely one of the best kickers we've had. No ifs ands or buts about it."

So the Cardinals are excelling offensively – through the air and on the ground – and on special teams, especially through the air. Their defense looks as if it has turned a corner, too. After allowing 64 points in two games to start the season, Webb City has allowed just 13 total points in two games against Carthage and Republic. Roderique thought before the season started that the team wouldn't be at the top of its game early on, and that's especially true of the defense. Twenty-three players have made tackles this season, and eight have made at least 10 stops.

The Cardinals will face another tough test in week five, though. They'll take to the road for only the second time and head to Nixa, where a clear leader in the Central Ozarks Conference race will emerge. The Eagles are undefeated and coming off a 35-0 trouncing of Willard last week, their second shutout of the season. The Nixa offense averages more than 38 points per game. Both teams are 2-0 in the conference. Both are also state ranked; Webb City still the undisputed first-place team in Class 4, receiving all 15 first-place votes, and Nixa is tied for seventh in Class 5.

The game even gets attention at the state capitol in Jefferson City, with state representative Charlie Davis, of Webb City, and Nixa state representative Kevin Elmer placing a friendly wager. The losing representative agrees to wear the winning team's tie for an entire day during the next legislative session.

"A powerhouse program like Webb City is something that needs to be respected by any opponent," Elmer says, "but I feel Nixa is as strong this year as they have ever been and there is the very real potential for an Eagles' victory."

Davis is a little more blunt.

"I hope Representative Elmer likes Cardinal Red," he says.

Webb City has won every game against Nixa since joining the COC in 2008, including a 49-21 win in 2012. The Cardinals also won games in 2006 and 2007, and prior to that the only time they played was in the 2003 state quarter-finals, a game Webb City also won, 29-15. Yet Nixa has established itself as a conference power, and even though the final score might not indicate it, they're one of those teams that plays Webb City tougher than most. Even in the 28-point win in 2012, Nixa's 21 points scored were the most by any team all season, including the playoffs and state championship game. Like Webb City, Nixa is good in all facets of the game – offense, defense and special teams.

Roderique acknowledges, somewhat grudgingly, the implications this game will have on the conference standings.

"That's certainly what people tell you," he says. "Somebody said everybody in the conference has lost already after just two weeks. I guess it could have ramifications as far as that goes for sure. You never know what the future holds, the next couple weeks, but certainly at this point in time it's two teams that are undefeated in the conference."

Nixa coach Rich Rehagen knows it too, though like his counterpart, he's somewhat reluctant to play up the significance too much.

"It's a big game in the conference. We're looking forward to it. Our players are excited about the opportunity," he tells *The Globe*.

It all came down to a matter of inches.

That's how close Nixa comes to beating Webb City for the first time ever. That's how close Webb City comes to losing its first game against a team from the state of Missouri in a decade, and its first game against a conference school in, well, ever. Yes, the week five showdown between undefeated Nixa and Webb City, undefeated in the conference, with first place in that conference on the line, goes down as an instant classic. And four quarters isn't long enough to decide a winner.

It's a warm evening on the last Friday night in September, with temperatures near 80 degrees and a slight breeze out of the south when the visitors take the field in all white. They're greeted by a packed house at Eagle Stadium on Joe Hawkins Track and Field, and many of those in the stands undoubtedly anticipate watching history. They'll see it all right, but it'll be another chapter in the rich history of Webb City football, as *Globe* sports writer Anvil Welch later writes.

From the very beginning the game lives up to the hype. Nixa strikes first when junior Alec Murphy scores on a two-yard run, but Webb City answers with a five-yard touchdown pass from quarterback Devin Pickett to receiver Maquel Harbin and the first quarter ends 7-7.

Webb City's defense stops the Eagles on a fourth-and-five in the second quarter, and the Cardinals score on a six-yard touchdown scamper by senior Kyle Baldassarre to take a touchdown lead. The defense is big again on the ensuing Nixa possession; junior Trent Para, a 5-foot-9, 155-pound defensive back, picks off a pass from Nixa's senior quarterback, Jacob Karlson. Karlson returns the favor a few plays later, however, intercepting a pass from Pickett with 2:17 left in the half that sets up Nixa's tying score. With Mason Rohr's 1-yard touchdown run, the first half ends with the game tied at 14.

Tyson Roderique, the 5-foot-10, 155-pound sophomore, takes over at quarterback in the second half, and momentum is still tough to come by. Nixa takes a 21-14 lead on a 16-yard run by Karlson, but Webb City counters with an 80-yard march and ties the game again with a 10-yard Baldassarre touchdown. As the fourth quarter begins, fans at other football games begin to take notice: Webb City and Nixa are tied in the fourth quarter! In Carthage, where the Tigers are hosting Neosho, the announcer provides frequent updates, which are greeted by either applause or loud groans. In Nixa, Webb City has a chance to pull ahead halfway through the quarter, with the ball on the Nixa 4-yard line and only six minutes left in the game. But the Cardinals fumble the ball, which bounces into the end zone for a touchback. A few minutes later, the Eagles are forced to punt.

Another Webb City fumble provides Nixa with its best chance to win the game in the final two minutes. The Eagles move the ball inside the Webb City 10, but lose three yards on first down and face a second-and-goal from the 12. On second down, the Eagles run the ball to the 3. Third down, less than a minute to go. Nixa runs the ball again, but is stuffed at the 1-yard line. Only 38 seconds show on the scoreboard, and Nixa faces a fourth-and-short with mere inches to go.

There is confusion on the field. Both teams are out of timeouts, but officials believe Nixa has called one anyway. The Eagles huddle on the sideline and officials decide to resume the game. When Nixa returns to the goal line, it sends its offensive unit out. Though it would be just an 18-yard field goal, likely for the win, and sophomore Logan Tyler, that "phenomenal" kicker has already booted four kickoffs into the end zone, Nixa head coach Rich Rehagen elects to pit muscle against muscle and go for the dagger, a touchdown. He has called for a quarterback sneak.

Karlson takes the snap and lunges for the goal line. The Cardinals get a great surge on defense. Karlson is stopped short. The game goes to overtime.

Each team gets a possession starting at the other's 25-yard line. Nixa gets the ball first. The Eagles run three plays, gaining six yards, but face a fourth-and-4 at the 19-yard line. This time, Rehagen sends Tyler and a holder onto the field. The sophomore bangs a 35-yard field goal, and Nixa goes up 24-21.

Roderique – the quarterback – and the Webb City offense take the field. The Cardinals need a field goal to force a second overtime, or a touchdown to leave town with a win. Roderique – the coach – decides this is the time to take that chance he said earlier in the week might be necessary. His son fields the snap, takes a three-step drop and puts the ball in the air for Kiante Hardin, who runs a fade route into the end zone. Hardin catches the pass, the Cardinals score, Webb City wins: 27-24, in overtime.

There are loud groans at K.E. Baker Stadium in Carthage.

Ironically, it's the same play Webb City had run in the third quarter, with the same quarterback, same receiver and same Nixa defender. The first time Hardin hauls in a 35-yard reception. The second time will be talked about for years.

"I knew if I threw it up there he'd make a play," Tyson says.

"We wanted to throw once and we wanted to do it on first down," says John.

Even Drew Gollhofer, the offensive line coach, wanted to take a shot at the end zone.

"When the o-line coach wants you to do it you do it," John tells the newspaper.

Rehagen takes a moment to compose himself afterwards, perhaps haunted by the decision to go for it on the ill-fated fourth-and-short at the end of regulation.

"It wasn't very far," he says. "We felt like the kids could get it and we wanted to show confidence in them."

A few days later, he says the coaches made the call to go for it, but the players wanted to go for it too.

"Webb City made a play. They stopped us. We'll move on. Hopefully, we'll build on it."

Nixa would go on to finish with a 9-2 record, losing to Kickapoo 45-14 in the Class 5, District 5 championship game.

Webb City rushes for 271 yards in the game on 53 attempts, a season-low average of 5.11 yards per carry. Trey Parra carries the ball 20 times for 125 yards and Baldassarre rushes 14 times for 62 yards and the two touchdowns. Roderique, playing exclusively in the second half, completes all four passes for 87 yards. Hardin leads the team with three receptions for 68 yards, and junior Tyler Davison adds 22 yards on one reception.

Senior Hunter Rhea makes seven tackles on defense, two for a loss, from the outside linebacker position. Hardin makes six tackles, and Harbin and senior Alex Lane, a defensive lineman, each have four tackles.

Willard and Webb City have played seven times in the last decade and it's been one of the most-lopsided series in the history of the Central Ozarks Conference. The Tigers have scored a total of 27 points in those seven games, and in the last three years the Cardinals have won by an average score of 50-0. Willard did manage a touchdown in 2009 in a 56-7 game, and the year before that it scored twice in a 42-14 contest. In 2004 and 2005 Webb City won 49-6 and 61-0, respectively.

In those seven games, Willard has never scored more than 14 points, and Webb City has never scored fewer than 41. However, the Tigers are a team on the rise in 2013 and they come to Cardinal Stadium in week five with a 4-1 record overall and a 2-1 conference mark. A week ago the Tigers blew out Ozark 55-24 and rushed for 615 yards, making Webb City take notice. It was Willard's first win against Ozark since 1992.

"All indications are that Willard is much improved and one of the teams in the top half of the league," Roderique tells *The Joplin Globe*. "They have several guys who can play for anyone in the conference. The program is going in a positive direction."

Always a team with substantial size, Willard has added speed in 2013 and three players have plenty of it, according to head coach Brock Roweton: Za-Korey "Z" Barr, Robert Richmond and Hunter Yeargan. Richmond ran for 261 yards against Ozark and scored three touchdowns; Yeargan ran for 187 yards and scored twice.

The first quarter of the game is all Webb City; Trey Parra scores on a 17-yard run and Nathan Gooch kicks a 30-yard field goal to give the team a 10-0 lead after 12 minutes of play. The Parra run comes after a Willard fumble and a 47-yard Cardinals drive. Pickett's 27-yard run was a key play, and Parra's touchdown comes on a second-and-17.

Eager to keep the game from getting out of hand before the half, things aren't looking good when the Tigers start a drive at their own 2-yard line. The running game that was so impressive a week earlier finally starts putting some good runs together and Willard marches 98 yards on 17 plays. Willard faces a fourth-and-5 with 5:32 left in the half and ZaKorey Barr runs it in from 14 yards out to make it a 10-6 game.

The Cardinals answer immediately with a 13-play, 84-yard drive. After junior Tyler Davison scores a 2-yard touchdown with 30 seconds left in the quarter, Webb City goes to the locker room ahead 17-6. It's a close game, but not too close.

The game gets a little bit closer in the third quarter. Each team scores a touchdown, but Willard converts a two-point try after Richmond's 27-yard touchdown run. For Webb City, Kyle Baldassarre scores on a 1-yard run to cap a 62-yard drive that also featured an 18-yard run by Parra and a 17-yard run by Baldassarre.

And so as the fourth quarter arrives, the Cardinals hold a 24-14 advantage, but not for long. Barely two minutes in, Willard suddenly makes everyone nervous when Richmond scores from a yard out to pull his team to within three points, 24-21. Willard is definitely living up to its billing as an up-and-coming squad.

Things almost take a turn for the worse; Willard's ensuing kickoff is a short one, but the Cardinals manage to come away with the ball at midfield and needing a score badly. They turn to Davison and Parra in the backfield, and the duo quickly takes the ball down to the Willard 22-yard line in just four plays. Davison then gets the handoff and scores at the 7:49 mark; Webb City leads 31-21.

The Cardinals' kickoff coverage, which on at least a few occasions so far this year has been shaky, is splendid after the touchdown. They pin the Tigers at their own 3, and in no time at all they're lining up to punt. It gives Webb City great field position, just 33 yards from the end zone, and on the first play Parra takes a handoff and scores with 5:16 left in the game.

In five minutes the Cardinals have turned a three-point lead into a 38-21 advantage, and they win by that score for their fifth victory of the season.

"Willard is a good football team and an improving one," Roderique says afterwards. "I've been telling people that all week."

Roweton tells the newspaper he's proud of how his team battled the Cardinals.

"We were with the No. 1 Class 4 team in Missouri in the fourth quarter," he says.

Willard gains one more first down than the Cardinals do, but Webb City's running game carries the night offensively. Parra and Davison each score two touchdowns and Parra rushes 13 times for 135 yards. As a team the Cardinals run for 338 yards and average 8.9 yards per carry. Willard still racks up 235 rushing yards.

Pickett throws the ball only four times and completes three of them for 20 yards; Kiante Hardin makes two catches for 22 yards, catching one ball from Tyson Roderique.

Defensively, Carson Johnson, a 5-foot-11, 170-pound senior linebacker, records nine solo tackles to lead the team, and Alex Lane, the 6-foot-1, 185-pound senior defensive lineman, has seven solo tackles.

If the 17-point win at home against Willard reinforces to some people the idea that Webb City just isn't as good in 2013, a road game at Neosho in week seven is enough to change their minds.

The top-ranked Cardinals sit at 5-1 overall and 4-0 in conference play; the win against Willard also catapults Webb City to the top of the district standings ahead of Springfield Hillcrest.

"We need to win to remain atop the conference as well as the district," Roderique tells Anvil Welch. "We need to keep winning."

Neosho hasn't won a game yet under the guidance of first-year head coach Dustin Baldwin, a former Neosho assistant and Miller head coach. But Roderique points to the Wildcat defense, which he says has been playing "pretty well," despite a rash of big plays.

"They have our respect," Roderique tells Welch. "You have to respect them. You never know from one week to the next."

But from the opening kickoff, which Kiante Hardin returns 98 yards for a touchdown, the game is a disaster for Neosho and a romp for Webb City.

"We didn't want the ball in his hands," Baldwin tells *The Globe* after the game. "That was not a good start."

Hardin hurts the Wildcats again on Webb City's first possession. Neosho, to its credit, shrugs off the kickoff return and mounts an impressive opening drive. The Wildcats get as far as the Webb City 35-yard line before the Cardinals' defense holds them on downs. Then, on first down, Hardin gets the ball on a reverse and gains 20 yards. Seven plays later, quarterback Tyson Roderique scores on a 1-yard run and Andrew Greek scores a two-point conversion following an encroachment penalty to make it 15-0 with 2:45 left in the first quarter.

Roderique starts in place of Devin Pickett, who misses the game with a shoulder injury. The sophomore completes eight of 12 passes for 111 yards; his only blemish is an interception.

Early in the second quarter, Trey Parra's 8-yard touchdown makes it a 22-0 game after the Cardinals move the ball 78 yards. Maquel Harbin catches a 28-yard reception on the drive, putting the ball at midfield, and Kyle Baldassarre adds 30 yards with a catch and 12 yards on a run to set up the team's third touchdown.

After three more touchdowns in the third quarter – each on the ground – it's a 42-0 game. Parra scores twice in the quarter and Baldassarre once. The lead grows to 49 points in the fourth quarter before Neosho finally breaks the shutout. But after fourth-quarter rushing touchdowns from Logan Cloyd and Kaleb Potts, Webb City wins 55-6.

"I normally don't tell the players this but I told them after the game: 'We'll bury this one and move on,'" Baldwin, the Neosho coach, says when it's over.

The Cardinals are, once again, a model of efficiency. They rush for 284 yards as a team and nobody rushes for more than 77 yards. Baldassarre gains 73 yards and averages 7.3 per carry; Parra averages 8.56 yards per carry with 77 yards; Cloyd rushes six times for 75 yards; Hardin carries the ball twice for 35 yards.

Among receivers, Harbin makes two catches for 45 yards, Hardin has five grabs for 35 yards, and Baldassarre has one 31-yard catch.

Defensively, 22 different players record tackles as Webb City limits the Wildcats to 72 yards on the ground and 88 yards passing. Trent Parra and Harbin each record interceptions. Nobody makes more than five tackles; Carson Johnson makes four solo tackles and one tackle for a loss, and Alex Lane makes four solo tackles and one for a loss. Hardin makes a tackle for a loss, as well, and Connor Badgley makes two on the defensive line.

It's John Roderique's 199th career win.

In only one game since 1995 has Webb City been shut out. It came in the 2003 semifinals, a 43-0 loss to Kearney, and that game is also the worst loss the Cardinals have suffered since John Roderique started coaching 17 years ago.

Through Webb City's 6-1 start to the 2013 season, and the first 218 games of Roderique's tenure, his teams are 199-19. His winning percentage in that time is 91.28. In those 19 losses, the Cardinals have lost on average by only two touchdowns – 14.7 points; if you remove the 2003 Kearney game from the equation that number falls to just 13.1 points per loss. On the flip side, in those 199 victories Roderique's Cardinals have won by an average of 28.66 points and have scored 5,704 points. The greatest single season in terms of margin of victory was the undefeated 2012 squad, which won by an average of 35.6 points.

Roderique also won the first 14 playoff games his teams played, and his career record in the playoffs is an astounding 45-6, including an 8-1 record in championship games.

Needless to say, it's been quite a run for Roderique and the Cardinals. His first win came in a 28-14 game at Branson to start the 1997 season. His 50th was a 58-7 win against McDonald County during the 2001 season. No. 100 came against Ozark in 2006, a 42-0 shutout.

Fittingly, with Roderique one win away from No. 200 for his career, his team heads to Ozark with the regular season winding down and district play right around the corner.

The Cardinals are 7-0 against the Ozark Tigers since joining the Central Ozarks Conference, and since 1996 Webb City is 12-0 in the match-up when factoring in playoff games. The Tigers are usually one of the better teams in the conference, though the 2013 Tigers aren't quite.

The Cardinals take the field in all white uniforms and white helmets and stretch in the end zone before the opening kickoff. It's a nasty night for football; a light rain falls and it's 50 degrees on the artificial turf with a wind that makes it feel several degrees colder. The Tigers emerge with about two minutes left before the game begins and they wear red helmets, black jerseys and white pants. They will get the ball to start.

Ozark's offense comes onto the field with the ball at its own 20 after a touchback. On first down, a reverse goes for a 5-yard loss. Three plays later the Tigers punt.

Yet again, the Cardinals have great field position, the ball at their own 44 before a penalty backs them up five yards. On first down, Kyle Baldassarre gains 12 yards. On second down, more penalties – two straight –move the ball all the way back to the Webb City 41, then Baldassarre takes a handoff up the middle, cuts to the outside and sprints down the Webb City sideline for a 59-yard touchdown run.

Ozark's second possession is even worse than its first. The Tigers gain a yard on first down, then lose it when outside linebacker Lakin Miner makes a tackle for a loss on second down. Third down is a disaster; defensive lineman Tayler Arterburn immediately sacks the quarterback for a 9-yard loss, and Ozark punts again.

This time Webb City starts at the Ozark 44-yard line, and after runs by Trey Parra, Devin Pickett and Baldassarre, Pickett throws a 24-yard touchdown strike to tight end Zach Davidson. Nathan Gooch's point after makes it 14-0 with 4:53 left in the first quarter.

Ozark starts at its own 17 after the kickoff, rushes for no gain on first down, passes for a yard loss on second down and throws incomplete on third down; another punt follows and the Cardinals start their third possession at their own 47. This time a penalty and a fumble in the backfield stalls Webb City and forces a punt.

By the time the second quarter begins it's raining heavily and the Cardinals are pinned deep in their own territory. Tyson Roderique enters the game at quarterback and immediately breaks a long touchdown run – but there's a flag for holding. His father isn't happy.

"In 17 years that's the most (poor) call I've ever seen," Roderique says, actually rather calmly, to an official on the sideline. He gets ejected.

Everyone is shocked. Ejected? For that? As their coach makes the solemn walk down the sideline and out of the stadium, Webb City's players get fired up. They know it's a milestone game, and they're as surprised as anyone Roderique won't be around for the rest of it. When they return to the field, they make Ozark pay. The Cardinals surge for 26 points in the second quarter and it's 40-0 by halftime. Then, they add three more touchdowns in the second half and though he isn't there to see most of it, Roderique gets his 200th victory in a dominating 59-0 rout.

By the time it's all over, Webb City has been penalized 17 times for 130 yards. The Cardinals rack up 500 yards of offense, rushing for 460.

John Roderique's ejection at Ozark is the first of his career, and according to Missouri State High School Activities Association rules, he must miss Webb City's next game against Branson, the final home game before district play starts.

He tells Anvil Welch of *The Joplin Globe* he's not sure how he'll spend his Friday night.

"I first thought about taking [wife] Heather to the movies or dinner, but she'll want to see our son play," he says.

In Roderique's absence, assistant coach Drew Gollhofer will call the plays on offense, and defensive coordinator Mike Smith assumes the role of head coach. It's not a new role for Smith, who has plenty of experience guiding a football program.

Defensive coordinator Mike Smith. Photo by Bob Foos.

Smith is another Pittsburg State guy; he played for the Gorillas from 1982 to 1985 and there he met Roderique, who started his Gorillas' career in 1986.

After college, Smith went on to spend 13 years as a coach at Stockton High School. After a six-year stint as the school's head coach, he decided he was ready to coach a bigger program, and he applied for the vacant head coaching job at Nixa. He was told, essentially, he wasn't a big enough fish, so he needed to boost his resume.

Smith talked with Roderique at a football clinic in Branson in 2001 and, figuring Webb City would be a good stepping stone, told him to let him know if he had any openings.

"He said, 'Don't say it unless you mean it,'" Smith recalls. "I said I meant it. I came here to boost my resume; it's worked, but I haven't left. I've had opportunities to, but I haven't left. It gets in your blood."

Smith has served as the Cardinals' defensive coordinator since 2001, and Nixa likely regrets passing him over; his Webb City defenses have allowed on average only 11.6 points against the Eagles in 10 games between 2001 and 2013 including two shutouts. And in his 13 seasons, the Cardinals have shut out their opponents 31 times, and they've allowed 7 or fewer points 81 times.

He's a coach in demand, and he'd likely have his pick of head coaching positions that open up every year. So why has he stayed? It all comes down to three things: God, family and football.

"I absolutely love the church I'm at," he says. "I can't fathom going anywhere else; that's strike one against leaving here. My family loves it here. It's close to my father-in-law, which is good for my wife and she gets to stay here close to him and her sisters. That's a positive. I never even make it to the third thing: football. There's always strike one and strike two, and there's no point going any further."

And the football ain't bad, either.

When Smith was hired in 2001 he replaced Aaron Hafner, who was an assistant at Webb City for three years and who since has gone on to an outstanding coaching career of his own. He left Webb City for Francis Howell Central in St. Peters, Mo., and after a year there he became head coach at Republic High School from 2003 to 2006. After Republic he spent seven years as offensive coordinator at William Penn University, and in January 2013 he was hired as the head coach at Luther College in Iowa.

That old problem Webb City football teams have dealt with for more than a century – the fact that they're almost always undersized – is actually used as an advantage in Smith's defense.

"We preach speed," he says. "You've got to be able to run. I always tell them if you can't run you can't play. We are undersized, but we're going to use that to our advantage, we think. That's our goal. We're going to be slanting, we're going to move around, we're going to stunt when we can. We're going to try to incorporate our assets that we think we have as a good, fast running team and we're going to try to utilize that to maximize our abilities. It's been pretty successful. There are times we get against bigger guys who can still move and we're in trouble. We've had those times, too, but fortunately there haven't been as many times that's happened."

And so Webb City defenses are usually on the smaller side, but very fast. That size can be misleading, too; they're almost always the hardest hitting team on the field. In addition to the requirement of speed, players must also know their assignments. Smith preaches speed, and he preaches assignment defense.

"And we play as a unit," he says. "We can't play as individuals because there are no standout individuals. We've had standout individuals, but they still play within a unit. That's the main thing with our defense. I get too much credit for a lot of things being the defensive coordinator. We have outstanding coaches. I get to go around and watch them coach and just how they teach the game of football and how they teach their position. It's amazing. It's amazing."

A great example of a Webb City defense playing as a unit is the 2001 team, which went undefeated and allowed only 100 points in 14 games. That's an average of barely seven points a game, and only twice all season did the Cardinals give up double-digit points. Smith says more players from that team went on to play college football than any other year.

"We had some outstanding, outstanding defensive players there," he says.

There is also the 2005 team, which lost in the quarterfinals but started the year off with four straight shutouts and held opponents scoreless a total of six times in 11 games. That team allowed only two rushing touchdowns all season, and gave up fewer than seven points a game. But Smith says it's impossible to pick one "best" defense he's coached.

"As far as the way they're graded around here, if they don't win a state championship maybe they're not there," Smith says. "I truly feel that it's not always about the rings. It's all about the relationships you build. Since I've been involved in this we've won seven rings; does that mean the other years that haven't won haven't been as important? I don't believe that at all. To pick out one, I couldn't do it. Now if you could pick an all-star team, man we'd be pretty good."

A Webb City defensive all-star team, at least since Smith arrived in 2001, would have to include Adam Spieker, a 2003 graduate who was a two-time all-state selection on the defensive line. He was also pretty good on the offensive line, too. Out of high school, Rivals rated him the No. 26 offensive guard prospect in the country, and he signed with the University of Missouri after receiving scholarship offers from Nebraska, Kansas State, Oklahoma State and Illinois. For the Tigers, he started 50 games at center and was a Rimington Trophy finalist.

"He was just an animal," Smith says. "He goes and sets a record at Mizzou for career starts. He was an animal. He was an unbelievable player."

So Spieker is certainly a good start.

"One of the most dynamic free safeties we've ever had was Marty Rodgers, who is now coaching in college," Smith says. "He's coaching defensive backs at the University of North Dakota."

Rodgers was a 2006 graduate who finished his career at Webb City with more than 2,000 rushing yards and 45 touchdowns his junior and senior seasons. Defensively, he made 15 interceptions and 260 career tackles for the Cardinals and was a two-time all-state selection. After high school he continued his career with Southern Illinois University, where he was twice selected to the all-Missouri Valley Conference team.

On Webb City's current team, Smith points to Kiante Hardin. He finishes the 2013 season with 41 tackles and four interceptions.

"Kiante's just unbelievable," he says. "One of the best corners who've come through here."

At linebacker, 2002 graduate Justin Smith is definitely on the list. He was a first-team all-state player in Smith's first season.

"He was just so intelligent on the field," Smith says. "He hit like a truck at linebacker, but he was so smart he probably knew more about the defense than I did and I'm supposed to be coaching him. And you've got guys like Grant McDonald and Aaron Davied and all these guys who have gone on and played in college. I also think about all the ones who could have gone and played college but didn't, who have gone and served our country and done things like that and I'm so proud of them. There have been some absolutely special players in terms of athletic ability here, but they're all special players because they're part of the family. I'm proud of them all. Any of them who have come out here. They've come out here and laid it down on the line to play for us. I'm proud of them all."

The one thing that drives both players and coaches alike, according to Smith, is the expectation of perfection.

"We expect excellence," he says.

But the coaches expect excellence both on and off the field. There's not a better reflection of life than the game of football, the way Smith sees it, and the sport is the perfect tool to prepare players for life after football.

"There are going to be times you get knocked down," he says. "It might be a glancing blow, but you might get a slobberknocker, you might lose your father. I've gone through those. Those are slobberknockers, those are immediate impacts. A parent might get diagnosed with cancer, something that just knocks you down, but what do you do? In a game you get back up and you get back in the play. That's what you have to do in life and I don't think there's a better reflection than football to teach that. We demand excellence. When they go out there and they do what you've coached them to do and they make that great play, you're like a proud father. A kid taking his first step, he goes out there that first start he gets to make and he goes out and just tears it up. You're just so proud of him you can't stand it.

"It's a process as you go along. They come as freshmen and sometimes they don't know what's going on. It's a process as they go through their maturation and they get to go out there on Friday nights. I'll take my son (Cooper) as an example. I never really coached my son because he was on the offensive side of the ball, but he didn't get to start until his senior year. There are a lot of teams, a lot of communities around here, they say, 'If I don't get to play as a sophomore or junior I'm not going to play.' That's not the way it is around here. These guys understand they'll have to do their time and wait their turn and then they have to earn a spot. There are still no guarantees. We're going to put the best people we can on the field to make plays and that's the way it is. We've got kids on the sideline who want to be out there playing. If we've got a mistake made out there, there's somebody waiting to go in and play."

The coaching staff wants the players it coaches to become better husbands, better fathers, better community members.

"It isn't all about football," Smith says. "It's about those relationships we build with them. That's the one thing that's been so fun about this program is the relationships developed. It's pretty special. Pretty fun to be a part of."

Even if the relationships developed and the process of turning high school kids into Friday night contributors is the most enjoyable part of football for coaches like Mike Smith and John Roderique, there's also got to be an intense competitive side to fully explain how Webb City can win more rings than can be worn on two hands. And they do enjoy those rings, but not for very long.

You won't see a single coach wearing a championship ring unless they're at a football clinic or a similar event.

"You won't see our rings on our fingers because we don't live in the past; we go for the next one," Smith says. "We put our rings on for a temporary time and then we take it off, put it in a box and go back to work for the next one. That's what we owe the kids. If you ever get to the point where you look back at what you've done, the disaster is right around the corner. You keep your eyes forward and always go to work for the next one because that's what these kids want. This next senior class, they want that next one so you're going to have to go out and work as hard or harder; we tell them every year your target gets bigger. We respect all but we fear none and that's the attitude we go in with."

The Branson game is significant for more than just being the Cardinals' Senior Night. With a win against the 4-4 Pirates, who have won three games in a row, Webb City will clinch another outright Central Ozark Conference Large Division championship. Nixa, the only other team that's close, is 5-1 in conference play, and the Cardinals are 6-0. A win against Branson would also go a long way in solidifying Webb City as the top team in the district. According to the seeding formula, the Cardinals lead Springfield Hillcrest 51.86 to 50.70.

The temperature is right at 50 degrees when the game begins, and for most of the first quarter it's a scoreless game. The first score comes after nearly 10 minutes. Roosevelt Edwards returns a punt 24 yards to the Branson 36-yard line, and later on the drive Trey Parra's 2-yard touchdown at the 2:42 mark puts Webb City on the board; Seth Rogers' point after makes it a 7-0 game. After a quarter of play, it's a very close game.

Perhaps motivated by their head coach's absence, the Cardinals turn it into a blowout before halftime.

Parra scores on a 66-yard touchdown run, then Kiante Hardin scores from 31 yards out on a play from the "Wildcat" formation. Parra adds a 54-yard score on a first-down run later in the second quarter – his third touchdown of the game – and it's a four touchdown game by the half. Parra's 66-yard run finishes off an 83-yard drive, and Hardin's score is due in large part to a fumble recovery by sophomore Kolesen Crane, a 5-foot-10, 170-pound outside linebacker.

By the time Webb City marches 56 yards on 11 plays and quarterback Devin Pickett runs into the end zone from the 2-yard line with 4:44 left in the third quarter, it's a 35-0 game and the running "courtesy" clock goes into effect.

But less than a minute later, Branson's Isaiah Daniels, a first-team all-state pick by both the Missouri State Coaches' Association and the Associated Press, scores a 78-yard touchdown to end the running clock.

It's the only highlight of the game for the Pirates, who go on to lose 48-7 after Tyson Roderique throws a 24-yard touchdown to Joseph Jones, a 6-foot-2, 215-pound senior tight end, and Keaton Burroughs, a 6-foot, 185-pound sophomore running back, scores on a 39-yard run.

Parra finishes the game with three touchdowns and 180 yards on 15 carries.

"We were on a mission," he tells *The Globe*. "We wanted to win for Coach Roderique. We talked about winning for him all week during practice."

And Smith's defense limits the Pirates to just 189 yards, while the Cardinals tally 477.

"This win is No. 201 for John Roderique," Smith says. "He prepared the team for this game."

Tyson Roderique completes 5 of 8 passes for 70 yards, a touchdown and an interception, and he and Pickett each run for 18 yards. Parra is the only back to eclipse 100 yards in the game. Kyle Baldassarre rushes five times for 36 yards, Tyler Davison rushes seven times for 46 yards, Keaton Burroughs gains 60 yards on six carries, Hardin has 28 yards and Logan Cloyd 17. Six different receivers make a catch: Roosevelt Edwards, Maquel Harbin, Parra, Hardin, Joseph Jones and Kolten Potts.

Another balanced defensive effort means just one player makes more than four tackles: senior outside linebacker Hunter Rhea, who finishes with five solo tackles and one assisted. Three of his tackles go for a loss, and Carson Johnson (senior linebacker), Steven Moore (junior linebacker), Trenton Moeller (senior defensive lineman) and Alex Lane (senior lineman) each add tackles for a loss. Rhea, Moore, Moeller and Lane each record sacks.

As football coaches like to say, the beginning of district play is a whole new season. Everyone's record is 0-0. Anything can happen. But with McDonald County visiting Cardinal Stadium after winning just one of its first nine games, and with the Cardinals having won eight of nine and seven straight, there isn't much suspense on this particular Thursday night in Webb City. The game is essentially decided in the first quarter.

As has been the case all season long, great defense and great field position lead to quick scores. In the first quarter the Cardinals score three times: Trey Parra from 25 yards, Kyle Baldassarre from 27 yards, and Logan Cloyd from the 5.

It gets uglier in the second quarter. Tyson Roderique finds Kiante Hardin on a slant pattern for a 3-yard touchdown, then the defense gets involved with the scoring. Sophomore linebacker Calem Nutting returns an interception 18 yards for a touchdown, then junior linebacker Royce Clark picks off a pass and returns it 30 yards for another touchdown.

By halftime Webb City leads 42-0.

In the second half, the reserves take over and keep their collective foot on the gas. Kaleb Potts scores a 1-yard touchdown in the third quarter, then Colton Adams scores from the 2 in the fourth quarter. While Nathan Gooch nails the extra points in the first half, Seth Rogers is perfect in the second half and the Cardinals win 56-0.

"Webb City is a great team," McDonald County head coach Chris Gwartney says afterward. "I'll put the Webb City program up against any program from around here. The coaches do a terrific job and tonight the team executed well."

Trey Parra gets just three carries in the game, and he gains 42 yards while eclipsing the 1,000 yard mark for the year. Baldassarre rushes five times for 110 yards and a score. Potts, the sophomore, rushes 13 times for 97 yards and a touchdown; Cloyd runs eight times for 39 yards and a score, and Adams, another sophomore, scores once and gains five yards on two carries.

The quarterbacks combine for another efficient game. Devin Pickett completes two of three passes for 19 yards, and Tyson Roderique completes 4 of 6 for 15 yards and a touchdown; he also rushes twice for 18 yards.

Potts makes three catches, Hardin two and Roosevelt Edwards one.

McDonald County's offense is shut down all night. The Mustangs complete 3 of 10 passes for 8 yards and rush 28 times for 69 yards. Part of the reason is eight tackles for a loss by the Cardinals. Senior linebacker Trevor Price, sophomore linebacker Calem Nutting and senior linebacker Hunter Rhea each make one stop for a loss, and junior defensive lineman Emilio Perez makes three tackles for a loss. Brett Busick, a sophomore tight end, records two sacks on defense.

While the two teams have been playing each other since at least 1905, the rivalry between Webb City and Carthage has been covered regularly since around 1910. Before the 1950 contest, local newspapers reported it was at least the 54th time the Cardinals and Tigers had played, and detailed the first half century of the series' history. Carthage dominated early on, winning 26 of 33 games between 1910 and 1949. Remember, the teams had played twice a year for some years. Between 1929 and 1949, the Cardinals won 11 of 20 games, and in the 1930s they won every year but 1933. But then the Tigers won eight games in the 1940s.

Between 1985 and 2014 however, the rivalry has become incredibly lopsided. The Cardinals are 32-2. The only years Carthage managed to win were 1987 (14-0) and in the 2007 sectional game on a thrilling last-second field goal. That 23-22 win for the Tigers has got to be seen as one of the program's biggest ever, if not the biggest.

Webb City had steamrolled through the 2007 regular season, winning all 10 games, and blasted Carthage 44-25 in the season's second game, played at Cardinal Stadium. But when district play concluded, the Cardinals traveled east to K.E. Baker Stadium for the rematch with the Tigers, who by then were 9-1 and ranked eighth in the state.

Jon Guidie became the first Carthage head coach since Ray Harding to beat the team's biggest rival. Photographs of the game, and of the kick, still hang in the fieldhouse at K.E. Baker Stadium. Zerkel, in his final game as a Cardinal before a record-breaking career at Missouri Southern, caught five passes for 116 yards and picked off two passes.

Of course, since that night at K.E. Baker Stadium, Webb City hasn't lost. The Tigers finished the 2013 regular season with a 5-4 record, and after demolishing Marshfield 80-22 in the first round of district play, make the short drive west for another rematch.

From the very beginning, it's apparent this won't be another 2007.

With temperatures hovering around 40 degrees at the opening kickoff, Carthage's kick sails out of bounds and the Cardinals start the game at their own 35. On their first snap, Devin Pickett passes to Kiante Hardin, who races down the home sideline untouched for a touchdown just nine seconds in.

The Tigers start at their own 32 after the quick punch to the gut, and they move the ball 20 yards but come up inches short on a fourth-down run at midfield; Webb City starts its second drive at the 48.

Again on first down Pickett looks to the air, and this time hits Roosevelt Edwards, the 5-foot-7, 145-pound senior, for a 31-yard gain. Pickett passes again, but this time the ball is dropped in the end zone. A play later, Kyle Baldassarre rushes to the Carthage 2, and then Pickett punches it in. It's a 14-0 game less than three minutes in.

The Tigers continue to have modest success offensively on their next drive, but again they are forced to try and convert on fourth down. Carthage rushes for a first down, but a holding penalty backs the Tigers up to their own 34 and they punt. Hardin returns the kick to the Carthage 28, and after two plays, Pickett scores on a 5-yard run.

Smelling blood, the Cardinals try a surprise onside kick and drill the Carthage player who recovers the ball. He hangs on, and the Tigers finally have decent field position. Five plays later, the Tigers are in business at the Webb City 22. A third-and-1 rush goes for no gain, and for the third time the Tigers line up on fourth down to go for it. Tim Bowers, a 6-foot-1, 175-pound senior linebacker, sniffs the play out and makes a tackle for a 1-yard loss.

Carthage finally gets on the scoreboard late in the first quarter. A 53-yard drive ends in a 32-yard Gabe Franklin-to-EJ Morgan touchdown pass, and the duo hooks up again for the two-point conversion. It's 21-8 after a quarter.

Webb City fumbles early in the second quarter and Carthage gets the ball at its own 47. Later in the drive, Franklin completes an 8-yard pass on fourth-and-4 at the Webb City 35, but on the following play Franklin's pass is intercepted by Hardin at the Cardinals' 10 and he returns it 47 yards. Three plays after that, Pickett throws another touchdown pass, this time for 31 yards to Edwards, and it's 28-8.

Carthage continues to move the ball, but the Cardinals' defense continues to bend but not break. The Tigers march 67 yards late in the first half, but Franklin's pass on first down at the Webb City 12 is intercepted by Kolesen Crane, the sophomore outside linebacker, at the goal line.

The second half is more of the same. Carthage tries to convert a fourth-and-5 at the Webb City 34 on its first possession of the third quarter, and Franklin is sacked by outside linebacker Hunter Rhea. On first down from his own 45, Baldassarre takes a pitch and rushes all the way down to the Carthage 4, and Trey Parra scores to make it 34-8.

Junior outside linebacker Lakin Milner picks off a third-down pass with 6:33 left in the third quarter, setting the Cardinals up only 24 yards away from the end zone. It takes seven plays, but Parra finally scores on a 3-yard run to make it 41-8. After a Carthage fumble at the 22, junior running back Tyler Davison scores a 6-yard touchdown to enact the courtesy clock with 1:36 left in the third.

Carthage does score in the fourth quarter when Franklin passes to Morgan again, but Franklin is sacked by Bowers on the two-point try. Franklin connects with Morgan for yet another touchdown with 4:51 left in the game, but junior outside linebacker Cameron Tournear blocks the PAT.

The scoring ends with a 40-yard touchdown by Webb City sophomore Keaton Burroughs, and the Cardinals walk off the field with a 55-20 win.

Devin Pickett is nearly perfect offensively. He completes three of four passes for 126 yards and two scores, and he adds two more touchdowns on the ground in just four carries. Other than handing the ball off, he's directly involved in just eight plays and accounts for four touchdowns.

"It's always a fun time against Carthage because of the big rivalry," he says on the field after the game. "Yeah, it's fun playing them."

As for the big 65-yard touchdown strike on the first offensive play of the game, he says the plan was to come out and try to hit the Tigers early with something deep.

"Our plan was to score, but if anything we were going to try to execute and get a lot of yards, at least."

It's pointed out that Pickett accounted for 159 yards and four touchdowns in the game, but he downplays his own effort, and instead gives credit to the linemen in front of him.

"The line played very well tonight," he says. "It gave us enough time to throw the ball and they got off the ball on run plays and we executed so it was pretty fluid."

Finally, Pickett is asked if the Cardinals, winners of nine straight after having scored at least 55 points in four of their last five games, are playing their best football of the season with the district championship right around the corner.

"Yes sir, I feel like we're playing pretty well," he says. "There's always room for improvement, but I feel like we're playing pretty well."

On the Cardinals' defense, seven different players combine for 10 tackles for a loss. Rhea makes three, and has eight total tackles. Sophomore Calem Nutting, senior Carson Johnson, junior Garrett Rogers, junior Tayler Arterburn and sophomore Colton Adams each make one tackle for a loss, and senior Alex Lane adds two more. Arterburn and Lane each have sacks; Crane, Hardin and Milner each have interceptions. Rhea, whose three tackles for a loss give him 13-and-a-half for the year, says the defense knew they would be seeing an improved Carthage offense after the Tigers had made some changes.

"They changed up their offense a little bit and do a lot more with the quarterback," he says. "He was effective; he could scramble, he could pass, and we did our best to defend it. We got a couple breaks and overall we were able to stop it pretty good.

"I feel like we're doing good," he says. "We can definitely improve, there's still a lot of things we need to work on and get better at. We'll be doing that, getting better, but there's still room for improvement."

It's a cold Wednesday night in Webb City, and for a few more hours the Cardinals will celebrate their berth in the district championship game after beating an old rival. And in five days, on Monday night, they'll play a huge game against another historic rival: Carl Junction.

Just as the historic rivalry with Carthage has been incredibly lopsided for the last 30 or so years, so too has the rivalry with nearby Carl Junction.

Since the Cardinals and Bulldogs played in 1981 – the last game for seven years after vandalism and the dissolution of the Big 8 temporarily put an end to the match-up – Webb City goes 20-0 against Carl Junction, with two more wins in 2014. But unlike Webb City's games against Carthage, with the occasional edge-of-your-seat finish, those contests against the Bulldogs have been even more lopsided. The 52-29 win against the Bulldogs to open the 2013 season is actually the closest game the schools have played since 2007, when Webb City won 28-6 the week before the infamous last-second field goal at Carthage. In recent years the Cardinals have won by 42 points, by 41, by 55, by 54, and by 36. And unlike Webb City's games against Carthage, which are an annual holiday in southwest Missouri football, the Cardinals and Bulldogs match-ups have become something of a rarity. Besides not playing between 1981 and 1988, the teams also didn't play after the 1994 season until 2006. With Carl Junction poised to join the Central Ozarks Conference, that should change.

The teams will play once more in 2013, however, and this time there's a real feeling around the area that this game could be a lot closer than the previous blowouts, and even closer than the 23-point game in week one. The Bulldogs come back to Cardinal Stadium ranked fifth in the state and 10-1 overall after inching past Springfield Hillcrest 29-28 on a touchdown pass with eight seconds remaining in the district semifinal. Earlier in the year, the Bulldogs won 50-46 at undefeated Lamar, ending the Tigers' long winning streak on a hook-and-ladder play to end the game. Carl Junction will play for the Class 4, District 4 title not having won a district championship since 2001.

The Bulldogs average 463 yards offensively with their high-flying spread offense guided by head coach Doug Buckmaster, a former Carthage and Joplin head coach. Quarterback Dustin Satterlee has passed for 2,310 yards and 21 touchdowns; receiver Matt Magee, who returned the opening kickoff for a touchdown in the season opener at Webb City, has caught 60 passes for 942 yards and seven touchdowns; receiver Tanner McMurtrey has 48 catches for 642 yards and five touchdowns; running back Keynan Scheurich has rushed for 1,313 yards and 22 touchdowns; Satterlee has rushed for 941 yards and 21 touchdowns.

This is, without a doubt, the most-hyped game between Webb City and Carl Junction since 1989, when the two teams opened the season against each other after the Bulldogs had gone to the state semifinals the year before and the Cardinals had gone to the quarterfinals.

"It's good for high school football in the area," Buckmaster tells *The Globe*. "It's great for the kids. It's all about the kids anyway, isn't it? You prepare as best you can and go play.

"It's exciting for our community. This is a big stepping stone for us as a

Carl Junction lines up during its first possession in the district championship game. Photo by Brennan Stebbins.

Kiante Hardin catches a touchdown pass from quarterback Devin Pickett against Carl Junction in the district championship. Photo by Brennan Stebbins.

Running back Tyler Davison gets to the edge in the district finals against Carl Junction. Photo by Brennan Stebbins.

football program."

Hours before the 7 p.m. game, fans are waiting in line to enter Cardinal Stadium. At 6:10 p.m., John Roderique stands in the north end zone doing interviews with Joplin television stations, which are broadcasting their sports segments live from the field. A half hour before kickoff, the wind picks up, gusting from the north and swirling around inside the stadium, and the sky starts spitting.

The Bulldogs take the field early, with more than eight minutes left before the game starts, and a couple minutes later, as Webb City players exit their locker room and start the walk down the hill, Carl Junction fans chant "Bulldogs" from the visitors' bleachers. The stands on both sides are jam-packed, and fans are lined up all around the fences.

With five minutes and 20 seconds on the countdown, the announcer introduces Webb City starters; Trey Parra, the senior running back, is the first player to run through the makeshift tunnel and burst through a blue, circular sign held by the cheerleaders. While players are introduced, the rest of the team huddles in the south end zone, and with three minutes, 50 seconds to go they run to the sideline as the home crowd erupts.

Captains head to midfield a minute later; from left the Cardinals send out

Parra, Hunter Rhea, James Fowler and Jordan Green. The running back, the linebacker, the linemen. Representing the Bulldogs: Chris Whelan, Kris Bird, Matt Magee and Dustin Satterlee.

The temperature plummets and the wind becomes even stronger.

Carl Junction wins the toss and wants the ball. The Bulldogs will begin the game facing north, into the wind. The ball is placed on the tee, then blows over. A few seconds later it sails into the end zone for a touchback.

Buckmaster calls Scheurich's name on first down; he gains three yards. On second down he runs for two more. A reverse to Magee on third down gains only a yard. The Bulldogs punt into the wind, and it goes only 20 yards.

Webb City's first possession starts at the Carl Junction 46-yard line, and Parra rushes for eight yards on first down. On second down, Tyler Davison takes a handoff, breaks outside and runs down the Webb City sideline. Just like that it's 7-0.

Carl Junction's second possession starts at the 22, and the Bulldogs quickly advance to the 39, but a high snap on first down is recovered by junior linebacker Steven Moore and he runs it back to the Bulldogs' 7. A Webb City false start moves the ball back to the 12, then Davison scores again. It's now 14-0.

This is a confident Bulldog team, though, and they shrug off the two quick touchdowns and start an impressive drive. Satterlee is sacked for a 5-yard loss on first down, but over the next 12 plays Carl Junction marches 82 yards and converts three times on third down. It sets up a fourth-and-1 at the Webb City 3, and Satterlee rushes up the middle for the touchdown. The point after is no good; it's 14-6 with 2:54 left in the first quarter.

Hardin returns the ensuing kickoff, a squib kick, across midfield and into Bulldog territory. With 31 seconds left in the quarter, Pickett passes to Hardin for a 25-yard touchdown, and it's a 21-6 game.

Carl Junction answers quickly. On first down, Satterlee takes the ball 65 yards to the Webb City 15, and on the very next play Scheurich scores; the Bulldogs have taken just 23 seconds to move 80 yards and pull within nine points, 21-12.

Trent Parra, a junior receiver, returns the kickoff to the 47 just before the quarter ends, and the Cardinals need only two minutes of the second quarter to score again. Trey Parra finds the end zone from six yards out, making it 28-12. Again, the Bulldogs answer. This time it's a long, methodical drive covering 67 yards and lasting more than six minutes. Three third-down conversions and another on fourth down set up a fourth-and-goal at the 3, and Scheurich gets the call again. This time Carl Junctions goes for two and Satterlee scores; it's now 28-20 with 3:53 left in the half and all of a sudden the game is living up to the hype.

The Cardinals have run only 14 plays so far in the half, but they've scored every single time they've had the ball. Now just a one-possession game, Webb

City must head into the wind for its last possession of the first half, which starts at the 35. Pickett, Davison and Parra are the only ones who touch the ball on the first eight plays, one of which is a 15-yard pass from Pickett to Parra, and Pickett gains five yards on a fourth-and-3 in the red zone. On first and goal from the 1 with 34 seconds on the clock, Parra gets the ball and goes up and over the line for another touchdown.

But with 26 seconds left in the half and the ball on their own 35, the Bulldogs still have time. Satterlee completes a 19-yard pass on first down, then Scheurich gets seven yards on a draw play to the Webb City 39. Satterlee is sacked on the next play, however, and the Cardinals leave the field with a 35-20 advantage.

As the third quarter begins, the Bulldogs find themselves in an especially precarious position. Webb City gets the ball to start, has the wind at its back, and Carl Junction hasn't been able to stop the Cardinals once all night. Immediately Davison gets an 18-yard gain on the first offensive play of the second half, Pickett gains 16 yards a few plays later, then Davison runs for 14, Pickett for eight and finally Parra scores from 11 yards out. It's now 42-20, and the game is almost out of reach.

And then the Webb City defense gets a huge stop, but a punt pins the Cardinals at their own 7. For once it's not Webb City but Carl Junction that plays the field position game, and when the Bulldogs force a punt, the kick is an especially short one and Carl Junction takes over at the Webb City 30 at the 5:14 mark of the third quarter. The Bulldogs gain five yards on first down, but lose two on second down. Satterlee passes for five yards on third down, but Carl Junction faces a fourth-and-2 and Scheurich loses two yards.

Almost five minutes after the Cardinals get the ball back, Parra scores a 21-yard touchdown early in the fourth quarter and even though the point after is blocked, it's 48-20 and the Cardinals look well on their way to the quarterfinal round of the playoffs.

In the game's final moments, Webb City has another chance to score but instead takes a knee on third-and-goal from the 1. The Cardinals win by four touchdowns, and they'll head to Westminster on Saturday.

The formidable spread offense of the Bulldogs, which had averaged 476 yards per game, is held to just 306 yards in the district finals. Webb City, meanwhile, gains 473 yards on the ground alone, and Pickett adds 52 more yards through the air on perfect 3-of-3 passing. Parra and Davison run all over Carl Junction; Parra rushes 18 times for 194 yards and four touchdowns, and Davison rushes 17 times for 168 yards and two scores. Pickett adds 80 yards on 10 carries.

"Our offense did a really great job rushing the ball tonight," Davison says. "Our offensive line did a fantastic job doing their assignments, getting people blocked, and that just opened up holes for me and Trey to get the job done."

Parra, Edwards and Hardin each make one catch in the game. And the Webb City defense again makes tons of stops behind the line of scrimmage – eight total against Carl Junction. Three juniors – defensive back Austin Carter, linebacker Steven Moore and defensive lineman Tayler Arterburn – sack Dustin Satterlee. Others making tackles for a loss are junior lineman Connor Badgley, junior outside linebacker Lakin Milner and junior lineman Drake Humphrey. Arterburn finishes with three tackles for a loss.

"It really means a lot," Davison says. "I really looked forward to playing this game all week. We all did. We just knew we needed to stay focused on the task at hand and just come out and play our best football.

"I feel like we have quite a bit of momentum," he adds. "Just that confidence we have from tonight's game offensive-wise. I think we only had to punt the ball one time. That's a real confidence booster for our offense, being able to go out and do that again."

Roderique says during the team's pregame meeting in the school theater he asked his players if they had to write down three reasons why they play football, how many would not include to have fun. Not a hand was raised.

"To a man, everyone said at least one of the reasons they do this is to have fun," he says. "We try to keep them loose that way and just have them focus on just enjoying the moment and enjoying the time with their buddies and with their teammates, the camaraderie. That's what we focused on, and I thought our kids handled themselves really well with everything."

In a game that featured two high-powered offenses and one dominating defense, field position was huge. The Cardinals started their first three drives in Carl Junction territory, at the 46, the 7 and the 46. After those three drives they led 21-6.

With Kyle Baldassarre battling a sore hip, the coaching staff opted to play him exclusively on defense, and he leads the team with six tackles from his position in the defensive backfield. With the junior Tyler Davison getting more carries in the last several weeks of the season, the district title game officially marks his coming out party in the Webb City backfield.

"Tyler's one of those guys like Kyle Baldassarre and Trey Parra were last year, a guy who probably hasn't played as much as he wanted to," Roderique says. "He'd be playing probably for a lot of other guys. He's been patient, he's been really unselfish. Whenever he's gotten his opportunity he's stepped up and done a great job with it. We decided that if Kyle has a bad hip flexor and we decided he could play we were going to play him on defense. He was able to go and he came over once or twice and asked about playing on offense. I just said, 'Stay over there.' We've got a lot of confidence in Tyler."

As far as the subject of momentum heading into a Saturday afternoon playoff road game, Roderique just says his team is fortunate to still be playing.

"That's the main thing," he says. "It doesn't matter how you win, it's just a matter of win and move on. I'm real proud of our guys and our coaches for the effort tonight. We live to play another day. That's what that means right now."

The Cardinals have won 10 straight since their winning streak was snapped at Springdale Har-Ber, and they've done nothing but gain steam since then.

Through 12 games they've scored 564 points and allowed 182. That equals out to an average score of 47-15. In their last six games, the Cardinals have really hit their stride. Since beating Willard by 17 points, they're averaging more than 50 points scored and fewer than 10 points allowed each week, a 45-point average margin of victory. The Carl Junction game is the closest contest in that period of time. It's basically been complete domination. One way to measure the difference between the first six games and the last six is the running game, which has gone from being very good to incredible.

The first half of the season the Cardinals threw the ball about eight times a game and tallied just under 100 yards through the air. The second half they're throwing the ball about seven times a game for 72 yards. The running game, meanwhile, averaged 291 yards per game those first six weeks, and 6.8 yards per carry. Since then, however, Webb City averages 384 yards per game and an astounding 9.1 yards per carry.

Whether coincidence or not, the improved running attack coincides with changes on the offensive line made after the Willard game in week six. Jordan Green, a 6-foot-1, 270-pound senior, started at center to begin the year and after Willard moved to strong tackle. James Fowler, a 6-foot, 220-pound senior, started the year at quick guard and then moved to center.

"It was just better for the team I guess," says Fowler, a few days before the Cardinals head east to face Westminster. "Whatever Coach Rod asks, we do it." Green and Fowler are both captains and anchors of an experienced offensive line. It's a line that Carthage coach Jon Guidie said was perhaps the best he's seen at Webb City after the week three game.

It's no surprise to anybody that Webb City likes to run the ball. It's been the team's bread and butter for basically a century or more. And even though every team the Cardinals play knows they're going to run the ball, nobody can stop it. Through 12 games Webb City has amassed 4,054 rushing yards and averages 7.98 yards per carry. The team has a ton of weapons to choose from in the backfield. Trey Parra leads with 1,234 yards and is averaging more than 9 yards per carry. Kyle Baldassarre has 931 yards and averages more than 8 per carry. Tyler Davison has 567 yards and averages right at 9 per carry. Devin Pickett has 459 rushing yards, and both he and Tyson Roderique have combined to give the Cardinals 702 yards from the quarterback position.

Jordan Green and James Fowler stand in the south end zone at Cardinal Stadium minutes after the conclusion of a brisk playoff practice and reflect on the season their team has had so far, and what it's like playing on the offensive line for perhaps the state's best rushing program historically.

"I take a lot of pride because that's pretty much the main thing we want to do is run the football," Green says.

Fowler, too, obviously takes pride in what he does on the field.

"Because Coach Rod says the most important key to the whole running game are the ones who block for the running backs," he says. "If we weren't there the game wouldn't even work."

Despite the importance of the job those offensive linemen do every week, it can be a thankless position, at least publicly. Seldom are the linemen mentioned in the newspapers and on television, but for Green and Fowler the reward comes in knowing the team's backs have a good game.

"I feel like that's enough reward for me, knowing I did my job so they could get those stats in the book," Green says.

"Sometimes we get a Twinkie or two," Fowler adds.

Webb City has had some tremendous offensive linemen throughout the years, as everyone knows, but Green and Fowler say they don't spend much – if any – time thinking about those Cardinal greats.

"Because it's kinda my turn to step in and try to be a great lineman in Webb City and move up the ranks," Green says. "Hopefully I'll be there one day."

"It's the same for me," Fowler says. "We talk about them sometimes, but that was in the past and we try to just focus on the present and get our job done."

When the Cardinals' offense takes the field on Saturday in the state quarterfinals, it does so behind 6-foot-4, 275-pound junior Dalton Ford at quick tackle; 6-foot-3, 270-pound sophomore Trystan Castillo at quick guard; Fowler at center; 6-foot, 275-pound senior Tony Carranco at strong guard; and Green at strong tackle. Six-foot, 255-pound senior Michael VanSlyke and 5-foot-10, 255-pound senior Aaron Gossard will see action there as well. They all look to Green and Fowler, captains of the team and of the line, for guidance.

"They voted us into these positions so that just shows how much they look up to us and respect us," Fowler says. "I just hope we can continue to have a good year and hopefully get all the way to state."

St. Louis Westminster Christian Academy advanced to the quarterfinals with a 28-20 win against Ladue Horton Watkins, its 10th win in 12 games this season. The combination of a dynamic offense and a stifling defense looks like it could pose a problem.

Westminster runs its offense out of the pistol and features two quarterbacks, one who throws and one who runs, and the team's leading running back has more than 1,400 yards. The defense features a 300-pound nose guard and a physical, aggressive style of play. Westminster has allowed 14 or fewer points in half its games so far.

The Cardinals leave town at noon on Friday and practice on the artificial turf at Waynesville High School. Neither school knows really what to expect on

Saturday.

"We don't play anyone that runs a veer," Westminster head coach Cory Snyder tells *The Joplin Globe*. "It's the players, of course, that make the offense. Webb City has an outstanding offensive line. The backs run very hard.

"Our No.1 concern against Webb City is its experience, tradition and depth," he says. "We have to play our best football, hang in and hope they make a few mistakes."

Roderique says the big threat his defense will face is 6-foot-2, 210-pound quarterback Brett Bond, who has already signed with the University of Missouri to play baseball.

The game, which is broadcast live on television in Webb City, opens with an 80-yard drive by the Cardinals. Devin Pickett's 9-yard run and Nathan Gooch's extra point stake the visitors to an early lead.

As everyone expected, though, Westminster's offense will be a challenge to stop. The Wildcats answer quickly with a 32-yard touchdown run by Bond, and they play aggressively for the lead and go for two; a pass falls incomplete and it's a 7-6 game.

Webb City gets the ball back at the 20-yard line again, and this time it takes only five plays to score. Pickett completes a 24-yard pass to tight end Cooper Strasser, and Trey Parra's 42-yard touchdown caps the drive.

In the second quarter, the Wildcats continue to move the ball, and they move deep into Webb City territory. Cornerback Kiante Hardin picks off a pass to kill one scoring threat, and when the Wildcats drive back to the Webb City 6, Hardin picks off another pass on a second-and-goal.

The Cardinals then march 93 yards with Tyler Davison rushing for 12 and 27 yards on two carries, and Parra eventually scores from the 16.

Hardin makes his third interception of the first half later in the quarter and returns the ball across midfield. Tyson Roderique comes in at quarterback and throws a 30-yard touchdown strike to Parra out of the backfield; it's 26-6 with 2:10 left in the half.

It's that critical point in the game faced by so many opponents when the Cardinals are on the verge of turning it into a rout. In the third quarter, they do, and they do it with field position.

Webb City's defense pins the Wildcats deep in their own territory, and a 8-yard punt sets the Cardinals up at the 33-yard line. Davison scores from the 29 at the 3:36 mark; it's now a four-score game.

Early in the fourth quarter, Cameron Tournear makes an interception, and that sets up a 27-yard field goal by Gooch with 9:33 to play. After its early touchdown response, and despite several more threats, Westminster never scores again. Webb City earns a berth in the state semifinals and leaves town with a 36-6 win on a rainy, overcast afternoon.

"Thank goodness for Kiante Hardin," John Roderique says after the game.

"The difference?" Westminster's Cory Snyder says. "They were better up front. They controlled the line of scrimmage on both sides of the ball. Also, we had too many turnovers."

Emilio Perez, Alex Lane and Easton Carver each make sacks in the game. Steven Moore, Connor Badgley and Drake Humphrey add tackles for a loss, and Moore leads the team with nine stops.

Offensively, Trey Parra scores three touchdowns and rushes for 127 yards, and Davison adds 97 yards and a touchdown.

There will be one last home game at Cardinal Stadium in 2013.

A crisp and clear afternoon greets fans at Cardinal Stadium on Nov. 23 as Webb City hosts Cape Girardeau Central in the Class 4 semifinals.

The sun is bright and there's a strong wind from the north; Webb City, in its red jerseys and white pants, wins the toss and defers to the second half. The opening kick sails into the end zone for a touchback.

The visitors are 10-4 on the season, having won eight straight after a 2-4 start. The Tigers have scored at least 56 points five times in that span and come to Webb City after eking out a 25-22 win against an 11-0 Miller Career Academy in the quarterfinals.

The first play from center is a preview of things to come. Webb City's Austin Carter, a junior defensive back, and Tayler Arterburn, a junior defensive lineman, combine to tackle a Central ballcarrier for a one-yard loss. The Tigers rush for two yards on second down. On third-and-long, quarterback Josh Morse scrambles and throws. His pass is intercepted near midfield by Webb City senior Kyle Baldassarre, who gives the Cardinals possession at the Central 38-yard line.

It actually takes the Cardinals eight plays to move 38 yards, and they have to convert on a fourth-and-1 at the 4 where senior Trey Parra rushes for two yards. He punches the ball into the end zone on the next play, and then Webb City executes a fake extra point. Sophomore quarterback Andrew Greek completes a pass to senior Hunter Rhea and Webb City leads 8-0.

Senior Kicker Seth Rogers sends his next kickoff into the end zone once again, and Central punts after three plays.

One of the game's big storylines is Webb City's excellent field position. After starting their first drive on the Central 38, the Cardinals start their second on the Central 39, and their third possession on the Central 37. Junior quarterback Devin Pickett keeps the ball on a veer play and scores a 35-yard touchdown, making it a 15-0 game, and the Cardinals strike again when another Morse pass is intercepted. This time junior Kiante Hardin picks it off and returns it for a touchdown.

After starting at the 37, Webb City takes nine plays to score again. Junior Tyler Davison finds the end zone from the 3-yard line on a fourth-and-goal.

Webb City leads 29-0 with 7:35 left in the half.

The rest is anticlimactic. Webb City rolls to a 46-0 win, and turns its attention to playing for a fourth-straight state championship.

On the field, after John Roderique has addressed the team, KNEO radio's sideline reporter, Scott Boudreaux, grabs the coach for a live interview.

"I guess a performance like today is what warms an old coach's heart up and makes you keep going, right?" Boudreaux asks.

"Boy, I tell you what, it really does," Roderique says. "Just thinking about the whole season, coming off of last year and what a great team, what a great season we had last year, thinking about how are we going to replace this guy, that guy and the other guy and just how the kids come together, come out and play in a game like this, that means so much. It just seemed like you kind of make your breaks but it seems like everything went our way today. The wind, the conditions. Gosh, I just feel very proud of this group of kids."

Against Central's prolific offense, the Cardinals not only hold the Tigers scoreless, their defense dominates the game. Webb City has seven tackles for loss, with junior linebacker Steven Moore recording two-and-a-half and senior lineman Easton Carver another one-and-a-half.

"The preparation had to be really intense this week knowing you had to stop a prolific offense the Tigers were going to bring you and it was evident those first couple of series that they had paid attention to detail because your defense came out, not only with the fire but also with the right stops," Boudreaux says.

"One thing coaching, you've got to be flexible and you've got to be able to understand what people are trying to do to you," Roderique says. "I'm so proud of our defensive staff. It's a great example of our coaches on defense putting our kids in a good position to be successful and then the kids going out and really executing what we tried to do. We kind of did some different things today that we've done throughout the course of the year and it really paid off."

The offense rushes for 302 yards and four touchdowns while averaging better than seven yards per carry. It does it despite missing senior James Fowler at center, who is injured in the game at Westminster.

Roderique fields more questions from media. Forty-six to nothing?

"Not in my wildest dreams did I think that would happen," he says.

"People all year long have been saying you aren't as good this year, and here you are 13-1, you just won 46-0 and you're going to St. Louis for the fourth year in a row."

"It feels pretty amazing," Roderique adds. "It's hard to fathom. When you start a season and we've got so many guys to replace, so many kids are going to be starting for the first time and you don't know about this, and then the second game of the year we give up 600 yards to a Har-Ber team, it's just one of those things where persistence pays off as a coaching staff. You try to get the kids to keep working and keep playing and keep doing things. Gosh, certainly we didn't expect this."

It's on to St. Louis...for a rematch.

The 1993 Webb City football team, with its undefeated record and nine shutouts, was one of the greatest Cardinals' teams in history. Twenty years have passed since that team beat Columbia Rock Bridge 20-7 for the school's third championship, and as the Cardinals prepare to play for their 12th title, that 1993 team is recognized on the field inside the Edward Jones Dome in St. Louis.

Webb City's marching band plays the national anthem. With nine-and-a-half minutes before kickoff, a familiar site emerges from the tunnel: Jefferson City Helias, decked out in all white with gold helmets, navy lettering and gold trim. This is the third time the two schools have met for the state championship. Webb City won by 35 points in 2012, and edged Helias in a 41-34 shootout in 2008. The Cardinals also won playoff games against the Crusaders in 2002, 2010 and 2011.

Webb City's players take the field about 30 seconds later, and players from both teams are announced. John Roderique accompanies his team's captains – seniors Trey Parra, Hunter Rhea, Jordan Green and Kyle Baldassarre – to midfield, then walks back to the sideline and shakes hands with an official and puts on his headset.

At 1:05 p.m., the game kicks off. Seven plays later, Helias leads 7-0 after the Crusaders march 70 yards and score on a 12-yard run by Garrett Buschjost just 2:29 into the game.

Barely a minute later, Helias has the ball back at midfield after a Webb City fumble, and quickly advances into Webb City territory before two intentional grounding penalties and a six-yard loss on a rush put the Crusaders in a fourth-and-47 situation at their own 22.

Webb City starts this time in Helias territory, and Trey Parra puts the Cardinals on the scoreboard with a 1-yard run at the 3:26 mark. The extra point is no good.

Helias' opening drive is an aberration and the Webb City defense clamps down. The Crusaders gain just two yards and punt on their second possession, and gain one yard and punt on their third. The kick does pin Webb City at its own 7, but the Cardinals then march 93 yards and take nearly five minutes off the clock in grabbing the lead on a 15-yard reverse run by junior Kiante Hardin with 6:21 left in the half. They lead 14-7 after quarterback Devin Pickett passes to Trey Parra for the two-point conversion.

This is our house," a player exclaims. "We own the Dome."

The key play of the drive is a fourth-and-1 at Web City's own 36. The Cardinals fake a punt, and Parra gains 31 yards on a run.

Helped by a pass interference call, Helias does manage to cross into Webb City territory on its fourth possession of the game. Junior Tayler Arterburn comes up with a big second-down sack for a nine-yard loss, and Helias punts two plays later. Junior lineman Connor Badgley picks off a pass on Helias' next possession.

At halftime, it's still a 14-7 game. The Webb City marching band performs again.

The third quarter is scoreless. Webb City comes up short on a fourth-down run, and then Helias punts. Webb City punts, Helias punts again. Webb City punts a second time, and Helias takes over at its own 30 with 1:28 left in the quarter.

This time the Crusaders move the ball. They move the chains on three straight plays while advancing to the Webb City 25. They convert on a third-and-2 at the 19, and another third-and-2 inside the 10. On first and goal, Tory Wiley gains five yards down to the 1, and on second down Buschjost punches it in. The game is tied with nine minutes remaining.

The Cardinals need a playmaker to rise to the occasion, and on the ensuing kickoff, one does. Hardin catches the kick at his own 14-yard line and returns it all the way to the Helias 19. Pickett rushes for six yards, junior Tyler Davison rushes for two more, and then Parra rushes for three. On first-and-goal, Parra scores on an eight-yard run, and Webb City leads 21-14 after the extra point by senior Nathan Gooch. Seven minutes, 12 seconds remain.

Helias gets the ball back at its own 17. The Crusaders get a first down at the 33, and another at the 44. With 4:35 on the clock, they face a fourth-and-seven at their own 47. Quarterback Wyatt Porter is sacked by a host of Cardinals, but a facemask penalty gives Helias new life – a fourth-and-1 just across midfield. The Crusaders rush for the first down, and it's close. Officials decide to measure. Helias is just short.

Webb City has the ball at its own 47-yard line just four minutes, 30 seconds away from its fourth consecutive state championship. Pickett keeps the ball on the ground and gains five yards on first down. Parra gains three yards on second down. On third-and-two, Webb City gives the ball to Parra again, and he doesn't stop running until he's in the end zone. Webb City leads 28-14.

The Crusaders still have 3:25 left to score two touchdowns, but they can't complete a pass and less than a minute later give the ball back to the Cardinals just 16 yards from the end zone. Parra rushes for a couple of yards on first down. Roderique starts pulling seniors off the field one by one.

Helias gets one last possession, starting at its own 8, with 1:33 to play. It converts a first down, and has the ball at the 31 with 55 seconds remaining. Hardin intercepts a pass, and then sophomore quarterback Tyson Roderique takes a knee.

"Going in, we knew we were facing a great opponent in Helias," John Roderique says in the postgame press conference. "If you look at their body of work over the season, they've really beat some good teams. We knew it was going to be one of those games where we were going to have to battle every second of the game. We just told our kids that.

"I'm so proud of our offense and defense. When you come in the Dome and play over here, things don't always go the way you expect them. There's a lot of adversity. Today was a great example of that for us. We had such untimely penalties in that game that really hurt. We took a couple chances, I think, in the first half and I think that was the key. It was huge for us being ahead at halftime, 14-7. That was a big deal for us in terms of momentum and being excited. Just having a little bit of momentum, having that edge. I told our guys if this was tennis it's our advantage right now and we hold the serve in the second half. I can't say enough about our kids, our players. A few times to our seniors, I said I don't know that very many people gave us a lot of credit as a group, a group of seniors or as a team this year. Last week I told them how proud I was they won that semifinal game and got a chance to play in the state championship because in July and August, back when we started this thing, I couldn't have imagined that we would be here, and I say that in all respect to our kids. Not in a negative way. Our kids look at me like, 'Are you stupid?' Our kids fully expected to be here. I really believe that. Even though sometimes they've got to convince us as coaches.

"It's been a fantastic year and I'm really, really proud of our guys, our seniors. We've had a lot of younger guys who have stepped up at times. It was one of those teams where everybody cares about each other, we always enjoy each other's time together. What a fitting way to end with a bunch of great kids."

The coach is asked what changed with Webb City's difference after Helias drove 70 yards and scored on its first possession of the game. Roderique says defensive coordinator Mike Smith made some adjustments; the team started attacking more, got into a three-man front.

"Our defensive coaches did a fantastic job making those adjustments and then the kids were just making plays," he said.

Helias rushes for 127 yards in the game and passes for 142, but the Cardinals still finish with more total offense despite not completing a single pass. Webb City gains 328 rushing yards on 54 carries.

Arterburn and senior Alex Lane each record sacks in the game, for a combined loss of 30 yards. Lane makes three tackles for a loss, and Webb City has seven total. Kiante Hardin, in addition to his 22-yard interception, breaks up two passes.

As for the fake punt, Roderique says it's the first time the Cardinals have done that all season.

"Honestly it's a deal between me and this kid right here, Trey," he says. "He looks over at me, I look out there, he's like, 'I think we can run it.' I just signaled to him from the sideline that I think it's there, let's run it. I think you've got to give kids an opportunity to play and you've got to take some chances once in a

Quarterback Devin Pickett carries the ball in the 2013 state championship game against Jefferson City Helias. Photo by Brennan Stebbins.

Kiante Hardin scores a touchdown against Jefferson City Helias in the 2013 championship game in St. Louis. Photo by Brennan Stebbins.

while. You've got to try to play to win games. I don't know if it was a smart call. I guess it was a smart call because we got it, but if we couldn't have gotten it it was a stupid call. That's just coaching."

A reporter asks Jordan Green what went through his mind as he stood on the sideline and realized he was about to win a fourth state title.

"It's just crazy," he says. "I was fortunate enough to get to come up here my freshman year and watch the other guys, the seniors. I was just kind of along for the ride. I got to state and then I knew it's my turn, it's my team, I'm a senior this year and I feel like we did a good job leading this team here. It just feels amazing."

"You're on the team as a sophomore and junior," Parra says. "Some of us stepped up and played and others didn't. When you're a senior, all eyes are on you. You have to put the team on your back and I think we did a really good job of that this year."

James Fowler is asked about the team's new nickname.

"Can you share with everybody what you were hoping this team would be called?"

"Are you referring to the Quad Squad?" Fowler says. "We've had that nickname since the summer. We were just hoping we'd be able to apply it to ourselves after this game."

Hunter Rhea, the senior outside linebacker, is asked about the fourth-and-inches stop with the Cardinals leading by seven.

"That was a big change of momentum in the game," Rhea says. "We knew they were going to come out and try to run it to get that last yard or so. Luckily we had some defensive linemen and linebackers who were there and able to fill it up to get that stop so we could hand it over to the offense."

"You can't even fathom what it's like down there; it's just crazy," Baldassarre says. "To stop them with like a yard or a foot and a half left, it's just insane."

"How much does it mean to you guys to have all those other guys who won a state championship there in the stands to cheer you guys on, as you were able to continue the legacy of Webb City football?" a reporter asks.

"Of course we do it for us and our coaches, but we do it for the tradition of Webb City," Parra says. "You don't want to let last year's team down and the year before that and 10 years before that. You keep going and you want to be part of that tradition that we have at Webb City."

The moderator says there's time for one last question.

"Got another one in you next year, coach?"

"Who knows, man. Who knows. We're going to enjoy this one, celebrate this and we'll get back to work. It's a process. You start that process here as soon as the season's over. We'll have a meeting, we'll have a little banquet here and we'll get back to work and see what we've got."

Richard Humphrey holds the 2014 state championship trophy while Webb City's football team celebrates on the field at the Edward Jones Dome in St. Louis. Pictured are Cameron Tournear (11), Austin Carter (25), Keegan Lumley (87) and Connor Badgley (56). Photo by Brennan Stebbins.

38. FIVE IN A ROW

For the fifth time in five years, Webb City football coach John Roderique sits at a table in the interview room deep inside the Edward Jones Dome in St. Louis. This time he's flanked by seniors Tyler Davison and Kiante Hardin, two of the team's biggest performers.

"Obviously every year is special, but five straight, it's unreal, can you put that into words?" a reporter asks.

His Cardinals have just blown out Cape Girardeau Central by four touchdowns in the 2014 MSHSAA Show-Me Bowl.

"I tell ya," he says. "It probably won't sink in until I retire from coaching. I'm sitting by myself sometimes here during Thanksgiving weekend, I start thinking about it. I'm driving down the road and I start crying about it. I'm tearing up. I just can't imagine having the opportunity to do this. The guys that ought to be answering the questions are the assistant coaches and all the players from the last five years. They're the guys that do it all. They're the guys that put the work in. This kid right here, I'm going to miss him. He's like a dang son to me." He pats Hardin on the back. "Tyler is, too. We've had some great kids. Here are two great kids right here. That's what makes it all worthwhile."

About 10 minutes later, the interview room takes on a decidedly more somber tone when Central head coach Nathan Norman and two of his players enter to talk about what might have been.

"It's tough," Norman says. "We talked about it all week. You're not playing Webb City 2014. You have to beat them in their past. I know that sounds funny. Everybody you talk to throughout the week is going to doubt you can win and you have to overcome that."

Only one school in Missouri history has ever won five straight state championships in football: Valle Catholic.

The little Class 1 private school in Ste. Genevieve, located along the Mississippi River, won five straight from 1988 to 1992. The first two games were played at Faurot Field at the University of Missouri, and Valle won 21-3 against Rock Port and 49-7 against Marceline. In 1990 the team beat Rock Port 49-21 at the Plaster Sports Complex in Springfield. A year later, Valle won 28-24 against Tarkio back at Faurot Field, and in 1992 Valle clobbered Hardin-Central 44-16 at the Plaster Sports Complex.

The five-year span was one of the most dominant stretches of football ever played in Missouri. Valle went 65-3 and almost won a sixth straight championship in 1993, but lost 19-12 to Milan. Two years later, in 1995, Valle won again, this time thrashing Wellington-Napoleon 63-13 at Hughes Stadium at Missouri Southern.

That marked the end of a 15-year period where Valle Catholic took home nine state championships, with the Warriors also winning in 1981, 1982 and 1983. The 1981 title was a tie with St. Pius X. Neither team scored at Busch Stadium.

Interestingly, the greatest Valle team ever didn't even win a state championship. Missouri didn't hold football playoffs until 1968, and the Valle team in 1966 put together "one of the most impressive seasons ever achieved by an American prep squad," according to the record book maintained by the Missouri State High School Activities Association. That 1966 squad went 10-0 and didn't allow a single point all season, while scoring a total of 535. The team's scoring average and points allowed per game are state records.

The Warriors amassed 221 first downs and allowed only 47. They rushed for 3,037 yards and allowed only 431. They passed for 974 yards and gave up 190.

Their defense came up with 22 interceptions. Their offense tallied 4,011 total yards, and their defense gave up just 621.

By 1995, Valle had won nine state championships, and Webb City had only three. It took the Cardinals until 2010 to win their ninth championship, and by then Valle was already out of a decade-long slumber. The Warriors didn't play in a title game after 1995 until they lost 21-17 to Penney in the 2009 championship game. In 2010, they beat Westran 22-21 to stay one ahead of Webb City on the all-time list with 10 championships.

It was the same story in 2011. Webb City edged MICDS in the thrilling 56-42 shootout, but Valle ripped South Shelby 49-7 for its 11th title, passing Jefferson City (10) on the all-time list. Finally, in 2012, the Cardinals caught up. Valle played for another title, but lost 60-34 to Penney. Webb City, meanwhile, defeated Helias 49-14. Both teams had 11 championships, both were tied for first place on the all-time list. In 2013, each won its 12th.

In 2014, Webb City would either be tasked with keeping pace with Valle Catholic, or given the opportunity, to pass it on the all-time titles list. The Cardinals, having won four straight championships, could also match Valle's record for consecutive titles and become just the second team in state history to win five straight.

The game that really gets everyone talking about Webb City in 2014 is the week two showdown at Rockhurst. When MaxPreps released its list in mid-August of the 20 most dominant high school football teams in Missouri over the last decade, there was little doubt who would be at the top.

Using a formula based on the high school sports website's own computer rankings each season, and awarding points for each state championship and second-place finish, the site awarded Webb City a whopping 406 points, 130 more than the second-most dominant team. The Cardinals compiled a record of 133-5 during the previous decade while catching up to Valle in state championships, winning six of them and placing in the top five second times.

A distant second on the list was Rockhurst High School, a private prep school for boys in Kansas City. Rockhurst won 96 games and lost 22 during the decade, and though it won just two championships in the last 10 years, the school isn't far behind Webb City, Valle and Jefferson City on the all-time list, with nine total in 14 trips to the championship.

It is no surprise, then, that the game of the week on the last Friday of August is at Rockhurst High School, where the Cardinals and Hawklets match up for a heavyweight bout of epic proportions.

The season, of course, begins a week earlier. It's a strange season opener for Webb City; the Cardinals head east to take on arch nemesis Carthage at K.E. "Doc" Baker Stadium, the first time the teams have played in week one since 1980. The game once played as a finale on Thanksgiving Day and usually reserved for late-season dramatics has taken place increasingly early in recent years, but almost never this early. It's also Carthage's first season playing in Class 5, meaning the season opener will be the one and only game between the two schools this season. It's so hot out, kickoff is pushed back to 7:30 p.m.

"I don't remember a game this hot," Roderique later tells *The Globe's* Anvil Welch.

The Cardinals have something like eight starters back from a defense that allowed just 13.4 points per game in 2013, and they also have several skill players back on offense. Carthage head coach Jon Guidie is weary of Webb City's depth – the Cardinals have 87 players on the roster, not including freshmen. That's 40 more than Carthage.

"They've got some Division I kids over there this year," Guidie tells *The Carthage Press*. "It's going to make them a pretty special team.

"They're always very strong up front and this year's no different," he says. "They've got some very nice-sized kids, very physical kids. The challenge there is to match the physicality the entire football game. We've really been on our kids. I think probably we're as big and as strong as we've ever been up front, I really believe that. They've got to understand it's going to be a very physical football game."

Guidie says the key to beating Webb City is to be balanced. It's not just about running the ball and working the clock, he says.

But then his Tigers come out and surprise everybody by abandoning their spread offense for a grind-it-out style of football. They rush the ball 42 times in 48 plays and chew time off the clock. The strategy works, for the most part.

Alex Derryberry intercepts a pass by Webb City quarterback Tyson Roderique, giving Carthage the ball at the 50 at the start of the game. The Tigers punt, but Webb City is pinned at its own 6-yard line. It takes just three minutes for the Cardinals to move 94 yards and take a 7-0 lead when Tyler Davison, the senior running back, scores with 5:26 left in the first quarter. Hunter Vanlue tacks on a 14-yard touchdown in the second quarter, and Maquel Harbin intercepts a pass at the Webb City 15 to halt another Carthage drive. Webb City almost scores again before the half. Kaleb Potts, on a first-and-goal with 17 seconds remaining, catches a pass at the 2. The Cardinals are out of timeouts, though, and can't spike the ball in time.

Carthage's offense improves in the second half. The Tigers drive from their own 31 to the Cardinal 14 but can't convert on a fourth-and-four. The defense stop is a turning point, because Webb City then marches 86 yards and takes a 21-0 lead on Davison's 23-yard run. Carthage answers with another drive into the red zone, this time to the Webb city 7, but the Tigers can't convert on a fourth-and-1.

Webb City wins 21-0.

"Everybody kind of feels a little bit down right now because it was a sluggish game, but that's part of it," John Roderique says when it's over.

"They threw a look at us that we have never seen before out of Carthage," says defensive coordinator Mike Smith. "That was interesting. They're normally a spread offense with one back and a quarterback all over the place, and now they're two back so that was interesting."

Tyson Roderique completes six of 10 passes in his season debut and rushes for 32 yards. Vanlue, the sophomore running back, rushes nine times for 73 yards, while Davison adds 78 and junior Keaton Burroughs finishes with 75.

Rockhurst starts the season off with a dominating 49-14 win on the road at Columbia Rock Bridge, a team thought by many to contend for a state championship in November, according to the *Kansas City Star*. The Hawklets are ranked fourth in Missouri Class 6, and the Cardinals are ranked first in Class 4. Longtime head coach Tony Severino tells *The Globe* his Rockhurst team will face a more physical team in Webb City. The Hawklets are quarterbacked by T.J. Green, a senior and the son of former NFL quarterback Trent Green.

Sam McDowell, author of *The Star's* Varsity Zone high school sports blog, predicts Rockhurst will beat Webb City 28-21.

As the game begins, it looks like McDowell might be right. Webb City fumbles on the third play of the game and Rockhurst scores seven plays later. The Cardinals then punt after three plays, and Rockhurst scores on a quick drive to lead 14-0 with 4:44 left in the first quarter.

"But that merely miffed the Cardinals," *The Star* wrote. They "took over the game with their efficient and grinding veer option attack."

On the first play of the second quarter, Webb City caps a 13-play drive with a 2-yard touchdown by Kaleb Potts. The Cardinals then force Rockhurst to punt, and Kiante Hardin hauls in a spectacular 37-yard reception from Tyson Roderique to make it 14-13. By halftime it's 27-14, after Roderique scores on a 5-yard run and throws a 29-yard touchdown to Potts. At the break the teams are forced to wait nearly two hours as a storm moves through the area. The second half doesn't begin until 9:52 p.m.

Hardin forces a fumble on Rockhurst's first possession of the third quarter, and Webb City launches a 97-yard drive – running on 19 of 20 plays – while eating 8:42 off the clock and increasing its lead to 20 points when Potts scores another rushing touchdown. The Cardinals add another touchdown in the fourth quarter, a 7-yard run by Tyler Davison, and win 40-14.

It's an all-around dominating effort. Rockhurst runs just 22 plays, while Webb City snaps the ball 69 times. Webb City possesses the ball for more than 33 minutes, and Rockhurst has the ball for only 14:25. Tyson Roderique is nearly perfect. He completes five of six passes for 100 yards and two touchdowns. Kaleb Potts catches one, the 29-yarder, and Kiante Hardin catches the other. Most of the damage is done on the ground, where Webb City rushes for

325 yards on 64 carries. Davison goes for 109 yards and a touchdown. Potts scores twice and has 81 yards. Roderique adds another touchdown and runs for 78 yards.

"When you play their offense for the first time, you know that can happen when you don't play as physical as they do," Severino tells *The Star*. "We were misaligned and making some wrong reads and when you do that against them, that's what happens."

The defense is just as good as the offense. Maquel Harbin, Kolesen Crane, Austin Carter, Calem Nutting, Connor Badgley, Emilio Perez, Tayler Arterburn and Jarren Taylor combine for an astounding 10 tackles for a loss. Nutting, a junior linebacker, has three of them and one of the team's four sacks. Crane, Carter and Taylor each record quarterback sacks, as well.

Junior Cory Duley adds four extra points.

A week later, Webb City opens its home slate, and the schedule doesn't get any easier. Coming back to town is Springdale, Arkansas Har-Ber, the team that ended Webb City's regular-season winning streak in 2013. That year the Wildcats advanced to the state quarterfinals in Arkansas' biggest class, 7A.

This year is no repeat. Webb City runs wild on the ground – 419 yards, an average of more than 10 per carry. Tyson Roderique rushes only eight times and gains 133 yards with a touchdown. Kaleb Potts scores twice and gains 99 yards. Tyler Davison adds 78, and Keaton Burroughs finishes with 60.

Kiante Hardin catches a touchdown pass. So does Trent Parra.

Sophomore Gage Sweet, a defensive end, makes 14 tackles, and senior linebacker Steven Moore makes 11. Cory Duley, the junior placekicker, is a perfect 6-for-6 on extra points.

It amounts to a 42-13 Webb City win. The Cardinals lead by only a touchdown after the first quarter, but explode for three scores in the second. They limit Har-Ber to just 8-for-22 passing, with two interceptions.

Already, two of what appeared to be Webb City's toughest games are behind the Cardinals, and they're still unbeaten. The schedule gets easier as the Central Ozark Conference slate begins with a road game at Republic. The Tigers are improved from 2013, but still no match. Webb City wins 49-14 and throws only four passes. Three different rushers – Tyler Davison, Keaton Burroughs and Tyson Roderique – top the 100-yard mark. Burroughs is the most prolific, with three touchdowns and 135 yards. Steven Moore has a huge game on defense, with 10 total tackles and two sacks.

The Cardinals return home to face a Nixa team that will go on to play for the Class 5 state championship. The Eagles lose 25-22 to Columbia Battle. At Webb City, the Cardinals win 47-7, even while possessing the ball for nearly 10 minutes less than Nixa. Tyson Roderique airs it out in this game, throwing the ball 11 times and completing six passes for 183 yards. It's a breakout game for

Kiante Hardin, who catches four passes and averages 37.5 yards per catch. He scores a touchdown, too. Not a single player makes more than four tackles on defense, but 33 different Cardinals make tackles in the game, and junior Nate Deadmond picks off a pass and returns it for a touchdown.

Nixa had played Webb City closer than anybody in 2013, losing by only three points in overtime after the infamous decision to go for it on fourth-and-goal. Willard played the Cardinals pretty close, as well, losing by 17, but the Tigers are no match for Webb City in 2014.

Royce Clark, Kaleb Potts, Tyler Davison, Keaton Burroughs and Tyson Roderique each score rushing touchdowns. Zach Davidson, a junior, punts only twice and averages almost 50 yards per punt. Webb City wins 46-15.

It's more of the same in week seven against Neosho. Tyler Davison scores three rushing touchdowns and carries the ball only eight times. Kiante Hardin has three catches for 81 yards. Junior Colton Adams returns a fumble recovery for a touchdown. The Cardinals roll 48-0.

On Oct. 10, the Cardinals host Ozark. They lead 38-0 before Ozark scores a fourth quarter touchdown, and the visitors possess the ball for 13 minutes more than Webb City does. Nine different Cardinals gain yards on the ground, but nobody rushes for 100. Outside linebacker Cameron Tournear returns a fumble for a touchdown.

The last week before district play begins is Oct. 17, and Webb City heads to Branson. The Pirates make a field goal in the second quarter and a safety in the fourth, but the Cardinals score four times in the first quarter alone. Tyson Rodcrique throws touchdown passes of 37 and 18 yards, rushes for a 5-yard score and then Keaton Burroughs scores on a 75-yard run. Trent Parra, a senior, catches both touchdowns and the Cardinals win 48-7.

As district play begins at home against McDonald County, Webb City comes into the game scoring an average of 41 points per game and allowing only eight. Both of those averages improve against the Mustangs. Tyler Davison scores from the 31, Maquel Harbin returns an interception 32 yards to the end zone, Trent Parra has a 55-yard interception return for a touchdown, Davison scores on a 22-yard run, and then Tyson Roderique passes to Kiante Hardin for a touchdown. Tanner Yokley makes all five extra points. And that's just the first quarter.

It's a 49-0 game at halftime; Webb City wins 71-0. The Cardinals average an offensive touchdown every five plays. Five different players score on the ground, and junior Colby O'Brien leads the team with 134 yards.

The Cardinals have another huge first quarter against Bolivar on Halloween night at Cardinal Stadium. Tyler Davison scores on an 82-yard run. Kiante Hardin rushes 15 yards for a touchdown. Junior tight end Bradyn Ansley catches a 14-yard touchdown from Tyson Roderique, and with about two minutes remaining, Devin Pickett scores from the 1.

Maquel Harbin comes up with two interceptions in the game, and seniors Austin Carter and Trent Parra each have one. Webb City wins 56-7.

Finally, on the first Friday of November, the district championship game arrives. It's a repeat of the 2013 district title game against Carl Junction. Webb City won that one 48-20. Both teams are 11-0 heading in, and the Bulldogs and head coach Doug Buckmaster have their usual prolific offense. They score on average 44 points per game and win by an average of 32. Their biggest win comes in Big 8 conference play, a 29-28 defeat of Lamar. It's the second straight year the Bulldogs have edged Lamar, the only time the Tigers lose.

Carl Junction's best offensive player is senior running back Keynan Scheurich. He's got 1,942 rushing yards on the season and three games with more than 200 yards. He's scored 39 touchdowns and is the team's all-time single-season rushing leader. The Bulldogs' best defender is senior linebacker Chase Johnston, who signs with Kansas State University three months later. Scheurich signs with Pittsburg State.

Webb City is 17-0 in the last 30 years against its old rival from the west. The Cardinals score on two of their first three possessions and win No. 18. The first touchdown is a 15-yarder by Keaton Burroughs, and it comes after a scary opening drive by the Bulldogs, who move 72 yards in 12 plays but come up short on fourth-and-3 near the Webb City red zone. Carl Junction goes for it on a fourth-and-1 at its own 37 on its second possession, and Scheurich is stopped short. Burroughs makes it a 12-0 game with his second touchdown, a 1-yard run, and he tacks on the two-point conversion.

Burroughs scores a third touchdown in the second quarter, and Tyson Roderique scores on a 7-yard run. Webb City leads 28-0 at halftime, 35-6 after the third quarter and wins the game 42-12. Not only is Carl Junction held to less than a third of its scoring average, but the Cardinals limit Scheurich to just 81 yards and a touchdown on 25 carries. The Cardinals don't complete a pass, but Roderique rushes for 158 yards, Tyler Davison goes for 143, and sophomore Hunter Vanlue adds a late touchdown.

In the quarterfinals, Webb City travels to Harrisonville. The Cardinals and Wildcats have played five times since 1996, and Webb City has won each game. Four have been played in the regular season, and Webb City won 35-8 in the 2010 semifinals.

The Wildcats are 11-1, having lost 14-12 to Savannah in week two, and boast a tremendous defense that has allowed more than 14 points in only one game, with six opponents held to single digits.

Keeton Marsh, a junior safety, sparks Webb City on the opening kickoff. His long return sets the Cardinals up inside Harrisonville territory. On their fifth play from scrimmage, the Cardinals take a 7-0 lead when Tyson Roderique throws a 16-yard touchdown to junior tight end Bradyn Ansley.

Harrisonville punts after three plays.

Webb City marches 62 yards on 13 plays, scoring when Tyler Davison pounds it in from the 1. Three plays earlier, he gains a yard on a fourth-and-short at the 5. The Cardinals, smelling blood in the water, catch Harrisonville completely off guard with a surprise onside kick. They recover it inside the 50-yard line, but have to punt. Even that works in their favor. Junior Zach Davidson's punt pins the Wildcats at their own 1, and on first down they fumble the ball into the end zone, where it's recovered by senior defensive end Connor Badgley as the first quarter ends.

When Harrisonville finally gets a drive going, starting at its own 10 and pushing inside the Webb City 40, junior Kolesen Crane intercepts a second down pass at the 32. The Cardinals get the ball back 68 yards away from the end zone with 1:37 left in the half. A roughing the passer penalty on third down gives Webb City a first down at the Harrisonville 46. Tyson Roderique throws incomplete on first down. On second, he passes to Keaton Burroughs, who makes the catch and tosses the ball to Kiante Hardin. The hitch and pitch.

With less than a second on the clock, Webb City faces a fourth-and-10 at the Harrisonville 32. The Cardinals line up with four receivers to one side, and Hardin all by himself on the other side against one defender. Roderique throws a jump ball into the end zone, which is tipped by a Wildcat right into Hardin's hands. Webb City leads 28-0.

Crane breaks up a big third-down pass in Webb City territory in the third quarter, and Webb City's final score is a 2-yard touchdown throw from Roderique to Ansley. Maquel Harbin picks off a pass in the third quarter. Webb City wins 35-0.

After the game, his team gathered and players taking a knee near midfield, head coach John Roderique tells them to hug each other and tell their teammates how much they mean to each other.

"Because our days are limited, men," he says. "I don't know how many more we've got, but enjoy it. Seniors, you guys enjoy this. This is what it's all about right here. Coaches, anything? Coach Hicks? I imagine you want the sophomores to get the equipment off the field. Anybody got anything? Seniors?

"Kearney's up 20-7 start of the fourth. Bottom line, if Kearney wins we'll play at home next Saturday." This elicits some cheers. "Be the last time on that field for a lot of you guys. Make it count. Great win, men. Put a smile on your face. You've got to have fun and enjoy it. Enjoy this. Enjoy the ride home. Enjoy this time right here because I'm telling you it goes too fast. Way too fast. Give your parents a hug, tell them how much you love them. Whoever you have here for you. Take your time getting out of here because we've still got 27 minutes before the pizza's supposed to be here, all right? Mazzios pizza." This elicits some more cheers. "Let's say the Lord's Prayer here."

Roderique's son, Tyson, throws the ball a whopping 22 times against Harrisonville, with 15 completions, three touchdowns and 160 yards. Ansley, the junior tight end, catches two touchdowns.

"That's exciting to me," he says on the field. "I only had one touchdown before this game."

What does it mean to beat someone 35-0 in the state quarterfinals?

"We're here to play," Ansley says. "We're here to go all the way and take home a state title."

The shutout is Webb City's fourth of the season. John Roderique says the Cardinals had to prepare for two different offenses because Harrisonville has changed in recent weeks.

"Our coaches work as hard as anybody in the business at it and hats off to our coaches," he says. "Hats off to our coaches, and our players did a really nice job executing."

Kearney, playing in a quarterfinal game against Jefferson City Helias, hangs on to win 23-20. The Bulldogs are the last team to beat Webb City in the playoffs. They won 38-13 at Cardinal Stadium in 2009 in the semifinals. They're 12-1. Webb City is 13-0.

"This is your seventh straight semifinal appearance, and eighth in nine years. What goes on when you hear that stat?" Roderique is asked.

"It just makes me tired," he says, and chuckles. "It makes me feel a little bit worn out. It's a good problem to have, being worn out because of that. I'm really proud of this team. Proud of all the teams that had the opportunity to play. It's really humbling to have the opportunity to play, to have a chance to play next week."

Since that 2009 semifinal loss to Kearney at home, Webb City has won 17 consecutive playoff games – 26 if you include district games in the new win-or-go-home format – and has won 39 straight games at Cardinal Stadium.
Just like that 2009 semifinal, this one is played on a Saturday afternoon. There's a strong wind blowing out of the south. Webb City wins the toss and defers; the Cardinals will kick with the wind.

The wind picks up just before kickoff, gusting as high as 30 miles per hour. It has an effect on the game almost immediately. Kearney, on its first possession, only loses yards thanks to a fumbled snap, and the Bulldogs' punt on fourth down is a low line drive that goes only 26 yards.

Webb City has great field position at the 50, but the Cardinals punt on a fourth-and-2 and the kick sails into the end zone. Kearney punts again on its second possession, and this one goes just 19 yards. Webb City gets the ball at the Bulldog 49. After a three-yard rush and a false start penalty, quarterback Tyson Roderique completes a 40-yard pass to Kiante Hardin to the 11. Three plays later, the two hook up again for a 7-yard touchdown.

Webb City continues to have great field position. The Bulldogs move the ball into Cardinal territory but are stopped for no gain on a fourth-and-inches.

Webb City takes over at its own 45, and Roderique passes to Hardin to the Kearney 22 on first down, but the Cardinals fumble on the very next play. Kearney punts again, and Webb City gets the ball at its own 43 just before the quarter ends and the Cardinals have to march into the wind. After eight plays, they settle for a 22-yard field goal by sophomore Cory Duley. It's 10-0.

Drake Humphrey, a 6-foot-2 defensive tackle, recovers a fumble on Kearney's next possession, and Webb City gets the ball at its own 36. Junior Keaton Burroughs is the featured back on this drive, and he scores on a 14-yard run with 7:10 left in the half that makes it a 17-0 game after Duley's extra point.

The Bulldogs finally get on the board with an 80-yard drive before the half, making it a 10-point game.

The Cardinals waste little time getting the points back once the second half begins. Keeton Marsh, the junior safety, has another great kick return and nearly scores, but is knocked out of bounds at the Kearney 1. Sophomore Hunter Vanlue gets the call on first down and scores easily, making it 24-7.

Junior Kolesen Crane intercepts a pass to stop a Kearney drive deep in Webb City territory. It leads to a 19-yard touchdown catch by senior Maquel Harbin, making it 31-7 with 4:51 left in the third. Senior defensive tackle Emilio Perez has a big sack on Kearney's next possession, which ends in a punt.

Early in the fourth quarter, Kearney gets the ball back at its own 24 after a Webb City punt. The Bulldogs rush for three yards on first down. On second down, senior linebacker Austin Carter sacks quarterback "Johnny Football" Weidmaier for a nine-yard loss. On third down, Carter sacks him again. Weidmaier fumbles the ball, and the Cardinals recover it at the 14. It leads to a 3-yard score by Tyler Davison, and the Cardinals lead 38-7.

The defense continues to harass Weidmaier. The Bulldogs start deep in Webb City territory after a long return, but on a fourth-and-6 at the 34, Crane comes untouched off the edge on a blitz and sacks Weidmaier.

Moments after the team's 31-point win, after players from both teams have slapped hands at midfield, the Cardinals gather in the south end zone, first to celebrate with the marching band, and then to take a knee and listen to their head coach.

"In about 10 minutes I want you to ask yourselves how you feel at 4 o'clock," says John Roderique. "Feels pretty darn good, don't it?" The players respond with a 'Yes sir.' "Man, golly. I looked up at that scoreboard at the end of the game, 38-7, I never would have thought. We talked about it in the pregame, we talked about a complete game, offense, defense, kicking game. If you look at that today it was every bit of that, every one of you. Every guy that got on the field today, all those influenced the game.

"Is there a better feeling than right now for you as a football team?" Roderique asks the players.

"Nah, nope," most say. But they pause, then start laughing when they realize there's still a game to be played.

"I'm with you brothers, I'm with you," Roderique says. "Today, this is a great feeling right now, but I hope it's not the last feeling like this that we have. Right now you have earned the opportunity to go play for a state championship." There's applause, some whistling. "Monday morning if you're not there you're not going. Does everybody understand that? If you're not there Monday morning at 7:15 you're not going." Roderique pauses. "No, I'm just kidding. You need to be setting five alarms. Guys, we're going to meet Monday afternoon. We will practice on Wednesday when we're not in school, on Thursday when we're not in school and on Friday when we're not in school. We will practice on all those days so plan on it. It'll be earlier in the morning but we will practice on those days. Golly, man my stomach just started settling down just about five minutes ago. Coaches, anything?"

"Proud of you guys, proud of you guys. Way to fight, way to play," says defensive coordinator Mike Smith.

"Guys make sure you thank your coaches for working you the way we have, maybe getting on you sometimes when you may need it," Roderique says. "Great team win today, though, men. Great team win."

The Cardinals, five days before Thanksgiving, have earned their fifth straight appearance in the Class 4 state championship game.

"It's just a great feeling all around for everybody," says Tyler Davison, after the team begins to disperse. "I thought we played a great all-around game today. Everybody really played hard, and it's the best feeling in the world right now to be able to go back there."

"Did you think you would win by 30-plus?"

"Definitely not coming in," he says. "We knew it was going to be a four-quarter battle. That's a very good football team over there on the other side and they've had a lot of success and we knew we'd have to come and play really hard if we wanted to win."

Davison says he was sitting in the stands when Kearney won at Cardinal Stadium in 2009. That game was on his mind, five years later.

"Yeah, definitely," he says. "Even not being in high school and not being on the team, after that loss it makes you feel bad. You don't feel very good after that and I think we all remembered the way we felt after that game and that really motivated us to put in a lot of work this week."

Austin Carter, who had the two big sacks and fumble recovery on consecutive plays, says they were probably his favorite plays of the season.

"With the rivalry that we and Kearney have, that was really fun," Carter says. The team watched film from the 2009 game during its preparations, he says.

"We all watched that whole game. We just didn't want it to turn out like that."

Kaden Roy celebrates a defensive stop in the 2014 semifinals against Kearney. Photo by Brennan Stebbins.

Maquel Harbin crosses the goal line on a touchdown reception in the 2014 semifinals at Cardinal Stadium. Photo by Brennan Stebbins.

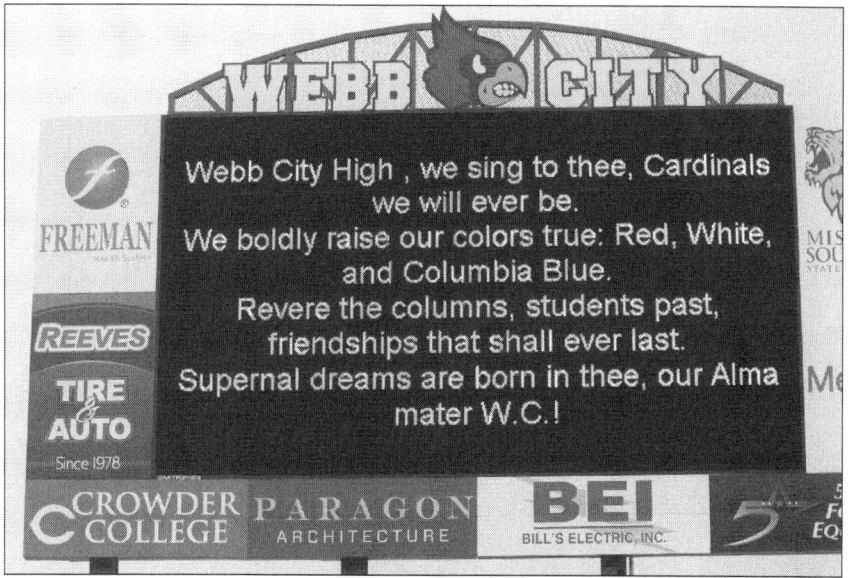

The video scoreboard at Cardinal Stadium provides words to the school fight song after Webb City's win in the 2014 semifinals. Photo by Brennan Stebbins.

Head coach John Roderique greets Tyler Davison on the sideline after a Webb City touchdown in the 2014 semifinals. Photo by Brennan Stebbins.

Carter was in junior high and remembers standing up in the stands. This time, the Cardinals shut the Bulldogs down.

"It was pretty simple. We just did what we were supposed to do, nothing too complicated. Just our assignments," he says.

Roderique, meanwhile, is speaking with reporters.

"It feels pretty good. It feels darn good," he says.

There is some doubt in the weeks leading up to the state championship if the game will still be played at the Edward Jones Dome in St. Louis. With a grand jury decision in the Michael Brown case due and tensions expected to flare in its wake, MSHSAA develops contingency plans to play the games elsewhere.

A week before, MSHSAA announces the games will be played, as planned, at the Dome. The first game of the weekend kicks off at 1 p.m. Friday, Nov. 28. It's the Class 3 championship pitting Oak Grove against John Burroughs. Oak Grove trails 14-7 after the first quarter but wins 49-27. At 4:15 p.m., the Class 1 game kicks off. It's Westran against Valle Catholic.

The Warriors from Ste. Genevieve have another incredible team. They're 14-0, give up only about nine points a game, and their offense scores more than 53. Valle, already having beaten Westran in the regular season 72-28, racks up nearly 600 yards of total offense in the title tilt. Junior quarterback Connor Basler throws five touchdown passes, tying a state championship game record set by Valle's head coach, Judd Naeger. Basler also throws for 419 yards, which ranks second all-time in a title game.

Valle scores first, and adds touchdowns on its final two possessions of the first half to lead 21-7. It's 21-13 after a Westran touchdown in the third quarter, but Basler throws a 65-yard touchdown just eight seconds later. Valle goes on to win 49-25. It's the school's 13th state championship, a new record.

"Once again, the Valle Catholic Warriors proved they're the best in the state – at least for a few hours," writes Jim Faasen in his story for the *St. Louis Post-Dispatch*.

"It doesn't really make any difference to me," Valle senior lineman Jacob Trautman tells the paper. "It's all about the team. We pulled this off as a team. We're not concerned with what Webb City does."

There's one more game inside the Dome on Friday evening, the Class 5 match-up. Columbia Battle beats Nixa 25-22.

The Class 4 championship game will be the first of the day on Saturday. Kickoff is set for 11 a.m. against last year's semifinal opponent, Cape Girardeau Central, which is 13-2 with a high-powered offense.

It'll be the last game for 25 Webb City seniors. Among them, offensive players like Tyler Davison, a running back who finishes the year with 1,255 rushing yards and 15 touchdowns; Devin Pickett and Royce Clark, who both score rushing touchdowns; Trent Parra, a receiver with three touchdowns; Maquel Harbin, a receiver with 13 receptions and a touchdown, and receiver Kiante Hardin, who makes eight touchdown receptions and 32 total catches for 684 yards. He also rushes 25 times and scores four touchdowns on the ground, and finishes with 1,224 all purpose yards.

Eighteen different seniors have made tackles on defense. Hardin has 32 while playing in the defensive backfield, and one interception. Lakin Milner, an outside linebacker, has 38; Cameron Tournear, another linebacker, has 45. Harbin, also in the defensive backfield, has 30 and leads the team with six interceptions. Clark, a linebacker, has 18 and a sack. Austin Carter, a linebacker, has 58, including eight for a loss, 5.5 sacks and an interception. Linebacker Steven Moore has 45 and two sacks. Linebacker Garrett Rogers has 22. Defensive lineman Connor Badgley has 38 and a sack and a half. Tackle Emilio Perez has 31 and 2.5 sacks. Lineman Drake Humphrey has 29, nine for a loss and two sacks. Tayler Arterburn, a lineman, has 26 and one sack. End Keegan Lumley has 19 and a fumble recovery. Defensive back Trent Parra has two interceptions.

On special teams, there's senior Tanner Yokley, who's made 21 of 22 extra point attempts.

In barely two months, six of them sign letters of intent on national signing day to play college football. Tayler Arterburn, a 6-foot-1, 245-pound guard and defensive end, signs with Eastern Illinois. Dalton Ford, a 6-foot-4, 270-pound tackle, signs with Arkansas State. He earns the team's Adam Spieker Award as the team's offensive line MVP. Kiante Hardin signs with Minnesota and Jerry Kill. He is named the overall Cardinal MVP and shares special teams MVP honors with Kolesen Crane. Maquel Harbin and Trent Parra each sign with Benedictine.

Drake Humphrey attends the signing ceremony. The 6-0, 235-pound defensive tackle and winner of the Grant Wistrom Award as defensive MVP has already signed with Pittsburg State University.

And a few months after that round of signings, standout junior offensive lineman Trystan Castillo becomes the latest Cardinal lineman to continue his career with a Division 1 school. The 6-foot-4, 280-pound Castillo is the first 2016 commit for the University of Missouri.

On the field inside the Edward Jones Dome, on the Saturday after Thanksgiving, the team's four senior captains – Dalton Ford, Kiante Hardin, Tayler Arterburn, Tyler Davison – take the field. The Cardinals win the coin toss and defer.

In the stands behind the Webb City sideline, one fan holds a sign that reads "Coach Rod for Pres." Another sign says "Coach Smitty minister of defense."

Webb City kicks off with a squib kick, Central gets the ball at its own 42. The Tigers cover the distance to the Webb City 5 in 10 plays, converting twice on third down and once on a fourth-and-4. Quarterback John Montgomery boots out to his left and scores, Central leads by a touchdown.

On Webb City's first play from scrimmage, Tyler Davison gains three yards. On second down, he gains 29. The Cardinals get as close as the Central 20, but Central safety Al Young intercepts a Tyson Roderique pass and returns it for a touchdown. The Cardinals luck out; there's a block in the back. But the Tigers go ahead and drive 59 yards and take a 14-0 lead with 1:34 left in the first quarter. There's some nervousness in the air.

Davison and junior Keaton Burroughs take turns bulldozing through the Central defense. Roderique rushes for 10 yards on a third down. On third-and-goal, the junior quarterback scores. Cory Duley's extra point is good, and Webb City trails 14-7 early in the second quarter.

On Central's next possession, the Tigers find themselves in a fourth-and-7 situation at their own 38. They line up to punt, but Montgomery, the quarterback, takes the snap and scrambles while looking for an open receiver. Drake Humphrey grabs Montgomery's jersey and drags him down.

The Cardinals cover the 35 yards to the end zone easily in six plays, and Roderique scores on another short run to tie the game with 5:27 left in the half. Central, ironically, faces another fourth down at its own 38 minutes later. This time the Tigers punt, and what follows is a 73-yard Webb City drive that ends when Burroughs crosses into the end zone with 35 seconds left in the quarter. The Cardinals lead 21-14.

The Central quarterback is heavily pressured on first down and throws up a prayer. Cornerback Maquel Harbin is there to intercept it, giving the ball back to the Webb City offense at the Tigers' 30. The Cardinals go for the dagger. On first down, Roderique throws a 30-yard strike to Hardin and Webb City leads 27-14 at halftime.

Linebacker Austin Carter sacks Montgomery on fourth down inside Webb City territory early in the third quarter. On Central's next possession, Hardin returns a punt down to the 16-yard line. He then scores on a reverse from the 15, making it 34-14.

The Tigers still have life when they score with 2:16 left in the third quarter, staying within two touchdowns. They try to recover an onside kick but Kolesen Crane fields the ball at midfield. About two minutes into the fourth quarter, sophomore Hunter Vanlue's touchdown makes it a 20-point game. Burroughs adds another short touchdown; it's a 48-21 game.

Central's last possession starts inside the 50 after it recovers a fumble with 5:40 left in the game. Montgomery is immediately sacked on first down, but the Tigers move the chains and drive closer to the end zone. Royce Clark sacks Montgomery on a second down, but the Tigers move the chains again by gaining five yards on a fourth-and-3. They have the ball at the 11 with 29 seconds on the clock. Webb City's first-team defense is still on the field.

Montgomery rushes to the 2 on first down. Fifteen seconds remaining.

Running back Braion Owens gets the ball and he's met in the backfield by senior Bradon Rogers, who delivers a punishing hit. Central calls another timeout, with nine seconds left and the ball still at the 2. The Tigers are determined to score. On third down, Montgomery keeps the ball. He's hit by tackle Emilio Perez behind the line, and the game ends. Webb City has won its 13th state title, 48-21.

John Roderique, flanked by seniors Tyler Davison and Kiante Hardin, sit behind their new trophy inside the interview room at the Edward Jones Dome. "I'm John Roderique, Webb City. The guy to my right, Tyler Davison, No. 35, running back, and then Kiante Hardin, No. 5, defensive back, receiver, running back, jack of all trades."

The coach scans the room. It's silent.

"Am I supposed to say something here? Or you guys want to ask questions?"

A reporter bites, says the 14-0 deficit was just like the game against Rockhurst. What did Roderique say to the players after that first quarter?

"Really didn't say a lot till halftime," he says "At least not that I could repeat here, probably. It was one of those days where we just kind of got real sluggish for whatever reason. Maybe mentally went into the game thinking...you know, the one thing I told them, I said, 'Guys, you can't sit around listening to what people say. Last year...' I think maybe our kids went into the game thinking we played these guys last year. That's what happens sometime when they're teenagers. We took some blows. We misfired on one, trying to throw the ball a little bit there, got tipped up and picked off. I didn't call a very good game myself. I'll take some credit for some of the things we didn't do very well. As I told them, that's how life is sometimes. It kicks you in the gut and you gotta suck it up and go. Can't say enough. We went down 14-0 and went into halftime 27-14. That just tells you about the leadership we have on our football team, the job our guys have done and just the poise and composure being able to just hang in there and keep battling."

"How much did the Rockhurst experience help your guys?"

Roderique says it had an impact. The 14-0 deficit was a very similar feeling.

"We have a philosophy that we believe in offensively and we're not going to start throwing it and doing all these crazy things just because we're down 14," he says. "We just tried to maintain composure and do what we do. I think we started getting back into it that way."

Scott Boudreaux, the sideline reporter for KNEO radio, asks Davison what he told the offensive unit after Central pulled within two scores in the second half.

"I could tell that some of the guys, it felt like they were panicking a little bit," says Davison. "They were losing their nerves and they weren't calm. I just told them we've got to calm down. The only time that we've been stopped was

Kiante Hardin scores a touchdown in the 2014 state championship game, with Evan Slaughter following him into the end zone. Photo by Brennan Stebbins.

when we stopped ourselves. Turnovers, too many penalties. We just had to keep going out there and doing what we know how to do. That was my message to them. We gotta stay calm and go out and execute."

"Coach, you get the 73-yard drive there to go ahead 21-14," someone says. "How key was that drive just in terms of setting you guys up right before halftime?"

"That gives you momentum, that gives you confidence, energy," Roderique says. "I really felt that during that drive sometime we got more energy and maybe they lost a little bit of energy. We were mixing it up a little bit, going on the line of scrimmage. Calling plays on the line of scrimmage a little bit."

A reporter asks Kiante Hardin about his 30-yard touchdown reception at the end of the first half. How much did it mean to him for the coaches to call his number in that situation, just like at Harrisonville?

"I think it shows that coaches believe in me, you know," Hardin says. "They believe in me, I have to make plays for them to get them to throw me the ball." Another question for Hardin. What's it mean to get the state title as a senior, the

Quarterback Tyson Roderique rushes the ball in the 2014 state championship game. Photo by Brennan Stebbins.

team's fifth straight?

"Junior year and sophomore year, they're big too but senior year, it's the biggest year," he says. "We got it done and I'm pretty proud of my team."

The Cardinals are now 13-2 in championship games. "What is it about Webb City that makes you guys so good in these title games?"

Roderique says it's preparation and staying loose.

"Maybe it happened after the 2004 season when we were here and we lost in overtime, I've told myself that we're not going to play to lose, we're going to play to win," Roderique says. "If we come here we're going to play to win.

We're not going to hold anything back. I think sometimes you can get a little bit tight in situations like this. Instead of playing to keep from losing a game you play to win a game. We're going to bring out everything we have at our disposal."

"Can you go ahead and put into words what it means – I mean, obviously every year is special, but five straight, it's unreal. Can you put that into words?"

"I tell ya," Roderique says. "It probably won't sink in until I retire from coaching. I'm sitting by myself sometimes here during Thanksgiving weekend, I start thinking about it. I'm driving down the road and I start crying about it. I'm tearing up. I just can't imagine having the opportunity to do this. The guys that ought to be answering the questions are the assistant coaches and all the players from the last five years. They're the guys that do it all. They're the guys that put the work in. This kid right here, I'm going to miss him. He's like a dang son to me." He pats Hardin on the back. "Tyler is, too. We've had some great kids. Here are two great kids right here. That's what makes it all worthwhile."

Richard Humphrey hoists the 2014 state championship trophy at the Edward Jones Dome in St. Louis. Photo by Brennan Stebbins.

AFTERWORD

In December 2012, when Webb City head coach John Roderique sat in his office and dissected the state of Cardinals football, the team had won 45 games in a row and three straight state championships since their last defeat. They had a 90-game regular season winning streak and 11 state titles in the trophy cases at the high school, which was tied with a small Catholic school on the other side of the state for most in Missouri history. Roderique, in 16 seasons, had earned eight of them.

Now, with the 2015 season on the horizon, the Cardinals have won 28 games in a row and two state championships since their last defeat. They've won five consecutive titles, and they have 13 trophies on display at the high school, which is still tied with Valle Catholic for most in state history. Roderique, in 18 seasons, has won 10 of them, and his career record is now 222-19. His winning percentage has improved to 92.1, which is still the highest in state history by a comfortable margin. Recall the legendary Pete Adkins, who coaching primarily at Jefferson City, won 405 games with a winning percentage of 86.8.

Adkins won 354 of his games and nine state championships at Jefferson City. He had a 71-game winning streak. He won his final championship in 1994 and then retired, after 37 years at Jeff City and 43 total as a head coach.

He was inducted into the Missouri Sports Hall of Fame in 1986.

In January 2015, the Webb City football program joined Adkins in the Hall of Fame. The Cardinals were inducted along with 15 individuals and the 1969 Missouri Tigers football team.

"I think a lot of our success over the years has to do with continuity," Roderique told the Hall of Fame. "We went a long time there, maybe eight or nine years, where we had the same exact coaches. I've been there 18 years. Kurt Thompson was there seven years before that. Coach (Jerry) Kill was there a couple years."

In the 27 years between Kill's hiring and Webb City's induction into the Hall of Fame, the Cardinals won 320 games and lost 32. They went undefeated 11 times.

In December 2012, after the Cardinals had won three straight championships, it seemed as good a time as any to declare that Cardinal football was at its highest point in the proud history of the sport in Webb City.

"Gosh, it'd be hard to say it's not," Roderique said then. "People ask a lot of times, 'What's the best team?' And that's not even fair, I think, to rank teams like that, but our football team this year was probably about as dominant as we've ever had since I've been here."

The same could be said for the undefeated Cardinals of 2013 and 2014. Now more than two years after declaring the peak of football in Webb City, all the Cardinals have done is rack up wins and titles, and there's no reason to think they'll slow down.

One of these years Webb City won't win a state championship. It might not even make the playoffs. It'll lose another regular season game. At some point in the future there will be a losing season. Records are made to be broken, and streaks don't last forever. Dynasties don't last forever, either.

At some point in the future, people will fondly recall those decades when Webb City was the greatest high school football program in the state of Missouri, and one of the very best in the nation. The Cardinals still are.

Bibliography

King Jack Yearbook photographs appear on pages: 18, 20, 22, 24, 28, 29, 37, 38, 39, 40, 43, 44, 47, 51, 52, 53, 54, 56, 59, 60, 67, 68, 75, 76, 81, 82, 91, 92, 97

Bob Foos photographs appear on pages: 98, 105, 127, 135, 136, 137, 144, 150, 152, 171, 194, 209, 226, 234, 235, 248, 264, 277

Brennan Stebbins photographs appear on pages: 292, 328, 329, 342, 344, 356, 357, 362, 363, 364

The New Century
The Daily Sentinel
The Webb City Daily Register
The Review
King Jack Yearbook
The Webb City Sentinel
The Joplin Globe
The Kansas City Star
St. Louis Post-Dispatch
Springfield News-Leader
The Carthage Press
Arkansas Democrat-Gazette

Webb City Area Genealogical Society
Maxpreps.com
Hooten's Arkansas Football
Athlon Sports

Pictorial History of Webb City, Carterville, Oronogo (2008)
Mrs. Wistrom's ABC's: What I Learned Raising Three All-Americans (2001)
Webb City Football: A History of Champions